2

Black Beauty, White Heat

A Pictorial History of Classic Jazz 1920-1950

By Frank Driggs & Harris Lewine

Introduction by Paul Bacon

Da Capo Press
New York 1995

Library of Congress Cataloging-in-Publication Data

Driggs, Frank.
    Black beauty, white heat: a pictorial history of classic jazz,
  1920-1950 / by Frank Driggs & Harris Lewine: foreword by John
  Hammond: introduction by Paul Bacon.—1st Da Capo Press ed.
        p.   cm.
    Includes indexes.
    ISBN 0-306-80672-X (alk. paper)
    1. Jazz—Pictorial works. I. Lewine, Harris. II Title.
ML3506.D74 1996
781.65—dc20

95-44844
CIP
MN

First Da Capo Press edition 1996

This Da Capo Press paperback edition of *Black Beauty, White Heat* is an
unabridged republication of the edition published in New York in 1982, with
the omission of the color insert. It is reprinted by arrangement with the authors.

Published by Da Capo Press, Inc.
A Subsidiary of Plenum Publishing Corporation
233 Spring Street, New York, N.Y. 10013

All Rights Reserved

Manufactured in the United States of America

This book was prepared for publication by Harris Lewine, New York City

Art Direction: Harris Lewine
Design: Robert Aulicino

Sources

(P. 19) "New Orleans," by William Faulkner, *The Double Dealer,* January– February 1925
(Pp. 20, 50, 68, Bottom, 148, 247,319) *Hear Me Talking To Ya,* Edited by Nat Shapiro and Nat Hentoff, Rinehart and Company 1955
(Pp. 22, Top, 25, Top) *Satchmo–My Life in New Orleans,* by Louis Armstrong, Prentice-Hall, Inc. 1954
(P. 26) Frank Driggs Interview with Harold Dejan, Decenber 28, 1980
(Pp. 26, 28, 35, Bottom) Frank Driggs Interview with Rene Hall, Brown Derby, Los Angeles, July 1969
(P. 30) *Storyville #86,* Laine Wright, December 1979– January 1980
(P. 33) Frank Driggs Interview with Richard Mackie, December 1980
(P. 33) "New Orleans Today," by George Hartman, *The Jazz Record,* January 1945
(P. 36, Bottom) "Louis Nelson and the New Orleans Navy," by Peter Vacher, *Jazz Journal,* 1975
(P. 43) "Back O'Town," by Barbara Reid, *Climax,* 1955
(P. 49) *Louis Armstrong—A Self-Portrait,* The Interview by Richard Meryman, Eakins Press 1971
(P. 50) "Going Down State Street," by Frederic Ramsey, Jr., *Jazzways,* Vol. 1, No. 1, 1946
(P. 50) *Chicago: City on the Make,* by Nelson Algren, Doubleday and Company 1951
(P. 71) Frank Driggs Interview with Preston Jackson, Chicago, April 1973
(P. 77, Top) "Wingy, Louis and Me," by Art Hodes, *The Jazz Record,* January 1944
(P. 91) *An Hour with American Music,* by Paul Rosenfeld, J.B. Lippincott Company 1929
(Pp. 97, Bottom, 219, 220, 242) *Duke Ellington,* by Barry Ulanov, Creative Age Press 1946
(Pp. 128, 129) Frank Driggs Interview with Greely Walton, New York, September 1973
(P. 149) Frank Driggs Interview with Kenny Rickman, New York, May 1975
(P. 150) Frank Driggs Interview with Buster Berry, Kansas City, Missouri, October 1957
(P. 155) Richard Smith Interview with Bus Moten (transcribed by Frank Driggs), April 1971
(P. 159, Top) *Early Jazz,* by Gunther Schuller, Oxford University Press 1968
(P. 163) *Jack Teagarden's Music,* by Howard J. Waters, Jr., W.C. Allen 1960
(P. 169) "Walter Page's Story," as told to Frank Driggs, *Jazz Review,* November 1958
(P. 173, Middle) Frank Driggs Interview with Ed Lewis, *Jazz Review,* October 1959
(Pp. 179, 215, 216, 217, 218) *Louis,* by Max Jones and John Chilton, November Books Ltd 1971
(P. 180) "Charlie Barnet," by Leonard Feather, *Down Beat,* September 21, 1951
(Pp. 181, 287) *The Kingdom of Swing,* by Benny Goodman and Irving Kolodin, Stackpole 1939
(P. 182) "Jelly Roll Morton," by George W. Kay, *Jazz Journal,* 1962
(P. 191) Frank Driggs Interview with Lorenzo Flennoy, Los Angeles, July 1969
(P. 205) *Henry Miller: Letters to Anais Nin,* G.P. Putnam's Sons, 1965
(P. 206) *Jazz from the Congo to the Metropolitan,* by Robert Goffin, Doubleday, Doran and Company 1944
(P. 206) "Lunar Caustic," by Malcolm Lowry, *Paris Review #29,* Spring 1963
(Pp. 208, Middle, 214, 222, 230, 232, 234) *Jazz Away from Home,* by Chris Goddard, Paddington Press Ltd 1979
(P. 213, Bottom) "Leon Abbey," by Ralph Gulliver, *Storyville,* October–November 1977
(P. 228) Frank Driggs Interview with Kieth Stowell, Montreal 1980
(P. 236) "Tommy Chase," by Frank Driggs and George W. Kay, *Coda,* March–April 1970
(P. 237) "Teddy Weatherford," by Peter Dark and Ralph Gulliver, *Storyville #65,* June–July 1976
(P. 239) "Colored Ideas," by Jack Mitchell, *Storyville #61,* October–November 1975
(P. 275) *The Big Bands,* by George T. Simon, Macmillan 1967
(P. 280) *The World of Duke Ellington,* by Stanley Dance, Charles Scribner's Sons 1970
(P. 282) "Don Redman," by Frank Driggs, *Jazz Review,* November 1959
(Pp. 315, 316, 324) *Bird Lives!* by Ross Russell, Charterhouse 1973
(P. 316) "The Blind King of the Ivories," by E. Burley Edwards, *The Melody Maker,* December 7, 1935
(Pp. 319, 322) *To Be or Not to Bebop,* Dizzy Gillespie with Al Fraser, Doubleday 1979
(P. 338) *Stan Kenton: Artistry in Rhythm,* by Dr. William F. Lee, Creative Press, Los Angeles 1980
(P. 343, Top) *My Life in Jazz,* by Max Kaminsky with V.E. Hughes, Harper and Row 1963

Contents

For Shirley. And for John Redmond Kelly (1918–1961),
who would have enjoyed this book.
—F.D.
For Louis Armstrong, child of the century
and its most enduring product.
—H.L.

AUTHOR'S NOTE

BLACK BEAUTY, WHITE HEAT IS THE RESULT OF THE intense stimulation and atmosphere provided by the late Professor Marshall W. Stearns, who founded the original Institute for Jazz Studies on Waverly Place in New York City in the mid-1950s. Stearns had gathered all the published jazz books and magazines into a formidable library, with a record collection to match. Coauthor Driggs was one of his acolytes.

This atmosphere, and the publication in 1955 of Bill Grauer and Orrin Keepnew's *Pictorial History of Jazz* and Nat Shapiro and Nat Hentoff's *Hear Me Talkin' To Ya*, moved Frank Driggs from being a jazz fan and record collector to becoming an accumulator of jazz memorabilia. The authors had become jazz fans and record collectors in the early 1940s, following a pattern set almost twenty years earlier by the great first-generation collectors, who began writing about their "collecting hot" discoveries and were unearthing personnels from musicians still active.

Frank Driggs, among a new group of writer-historians, built on that early research and accumulated files of archival material from which the majority of the material in this book was chosen.

Black Beauty, White Heat encompasses the years 1920–1950 because they were the decades of the greatest ferment and spread of jazz; it reaches back to 1917 for the Original Dixieland Jazz Band—the first to make jazz records—and moves ahead to 1951 to make a point regarding an important gathering of stellar modern jazz artists. The authors chose the classic period of jazz because its music continues to nurture long after most of its practitioners have passed on. We had many friends among those players and wish it had been possible for this book to have been published while most of them were still living.

There is no chapter devoted to the blues. This may upset some enthusiasts, but throughout these pages they will find the blues artists who worked frequently with jazz bands and jazz players, from Mamie Smith to Jimmy Witherspoon. The blues is a separate story, told in many works here and abroad.

Some special acknowledgments are due individuals who went out of their way to help make this book possible, not only in the past five years while it was being thought out and prepared, but over the past twenty-five years in allowing access to scrapbooks and sharing their memories. We have listed them as a "table of contents" of generosity.
New Orleans: Richard B. Allen, Danny Barker, Harold Dejan, Karl Gert zur Heide, Rene Hall; Curtis Jerde and the William Ransom Hogan Jazz Archive, Tulane University; Richard Mackie, Sr., Joe Mares, Jr.; Don Marquis and the Louisiana State Museum; Al Rose, and William Russell. *Chicago*: Ralph Hancock, Dennis Hess, Frederic Ramsey, Jr., Banjo Ikey Robinson, John Steiner, and Hal Williard. *New York*: Clyde Bernhardt, Paul Burgess, Lawrence Cohn, Stanley Dance, David Griffiths, Edgar Hutto, Paul Larson, Jr., Jack Lomas, Charles Nadell, Carline Ray Russell, Freddie Skerritt, Peter Tanner, Dr. Albert Vollmer, and Greely Walton. *Kansas City*: Buster Berry, Wesley Collins, Curtyse Foster, Al Gilbault, Cliff Halliburton, Eddie Johnson, E. Tim Kelly, Andy Kirk, Milt Larkin, Ruth Towles Lesley, Ed Lewis, Clarence Love, Kenny McVey, Gene Ramey, Eddie Randle, Dr. Charles W. Reiley, Leslie Sheffield, Ligon Smith, Marshall Van Pool, Will Warner, and Ben Young. *California*: Andy Blakeney, Benny Booker, Peter Carr, Buddy Harper, Floyd Levin, Preston Love, Barry Martyn, Horace Moore, Forrest Powell, Peppy Prince, Leon Rene, Reb Spikes, and Stan Wallman. *Europe*: Fletcher Allen, Tommy Benford, Jan Breuer, Arthur Briggs, Garvin Bushell, Buck Clayton, Charles Delaunay, Bertrand Demeusy, Juan Duprat, Harold Flakser, Chris Goddard, M. Russel Goudey, Juan Rafael Grezzi, Ralph Gulliver, Jacques Helian, Max Jones, Harold Kaye, Jack Mitchell, Francis Paudras, Robert Pernet, Warren Plath, Henri Renaud, Johnny Simmen, Keith Stowell, Louis Vola, and Laurie Wright. *Swing*: Robert Altshuler, Elmer Crumbley, Lester Glassner, James T. Maher, Vito Marino, and Arlene Thompson. *Film*: Don Brown, David Chertok, Duncan P. Schiedt, and Ernest Smith. *Modern*: Leonard Feather, Sheldon Frummer, Milt Hinton, Don Lanphere, Roy Porter, Nat Shapiro, Jerry Valburn, and Art Zimmerman.

Finally an acknowledgment to the immediate past: Allen Goldberg and Modernage Photographic Services, Inc.; Arlene Muller and John McKellen, MCA Music, Inc.; Mario Conti, Peer International Corporation. Special thanks go to Dan Morgenstern, Ed Berger, and the staff at the Institute of Jazz Studies, Rutgers University, Newark, New Jersey; to designer Robert Aulicino, always at the stop-and-go ready, for his untiring devotion; to Elliot Saunders, for his eyes and ears; to John Hammond, for his inspiration and enthusiasm; to Bob Bender, our original William Morrow editor, who was "fan," believer, and smoother-outer; to Albert Goldman, author, critic, and "Jazz Spritzer," who confirmed what we hoped was true; and finally to Paul Bacon, for his generosity, friendship, and wise counsel (often after midnight), without which this book couldn't have been completed.

Frank Driggs
Harris Lewine
Summer 1982

MEMORABILITY
A Foreword by John Hammond

I T IS EXTRAORDINARY, WITH SO MANY BOOKS DE-
voted to the subject of jazz published during the last
fifty years, that one should now come along that is
absolutely an essential part of every aficionado's
library. *Black Beauty, White Heat* brings back innumerable memories of my early days as a would-be entrepreneur, memories instantly evoked by the more than
1,500 photographs, advertisements, and record labels,
many of which were unfamiliar even to me.

During much of the 1920s I was away in prep school and
college, but somehow I managed to get to New York on
weekends, not only to listen to jazz, but to play in a string
quartet and hang out in Harlem speakeasies after theory
lessons and rehearsals. Here are some of the finest pictures I have seen of New York night life, which I first
tasted at the old Alamac Hotel on upper Broadway when
Paul Specht's band was playing in 1923–24. Shown here
(Page 94, Middle, R) recording at the old Columbia Studios at 20th Street and Sixth Avenue, they had good
soloists like Arthur Schutt on piano and Frank Guarente
(who was the leader of a small group of virtuosi within the
band called the Georgians) on trumpet. Here too is Duke
Ellington's original group (Page 97, Top) with Bubber
Miley and Toby Hardwicke, which played at a basement
joint called the Kentucky Club on West 49th Street.

How he has done it, I don't know, but Frank Driggs has
come up with an advertisement (Page 96, Middle, R) for
my very first theatrical venture, the presentation of
Fletcher Henderson's band at what was then called the
Public Theatre at Second Avenue and 4th Street on April
15, 1932. The ad says "astonishingly low prices, 15 cents
balcony on matinees, and 35 cents at night in the orchestra." All this included a line of sixteen chorus girls, the
best jazz band in the world—Fletcher Henderson—and
many supporting acts, including the funniest comedian in
the business—Dusty Fletcher—who was not even billed.
He later became famous for a record called *"Open the
Door, Richard."* There was even a grade-Z movie: *X
Marks the Spot.*

One of the virtues of this book is its reproductions of the
great old record labels, most of which are long gone and all
of which are almost completely unknown to today's record
buyers. All during the 1920s and 1930s I was an avid record
collector. It was almost impossible to find my favorite
records in downtown stores, so I found myself hanging out
in tiny little stores in Harlem, Brooklyn, and the Bronx.
Such searching is summed up in a superb essay by Paul
Bacon on the joys and trials of record collecting in the
days of the 78-rpm disc. I have experienced all the frus-
trations and thrills he has recounted so eloquently. These
fine old labels appear at the end of each chapter and
form a remember to remember pantheon of jazz. Almost

unbelievable in their number and variety, the European
labels that featured black American jazz are also included.

I got to my first recording session in 1927, when I was
down from Hotchkiss for Easter vacation. There, at the
old Cameo Studios at 116 East 32nd Street, I knew that
the world of banking and law would never be for me and
that one way or another I would end up in the music business. That business was a strange mixture of genuinely
popular white music and slightly underground black jazz,
which was known and appreciated by the white musicians,
if not by the public. Here you will find a photo of one of the
earliest mixed sessions (Page 114, Top, R), very much
frowned on in those years, with Benny Goodman and an
all-star band featuring Coleman Hawkins; a photo of the
incomparable Count Basie band with Lester Young, Buck
Clayton, and my own favorite trombone player, Vic Dickenson (Page 115, Bottom); and one of Billie Holiday,
accompanied by the equally incomparable Roy Eldridge on
trumpet (Page 115, Top, R-and M). I was fortunate
enough to have supervised all these sessions and many
others, and they have stood the test of time.

I am especially pleased to see a picture of the Reno Club
in Kansas City (Page 161), where Count Basie's nine-
piece band played. I first heard them over shortwave radio
while I sat in my car during intermission between sets of
the Goodman orchestra at its peak at the Congress Hotel
in Chicago.

The kind of jazz I liked appears throughout this book,
and it was not written about in the trade journals of the
time, nor in the music papers like *Metronome* and *Orchestra World.* New York was a completely Jim Crow town,
and I finally became correspondent for two British papers
in order to write about what was really going on in places
like Small's Paradise, the Saratoga Club, and the Savoy
Ballroom; one of those British papers, *Melody Maker,*
appears in the chapter on Europe (Page 226).

I might easily comment on almost every photograph in
Black Beauty, White Heat, but to do so would deprive
readers of the pure experience and surprise of seeing
them—documents of the most vital era in jazz history—
for the first time. I expect this book will be the focal point
of endless discussions regarding the time that it covers so
eloquently. Frank Driggs has been my friend for well over
twenty years, and there is nobody in the country who has
a wider or more detailed knowledge of classic jazz history.
In Harris Lewine he has the perfect partner, an ideal colla-
borator whose superb taste and outstanding art direction
are further enhanced by a lifelong immersion in jazz. In
Black Beauty, White Heat, they have brought together all
of my old favorites (and some who were not), and I for one
look forward to renewing many rich and enduring associations with the pantheon of artists gathered here.

JAZZ FAN
A Memoir by Paul Bacon

For Evelyn Dorfman, Rosemary Hermansader,
and John Van Bergen, once and forever members of
the Hot Club of Newark

NEWARK, NEW JERSEY. MAY, 1941. A COLLECTOR OF *hot jazz records, who is, in real life, an office boy in a small advertising agency in Newark, leaves his rooming house on High Street. He has a purposeful air. Striking out with a light but obsessed heart, he heads for any of the several black sections of the city, preferably one he hasn't seen before (or one not known to have been scoured by Phil Stein); in his pockets are a pack of Luckies and seventy-five cents (approximately 5 percent of his week's pay), with which he intends to buy as many as nine records, or as few as three.*

Newark has buses, but nickels have more important uses, and the city is small, so he walks. It is Saturday, it is sunny, the auguries are good. Who knows what lies in wait—in an old store, in a closet, in a junk shop, in an old Victrola, in anything?

But today's is one transaction, one aspect of the quest. The collector finds himself on the north side; he has been here before, but not in this particular spot. He enters a side street: small frame houses, a grocery, a couple of open lots, and, crucially, an eight-year-old kid, who gives him a wary eye (as well he may; he is looking at a sloppily dressed white youth, about nine years older than himself, wearing a fevered countenance).

"Hi," says the collector.

"Huh," replies the kid, toe-tracing a line on the sidewalk.

"Listen, does your mother have any old records?" No matter how ludicrous it may seem forty years later, this is the dialogue.

"She got a gang of ole records," says the kid, looking at the ground, the sky, and, fleetingly, the collector.

"Well, uh, I buy old records, and, uh...is your mother home?"

She is home. The kid leads the way up the outside stairs to the second floor, goes inside; the collector can hear little bits of the explanation: "a man(!)...don't know who...old records..." At any rate, he is allowed to enter. In the kitchen he meets a not particularly hostile, but skeptical and bemused, woman, about forty years old. (This scene needs a little background. It is the tail end of the Depression; the United States is the Arsenal of Democracy. People are beginning to have jobs, but nobody really has any money. The collector is wearing his one pair of shoes, his one sweater, etc. The family in whose kitchen he is standing is living on the edge of genuine poverty, which is several stages below his own merely broke state. He is undoubtedly an exploiter, but he doesn't feel like one—he is only a zealot on the hunt, sacrificing butter money for the cause.)

"What you want with old records?" inquires the woman. This is a delicate question, requiring an honest answer, but not too honest, not too close to the reality of collecting jazz records, which is that they are worth more than the collector is prepared to pay for them—a lot more, in some cases. So the collector explains that he likes them, especially Bessie Smith, Ma Rainey, Louis Armstrong, people like that. He plays them; he and his friends are looking for ones they really like. And so on.

"What you pay for these old records?"

"Well, I pay three for a quarter. Sometimes I might buy a whole bunch, and then I pay a nickel apiece."

She considers this, nods, and moves to a closet off the kitchen. Digging around, she finds a stack (what a moment!) and brings them to the table. She stands there, arms folded, as the collector moves in for what he prays is a strike. These are 78s, remember, which have not been played, probably, in close to ten years; they are sleeveless, to say the least.

The day in question is not to be a fabulous one, just routine, so the little stack on the kitchen table may include four Bessie Smiths (one chipped), one Tampa Red, a wonderful Clara Smith, Kitchen Mechanic Blues *(Columbia 14097);** *a Cab Calloway, a Lonnie Johnson guitar solo, and a few of no interest whatever. The collector picks out two of the Bessie Smiths, the Lonnie Johnson, and, especially, the Clara Smith: it's a black Columbia, in very good condition.*

She brings out the second (and last) small stack. It is much like the other: three more Bessie Smiths, a Lemuel Fowler piano solo (rather an odd item), some more duds, and one real tragedy. There is a great and rare Louis Armstrong accompaniment, Lonesome, All Alone and Blue *by Chippie Hill (Okeh 8339), and it is hopelessly cracked. He buys it, just to have it, along with a third Bessie. So he has bought six records. None are in excellent condition; all, however, are playable except the Chippie Hill. One Bessie is a duplicate, but he thinks it is in better shape than the one at home. He has a quarter left for staples like cigarettes or phone calls. He has had a passable day.*

What is a jazz fan? If you have to ask, you haven't met one (forgive me for mangling the famous quote, which is probably apocryphal anyway). Well, that's not exactly true, although jazz fans have something elusive about them, as does the music. But they come from somewhere. I have thought a lot about this question, and I can at least wrestle with it.

To begin with, jazz fans go back to exactly that—the beginning. My brother Jack and I suspected that we were of the breed in late 1937, and we were johnny-come-latelies. There had been jazz writers and collectors, serious ones, since the early 1920s; some sort of prescient hipness award should certainly have been given to Gerald Murphy, that aesthetically remarkable man, when he had a copy of the Armstrong-Hines *Weatherbird* (Okeh 41454) built into

**Whenever a record is named, it will be identified by label and serial number out of reverence for the whole collecting process.*

the keel of his yacht, *Weatherbird,* in 1929!

An essential point is that Jack and I knew nothing about all that; even though it was tempered by a lot of developments in that period between 1923 and 1937, the same process that captured our predecessors captured us. What that process was may not be objectively explainable, but I'm convinced that fan A's experience would sound very familiar to fan B. I can actually remember the discovery, not of jazz, but of music itself; it wasn't all one thing—it had large and unknown dimensions, unimaginable colors and feelings barely hinted at until then. What had happened?

Ours was a musical family, in the most casual way. We had no cultured European tradition of sibling string quartets, but my mother had studied voice and my father was exactly of the age and disposition to have seen Husk O'Hare's band in Florida, Goldkette in New York, whatever was going, in that Flaming Youth time. He played a little banjo (a Bacon banjo, by God, though no relation) and taught us ukulele, and we were all barbershoppers. I remember, in fact, a carful of parents and friends rushing home to hear a broadcast by the Mills Brothers, in what must have been 1933, and similar attention to the Boswell Sisters. In those summers, my brother went to camp in Maine; he fell in with a kid named Jimmy Poe, who not only had a set of drums but read *Down Beat.* (Precocious Jimmy became James Poe, a noted screenwriter; he died in 1980.) When Jack came back in the fall, he was singing things alien to the old homestead, and he could tell the difference between this dance band and that. I pricked up my ears.

From then on everything led, apparently, to our becoming jazz fans. Everything also led, apparently, to our not becoming lindy-hoppers and eventual Glenn Miller idolators. Speculation about that (it was true of almost all jazz fans we knew) does suggest that jazz fans are outsiders. Jazz is powerful stuff; it usually seizes you at the same time as sex, and it is deeply affecting to many of its converts throughout their lives—enough so to make bearable a slight alienation. There is a chicken-or-egg question implicit in this: which came first, the groping toward the art we dimly perceived or the unwillingness (inability?) to join our more extroverted fellows? Certainly there were people who managed both worlds, and there were people who had profound musical feelings who never could take jazz seriously—there still are. But my friends and I were led almost inexorably along a path toward a maverick stance. Maybe if we had been born dancers we would have taken that other fork; as it was, the big-band era told our story. Our dancing friends would do the shag; we listened. They didn't know that Artie Shaw's piano player was Bob Kitsis; we did. However, I remember being jealous of those shaggers. I don't think they were jealous of me.

Whatever the emotional responses to jazz are, wherever

they come from, they are unifying in their strength. My brother and I traveled our peripatetic course, listening to the Chick Webb band in rural Connecticut, Mildred Bailey in Baltimore, the Goodman band in suburban New York—all the typical music of the late thirties—almost always on radio. We didn't have a phonograph, or records, although friends might. We knew nothing whatever about Roger Pryor Dodge, or Charles Edward Smith; I do remember an article in *Esquire,* in 1937 or '38, in which I saw, for the first time, the name Bessie Smith. Whoever the writer was, he alluded to Bessie in such a way that I knew she must be something special, in the way that one senses those things; some names have a resonance that defeats ignorance.

By the time we reached Newark, New Jersey, in the spring of 1939, we knew enough to be classed as budding fans—emphatically without portfolio. I think we had *From Monday On* by Whiteman (Victor 21274) and a few others. Then we discovered the Hot Club of Newark. We were on the threshold of the Real Thing. These were not jazz buffs (I have always thought of a jazz buff as someone who calls Louis Armstrong "Satchmo"), but jazz fans. Cadre, hardcore. The kind who seized you by the arm and told you that the clarinet solo by Bill Creger on *She Wouldn't Do What I Asked Her To* by Naylor's Seven Aces (Gennett 5376) was the best damned unknown solo by a white musician... and so on.

The Hot Club of Newark was a tightly knit band despite wildly disparate origins. They were a family; we were strangers and they took us in. The club dated from early 1939; we joined in 1940 and fell, gratefully, into the world of *Jazzmen,* Delaunay's *Hot Discography,* and people who actually had record collections, however small. It's difficult, now, to remember how powerful the effect of those two books was, and how fertilizing to our presumably fecund imaginations and ambitions; *Hot Discography* was, literally, a revelation. Keats's looking into *Chapman's Homer* shrank in comparison. Here were all the things we had—and here were all the vast number of things we didn't have, and hadn't heard of. I think three of us had copies, grudgingly lent and assiduously memorized; I can still recall whole pages. The lucky ones who had them marked them with little checks or *x*'s. The names were so exotic and desirable: Harry Dial's Blusicians, Albert Wynn and his Gutbucket Five, Bix and his Rhythm Jugglers, Luis Russell's Heebie Jeebie Stompers. Talk about music!

Jazzmen was another thing entirely, a romantic book about the most romantic figures we could imagine—described in very satisfactorily charged prose, exactly to our liking. For a barely post-adolescent already deeply hooked on the music of these great heroes, reading *Jazzmen* was enough to engender the vapors. And, in soberer moments, provocative; who, one wondered, was Ernest

Ansermet, and what was he doing writing about Sidney Bechet before one was born? (I was born the day after King Oliver recorded *Mabel's Dream* for Paramount (20292); my mother was called Mamie by her brother; I wish I could make something more of that, but I can't.)

Back to the Hot Club. It met on Monday nights in the Fuld Neighborhood House, a Jewish community center on the edge of the black section. We, the members, had a communally owned record player (the best we could get for $35), fierce loyalties and disagreements. We also had access to a gold mine.

By 1940 most of the great collections already existed, and the world wasn't exactly unaware of the presence of record collectors, valuable rarities, and so on. So it is interesting to consider a few facts about Newark in 1940: there was, for instance, McGarry's. McGarry's was a piano and music store, downtown, rather faded but genteel, presided over by formal, soft-spoken men; on the left side of the store was a long glass counter, behind which were extremely neat shelves of records. You went up to the counter, waited for one of the grave gentlemen to move behind it, and then requested the catalog—the Victor Catalog. It would be handed to you, whereupon you would find the right section, clear your throat, and say, "Um, do you have 20221?"

The man would turn to the shelves, thumb his way along, pause—extract!—and return with a crisp envelope containing *Black Bottom Stomp* by Jelly Roll Morton's Red Hot Peppers. That would be fifty cents, please, the going price for any black Victor. McGarry's didn't care that this one was fourteen years old.

Regrettably, this was more unusual than I make it sound; they really didn't have many left—but it was incredible that they had *any.* The omnipresent Depression was largely responsible, of course: who could afford fifty cents for a record? But there were some, and most of us got two or three, particularly Mortons, which weren't heavily collected at that time.

Then there was the mysterious little record shop in the Italian section; I was really too late on that one, but not shut out completely. It sold nothing but Harmony records, a peculiar circumstance entirely. When I stumbled upon it, the vultures had left only a few remnants, as I found when I asked for (inevitably) *There Ain't No Land Like Dixieland* by the Broadway Bellhops (Harmony 504). A young Italian girl stood behind the counter. She had a dog-eared catalog—shades of McGarry's, but only shades—from which I did elicit one splendid Dixie Stompers, *I'm Feelin' Devilish* (Harmony 974), but the bones were just about clean.

Those were Newark experiences, but similar ones weren't rare in other places. A nice one concerned a friend of the club, in 1939 or '40: while walking through the subway passageways at 34th Street, in New York, he passed a display window belonging to Gimbels'; in it were articles from the store's music department—a portable player, a plastic case to carry records in, that sort of thing. Near the glass was one of those triangular wire racks meant to hold fifty records upright, and there were two or three records in it. Our man took a good look at those records and froze like a Gordon setter. The one he could read said James P. Johnson. He went forthrightly to the personnel office, got hired, and spent six lovely months discovering the many pearls in Gimbels' record department, clerking happily away, buying 1920s Okehs and Columbias at his employee's discount.

There were many legendary windfalls, some strange indeed. John Hermansader, the resident grownup and president of the Hot Club of Newark, once found in a junk shop (in Pittsburgh, I think) nothing but an entire box— twenty-five copies—of *Take Me for a Buggy Ride,* by Bessie Smith (Okeh 8949). How come? No one knows.

For the most part, collectors depended on solo forays; door-to-door as in the beginning of this essay, or in junk shops and other places likely to have either used or, one hoped, new records. The Salvation Army produced a number of things, and they were cheap, but rarely in good shape. There were other sources, such as a well-known store—I can't remember the name—on Chambers Street, in New York, that had large batches of records, many of them new ones; it was a streaky place, having nothing one week and Sutter's gold the next. I think every one of us in the club got a new copy of *Dee Blues/Bugle Call Rag* by the Chocolate Dandies (Columbia 2543) on Chambers Street.

But the happiest situation was to have a source of one's own, and fortune smiled upon me. One Saturday in 1941 I was junk-shopping with my cousin Dick Farley; we were ambitious but still innocent in many areas; once, when we found *Sensation/Lazy Daddy* by the Wolverine Orchestra (Gennett 5542), Dick cheerfully let me have it, because he thought it should have been by "The Wolverines"—and so did I, but I hoped we were wrong. We were, and I had my first Bix Beiderbecke Gennett. Today we ranged beyond our usual perimeter, in this case west on South Orange Avenue, a mildly hilly section, run-down and quiet. There were stores and small buildings along both sides of the avenue, and the area was largely white, so I'm not sure, thinking back, why we thought we were in collectors' territory. But you never knew.

We entered a small store, a junk–novelty–old magazine store, on the north side of the avenue. Inside the door was a slight, elderly (to us, that is; he was probably about fifty) man with glasses, a kindly looking man, in a little cash register alcove. Not ten feet from him, on the floor, right in front of the door—records. A stack of records, obviously

used, about a foot high. We didn't try to look casual: we went straight to the stack.

As Dick reached for the top one (which was, I believe, *Ride, Red Ride* by the Mills Blue Rhythm Band (blue Columbia 3087), the kindly looking proprietor's voice floated through the dust motes.

"You boys looking for records?" Oh-oh. A dreadful, ominous pause. But then the same voice said, "Well, those are three for a quarter. They aren't new." Paradise enow. We resumed the search, and we were dumbfounded; the stack was made up largely of things like the top one, things like Ellington's *Bundle of Blues* (Brunswick 6607), *Pardon My Southern Accent* by Henry Allen's group (Perfect 15970), etc.; nothing before 1928 or '29, nothing after 1937, all worn but eminently playable—let's say G−. No blues, no white bands. Hmmmm.

That day we bought nine, I think, exhausting the exchequer. The whole transaction seemed oddly normal, if that's viable English; too good to be true. But two weeks later, having amassed a dollar, we went back. The proprietor, whose name was Frank, was still there, the records were still there—in fact, there were a few more. This time we talked to Frank, who hadn't the slightest compunction about telling us that his source was a man in Newark who supplied music for various functions; he had a small truck, a portable record player, and lots of records. As times and tastes changed, he sold the older ones to Frank. How remarkable, simple, and fortuitous! But the best was yet to come.

A week or so later, I had a conversation with Frank about records and music. (My cousin didn't live in Newark, so Frank's was deemed my turf.) He seemed to know all about what he had, but didn't care in the least about age or value (shades of McGarry's again); he was a storekeeper and this merchandise was three for a quarter. "Of course," he said, "any new ones would be more—maybe fifty cents."

"New ones?" "Why yes, there are some new ones"— he glanced at the rich mélange of magazines, bed springs, playing cards, lampshades, and God-knew-what surrounding him—"around here someplace. This used to be a record store," he said.

I was galvanized. "When was that, Frank?"

With outward calm I listened as he described a situation made in Jazz Fantasy Land. He had run the store, selling sheet music and records, until 1931, when the record business almost literally died. And it had been a Race Record store, specializing in Vocalion and Paramount records.

I asked if it would be okay if I looked around, and he said it would be. (It must be noted that this was ten years after the failure of the music store, ten years in which any collector before me—and there were plenty of them, including

the aforementioned Phil Stein—could have had the same luck; why none did remains a mystery.) For a year, a little bit at a time, I looked. I peered and pried, I edged sideways between cartons and stacks of junk, I lifted magazines, I moved anything movable. And the treasure was there—in tiny quantities, but there. I found probably fewer than forty records in all, but some were extraordinary, and all were unplayed, in the original sleeves. There might be two, sandwiched between musty magazines and a carton of china. Two, one being *Smoke Shop Drag* by Junie C. Cobb and his Grains of Corn (Vocalion 1269), the other being *There'll Come a Day* by the Dixieland Thumpers (Paramount 12525).

Once I found a shipping carton, one of those metal-edged gray ones that were meant to hold twenty-five records; on it was written, in Frank's handwriting, REAL OLD BLUES. The box held six or seven records, all black Paramounts: Elzadie Robinson, accompanied by Will Ezell; late Ida Coxes with Jesse Crump; and the first (I think) Bill Broonzy.

Frank would say, as I slithered out of some cranny, "Well, you got something?" And he would remember them. He would say, "Oh, yes, she was a good singer, popular singer in those days...."

By late 1942, I had mined out the vein, but not before my most precious one-record nugget, which I will come back to later.

Jazz was, at this point, busting out all over (it had been for some time, what with Muggsy Spanier's Ragtimers playing in New York in 1939, among other things, but 1940 was really it for us in Newark; partly a matter of our age, partly a matter of money, partly a matter of events). The magazine *Jazz Information* was being founded by Eugene Williams, Ralph Gleason, and Ralph de Toledano; George Hoefer was scolding the jar-heads in his *Down Beat* column, "The Hot Box." Re-issue programs were fomenting; Ralph Berton had a daily radio program on WNYC, emanating from the Municipal Building in lower Manhattan (I used to sprint home from Arts High School, on High Street, to catch *West End Blues*, the theme, at lunchtime). The *HRS Rag* was rivaling *Jazz Information*. The small labels were appearing like lovely stars: Blue Note, Signature, Solo Art. And there were the two fabled record stores in New York: the Commodore Music Shop, just handy to Grand Central Station, with its own label to boot, and the HRS Record Shop, on Seventh Avenue, with label ditto. There would be other places to buy jazz records, then and later, through and after the war, like Berliners, the Music Room, and the Record Rendezvous, but we didn't get to them all. In the performing world, the Ellington band was hitting a spectacular peak; I think *Cottontail* (Victor 26610) had an impact almost like the famous *Body and Soul* by Coleman Hawkins

(Bluebird 10523) had had the year before.

And the strange, contentious quirks that were typical of many jazz fans, collectors, and critics were peaking at this time, too. A classic example was a discussion that went on in *Jazz Information* about whether or not Louis Armstrong was present on *New Orleans Stomp* by Johnny Dodds's Black Bottom Stompers (Vocalion 15632); opinions were quoted (some Armstrong experts said it "didn't sound like Louis" to them) about a record that was made in 1927 by seven musicians, at least five of whom were, in 1940, alive and playing. To be fair, I must say that pianist Earl Hines *was* consulted and he said flatly that "that was Louis."

And Hines's was not the final word—some few experts weren't convinced.

But that was all happening in New York. In Newark (which was then, as now, crawling with musicians), there were one or two places to hear live music (aside from big-band appearances at the Adams): Art Tatum sometimes played at the Dubonnet, and at the Alcazar you could find Gus Young's band; the trumpeter was Jabbo Smith.

The Hot Club was introduced to Jabbo by Phil and Gertrude (at that moment she was Gertrude Goodkin) Stein, who were astounded to discover the legendary Jabbo not only playing, but practically around the corner. In guitarist Will Johnson's words, "When Jabbo was young, he was worried about nobody—and I mean *nobody*." He was playing very lyrically and personally, as he always had, and he was indulgent to us; *Jazz Battle* and *Boston Skuffle* (Brunswick 4244, 7101) on UHCA's re-issue label, proved what Will Johnson was talking about.

The Hot Club gave two jam sessions starring Jabbo Smith, one including Gus Young's clarinetist, Larry Ringgold, and I think all of us had proprietary feelings about Jabbo from then on. The war (World War II, that is), which was looming before us, caused a slight pause in our connections—I saw Jabbo again in 1980, when he came to New York in a hit show, *One Mo' Time*.

Whenever we had the price we would go, in threes and fours, to Manhattan, on Sunday afternoons, to either of two clubs: the Village Vanguard, on Seventh Avenue, downtown, or Jimmy Ryan's, on 52nd Street. Both had the intelligent policy of charging one dollar for admission and not hounding you to drink, and both had music varying from okay to wonderful, starring practically every musician in the area: Henry Allen, J. C. Higginbotham, Willie the Lion Smith, Kansas Fields, Charlie Shavers, Hot Lips Page, Frankie Newton, Sidney DeParis, Rod Cless, Pee Wee Russell, Max Kaminsky, George Wettling, Tony Spargo, Buster Bailey, Art Hodes, Wild Bill Davison, Zutty Singleton, Pops Foster, Sid Catlett, Cliff Jackson, James P. Johnson, Brad Gowans, Georg (as he was calling himself) Brunis, Sandy Williams, and many more. Of course, other notable musicians were playing in big bands, so we had little chance to hear them at sessions.

If we were flush, as was sometimes possible after Pearl Harbor, we would go to Barney Josephson's Café Society Downtown, where the roster might include (on one bill) the Golden Gate Quartet, Albert Ammons and Pete Johnson, the Revuers (Betty Comden, Adolph Green, and Judy Holliday), all intertwined with the elegant Teddy Wilson band, featuring Emmett Berry and Benny Morton, sometimes starring the even more elegant Helena (as Mr. Josephson billed her) Horne.

That period seems very compressed and intense as I look back; there was little else in our lives that we cared about but jazz. We were engaged in survival, naturally, in such things as food, clothing, and shelter, but we spent as little as possible on them; jazz was what we lived on. We published a mimeographed newsletter/magazine called *Jazz Notes,* which we sent to an enterprising list, thereby getting into correspondence with some of our heroes, writers of the *Jazzmen* stripe; we gave a jam session that started out to be a disaster, but turned out to be fabulous. It was to have starred Max Kaminsky and Bud Freeman, but things started to go wrong and we had to go elsewhere. I don't remember the details, but we wound up with a band comprising Sidney DeParis, Rod Cless, James P. Johnson, Danny Alvin, and Earl Murphy; I may be mistaken, but I think they hadn't played together before that night. The chemistry was explosive, and people talked about that session for years afterward.

When the re-issue programs were really underway, some of our ideas about collecting changed—though never completely. No matter how pragmatic and pure music-oriented you were, playing a brand-new Columbia re-issue of *Gut Bucket Blues* by Armstrong's Hot Five (Columbia 36152) lacked that little soupçon, that lagniappe, that you breathed in when you played your VG copy of Okeh 8261—whether you admitted it or not. But the facts had to be faced: records of quality and rarity beyond our wildest fancies were mushrooming, and they were available—pricey, but available—on many labels.

The first, and most influential, re-issue program was Columbia's, run by George Avakian. It was devoted to the truly classic: Louis Armstrong's Hot Fives and Sevens, Teddy Wilson/Billie Holiday sessions, etc.—real cornerstone records. Most of us had few Hot Fives, and the ones we did have were seldom in good shape; here came all those seminally great records, newly pressed and available at your local record shop. And I can still remember the news that George Avakian had found un-issued Armstrongs! Today they are standard parts of the Armstrong discography, but at that juncture I don't think any collector believed that there could be major Hot Five and Seven dates lying unknown and unheard in the Columbia files in Bridgeport. There they were, however, and out they came into the light.

Meanwhile, *Jazz Information* was getting into the more mysterious rarities, removed from all but the most heavy-weight collectors' sensibilities: *No. 29* by Wesley Wallace (Paramount 12598), *Jab Blues* by Jabo Williams (Paramount 13141), and the irresistible *Hastings Street* by Charlie Spand and Blind Blake (Paramount 12863). They reflected, in some ways, the still-warm national love affair with boogie-woogie, which had been going strong for some time; its doyens were Pete Johnson, Albert Ammons, and Meade Lux Lewis. The *Jazz Information* sides deftly showed us that the style was deeply rooted—much older than we thought (though we knew Pinetop Smith's and Montana Taylor's records from the late twenties)—and had been practiced brilliantly by virtually unknown artists, some of whom had made only one record, but one of such quality that it became a permanent jewel. The Wesley Wallace piece was one such (although he reportedly made a couple of blues accompaniments), and another was *Louisiana Glide* by Blind Leroy Garnett (Paramount 12879), which wasn't re-issued until after the war.

While all this was going on we were living rather insular lives (in a jazz-fan sense). We were concerned with our own collections and enthusiasms, and although we had heard of the famous collectors—some were even on the *Jazz Notes* mailing list—they were just names to us: Bill Love, Hoyt Cline, Bill Coverdale, Marshall Stearns, George Frazier, John Hammond, John Steiner, Dave Stuart, plus the ones involved in more accessible pursuits, such as record labels and stores, like Steve Smith and Bob Thiele, for whose magazine, *Jazz,* I did some drawings. And there was William Russell.

I encountered that most diffident and scholarly man by mail, in 1942. I had had a bit of ridiculously good luck; visiting one of my regular Newark haunts, not a particularly fertile one at that, I found the owner waiting for me. He said he had a record he bet I would pay a dollar for. Since a dollar was exactly one-fifteenth of my weekly income, I was dubious. He produced the record. It was *Fish Tail Blues/High Society* by Jelly Roll Morton's Kings of Jazz (Autograph 606), in N— condition. I was as wan as Chopin in those days, so he probably didn't see that I had turned pale. I paid the dollar. Now what?

For one thing, as all of us in the club reluctantly agreed, it wasn't a very good record. It should have been marvelous, what with Jelly and trumpeter Lee Collins, who was then a hero of ours. But it was stumbling, muddy, and a deep disappointment; it was also that strange collecting anomaly: a luxury item no small collector could afford to keep. So the next issue of *Jazz Notes* simply mentioned that

I had Autograph 606 and would trade it.

In a week or so, word reached me that I should call *Jazz Information*'s Gene Williams, so I did. Williams was not really the languid snob he allowed himself to appear, but there was no doubt that he thought that kid jazz fans from Newark, New Jersey were probably not the 24-karat stuff. At any rate, he wanted to know what I was after. What I really wanted was *Georgia Bo Bo* by Lill's Hot Shots (Vocalion 1037); the Morton was much rarer, but not nearly as good, and I would have thought it a fair trade. Well, Williams didn't know of one nearby— had I thought of Bill Russell? He would be talking to Russell and would mention the idea (this was typically generous of him).

About a week later, I received a penny postcard, which I wish I still had, a classic bit of Williamsiana. It said, as I recall, "Dear Bacon, Bill Russell hasn't got an odd copy of Georgia Bo Bo, but he has quite a number of other things. Why don't you write him—" and the address.

I did write Bill Russell. Back came a letter and a list of duplicates. The letter said that he would indeed like to have the Jelly; since it was so rare, I should pick out a number of things, and we would work out a deal.

The list of duplicates absolutely floored me, being enormously better than my entire collection. This was the Real Thing, and no mistake. That list is given here; I still marvel at it, almost forty years later.

647 Means Ave.
Bellevue, Pitt. Pa.
Sept. 24, 42.

D.P.

Rec. your letter but was too busy to write & had a cold last 2 nites & had to go to bed as soon as I got home from work.

The Autograph trade is OK as you list it.

Also perhaps we can work out a deal on the other stuff.

I don't need the Cow Cow you list. The Clar. Wms might interest me if K. Ol really plays solos etc. I have a few of the Col. Cl Wms with K. Ol. & 3 or 4 of the Q.R.S. & as far as I can remember, except for a solo on Sister Kate, Ol. doesn't do much & they aren't so hot, but perhaps the *Bozo–Bimbo* is good. However I have between 50 or 60 Clar Wms assorted bands which are already in my junk pile so unless it is fairly good there would be no point in having it....

Record List

Armstrong	OK 8519—Weary Bl. n.	4.00
	8300—Muskrat R. n.	3.00
	8641—Two Deuces g to vg	2.50
	8566—Barbeque g–	1.50
	8261—Gutbucket g	2.00
	8396—King of Zulus f	1.00
	8535—Savoy Bl fg	1.00
	8318—Geo Grind f to fg–	.75
	8379—Big Fat Ma f to g–	1.50
	8423—Big Butter & Egg f+	1.00
	8343—I'm Gonna Gitcha n.	4.00
Louie with Dodds		
	Br. 3567—Melancholy-Wildman g.	2.00

Accomp. with Louie

Lilly Delk Chris	OK	8607—Last Night n.	2.50
Bessie Smith	Col	14079—Good Ole Wagon n.	3.00
Bessie Smith	Col	14079—Good Ole Wagon f+	.50
Bessie Smith	Co	14083—Careless Love f	.50
Bessie Smith	Co	14056—Reckless Bl g−	.75
Clara Smith	Co	14073—Court House f	.75
Clara Smith	Co	14058—Nobody f	.50
Ma Rainey	Para	—Jelly Bean Bl g	1.00
N. Welsh	OK	8372—St. Peter Bl (small crack 1″) f	1.00
Chip. Hill	OK	8312—Trouble in Mind fg	.75
Sippi Wallace	OK	8212—Baby I Can't Use Your Trouble with Cl Wms. Bl. 5 f+	.50

Armstrong with Er. Tate Vendome Ork. Voc. 1027

Stomp Off—Static Strut (I got this one at an auction listed as *ex,* but I'd say its not quite an ex, perhaps vg is more correct)   8.00

Armstrong & Cl. Wm Bl 5

	OK	8181—Everybody Loves My Baby vg to ex	2.00
	OK	40321—Cake Walkin Babies fg	4.00

Armstrong & King Oliver

	OK	4806—Sobbin Bl-Sweet Lovin Man g−	2.00
	Col	14003—London Bl f+	1.50

Also several Louies with Henderson including a good copy of *Alone At Last* (So. Serenaders). However these Hendersons are not too interesting musically.

Jelly Roll

Vic	38125—Ponchatrain Bl ex	1.25
Vic	20948—Pearls-Beale St (different masters than B. Birds) vg	.75
Vic	20252—Deadman vg to ex	1.25
Genett	5323—Pearls (pf solo) g−	1.75
Gen.	5220—New Or. Rhy Kings with Jelly Roll, Mr. Jelly Lord vg	3.00
Gen.	5221—London Bl (N.O.R.K.) g	2.00
Voc.	1154—Mr. Jelly Lord (Levee Serenaders) 1″ crack but surface is good	1.50

Pinetop

Voc	1256—Big Boy-Nobody Knows You n.	3.00
	1266—I'm Sober Now n.	4.00

Celler Boys	Voc	1503—Wailing Bl n.	8.00
Bud Freeman	OK	41168—Crazeology n.	4.00
Miff Mole	OK	41445—Shimme Sha Wabble ex	2.00

In case you like Bix I have vg to ex copies of

Wolverines	Gen. Copenhagen or Big Boy	3.00

Orig New Orleans Rhy Kings

OK 40327—Shes Crying—Golden Leaf fg   1.50

Tenn Music Men (Mound City B.B.—Muggsy, Hawk, etc)

Har 1375—Geo. On My Mind—I Cant Believe ex   1.00

Cook	Col.	862—Side Walk Bl. with Keppard fg	.75
Cook	Col.	813—High Fever, Brown Sugar with Keppard g	1.25
Cook	OK	8369—High Fever (⅛″ bite out of edge but not as far as grooves) fg	1.50
Harry Dial	Voc.	1515—Funny Fumble—Dont Give it Away with Jabbo & Simeon fg	1.00

<u>Jabbo Smith</u>	Br. 4244—Jazz Battle vg		1.50

<u>Chi. Rhy Kings</u>

      Bl. Bird 6371—Little Sandwich Wagon—
                       Shanghai Honeymoon—
                       (Good rough N.O. record
                       led by trombone Roy Palmer) vg+   1.25

<u>Ar. Sims & Creole Roof Ork</u>

              OK 8373—Soapstick Bl g   1.50

<u>Ch. Webb</u> (& J. Harrison)

              Br. 6895—Heebie Jeebies n   1.25

<u>Al Wynne</u>   Vo 1218—Crying My Bl. Away (unfortunately
                               not as good as Parkway) fg   1.00

<u>K. Oliver</u>   Br. 3373—Someday Sweetheart vg   1.00

<u>Ida Cox</u>   Par 12307—Long Distance Bl (good <u>Ladnier</u>) f   .75
                     12291—Black Crepe Bl—very good Ladnier f .50
                     12282—Cold Bk Ground Bl n   1.00

<u>Ellington</u>
(Washingtonians)

        Cameo 8188—Take it Easy g   .75
(Greer)   Col 1868—Beggars Bl g   .75

Prob. have several other Ellingtons & would also take out some of my collection if you're especially interested in Ellington.

Also have a large selection of Bessie Smiths, (but many are not extra good cond.)

Ordinarily there would be no hurry about arranging a deal, if one is possible, but Gene Williams will be here about Oct. 8 (at latest reports—he should have been here in Aug. according to 1st plans) & he plans to stay a week so as to play over most of my collection, so if possible I'd like to have the Jelly by, let's say Oct. 10, so he can hear it here.

                                          yt
                                        R.

After the Autograph trade (in which Bill was far too open-handed) he suggested that he would dub anything I was interested in if I would pay for the blanks. A bonanza! I kept those Wilcox-Gay Recordio acetates (this was well before the tape era) until long after the war, when they became too worn to play. They were my access to gems I had little hope of finding: the Bertrand/Dodds/Armstrong Washboard Wizards (Vocalions 1099 and 1100), and the Blythe/Dodds Washboard Wizards *Oriental Man/My Baby* (Vocalion 1184), which is still my favorite Johnny Dodds record; and *Livin' High* by the Clarence Williams Blue Five (Okeh 8272); and other blue-chip prizes I had never seen.

William Russell still lives in New Orleans, as he has for many years. He has been so valuable to the jazz world for so long that there isn't any point in trying to list what he has done. He plays violin with the New Orleans Ragtime Orchestra for fun.

About a year before this, in 1941, there had been a meeting of the Hot Club, a special one, with guests. They turned out to be Alfred Lion and Francis Wolfe, the ex-Berliners

who had founded Blue Note Records a couple of years earlier. Meeting them left us slightly awestruck, especially when we saw what they had brought to play for us.

What they represented was an entirely different, and to us unknown, aspect of the world of jazz records, and I use the word "world" advisedly. We knew that Europeans had responded to jazz from the first day they were exposed to it, had collected records with equal alacrity, and wrote about them with profound insight—sometimes to the consternation of their United States counterparts. But few of us had seen such exotica as Vox, Odeon, and Spanish Parlophone issues, not to mention other Continental versions of records familiar to us on American labels.

When they started out with a couple of Sam Woodings, one on Vox and another on Spanish Parlophone, both of which they had bought in Berlin around 1926, we sailed into euphoria.

After that meeting, we began, by ones and twos, to visit Alfred Lion and Frank Wolfe at their small apartment on First Avenue in Manhattan. Despite their feral names, they were shy, intensely European, in that old-wine and full-of-history way; we were bouncy, they were deep. They were amused by us, and they liked us. They greatly enjoyed stunning us with some unimaginable treasure, like *Honky Tonk Train Blues* by Meade Lux Lewis (Paramount 12896). New! They would smile small Mona Lisa smiles and stun us again with *Jockey Blues* by Sammy Brown (Gennett 6337), which turned out to be a Cripple Clarence Lofton—indistinguishable from *Streamline Train*, in fact.

I can still see that apartment. It seemed a powerfully romantic place to me, cosmopolitan, full of riches; there was a lamp made from a tube of parchment, with a bulb inside it, and a red bandanna draped over the top; there were photographs by Frank, abstracts with titles like *Four or Five Times* and *Church Street Sobbin' Blues*.

I can also remember passing a kind of test in that apartment. I would occasionally trade with Alfred and Frank; they had amazing duplicates, especially late Paramounts, such as John Williams's Synco Jazzers (the earliest Andy Kirk group, except that Kirk wasn't on it but Mary Lou Williams was, under her maiden name of Burley), and Tiny Parham's Forty Five; if I found something worthwhile, I would bring it along, hoping they didn't have it. One day I was anxious to hear a record that had been talked about at a club meeting; it was *Willie Kelly Special* by Willie Kelly (Victor 23259). They had it, in their low-bookcase set-up, and it was duly played. I listened until the end and said, "Well, it's not bad, but—" Frank nodded and said, "Ja, Paul. Have some sandwich." Which I did, washed down with the mixture of bottled German raspberry juice and seltzer that they liked in warm weather. They had decided that I had possibilities; I was content.

The small triumph I referred to before—a find at Frank's ex-record store in Newark—concerned Alfred Lion. He had played one of his and Frank's favorite records, a piano solo by Jimmy Blythe called *Chicago Stomps* (Paramount 12207), a complex, impressive performance. He had other Blythes, but he said, wistfully, that the really tough one was *Alley Rat/Sweet Papa* (Vocalion 1181). He and Frank had never even seen it.

Well, one of my last finds at Frank's shop was *Alley Rat*. It was so exactly what I would have wished to find that, if I had wished for it, I might have feared the loss of my soul to Mr. Scratch. When I showed it to the Blue Noters, they looked at it, looked at me, and said something like *"Alley Rat* [a short laugh]. Ja, *Alley Rat* [another laugh, longer and full of pleasure at the unaccountability of life]!"

Considering all that, it's strange that Alfred and Frank were my first real connection with modern jazz, the bop strain, after the war. I should mention that their connection with the Hot Club of Newark had entered a new phase, during the war years, because Alfred married one of us—Lorraine Stein (Phil was her brother). By early 1943, most of us who were eligible for service were long gone, but we corresponded in the standard hit-or-miss fashion. None of us, as far as I know, sensed any new directions in the music; I had heard of Dizzy Gillespie (as a wild kid in the Cab Calloway band), but I certainly didn't think he represented a trend. The club had a few members who didn't like anything much but classic New Orleans ensemble jazz, but there were others who liked Lester Young, Don Byas, Nat Cole—I remember with embarrassment some of us being patronizing about Art Tatum, opining that he had a hell of a technique, but was it really jazz piano? So we disappeared into the war as classicists. Most of what we heard, in the services, was Jo Stafford, Frank Sinatra, Tommy Dorsey, Dick Haymes, and the Mills Brothers; but something was going on, and I got my first taste of it in northern China, where I wound up after the war ended: Armed Forces Radio played some new records by Woody Herman. The brass figures in *Your Father's Mustache* (Columbia 36870) sounded like nothing I had ever heard; it wasn't a case of instantly seeing the light, by any means, but I knew I had heard something.

When I got home I heard a lot more, from every segment of the spectrum. In April 1946, my brother Jack and his wife hustled me to the Stuyvesant Casino, in downtown New York, to see more or less the tail end of the Bunk Johnson phenomenon; but on the radio we heard *Koko* (Savoy 597) and *Shaw Nuff* (Guild 1002) by Charlie Parker's Re-Boppers and the Dizzy Gillespie All-Star Quintet. Who was Charlie Parker? We had no idea. We were about to find out, and not only about him. Music was exploding.

When I got to see Alfred and Lorraine Lion and Frank Wolfe again, Blue Note was continuing its commitment to classic jazz, with special attention to Sidney Bechet and the unique Ike Quebec sessions; but they were on the verge of new ground. Early in 1947, I was visiting the Blue Note office, and Alfred asked me what I thought about "all this modern stuff." I replied that I didn't know much about it, but I was fascinated by it and I knew it was hard to play. Not long afterward, Alfred and Frank played me the first tests of their first modern date: *The Squirrel* and *Our Delight* by the Tadd Dameron band (Blue Note 540). I was bowled over, and by this time I had heard enough to know what was there. From that day I began an intense involvement and, thanks to Blue Note, exposure to that most remarkable period in New York, when the New Sound was everywhere: Thelonious Monk and Art Blakey at Mintons, Fats Navarro and Tadd Dameron, Miles Davis, Charlie Parker, tenor players in droves—Wardell Gray, Dexter Gordon, Allen Eager, Lockjaw Davis, and on and on. It was a chaotic and violently exciting time.

Not long into that time I became the modern jazz reviewer for *The Record Changer* (slight overtones of the blind leading the blind), and began a long association with Bill Grauer and Orrin Keepnews, who were proving, as the Erteguns, Avakians, Qualeys, Lions, and Wolfes had first posited, that this consuming hobby could indeed be a vocation. Most of us had heard, from parents and others interested in our welfare, that jazz was a foolish dead end; we were a little surprised to find that they were wrong.

NEWARK, NEW JERSEY, SOMETIME IN THE FALL OF 1942. ON THE corner of Plane and Market streets sits the Radio Record Shop, presided over by Herman Lubinsky. In this shop the members of the Hot Club of Newark have bought records for years; old ones in bins, new ones over the counter. A member once passed up Monkey Man Blues *by Cripple Clarence Lofton (Vocalion 02951) in the 19¢ bin, but another bought it half an hour later. The members refer to Herman Lubinsky as Simon Legree. He knows, and laughs like hell.*

On this day the floor of the Radio Record Shop is groaning under the weight of thousands of records, in boxes, in stacks, cracked, broken, crunching underfoot—records everywhere. What is happening? There is a war on. Uncle Sam needs not only Lucky Strike Green but shellac, and 78-rpm records are a prime source of reclaimable shellac, so there is a drive: bring in your old records! Our boys need the shellac!

Newark is answering the call. Bessie Smiths and King Olivers and Louis Armstrongs and Fats Wallers and Troy Floyd's Dreamland Orchestras and Ma Raineys and Banjo Ikey Robinsons and Frankie Half Pint Jaxons and Sam Morgan's Jazz Bands and Bix and His Gangs and Jimmie Noones are heading for the hopper, at a few cents a pound.

Collecting will go on, great collections will become greater, The Record Changer *will be the medium for innumerable transactions: auctions, trades, outright sales; but the sources are drying up. The scrap drive is Gotterdammerung. Eventually, by the seventies and eighties, there will be LPs of practically anything ever recorded, from delta blues to obscure airchecks. But here, in the middle of World War II, the golden age of collecting hot jazz on 78-rpm records is about over.*

New Orleans
Joys, Tears, and Revival
1919-1950

"New Orleans…a courtesan whose hold is strong upon the mature, to whose charm the young must respond. And all who leave her, seeking the virgin's unbrown, ungold hair and her blanched and icy breast where no lover has died, return to her when she smiles across her languid fan…New Orleans."
—William Faulkner, "New Orleans," *The Double Dealer*, 1925

New Orleans was unlike other cities. Music was part of its daily life. You didn't have to go out to hear it; it came from street vendors, chimney sweeps, from ethnic strains sung by carousing sailors from a dozen countries, yet the sounds could rarely be pinpointed. Veteran New Orleanian Danny Barker recalled: "A bunch of us kids, playing, would suddenly hear sounds. It was like a phenomenon, like the Aurora Borealis—maybe. The sounds of men playing would be so clear, but we wouldn't be sure where they were coming from. So we'd start trotting, start running—'It's this way!' 'It's that way!'—And sometimes, after running for a while, you'd find you'd be nowhere near that music. But that music could come on you any time like that. The city was full of the sounds of music."

The closing of Storyville's "district" in 1917 and the exodus of outstanding players like King Oliver, Freddie Keppard, and a little later, Louis Armstrong, did not immediately diminish the strength of jazz in New Orleans. There were opportunities for work throughout the city, and horn players like Chris Kelly, Kid Rena, Buddy Petit, and Lee Collins made one aware of the depth of talent.

Hotels, new ballrooms, and restaurants hired bands, and the Lake Pontchartrain resorts of West End, Milneburg, Spanish Fort, Bucktown, and Little Woods used bands of varying size and quality well into the Depression. Suburban roadhouses in the parishes had gambling as well as jazz, and New Orleans's then forty-year-old brass band tradition continued at parades, at store openings, picnics, and the inevitable funerals with strong young players.

More than twenty halls throughout New Orleans were in constant use by the more than thirty black social clubs like the Bulls Pleasure and Aid Society for their dances; the various cotton, lumber, sugar, molasses, and other "kings" of white business gave parties with music at their lavish homes. The riverboat companies, led by the Streckfus lines in St. Louis, used New Orleans bands and jazzmen for more than two decades.

Despite all this activity and the dozens of fine players New Orleans produced between the two world wars, the focus had shifted to Chicago and then New York in the 1920s. New Orleans bands reflected developments taking place there by increasing their size and using printed orchestrations and saxophones in pairs and trios, thus diluting the purity of the classic New Orleans front line of cornet or trumpet, trombone, and clarinet, which had fallen out of favor.

Tradition never entirely disappeared in New Orleans, but after the middle 1920s, one had to search awfully hard to hear it. Then it was only an echo of bygone times played by a few men like Emile Barnes, "Big Eye" Louis Nelson, Albert Burbank, or George Lewis, who stuck with their clarinets and found it hard to get jobs. Younger black players, and many whites as well, took to the saxophone in droves, and many fell so in love with their new horns that they refused to play clarinet any longer. Gifted saxophonists like John Handy, Ted Purnell, Harold Dejan, and Son Johnson worked steadily in nightclubs, roadhouses, and on the riverboats.

The ambitious players left New Orleans. Most of the black men like Lee Collins, Herb Morand, Barney Bigard, and Albert Nicholas went to Chicago. Their white counterparts like Ray Bauduc, Eddie Miller, and Sidney Arodin went to New York.

Those who stayed behind found plenty of work on Bienville Street in the late 1920s at clubs like the Nehi and the Whip, and later, around 1935, Decatur Street had small jazz combos for a year or so. Bourbon Street, not then the tourist attraction it became in the late 1940s, had the Shim Sham Club, where Guy Lombardo discovered Louis Prima, and veteran Halfway House trumpeter Abbie Brunies, who played for floor shows to stay in music rather than take a day job. Clarinetist Raymond Burke doubled on alto sax with the Melon Pickers and kept working.

Well-connected leaders like Papa Celestin, Sidney Desvignes, and A.J. Piron stuck to their riverboat and country club jobs, sometimes playing nightclubs and one-nighters in nearby Mississippi or Alabama, but found it unnecessary to go on lengthy road tours.

The rediscovery of trumpeter Bunk Johnson helped bring about a revival of interest in classic traditional jazz, so that for the first time since the 1920s, many of the older pioneers found themselves able to make a living from music.

Tradition was strongly entrenched in New Orleans and bebop never really took hold; although many younger players did try it, most of them in the city found it far easier to move into the burgeoning postwar rhythm-and-blues field led by Smiley Lewis, Paul Gayten, and Fats Domino. These men could often be found working side by side on Bourbon Street (by then a tourist venue) with Papa Celestin and the Dukes of Dixieland. The Crescent City was un-American; it had stuck to its roots.

Rediscovered but unrecorded William Geary "Bunk" Johnson posed in a New Iberia photo studio (with borrowed trumpet and without teeth) at the request of authors William Russell and Fred Ramsey for their fall 1939 book *Jazzmen*. Bunk wrote critic Eugene Williams: "I can really play yet. All I need is something to play with, and three men besides myself, and I can really stomp 'em down. 'Cause what it takes to stomp 'em, I really knows it yet...." Certain writers, record collectors, and budding jazz historians who hated swing and the new directions in which jazz seemed to be moving had elevated sixty-two-year-old Bunk Johnson to a cult figure by the time he made his first records in 1942. Bunk had been out of New Orleans since World War I and out of music since 1933, laboring in the rice fields around Bayou Teche and teaching music for the WPA. Most black musicians hadn't played his kind of music for nearly twenty years, but his recordings for Jazz Information, Jazz Man, and American Music created a sensation. His biggest success came in 1945 and 1946 at the Stuyvesant Casino in New York, where he and his New Orleans Band became media celebrities. They were lauded in print by no less an eminence than the distinguished composer and *Herald Tribune* music critic Virgil Thomson, who wrote of "the master of the darkest trumpet tone" and of "the greatest master of blue or off-pitch notes." Johnson died in 1949.

The Fate Marable Orchestra aboard the Streckfus Line flagship, the S.S. *Capitol,* New Orleans, 1919. Marable, here on piano, was the best-known leader and hardest taskmaster on the boats. He joined the Streckfus Line from his home in Paducah, Kentucky, in 1907, became leader by 1917, and worked the river until 1940. Louis Armstrong (third from R) remembered how he learned to read music under the red-haired leader: "In that orchestra David Jones [fifth from R] played C-melody sax and mellophone.... I mention him particularly because he took the trouble between trips to teach me to read music.... Br'er Jones, as I later called him, taught me how to divide the notes so that whenever Fate threw a new arrangement I was able to cope with it." Other "sight" readers were Boyd Atkins (second from L), Johnny St. Cyr (fourth from L), and Baby Dodds (extreme R).

Ed Allen's Whispering Gold Orchestra, S.S. *Capitol,* 1922. Nashville trumpeter Ed Allen (fourth from L) was working around St. Louis, Streckfus Line headquarters, when he was given leadership of one of the boat bands for two seasons. Pops Foster bought a tuba because the bands were now using three saxophones and it was sometimes hard to hear the bass. Lead trumpeter Sidney Desvignes (second from L) took over after Allen left, beginning a riverboat career that lasted until 1945. Tenor man Gene Sedric (extreme R) became a star with Fats Waller in the swing era. Ed Allen went to New York and became composer Clarence Williams's favorite recording trumpeter after 1926. In the 1940s and 1950s Allen finished out his career at the New Gardens Dance Palace, a dime-a-dance "rub" joint on 14th Street in New York.

Several fine second-generation brass men matured during the twenties. Lee Collins (L) was good enough to join King Oliver at the Plantation in Chicago in 1924, replacing Louis Armstrong, and lucky enough to record, at his peak in New Orleans, the famous 1929 Jones and Collins Astoria Hot Eight sides for Victor. Unrecorded Buddy Petit (Top, R), 1920, was "one of the greatest hot cornets," according to Jelly Roll Morton. Henry "Kid" Rena (originally René) (Middle, R) played in the Waif's Home band with Louis Armstrong and replaced him in Kid Ory's band in 1919 when Armstrong went on the boats. Heavy drinking and the Depression grind of taxi-dance-hall jobs depleted Rena's terrific endurance, range, and ideas. His only recordings, for Heywood Hale Broun's Delta label in 1940, though disappointing, helped initiate the New Orleans revival of the forties. (Bottom, R) The Elton Theodore Band, Algiers, 1930. Kid Thomas Valentine (extreme R) had endurance and range, but not enough style or polish, and spent most of his career playing backcountry towns until he was discovered and recorded in the 1950s.

Dance Classique

A. J. Piron and his Non-Pareil Orchestra cordially invite you to be present at their

Grand Soiree Dansante

at the Parisian Roof Garden, Saratoga and Gravier

On Monday Night September 24, 1923

This being their first appearance before the New Orleans public after seven consecutive years at Spanish Fort and the New Orleans Country Club. Having spent many years in perfecting his aggregation Mr. Piron brings to you the following artists of ability.

Steve J. Lewis, Pianist Chas. Bocage, Banjoist-Entertainer
Johnny Lindsey, Trombonist Lorenzo Tio, Clarinet and Tenor Saxophone Lewis E. Warnicke, Alto Saxophone Soloist Peter Bocage, Cornet & Xylophonist Lewis A. Cottrell, Trap Drummer. Clarence Ysaguerre, Bass Soussaphone Armand J. Piron, Violinist-Conductor

MUSIC BY

A. J. Piron & his Non-Pareil Orchestra
And The Famous Parisian Roof Garden Orchestra

Armand J. Piron and His Novelty Orchestra, Tranchina's Restaurant, Spanish Fort, New Orleans, 1922. Piron, a Creole, played violin left-handed, wrote songs *(Sister Kate, Day by Day, Kiss Me Sweet,* etc.), and played the New Orleans Country Club and Tranchina's Restaurant from 1916 to 1934. He wouldn't hire a player who couldn't pass for white. The band played stock orchestrations, but Piron allowed occasional solos by gifted pianist Steve Lewis (Top, R) and clarinetist Lorenzo Tio, Jr. (Bottom, fifth from L), teacher of many of the city's finest second-generation players (Noone, Dodds, Nicholas, and Bigard among them). His success took him to New York in 1923 to play Roseland Ballroom and the Cotton Club, and with the help of Werlein's Music Store on Canal Street he landed a Victor and Columbia records contract. After 1928 he hired younger players who lured him from the country club onto the riverboats in 1934. His social standing diminished, Piron had to play nightclubs and take black jobs. He later got back on the boats and played his violin until his death in 1943.

The Albert Nicholas Band, Tom Anderson's Café, Basin and Iberville, 1923. Albert Nicholas (extreme R), who, though leader, got only sideman's pay, and Barney Bigard (who missed the photo session) were a team; Nicholas, on clarinet, and Bigard, tenor sax, modeled themselves after the white duo of Tony Parenti and Tony Papalia. With drummer Paul Barbarin and pianist Luis Russell (third from L) they joined King Oliver's Dixie Syncopators in Chicago in 1924, despite banjoist Willie Santiago's fear: "Say, what you-all doin' goin' up there and freeze to death up North?"

The Original Tuxedo Orchestra, 1924. At first a brass band, the Tuxedo switched to dance work in the twenties. Co-leader William "Bebé" Ridgley (fifth from L) left in 1925 to form his own Tuxedo Band. Oscar "Papa" Celestin (seated, third from R) continued with such top players as Kid Shots Madison (second from R), pianist and multi-instrumentalist Manuel Manetta (standing, fourth from R), and alto and clarinet man Paul Barnes (second from L). Celestin's Original Tuxedo Orchestra recorded for Okeh and Columbia in the twenties. Primarily a lead trumpet player, Celestin retained his popularity through the thirties and forties and became Bourbon Street's main jazz attraction after 1949.

(Top) Manuel Perez's Garden of Joy Orchestra, S.S. *Sidney*, 1925. Perez (fifth from L), a cigar maker by trade, was one of the greatest parade cornetists in the city's history, playing with the Onward Brass Band from 1899 until its demise in the late 1920s. He founded the Imperial Orchestra in 1899 and went to Chicago in 1915, before King Oliver, and again in the late 1920s. The group featured Eddie Cherie on tenor sax (fourth from L); the rhythm was driven by Buddy Bolden's original bassist, Jimmy Johnson (extreme R). Perez stopped playing during the Depression and returned to his trade. He died in 1946, refusing to talk to anyone about the old days. (Middle) Nat Towles's Creole Harmony Kings, 1926. Towles (R) apprenticed in the Tuxedo Band and with Jack Carey and Henry "Red" Allen, Sr., before putting this group together. He was ambitious and became one of the Southwest's most prominent leaders in the mid-1930s. Trumpeter Herb Morand (second from L) went to New York and then settled in Chicago, working and recording with the Harlem Hamfats. Bill Matthews (L) spent most of his career with Papa Celestin. Banjoist Frank Pasley (second from R) spent years on the road before succeeding as a blues and rhythm-and-blues guitarist. He soloed on Les Hite's famed 1940 recording of *T-Bone Blues* and worked the early R & B circuit after the war with Deacon Joe Liggins's Honeydrippers. (Bottom) Sam Morgan's Jazz Band, Pelican Roof Ballroom, South Rampart Street, 1927. The Morgan band read music, used stock arrangements, and played jazz as well, spending most of their time playing small towns in Louisiana and the surrounding Gulf Coast states. Sam Morgan (seated, third from L) was highly regarded as a trumpeter until he suffered a stroke in 1925. He recovered a year later and rebuilt the band with Jim Robinson on trombone, Earl Fouché on alto sax, and brothers Isiah (seated, second from L) on lead trumpet and Andrew on tenor sax. The eight sides they recorded for Columbia Records on April 14 and October 22, 1927, in Werlein's Music Store on Canal Street, are the best representation of what was left of the earlier ensemble style of music. The recordings feature Earl Fouché on alto; his fluid lead and call-to-response playing is especially effective on *Mobile Stomp, Sing On,* and *Bogalusa Strut.* Saxist Harold Dejan told Frank Driggs: "Son Johnson, he used to cut everybody's ass...but my favorite alto player was Earl Fouché. He used to help me a lot.... you know he was a great soprano player too, oh, man, he'd play that soprano.... he was a humdinger, that Earl Fouché." Bogalusa, Louisiana, was one of the bigger towns on the Morgan tour. Banjoist René Hall explained: "The first band I left home with was Sam Morgan's band out of New Orleans....they all believed they had a gift for finding buried treasure...used to carry divining rods in their car and they'd get to a town and go around and charge people money to dig for buried treasure on their backyards....they had the whole thing sewn up...rent the hall, sell the lemonade—they carried a tub with them—for five cents a glass, check the coats and everything and divide the money." Sam Morgan had another stroke in 1932, and the band broke up the following year. Jim Robinson joined alto man John Handy at the La Vida Dance Hall, and Earl Fouché played with Steve Lewis and Bebé Ridgley.

Henry "Red" Allen, Senior's, Brass Band out of Algiers, Louisiana, was constantly in demand for parades, funerals, and other social functions that were an integral part of black life in the Crescent City. From 1907 through the 1940s most of the city's top brass and percussion men worked with him. The fluctuating lineup included Peter Bocage, Joe Howard, Papa Celestin, Bunk Johnson, King Oliver, Louis Armstrong, Henry "Red" Allen, Jr., and even occasionally Sidney Bechet, trumpets; Jack Carey, Buddy Johnson, Yank Johnson, Harrison Barnes, trombones; Lawrence Duhé, clarinet; Wallace Collins, bass horn; James A. Palao, alto horn; Bebé Matthews, snare drum; Clay Jiles, Red Allen, Sr., bass drum. For Mardi Gras, 1926 (L), Allen and Louis Dumaine (face hidden by music) are the trumpets; Ramos Matthews is on snare drum.

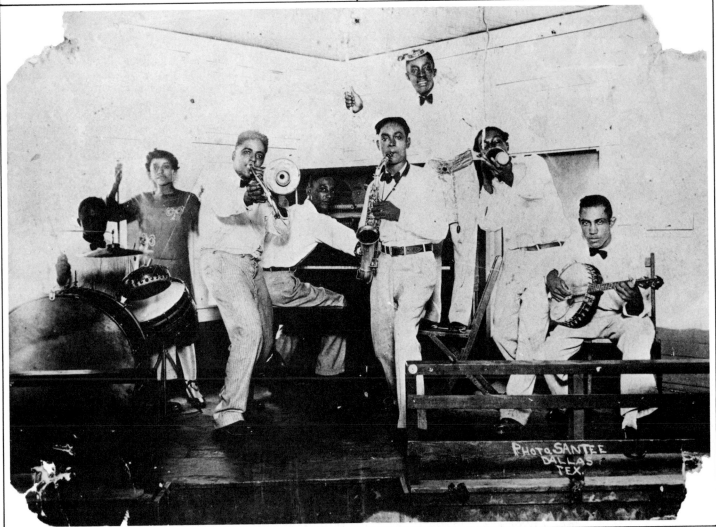

The Lee Collins Band, Tip Top Inn, Dallas, ca. 1925. New Orleans musicians were in great demand out of the city and often worked in bands in the Southwest, but rarely did a visiting player crack the "clannishness" of New Orleans bands. Lee Collins (standing, second from R) was well established, having succeeded with King Oliver in Chicago early in 1925. The Tip Top was Dallas's best club for black bands. Pianist Octave Crosby (fourth from L) and banjo player Percy Darensburg (R) were already well known in New Orleans. Crosby worked constantly and eventually took over from Papa Celestin at the Paddock Lounge, Bourbon Street, in the fifties and early sixties. Darensburg stayed in Texas and recorded with the legendary trumpeter Polite Christian. After Lee Collins recorded for Victor in 1929, he left the city for good.

In 1928 Creole trumpeter Sidney Desvignes realized his Southern Syncopators (Top) wouldn't always play jobs like the S.S. *Island Queen*. When they played for black audiences at San Jacinto Hall, they couldn't get away with stock arrangements or Creole players who couldn't improvise, so to compete with Papa Celestin and other uptown hot bands he hired darker players like trumpeter Eugene Ware (fifth from L) and alto man Ted Purnell (fourth from R). He also let pianist Fats Pichon (sixth from L) and saxist Adolphe Alexander (third from R) write special arrangements. Desvignes himself (fifth from R) was strictly a melody player, but he learned to be flexible. René Hall spoke of the color line of the Creole clubs: "I remember the clubs, like the Young Men of Illinois, the Old Men of Illinois, they wouldn't have dark musicians at their affairs. I'll take that back, you could be dark, but you had to have hair, good hair." Backcountry bands like the Yelping Hounds Jazz Band (Middle) of Crowley, Louisiana, competed with the Banner Orchestra (Bottom) and the Morgan brothers for jobs in northern Louisiana, Texas, and Mississippi. The best player in this group in 1925 was alto man Baker Millian (fifth from L), who became a tenor sax specialist with Boots and His Buddies in Texas in the thirties and played on many of Ivory Joe Hunter's records in the postwar rhythm-and-blues era. (Bottom) Trombonist-leader Gus Fortinet's (L) Banner Orchestra was one of the best reading bands, working out of New Iberia in 1928. Fortinet hired Bunk Johnson and Evan Thomas (second and third from L) whenever they weren't working in Thomas's own Black Eagle Jazz Band. Bunk and clarinetist George Lewis were in the Black Eagles playing a dance in Rayne in 1932 when Thomas, a ladies' man, was stabbed to death by a suspicious husband.

The Louisiana Shakers, 1930. Leader John Handy (seated, third from L) was one of the city's greatest alto men, a serious competitor in jam sessions. He and his bassist brother Sylvester formed the Shakers in 1930 but were unable to find enough work to keep it going more than a year. Handy played at the La Vida Dance Hall at St. Charles and Canal for the rest of the decade. His unique solo style, said to have been an influence on Earl Bostic and Tab Smith, sounded not unlike that of Pete Brown. Handy was not recorded until the 1960s.

The Creole Serenaders, Absinthe House, 1930. Louis Warnecke (third from L) and Peter Bocage (L) organized this band after A. J. Piron cast them aside in 1928. By playing in an older dance style, they soon surpassed Piron in popularity to become one of the more successful bands in New Orleans. They played mostly in this one club and broadcast over WWL throughout the 1930s. Bocage played violin, trumpet, trombone, banjo, and xylophone, which gave the group a unique sound. Pianist Dwight Newman (fourth from L) lived to see his trumpet-playing son Joe become a star with Lionel Hampton's band. Bocage sold life insurance when things slowed down and recorded with his Creole Serenaders for Riverside Records in 1961 at the age of seventy-five.

CLASS OF SERVICE

This is a full-rate Telegram or Cablegram unless its deferred character is indicated by a suitable sign above or preceding the address.

NEWCOMB CARLTON, PRESIDENT   J. C. WILLEVER, FIRST VICE-PRESIDENT

DL = Day Letter
NM = Night Message
NL = Night Letter
LCO = Deferred Cable
NLT = Cable Night Letter
WLT = Week-End Letter

The filing time as shown in the date line on full-rate telegrams and day letters, and the time of receipt at destination as shown on all messages, is STANDARD TIME.

Received at

1931 JUL 25 PM 8 59

NF236 127=NEWORLEANS LA 25 655P

MR ZOOTY, GATE SINGLETON CARE LAFAYETTE THEATRE
=131 AND 7 AVE=

OH YOU DOG I KNEW YOU COULD DO MORE POWER TO YOU PAL AM SO
GLAD TO HEAR OF YOUR BREAK WHICH YOU HONESTLY DESERVE POPS
I COULD CRY IM SO HAPPY OVER IT ALL HONEST I AM LIL SENDS
LOVE TO YOU AND FAMILY ALWAYS REMEMBER SATCHEL THAT YOU WILL
ALWAYS BE THE SAME ZOOTY TO ME YOU WAS WHEN WE WERE BOTH
YOUNG I PASSED BY THE PLACE WHERE WE USED TO EAT THOSE HOT
DOUGHNUTS HA HA HA WELL ZOOT WORK HARD AS YOUVE ALWAYS DONE
AND SUCCESS SURE TO STICK WITH YOU REGARDS TO NINA MAE YOUR
ORCHESTRA & COMPANY ALSO TELL YOUR MOTHER & MARY THAT I
THINK OF THEM OFTEN TELL ALL THE CATS ON THE STROLL HOWDY
FROM YOUR BOY=
    :LOUIS ARMSTRONG=

The Louis Armstrong Orchestra, Suburban Gardens, Jefferson Parish, summer 1931. Louis's favorite band, and one of the few of his own choosing, made a triumphal return to New Orleans and broadcast nightly over WSMB. Led by trumpeter-arranger Zilner T. Randolph (second from R), it featured New Orleans musicians Preston Jackson (R), trombone; Tubby Hall (top row, L), drums; Charlie Alexander (mugging with Louis), piano; and John Lindsay (top row, R), bass. Alto man George James (second row, third from L) recalled: "It was a beautiful place...at that time New Orleans was just like Las Vegas....we stayed there all summer and you couldn't get near the place....Louis was just terrific, and that guy was very fair; the more money he made, the more we made. He raised our salaries about three times while we were there." Louis found time to congratulate Zutty Singleton (Top, L), provide for a local baseball team—Armstrong's Secret Nine (Top, R)—and push his recently marketed cigar, the Louis Armstrong Special.

For ten years or so the Halfway House (Middle, L) at City Park Avenue and Pontchartrain Boulevard featured jazz groups, usually directed by trumpeter Albert "Abbie" Brunies. The Four Jazz Babies (Top, L), ca. 1920, featured trumpeter Brunies and blind singer and banjo player Emile "Stalebread" Lacoume, whose own Razzy Dazzy Spasm Band of young boys had worked the Storyville streets as early as 1897. "Originator of Jazz Music" is the family claim on his headstone. The group that achieved the greatest fame and recorded for posterity was the Halfway House Dance Orchestra: (Bottom, L to R) Charlie Cordilla, Mickey Marcour, Leon "Rap" Roppolo, leader Abbie Brunies, Bill Eastwood, Joe Loyacano, and Leo Adde. Soon after their first recordings for Okeh Records, *Pussy Cat Rag* and *Barataria,* January 22, 1925, the gifted alto and clarinet player Leon Roppolo began slipping mentally and had to be institutionalized. When he was released for a while in 1928, he began playing alto sax at the La Vida Dance Hall. Survivors still talk about his memorable saxophone chase choruses there with the younger and equally gifted Nunzio "Scag" Scaglione. Abbie Brunies's younger brother George (Top, standing R), shown with Charlie Cordilla (L) and Alfred "Pantsy" Laine (seated), trumpet-playing son of brass-band pioneer Jack Laine, left the city in 1921 to play trombone with the New Orleans Rhythm Kings in Chicago. Laine led his own jazz and dance bands in the city for twenty years.

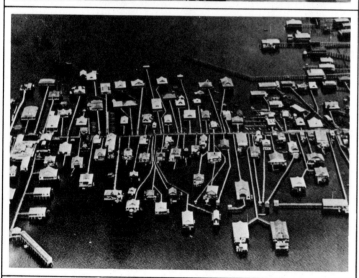

(Top) The Johnny Bayersdorffer Band, Tokyo Gardens, Spanish Fort, ca. 1922–25: (L to R) Chink Martin Abraham, Tom Brown, Johnny Bayersdorffer, Leo Adde, Johnny Miller, Steve Loyacano, Nunzio Scaglione. Bayersdorffer worked for the U.S. Civil Service by day and played good trumpet at night. His recording of *Waffle Man's Call* for Okeh in 1924 featured clarinetist Scaglione (extreme R). When he felt the band was good enough to play up North he quit the civil service, but the band wouldn't leave town, so he hired younger musicians like banjoist Nappy Lamare and drummer Ray Bauduc and played in California, Indiana, and Chicago. He stayed in Chicago after the band broke up but went home to participate in the post-1950 revival. Musicians who worked with cornetist Emmett Hardy (Middle, R, extreme R) claimed he was the best of all time. He was good enough to play professionally in 1919 alongside Leon Roppolo in the Carlisle Evans Band in Davenport, Iowa (Middle, L), and players of the period always claimed he influenced Bix Beiderbecke. He died of tuberculosis in 1925, without having recorded. The myriad Milneburg (pronounced "millenburg") camps on Lake Pontchartrain (Bottom, L, as seen from the air in 1921) had fishing, eating, drinking, dancing, carousing, *and* music from the end of World War I until the WPA put in a seawall in the 1930s. (Bottom, R) The Six and 7/8 String Band, on board Commodore Ernest Lee Jahncke's houseboat, *Aunt Dinah,* 1921, included amateur as well as professional musicians. Edmond Souchon on twelve-string guitar (kneeling, second from R), one of the organizers, became a leader in the medical profession. He was instrumental in the post–World War II New Orleans jazz revival and was at one time president of the New Orleans Jazz Club and editor of the jazz magazine *The Second Line.* The group played private parties for over fifty years. Many of the other players also became leading business and professional men.

(Top) Louis Prima's Kid Band, ca. 1923. There was so much casual work after World War I that bands of youngsters barely in their teens were able to gain valuable experience playing lawn parties and private affairs at the Milneburg camps. Thirteen-year-old Prima (L) and twelve-year-old Irving (Fazola) Prestopnick (fourth from L) became nationally known stars during the swing era after playing in most of the best local bands. Clarinetist Fazola was in the big bands of Ben Pollack, Glenn Miller, and Bob Crosby; trumpeter Prima played with small combos in the 1930s and found big-band success in the 1940s with such hits as *Angelina* and *There, I've Said It Again*. Pianist Ayars Lamarr (third from L) became a successful Midwest territory leader in the 1930s. (Middle) The New Orleans Owls, Fountain Lounge, Hotel Grunewald, 1923. The Owls were organized by onetime guitarist Lester "Monk" Smith, who turned to clarinet and tenor sax after 1920. (Their nominal leader was drummer Earl Crumb.) In 1921 they hired a fifteen-year-old cornetist, Richard Mackie (R), an admirer of Louis Armstrong, who helped build the Owls' reputation as the finest band in the South during his four-year stay. The Owls broke into what had been the exclusive territory of the Creole society bands and played "knocked-out barrelhouse jazz," in Mackie's words. He left for college shortly before the band began recording for Columbia in 1925. For the recording session the Owls raided their chief rival, the Princeton Revellers, for Mackie's replacement, trumpeter Bill Padron (Bottom, extreme R), and for clarinetist Pinky Vidacovich. *Stomp Off, Let's Go* and *Oh Me! Oh My!* introduced a rocking, swinging band whose output outranks that of most other white bands in 1925. *Stomp Off*...features Padron taking Oliver- and Armstrong-type breaks, a tromboneless front line, and a tempo that is very close to that of the famous Erskine Tate Vendome Orchestra recording of the same tune, featuring Louis Armstrong, made nine months later. The Owls split into two groups not long after their last recordings in 1927. Eddie Miller (Bottom, second from L) went with the second group, along with Padron and the city's finest young pianist, Armand Hug (second from R). Trumpeter George Hartman recalled: "There was Eddie Miller, who was considered a fine clarinet player before he switched to sax, and Sidney Arodin, Hug, Schilling, and others. After Bucktown's famous days, when it was dying out, the West End Roof opened. It was sort of an exclusive place with high prices. The best band in the South in those days was the Owls. The Owls went from the West End to the Roosevelt [the Grunewald], in the Venetian Room [now the Blue Room], and then the band broke up." After the Owls disbanded in 1928, Bill Padron left the business. Eddie Miller went to New York to join several bands; he switched to tenor sax when he joined Ben Pollack in 1930. When Dick Mackie went home after college and a year or so on the road with Hal Kemp and Kay Kyser, he found that reading bands held down the best jobs in town. He began a career as leader of one of the South's most successful bands and worked out of New Orleans well into the Depression years.

(L) The Dominos, 1929. Trumpeter Tony Fougerat was a primitive but popular player who led his own dance bands well into the 1960s. This group played mostly one-nighters in and around New Orleans and featured the clarinet and tenor sax of Lester Bouchon, trombone by veteran Frank Christian, and the young but experienced banjo player Hilton "Nappy" Lamare, who would achieve national acclaim with the Bob Crosby band of the thirties and forties. (R) Anthony Parenti and His Famous Melody Boys, La Vida Dance Hall, 1924. Tony Parenti (standing, hands folded) was a child prodigy on clarinet, having been featured with ragtime bands as far back as 1912. He refused offers from the Original Dixieland Jazz Band and from Paul Whiteman, although the latter arranged a Victor recording date in 1925. Parenti worked and recorded steadily in nightclubs, ballrooms, and theaters until late 1928, when he went to New York to become a highly paid studio musician.

(L) The Original Crescent City Jazzers, Mobile, 1926. Their reputation as Mobile's hottest band was helped in no small way by having New Orleanians Felix Guarino on drums and Johnny Riddick, piano. Mobile trumpeter Sterling Bose (second from L) sat in around the city, worked with Norman Brownlee, and was considered a "New Orleans musician." He became a featured hot soloist with Ben Pollack, Benny Goodman, Tommy Dorsey, Bob Crosby, and Glenn Miller. (R) The Happy Schilling Orchestra, 1924. Trombonist George "Happy" Schilling led some of the city's pioneer dance bands, playing hotels, nightclubs, and at Heineman's Ball Park for the New Orleans Pelicans' games. Outstanding members of this band were trumpeter John Wigginton Hyman (Johnny Wiggs), drummer-cornetist Monk Hazel, and pianist Frank Pinero, who played with most of Louis Prima's swing-era bands.

(L) The Johnny DeDroit Orchestra, 1924. Trumpeter Johnny DeDroit's (DeDroit, at piano) groups were among the city's most popular for three decades. His brother Paul usually played drums, and for a recording date in New York the band featured pianist Frank Froeba (third from R, leaning on piano). Froeba remained in New York and enjoyed a successful career that ranged from being a pianist with the first Benny Goodman Band of 1934–35; to solo residencies at the 18 Club, Jimmy Ryan's, and WNEW; and being house pianist for Decca Records. (R) The New Orleans Harmony Kings, Ringside Café, Dauphine and Bienville, 1927. Trumpeter Joseph "Sharkey" Bonano (third from L) and clarinetist Sidney Arodin (third from R) combined to make this one of the last real jazz units of the 1920s. The following year Bonano and Arodin recorded *Panama* with Johnny Miller's New Orleans Frolickers, a side that is often considered the apogee of white New Orleans jazz in the twenties.

The Abbie Brunies Band, New Slipper Night Club, 426 Bourbon Street, 1933. Brunies (front, R) made enough business connections during his Halfway House Orchestra days to keep working through the Depression when Dixieland went out of style. He spent most of the 1930s playing nightclubs on Bourbon Street. To ease the pain of accompanying floor shows, he persuaded his old friend Sidney Arodin (fourth from L) to work with him on tenor sax. Arodin stuck it out for a year before leaving for New York to work and record with Louis Prima and Wingy Manone. Abbie Brunies did defense work during World War II and in 1945 moved to Biloxi, Mississippi, where he led bands until 1960.

The Prima-Sharkey Orchestra, Tony Dinapolis's Little Club, Rampart near Common, 1930. Trumpeters Sharkey Bonano and Louis Prima's elder brother Leon (seated, second and third from L) combined forces to form one of the best big bands in the city. Trombonist Charlie Hartman, altoist Irving Fazola (seated, third from R), and a fine young tenor man, Nino Picone (extreme R), gave the band plenty of depth. Drummer Augie Schellange kept the good beat. They were popular for a year, working on the riverboats and at the Club Forrest, a supper club and gambling establishment in Jefferson Parish. René Hall remembered: "When radio first came in, a lot of white bandleaders would let colored soloists broadcast with them, to make the band sound good, because you couldn't see them. I made a lot of those broadcasts with Leon Prima over WSMB with Prima-Sharkey's Melody Makers. It was ten-thirty at night and the radio station was dark, no fans hanging around, so they could have a couple of colored soloists."

(L) Sammy Lee, ca. 1934. Tenor saxophonist Lee, a third-generation musician, worked in all the city's best bands and is still active today. (M) Louis Barbarin, 1932. "Lil Barb," younger brother of famed New Orleans drummer Paul Barbarin, was a very smooth and swinging drummer, much in demand. He worked with Desvignes, Celestin, and Piron and is still active. Many musicians preferred him to his brother. (R) Creole George Guesnon, 1936. A superb musician and musicologist known for his driving rhythm, Guesnon worked with Kid Clayton, Papa Celestin, Willie Pajeaud, Sam Morgan, Little Brother Montgomery, and George Lewis. In the 1960s he vowed: "This year I put up my banjo and guitar, never to play them again. . . . Al Hirt gets $8,500 a week, Pete Fountain the same, and Audio Fidelity Records gives the Dukes of Dixieland a check for $100,000. . . all this while the true creators of this art are playing for nickels and dimes. . . . I'll find one consolation; at least I could carve the pants off any banjo player in New Orleans when it came to playing jazz."

The Sidney Desvignes Orchestra, S.S. *Capitol,* 1935. Trumpeter Desvignes (sixth from L) finally achieved his dream of having the best band in New Orleans. Trombonist Louis Nelson (L) described it: "It was a swing band, just like Basie and them. We'd run from New Orleans all the way up the river to St. Paul, that was every summer. During the off-season we'd play New Orleans. It was two nights for colored. Every Monday we was on at the Pythian Temple, they call it the Roof Garden; and every Tuesday the Bulls Aid and Pleasure Club and the rest of the week was for white. . . . We used stock numbers except when the banjo player Emmanuel Sayles [fourth from L] and Eugene Ware [third from L], the trumpet player, would write and do the arrangements. . . . You had to read to be in there. . . . We didn't play no head numbers at all. The trumpet players would take jazz solos and I'd take one every now and then. You know, mix them in. And then some of the solos would be written out. You had to play what the other fellows wrote. . . ."

(Top) The Kid Rena Band and entertainers, Gypsy Tea Room, Villere and St. Ann, 1936. Rena (seated, fifth from R) played taxi-dance halls and nightclubs like this for nearly twenty years—seven nights a week for floor shows and dancing, a chorus a minute, and no intermissions. The constant grind and heavy drinking took their toll; rarely could he summon the drive for which he was noted as a younger man. His group included alto man Harold Dejan (seated, fifth from L); Pleasant "Smilin' Joe" Joseph (standing, eighth from R), dancer-vocalist and guitar; and three rhythm. Rena's health gave out in 1947 and he died two years later. His 1940 Delta records are his sole legacy. (Second) The Ernest "Kid" Moliere Band, Four Rose Club, St. Philip and North Robertson, 1935–36. Clarinetist Moliere (standing) played this typical uptown black club that barely stayed alive in the Depression. (Third) The Fats Pichon Orchestra, S.S. *Capitol,* 1939. Pichon was a fine arranger and orchestral pianist who knew how to put a good band together by mixing seasoned veterans, like bassist Chester Zardis (second from L) and pianist Burroughs Lovingood (fourth from R), with strong young players, such as trumpeters Dave Bartholomew (fifth from R) and John Brunious (fifth from L). Pichon asked his old friend, songwriter Harrison Smith, to try to get them work in New York, to no avail. Pichon survived to become one of the French Quarter's biggest tourist attractions with his spur-of-the-moment song parodies. (Bottom) Joe Robichaux's New Orleans Rhythm Boys, Rhythm Club, Jackson Avenue, 1938. In 1930 Robichaux (Bottom, R) organized his own six-piece band; three years later it was the hottest swing band in New Orleans with trumpet, alto and tenor (both doubling clarinet), and four rhythm. They recorded twenty-two sides for Vocalion Records in New York in August 1933, one of which—*King Kong Stomp*—deserves serious consideration on any all-time "greats" list. The records opened doors, and agents told Robichaux he could get bookings up North if he had a *big* band. In 1935 he built one around Sidney Desvignes's star alto man-arranger Earl Bostic and went on the road playing one-nighters. Decca recorded (but never released) them a year later, and many of the city's best third- and fourth-generation brass and reed men joined. Arrangers Gene Ware and Henri "Kildee" Holloway (fifth from L and L) wrote simple scores that allowed soloists John "Turkey" Girard (third from L), Frog Joseph (second from L), and Clem Tervalon (fourth from L) considerable freedom. Vocalist Joan Lunceford (holding baton) was considered the Ella Fitzgerald of the South. Their biggest success came in Havana, Cuba, in 1938; they kept working until the draft split them up.

Burnell Santiago, ca. 1942. After Steve Lewis, no pianist in New Orleans was more highly regarded than Burnell Santiago, born in September 1915. He usually worked as a single or with guitar and bass as a trio, but for a while he was on the S.S. *Dixie* with Harold "Duke" Dejan's Dixie Rhythm Boys (Opposite Page, Top, R). He worked with Big Eye Louis Nelson during Mardi Gras, 1939, and was often billed as "Boogie Woogie King," although he himself usually yielded that title to the unsung Willy Forrest. He died in 1943.

The Kid Howard Band, San Columbo Club, 308 Bourbon Street, ca. 1938. Avery "Kid" Howard (L) played drums and learned cornet under the tutelage of the legendary Chris Kelly, who died in 1927. His first band played L & N Railroad excursions to Chicago. During the Depression he worked in pit bands at the Palace, Gem, and Lincoln theaters and played with alto man John Handy's band at the La Vida Dance Hall. When Kid Rena's lip went down, Howard became king of trumpet players. His fiery, driving playing on the 1943 George Lewis Climax recordings made them some of the best records of the revival era. Howard continued playing well into the 1960s.

(Top, L) The Herb Leary Orchestra, Rhythm Club, Jackson Avenue, 1939. Pianist Leary (standing, second from R) had worked with Dejan's Black Diamond Orchestra in the late 1920s before organizing his own band. During the swing era he competed successfully with Papa Celestin, Sidney Desvignes, and other leaders for the better social-club dances. He did some arranging, but mostly used stocks of Ellington tunes or had them taken off records. Because he worked frequently, he had many of the city's best younger players, men who preferred cleaner jobs to the dance-hall grind so many combos had to endure to keep working. He used two basses for a period, just as Duke Ellington did when Jimmy Blanton joined his band in 1939. Trumpeter Ernie Cagnolatti (L) liked Red Allen's style, although most of his work was playing lead. Joe Phillips (seated, second from L) did melody solos and Lawrence Douroux (seated, third from L) the hot work. Son Johnson (seated, third from R) was the most outstanding alto man in New Orleans but refused to leave town. (Middle) The Percy Gabriel Band, Moulin Rouge, Bourbon and Bienville, 1939. Bassist Gabriel worked with the small combos of Kid Rena and Harold Dejan and the big bands of Sidney Desvignes and Herb Leary, and later Don Albert and Jay McShann on the road. For nearly two years he had small units at the Moulin Rouge, this one with Manuel Crusto, trumpet; Jack LaMothe, alto sax; and his older brother Clarence on piano. (Bottom) Adam Lambert's Brown Cats, Club Rio, Springfield, Illinois, 1942. Adam Lambert on guitar and his pianist brother Phamous (second from R) and their string unit opened Hyp Guinle's Original Famous Door on Bourbon Street in 1941. They were immediately successful, along the lines of the Spirits of Rhythm, the Ink Spots, and the Cats and the Fiddle. Thomas Jefferson joined on trumpet that year and stayed with them on the road until 1944, when he was replaced by a very young trumpeter from St. Louis named Miles Davis. (Top, R) Harold "Duke" Dejan's Dixie Rhythm Boys, S.S. *Dixie*, New Orleans–New York, 1936. This group often worked the Lake Pontchartrain steamers in the 1930s and occasionally this New Orleans-to-New York run. (L to R) John Brunious, trumpet; Lester Santiago, piano; Dejan, alto sax; Pleasant "Smilin' Joe" Joseph, guitar and vocal; Percy Gabriel, bass.

(Top, L) Bunk Johnson, Conrad's Rice Mill, New Iberia, May 23, 1945. After recording nearly one hundred tunes between 1942 and 1945 (only a third were released) and being the subject of continuing and intense admiration in and out of print, Bunk Johnson was still working in the rice fields of New Iberia, his home since early 1933, not much better off than the "backyard" trumpet player (Top, M) of 1938. He had played only irregularly in California, in 1943–44, rarely in New Orleans itself, though he would play Mardi Gras, 1946, with Jim Robinson and George Lewis (Bottom), and he accepted occasional jobs and recording dates for Bill Russell's American Music label with brass bandsmen like Kid Shots Madison (Top, R). His initial appearances in New York and in Boston (with Sidney Bechet) were not resounding successes, but despite this, the early New Orleans sound in its postwar incarnation was built around him and the playing of the older classic ragtime and jazz standards. Part of the problem was Bunk's feeling that the other musicians he was working with were "emergency musicians," used only because his preferences were unavailable. Nonetheless, many of the recordings he made during this period are magnificent examples of this form of jazz. (Opposite Page, Top, L and R) Artisan's Hall (pronounced "artesian" in New Orleans), 1460 North Derbigny Street, was one of twenty-odd halls that social clubs hired for their dances. Many of Bill Russell's American Music recordings were made in Artisan and San Jacinto, the latter hall for years having been the site of battles of bands among Desvignes, Celestin, Leary, Robichaux, and others. Trumpeter Wooden Joe Nicholas (Middle) was four years younger than Bunk Johnson and still one of the strongest players in the city. Russell recorded him at San Jacinto Hall with trombonist Jim Robinson, drummer Josiah "Cié" Frazier, and the gifted clarinetist Albert Burbank, whom many liked just as much as they did George Lewis. Nicholas was then playing a black club, the Shadowland, which did not admit whites. Albert Nicholas was his much-traveled and successful nephew. Wooden Joe never left the city, yet his powerful, driving style failed to attract the same critical attention given Bunk. He died in 1954. (Bottom) Three second-generation men who achieved success beyond the confines of their home city went back for a visit in 1944. Bassist Pops Foster, drummer Paul Barbarin, and soprano saxist Sidney Bechet (second, third, and fourth from L) are shown surrounded by Big Eye Louis Nelson (L), bassist Albert Glenny (second from R), and clarinetist Alphonse Picou (R). Glenny was long retired and had been one of the city's finest players. Nelson was working at Luthjen's, and Picou was playing casual jobs but usually could be found tending his own bar.

George Lewis and Jim Robinson (Top, L and M) found new audiences after the war, and Lewis was finally able to give up his longshoreman's job when he began playing on Bourbon Street in 1950. By then he had most of Bunk's band, with the addition of trumpeter Elmer Talbert, seen here with Jim Robinson (Middle, L), who he said was his favorite because he played good lead and also sang good blues. Herb Morand (Middle, R) came back from Chicago in 1941 and usually led his own bands at Mama Lou's on Lake Pontchartrain, Manny's Tavern, and the Rainbow Inn, but had to stop playing in 1950 because of ill health. When he died in 1952, his older sister threw out all his scrapbooks on early New Orleans jazz because she felt playing jazz was nothing to be proud of. Bill Phillips (Top, R) had led his own brass band and dance groups since the twenties but failed to get much public recognition. Papa Celestin (Bottom, clapping), on the other hand, bathed in the limelight. Much of the renewed local interest seemed to focus on him, as he gathered old associates like Alphonse Picou, clarinet, and Bill Matthews, trombone, and began a long stand at the Paddock Lounge on Bourbon Street in 1949.

There may not have been as many brass bands in the 1940s as there had been in the great days, but some, like the Young Tuxedo Band (Top), were organized to maintain the older traditions and play for funerals since so many older players were dying off. There was one significant change: the bands now used alto and tenor saxophones in place of the alto and baritone horns used originally. It was much easier to get a saxophone player, and in this way some younger fourth- and fifth-generation musicians could participate in the city's heritage even if they didn't want to play older jazz styles at dances or concerts. But not all the heritage was maintained! In 1949 Lulu White's famed Mahogany Hall (Bottom, R) was torn down, and the tradition of small neighborhood clubs where one could go dancing, like Luthjen's (Middle) at Marais and Almonaster or Mama Lou's on the lakefront, just off Little Woods Road (Bottom, L), was slowly coming to an end. Jazz fan Barbara Reid described those last days: "...During the week the dance hall [Luthjen's] is closed but on Friday, Saturday, and Sunday a four-piece band keeps the place packed. There are streamers, gaudy lights, soggy tablecloths, and wonderful music. Billie Pierce, the warm friendly woman at the piano, has a voice reminiscent of Bessie Smith....Her husband, DeDe, plays a strong wild trumpet...and he shouts his own inimitable Creole versions of all the favorite numbers...that can only be described as Picnic Style Swing. Luthjen's has been known for some years among the musicians as the 'Old Folks' Home' because of its steady popularity with the people of the neighborhood. Most of these people have been spending their nights out at this establishment since they themselves were young....Signs all around the wall warn against jitterbugging; but we might suggest you beware what we term 'The Cajun Stomp.' The Kitty is passed occasionally. No request is ignored and even the most boring of top tunes is made enjoyable by the band." It lasted into the fifties, later than anyplace else in the country, but it too had to end.

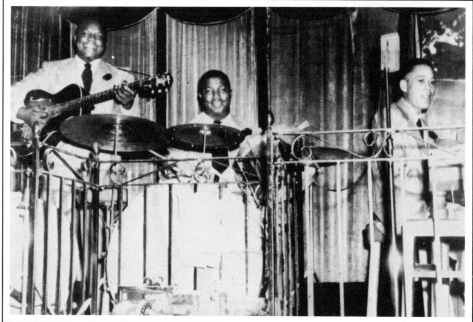

The Jazzfinder

Published monthly at 439 Baronne Street,
New Orleans 13, La.

Orin Blackstone, Editor

Vol. I, No. 5   May, 1948

CONTENTS

EDITORIAL: Address all manuscripts to
the editor, THE JAZZFINDER, at
439 Baronne Street, New Orleans
13, La.
SUBSCRIPTIONS: Annually, $2; Single
copy, 20 cents.

Jazz concerts replaced dancing in the later 1940s. The New Orleans Jazz Club started in 1948, the same year *Times Picayune* editor Orin Blackstone published his monumental *Index to Jazz,* the first serious effort to document all jazz records since Charles Delaunay's work a decade before. He also published a magazine, *The Jazzfinder,* and changed its name to *Playback* before he closed it in 1950. Pianist Armand Hug (Top) played concerts, but preferred working at the Pontchartrain Hotel as a soloist. Younger black musicians left town with traveling bands like Ernie Fields's, as trombonist Bennie Powell did in 1948. Or they became part of the burgeoning rhythm-and-blues field, as trumpeter Dave Bartholomew did. This was instrumental and vocal blues with saxes and electric guitars, and many talented New Orleanians became successful in it after 1947. Singers and players like Smiley Lewis (Middle, L) used veteran pianists like Tuts Washington (R) at the El Morocco in 1949. Paul Gayten, Roy Brown, Professor Longhair (a.k.a. Roy "Baldhead" Byrd), and Fats Domino all played small clubs in and out of the French Quarter until they began touring. Bebop and modern jazz never took hold here; the music was too open, and the "traditional style" was too well entrenched.

After World War II New Orleans finally began to take pride in its music. The newly founded New Orleans Jazz Club, along with prominent professional men like Dr. Edmond Souchon, Joe Mares, Jr., and others, helped bring about public acceptance of Dixieland. Many veterans who had retired began playing, lecturing, and doing concerts on radio, as cornetist Johnny Wiggs did weekly over WSMB in 1946 (Middle, R) with top musicians like (L to R) Julian Laine, Monk Hazel, Chink Martin, Armand Hug, and Bujie Centobie. This was a staff band! Trumpeter George Hartman (Top, R), who had recorded in 1941 and again in 1945, got a new lease on life at the Three Deuces (Bottom, L) with Julian Laine, trombone, and Buji Centobie, clarinet. Jazz concerts brought together veterans and newcomers (Middle, L) like trombonist Tom Brown, who had one of the pioneering jazz bands around World War I, trumpeter George Girard, bassist Sherwood Mangiapane, and clarinetist Raymond Burke. The best new group was George Girard's Basin Street Six (Top, M, and Bottom, R) with the leader on trumpet, trombonist Joe Rotis, and clarinetist Pete Fountain. Girard and Fountain were bound for success, but cancer stopped Girard in 1957. The Roosevelt Hotel, which had for so many years booked name bands, began using good locals like Sharkey Bonano (Top, L), and New Orleans seemed to offer as many opportunities to play as it had in twenty years. Jazz had come full circle.

ZULU SOCIAL AID
AND PLEASURE CLUB
—PRESENTS—
LOUIS ARMSTRONG
and his Esquire All Star Band

1949   1949

KING ZULU

Sunday, February 27th, 1949
BOOKER T. WASHINGTON
AUDITORIUM
DOORS OPEN 7:00 P. M.

In 1947 Louis Armstrong gave up the big swing band that he had fronted since 1935; the band era was over. His All-Stars, featuring Jack Teagarden, Barney Bigard, and Earl Hines, were greeted with tremendous enthusiasm and made a triumphal visit to Europe in 1948. His hometown could bestow upon him no higher honor than to name him King of the Zulus for Mardi Gras, 1949. Louis was an international figure, no longer just a great jazz artist, a man whose person transcended music. Later that year he was on the cover of *Time* magazine as well. This single act, as much as anything else, announced to the world that New Orleans was willing to go all the way, at least in this instance, to redress thirty years of omission. Louis really came home in style. Seven years earlier no studio in New Orleans would have allowed blacks to use its facilities for recording.

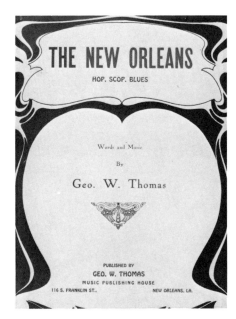

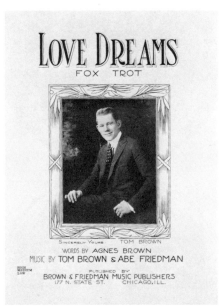

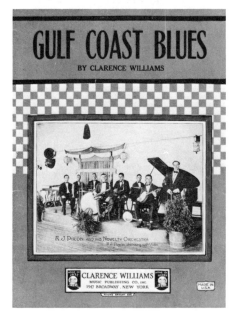

Columbia
Viva-tonal Recording
ELECTRICAL PROCESS
Fox Trot
UP JUMPED THE DEVIL
(Brunies and Lyons)
PARENTI'S LIBERTY
SYNCOPATORS
836-D
(142000)

Columbia
Viva-tonal REG US PAT OFF Recording
ELECTRICAL PROCESS
Fox Trot
Vocal chorus by
Charles Gills
MY JOSEPHINE
(Barnes)
CELESTIN'S ORIGINAL
TUXEDO JAZZ
ORCHESTRA
636-D
(142015)

Columbia
Viva-tonal Recording
ELECTRICAL PROCESS
Fox Trot
PRETTY BABY
NEW ORLEANS OWLS
1045-D
(142022)

Brunswick
U.S. PAT. 1,637,544
Fox Trot
GIT-WIT-IT
—Arodin—
MONK HAZEL and HIS BEINVILLE
ROOF ORCHESTRA
Direction of Sharkey Bonano
THE BRUNSWICK-BALKE-COLLENDER COMPANY
4182

VICTOR
Orthophonic Recording
"HIS MASTER'S VOICE"
For best results
use Victor Needles
V-38576-A
ASTORIA STRUT
(Lee Collins-David Jones)
Jones and Collins Astoria Hot Eight
Orchestra
Victor Talking Machine Co.
Camden, N.J.

Vocalion
U S PAT 1 637.544
Not Licensed for Radio Broadcast
2539-B
KING KONG STOMP
Novelty Dance
Joseph Robechaux and his
New Orleans Rhythm Boys
BRUNSWICK RECORD CORPORATION

Vocalion
Not Licensed for
Radio Broadcast
(20368)
Fox Trot
Vocal Chorus
Sharkey Bonano
WHEN YOU'RE SMILING
—Fisher-Goodwin-Shay—
SHARKEY and his
SHARKS OF RHYTHM
3400
U.S. PAT. 1,637,544 BRUNSWICK RECORD CORPORATION

Delta
B 801-A
GETTYSBURG MARCH
(Traditional)
KID RENA'S JAZZ BAND
Henry "Kid" Rena, Trumpet; Louis Nelson, Clarinet
Alphonse Picou, Clarinet; Jim Robinson, Trombone
Willie Santiago, Guitar; Albert Gleny, Bass
Joe Rena, Drums

11
THE THRILLER RAG
(May Aufderheide)
Recorded in New Orleans in 1942 by
BUNK JOHNSON'S JAZZ BAND
JAZZ INFORMATION
Willie "Bunk" Johnson, trumpet; Albert
Warner, trombone; George Lewis, clari-
net; Walter Decou, piano; Lawrence
Marrero, banjo; Chester Zardis, bass;
Edgar Mosley, drums.
RECORDED BY JAZZ INFORMATION
Exclusive Distributors:
COMMODORE RECORD CO., INC.
415 Lexington Ave., N. Y. C.
4660-4A

No. 9 (137)
BUNK JOHNSON'S
ORIGINAL SUPERIOR BAND
Co-sponsored by Jazz Information

Jazz Man
MOOSE MARCH
Traditional
Bunk Johnson, Trumpet; George Lewis, Clari-
net; Jim Robinson, Trombone; Lawrence
Marrero, Banjo; Austin Young, Bass; Walter
Decou, Piano; Ernest Rogers, Drums.
Recorded June 1942
FOR HOME USE ONLY
RELEASED BY JAZZ MAN RECORD SHOP—4351 SANTA MONICA BLVD—HOLLYWOOD

CLIMAX
DAUPHINE ST.
BLUES
(TRADITIONAL)
GEORGE LEWIS AND HIS
NEW ORLEANS STOMPERS
(CD 113)
104-B
GEORGE LEWIS .... clarinet
AVERY "KID" HOWARD .... trumpet
JIM ROBINSON .... trombone
LAWRENCE MARRERO .... banjo
EDGAR MOSLEY .... drums
CHESTER ZARDIS .... bass
DISTRIBUTED BY
BLUE NOTE RECORDS, N.Y.C.

CREOLE
SLOW BLUES
RAY BURKE'S
NEW ORLEANS BLUE FOUR
1 B

Chicago
Jazz on the Make
1919-1950

"I raved over Chicago—bright lights, nightclubs everywhere, big shows, everything open till 4 or 5 o'clock. I'd never seen anything like that before. Al Capone with his army or his entourage or whatever you call it used to come to enjoy our music. He was a nice little cute fat boy—young—like some professor who had just come out of college to teach or something."
—Louis Armstrong, from the interview by Richard Meryman

Jazz didn't come up the river from New Orleans. It took the Illinois Central Railroad into LaSalle Street Station. It came in box-back coats and high-button shoes, with clarinet sticking out of back pocket and trombone wrapped in newspaper. It brought blacks from all over the South, musicians who sometimes cooked their own meals right on the bandstand—odd behavior in the hard, lawless atmosphere of "Big Bill" Thompson's Chicago.

Thompson ran the town wide open from 1915 to 1923 and again (after a reform movement failed) from 1926 to the end of the decade. His syndicate and gangsters like Al Capone made a farce out of Prohibition. Thompson's cynical post-election greeting was "fellow hoodlums."

Chicago's population of 800,000 blacks was more than three times that of New York, and 25 percent of the total for the city. The South Side had three times as many theaters and nightclubs as New York until the Crash in 1929.

Starting with the "stroll" on South State Street from Twenty-sixth to Thirty-fifth streets, the Elite, Panama, and Dreamland cafes, Monogram and Vendome theaters ran full blast. In full command, King Oliver worked with Bill Johnson's band at the Royal Garden Cafe and doubled at the Dreamland late at night. Later he took his own Creole Jazz Band into the Dreamland with Louis Armstrong and the Dodds Brothers, playing nothing but pure jazz, vying with big bands (up to thirteen pieces) led by Doc Cooke, Charlie Elgar, Sammy Stewart, and Carroll Dickerson. At the Vendome, Erskine Tate hired every leading jazzman in Chicago from 1919 to 1927 to play one-hour jazz concerts between showings of silent films.

The Black Belt jazz bands inspired white groups like the New Orleans Rhythm Kings, led by trumpeter Paul Mares, at the Friar's Inn downtown on Wabash Avenue. They recorded before King Oliver, and their music was equally uncompromising.

Incredible events, such as the "Cabaret and Style Show" staged by Okeh Records and organized by pianist and recording supervisor Richard M. Jones in 1926, presented (to 10,000 people at the Coliseum) thirteen different big bands, plus Louis Armstrong's Hot Five, demonstrating their recent records. Earlier that year Okeh ran "Okeh Race Records Artists Night," with fourteen different artists and bands at the same venue.

The Black Belt shifted in the mid-twenties to Thirty-fifth and Calumet, where the Sunset Cafe, the Plantation Cafe, and the Apex Club were located. Louis Armstrong's

Stompers (with Earl Hines directing) at the Sunset, King Oliver's Dixie Syncopators across the street at the Plantation, and Jimmie Noone at the Apex caused the Chicago *Defender* to comment, "They ought to line 35th Street with asbestos to keep the hot music from scorching passersby." Battles of bands were being held at Midway Gardens, Riverview Park, the Dreamland Ballroom, and the Coliseum.

An intense group of teenagers at Austin High School formed a band around Jimmy McPartland, cornet, his brother Dick, banjo, Frank Teschemacher, clarinet, Bud Freeman, tenor sax, and an intellectual drummer from Oak Park named Dave Tough. These men, along with Indiana banjoist Eddie Condon, pianist Joe Sullivan, and several others, wore out Gennett and Okeh records by Oliver, NORK, and the Wolverines and developed their own "Chicago style," which, through the efforts of Condon and Red McKenzie (leader of the Mound City Blue Blowers), made several brilliant records in 1927-29, despite the fact that they rarely got jobs playing this style with one another.

Jimmy McPartland later explained the devices used: "We had names... like the explosion... in the middle of a chorus, we would build up to an explosion, then go way down soft; 'way down,' we would say. Like, for instance, that final chorus of *Nobody's Sweetheart*. Then, at the end, we used to break out and ride. We called that the 'ride out.' These things were largely Davey Tough's ideas."

Black Belt night life shifted to South Parkway (now Martin Luther King Drive) from Thirty-eighth to Fiftieth streets when the Regal Theatre, Savoy Ballroom, and Grand Terrace Cafe opened in 1928. After the Crash the Regal and Savoy began importing name bands from Detroit and New York. By this time King Oliver, Jelly Roll Morton, the Austin High players, and even Louis Armstrong had all moved to New York.

For a time along West Fifty-fifth Street, Dave's Cafe, The Golden Lily, and the El Dorado kept Carroll Dickerson, Punch Miller, and others working, but Chicago had only Earl Hines, the Dodds Brothers, and Jimmie Noone working on a steady basis. Clubs opened and ran for a time, but Chicago never regained its foothold again.

Chicago's voice, Nelsen Algren, summed it up: "You can belong to New Orleans. You can belong to Boston or San Francisco. You might conceivably belong to Philadelphia. But you can't belong to Chicago any more than you can belong to the flying saucer called Los Angeles. For it isn't so much a city as it is a drafty hustler's junction in which to hustle awhile and move on out of the draft. That's why boys and girls grow up and get out."

Louis Armstrong was, in 1927, known only to musicians, show people, Tenderloin hangers-on, and handfuls of white jazz fans, but his Hot Five and Hot Seven recordings on Okeh would become some of the most influential jazz recordings in history. *Hotter Than That, Potato Head Blues, Cornet Chop Suey, Heebie Jeebies,* and a host of others were master's degrees for jazz musicians for the next decade, but these records were just another job to Armstrong, Johnny Dodds, Kid Ory, and the others, a way to play their music among friends and to make some money. Just how far-reaching these recordings were was echoed by trumpeter Bill Coleman: "Armstrong was my first inspiration. . . . Now this particular number, *Knee Drops* . . . It's in B flat. I used to play it on my horn along with the record. . . . Oh, Louis had some technique, and harmonically he was years ahead of his time. . . . When he plays the introduction he makes a phrase any trumpet player of today would consider modern, and when he comes in with his solo he plays some very unexpected things. . . . All those old records with Pops, I knew them. *Money Blues* with Fletcher Henderson, that was my first impression of Louis."

Chicago boomed with wartime industry, and thousands of Deep South blacks poured in to fill factory jobs. Storyville's closing brought numerous great jazzmen to the "City of the Big Shoulders." They were welcomed by longtime city favorites such as pianist Tony Jackson (Top, L), whose songs like *Pretty Baby* were sung by the Panama Trio (Florence Mills on piano edge, R) at the Elite #1 and the Pekin Cabaret since 1915. Tony worked until only months before his death in April 1921 (Top, R). Cornetist Freddie Keppard (Bottom, L) left New Orleans in 1912 with the Original Creole Band, snubbed a Victor recording contract in 1916, toured until 1918, and finally settled in Chicago. Keppard was a king down South, and he remained one, as did fellow New Orleanian Willie Hightower (Bottom, R). Hightower and Keppard were the same age; one was reserved, whereas the other, known as "Ol' Whalemouth" and "Geechee," was flamboyant and suspicious. The former made one great recording, *Boar Hog Blues,* on Black Patti, with his pianist wife Lottie Hightower's Night Hawks; Keppard failed to leave much of an impression, though he recorded at least a dozen times a decade after his prime. Jelly Roll Morton recalled the Keppard of 1916: "I never heard of a man that could beat Keppard—his reach was so exceptional, high and low, with all degrees of power, great imagination, and more tones than anybody." Keppard burned himself out and died in 1933. Hightower saved his money, his wife was secretary of the union, and he was able to retire after years of theater work.

AMERICA'S GREATEST ROADHOU
"THE HOUSE THAT JACK BUIL"
LOCATED ON MILWAUKEE ROAD
40 MINUTES NORTH OF THE CHICAG

Trumpeter Jimmy Wade (L) was not a New Orleanian but was born in Jacksonville, Illinois. He led Lucille Hegamin's Blue Flame Syncopators, a touring band. He settled in Chicago, worked for a time with Doc Cook, and then led his own band, which featured director-violinist Eddie South and pianist Teddy Weatherford, at clubs like "The House That Jack Built" (Bottom), near suburban Glenview, until he died of tuberculosis in 1933. His Moulin Rouge Orchestra recorded for Paramount in 1923. Teddy Weatherford (Middle) went to Chicago from Bluefield, West Virginia, in 1921 and upset everyone. His huge hands ranged all over the keyboard, and he seemed able to play anything. Earl Hines learned a lot from him, then surpassed him, because Weatherford decided to go to China in 1926 before he had a chance to challenge Hines's brilliance. Pianist Dave Peyton (Top, R) had been active in Chicago before World War I and led bands at all the leading theaters and some of the best nightclubs well into the Depression years. This 1924 band had drummer and washboard player Jasper Taylor, trumpeter Raymond Whitsett, violinist and later bandleader Jimmy Bell, and saxist Oscar Lowe. Peyton opened the last South Side theater to use live music, the Regal, in 1928, with the brilliant, eccentric showman Fess Williams directing. During the 1940s Peyton played solo piano and ran a dry-cleaning business.

Doc Cook and His Dreamland Orchestra, Paddy Harmon's Dreamland, South State and 35th, 1923. Charles "Doc" Cook was born in Detroit and became prominent there before moving to Chicago after World War I. His large orchestra replaced Charlie Elgar's (Bottom) at the Dreamland in 1921, and he held many good jobs in Chicago until Radio City Music Hall in New York hired him as staff arranger in 1930. His big band and jazz unit (featuring Freddie Keppard, cornet, and Jimmie Noone, clarinet) recorded for Gennett, Okeh, and Columbia. Cook directed and played organ. Jimmie Noone (third from R) was featured for seven years before taking Jerome "Doc" Poston (seventh from R) and forming his own band at the Nest, renamed the Apex Club in 1926.

Elgar's Dreamland Orchestra, 1921. Violinist Charlie Elgar (L) played classical music in New Orleans and settled in Chicago in 1913. A year later he led a five-piece unit at the Fountain Inn, and he soon became one of the city's most prominent bandleaders, directing orchestras at ballrooms, theaters, and nightclubs in Chicago and Milwaukee until 1930. This unit featured legendary trumpeter Joe Sudler (standing, R), reputed to have invented the mute for trumpet (patented by Paddy Harmon); Clifford "Klarinet" King; and a precociously gifted clarinet and violin player named Darnell Howard (seated, second from R, and R). After 1930 Elgar became an official of Local 208.

When Joseph "King" Oliver (Top, L) arrived in Chicago (from Pete Lala's Café in New Orleans) in 1918, he was met by delegations from two bands. Always the businessman, he joined both. He played in bassist Bill Johnson's band at the Royal Gardens on 31st and State and in clarinetist Lawrence Duhé's band at Bill Bottom's Dreamland Café. A White Sox fan, Oliver found time to appear at Comiskey Park for the 1919 World Series (Bottom), joining (L to R) drummer Minor Hall, trombonist Honoré Dutrey, (Oliver), first clarinetist Lawrence Duhé, second clarinetist Willie Humphrey, and tenor saxophonist Jimmie Palao (banjoist Bud Scott and bassist Wellman Braud not shown). After a successful but exhausting year's stay in California in 1922, Oliver brought his own band to the Lincoln Gardens, the newly refurbished Dreamland. He decided the pace was too wearing, so he sent to New Orleans for his young protégé, Louis Armstrong, who joined him during that summer (Top, R). Thus began an era that made jazz history.

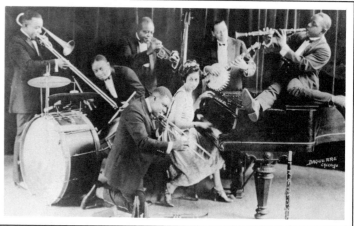

King Oliver's Creole Jazz Band (Top, R) did tremendous business at the Lincoln Gardens, which held nearly a thousand dancers. (L to R) Honoré Dutrey, Baby Dodds, Louis Armstrong, King Oliver, Lil Hardin, Bill Johnson, and Johnny Dodds. Musicians from all over the city came to listen, to try to discover the secret of the two-cornet breaks that Armstrong and Oliver tossed off with such ease and inventiveness. Beginning in April 1923, the Creole Jazz Band recorded forty titles for four companies—Gennett, Okeh, Columbia, and Paramount—the last three contracts being secured by Oliver's longtime friend, pianist and talent scout Richard M. Jones. Their ballyhooing in the old tailgate tradition (Middle, R) helped sell some of their Okeh recordings that year. Some key players, including the Dodds brothers, left at the end of 1923 over contract and royalty differences, and Oliver had to have new photos made (Bottom) for the tour in 1924. Changes included Charlie Jackson, sax; Snags Jones, drums; Buster Bailey, clarinet (first, second, third from L); and Rudy Jackson (extreme R). Clarinet and alto saxophonist Jackson took Oliver's *Camp Meeting Blues* to Duke Ellington's band in 1927, and there it became *Creole Love Call*.

(Top, L) Ma Rainey and Her Georgia Band, 1925. With a few exceptions like Lonnie Johnson, the blues throughout the 1920s were the property of gifted, mature women like Georgian Gertrude "Ma" Rainey. She was active from 1904 to 1935, playing the TOBA theater circuit, tent shows, and carnivals, and she recorded ninety songs in exactly five years, 1923–28. Her Georgia Band included Al Wynn, trombone; Dave Nelson, trumpet; and pianist-composer Thomas "Georgia Tom" Dorsey, later renowned for such gospel favorites as *We Shall Overcome*. Ma died in 1939. (Top, R) Albert Wynn's Paradise Orchestra, 1926. Wynn (seated, with cape) was a smooth, well-trained trombonist, equally at home playing jazz, blues, and show tunes, as he often did. His equally adept trumpet soloist (seated, L) was Adolphus "Doc" Cheatham. Both men worked in Europe and in many outstanding big bands before returning to smaller groups.

The Carroll Dickerson Band, Sunset Café, 1923. Violinist Dickerson was one of Chicago's best-known leaders and led at this club twice for long periods in the 1920s. Clarinetist Buster Bailey (L) and alto man Rudy Jackson (fourth from L) joined King Oliver in 1924. Dickerson toured the Pantages Circuit for nearly a year, led bands at Connie's Inn in New York, directed the Mills Blue Rhythm Band, recorded, but remained known only as a Chicago bandleader. This floor show, produced by actor Clarence Muse, presented singer Mary Stafford (front row, hands raised), an early rival of Bessie and Mamie Smith, and singer-dancer Frankie "Half-Pint" Jaxon (doing splits). Joe Glaser's mother reputedly owned the Sunset, a background that would later stand him in good stead as a booking entrepreneur and, eventually, Louis Armstrong's manager.

The New Orleans Rhythm Kings, also known as the Friars Society Orchestra (Bottom), were *the* white band of the early 1920s. New Orleans players still led the way, and this group brought jazz to most white audiences over a three-year period, 1921–24: (L to R) George Brunies, leader Paul Mares, Ben Pollack, Steve Brown, Lew Black, Mel Stitzel, Leon Roppolo, Volly De Faut. Pollack, De Faut (Top, M), and Stitzel were Chicagoans. The New Orleans players—Brunies (Middle), Mares (Top, L), and bassist Steve Brown (Top, R), who replaced Arnold Loyacano in 1923—drove this band, especially when new prodigal drummer Ben Pollack joined. They dispersed in 1924 when Friars Inn management instituted a floor show and "funny hats" policy. The NORK wasn't a reading band, and when no other work was available in Chicago, George Brunies joined Ted Lewis and stayed for ten years. Paul Mares and Roppolo joined Al Siegal's nightclub band in New York, and then both went home. Steve Brown joined the Jean Goldkette organization. Pollack soon formed his own band. Mares and Roppolo got together again in New Orleans for a final unsuccessful attempt to keep the New Orleans Rhythm Kings together in 1925. Mares went into the family fur business, and Roppolo went into the sanitarium.

Bix Beiderbecke (Top, L), photographed August 30, 1921, Davenport, Iowa, would become the most talked-about and imitated player of his generation. There was something ethereal in his cornet solos that only a handful of musicians have ever been able to grasp. His lines seemed to float separately from what the other players were doing, and yet they were still part of the ensemble. Bix played in the Original Wolverine Orchestra (Top, R) from late 1923 to late 1924: (L to R) Min Leibrook, leader Dick Voynow, (Bix), Vic Berton, George Johnson, Jimmy Hartwell, and Bob Gillette (trombonist Al Gande not shown). Bix's tone, conception, and will-o'-the-wisp personality all contributed to the legend. He didn't have the inexorable drive of a Louis Armstrong, or the same kind of room-filling sound, but what he had he was able to aim right at the heart, no matter what the circumstance. Bix's most successful band associations were the Wolverines and the Frankie Trumbauer Band (Bottom), which worked for part of 1925 and 1926 at the Arcadia Ballroom in St. Louis. Pee Wee Russell (third from L), Trumbauer (with bass sax), and Bix (standing, second from L) were the stars of an unrecorded legend. Bix and Trumbauer joined the Jean Goldkette organization in Detroit in May and later that month took a jazz unit (including Pee Wee Russell) to Hudson Lake, Indiana, to play the Blue Lantern Inn for the summer.

*The Jean
Goldkette
ORCHESTRA
VICTOR RECORDS*

The Jean Goldkette Orchestra, May 6, 1927, University of Pennsylvania, prom date. White jazz achieved the height of perfection in the number-one Jean Goldkette band in 1926–27. Only one other band, Ben Pollack's, came even close in reconciling "commercialism" and real jazz. Goldkette was a classically trained pianist who had dominated music in Detroit since the end of World War I. At his peak, in the mid-twenties, he had nearly twenty bands working, built the giant Graystone Ballroom, and was *the* name in the Midwest. The men in this star-studded band were practically all handpicked for their superior sound and reading skills; they provided a foundation for the soloists: Don Murray, clarinet; Frank Trumbauer, C-melody sax; and Bix Beiderbecke, cornet (seated, L, second from L, and fifth from L). Bassist Steve Brown (standing, fourth from L) and drummer Chauncey Morehouse (seated, second from R) were a superb rhythm team. They were unlucky recording for Victor; the rigidly conservative recording director, Eddie King, shelved their many outstanding, inventive Bill Challis arrangements. The band fared better under the recording supervision of Nat Shilkret and house arranger Eddie Sheasby. *My Pretty Girl, Clementine (from New Orleans), Idolizing, Proud of a Baby Like You,* and *I'm Gonna Meet My Sweetie Now* are the few sides that feature the great swing and solo work of Bix, violinist Joe Venuti, Trumbauer, Murray, and trombonist Bill Rank. The large payroll and the cost of maintaining the Graystone broke up the band later in 1927.

(Bottom) Louis Armstrong and His Hot Five, Chicago, 1925: (L to R) Louis Armstrong, Johnny St. Cyr, Johnny Dodds, Kid Ory, Lil Hardin Armstrong. This was an all-star recording unit, one that made only one or two appearances in public (at the Okeh Race Records Artists Ball, 1926, for one), but whose artistic achievements in sixty sides recorded over three years are still being rediscovered today. These recordings—a return to New Orleans barrelhouse—were a reaction to all that "reading and writing" Armstrong had had to do with Fletcher Henderson's band in New York. The raw, emotional Armstrong trumpet and Johnny Dodds clarinet were balanced by Kid Ory's gruff, basic trombone and the strong foundation of Lil Armstrong's chorded piano and Johnny St. Cyr's banjo. Lil, who married Louis while they were in King Oliver's band, helped shape and direct him toward stardom. When he appeared with her band at the Dreamland in November 1925 (six days later they began making the first Hot Five recordings), she arranged for a five-foot-high banner billing him as the "World's Greatest Jazz Cornetist"—which he was, despite similar claims made for players as disparate as Freddie Keppard and Reuben "Red" Reeves, whom Louis replaced in December 1925 with Erskine Tate's band at the Vendome Theatre. (Top) A previously unpublished Hot Five pose.

"JELLY ROLL" MORTON

KING OF JAZZ PIANISTS

COMPOSER OF MANY POPULAR NUMBERS SUCH AS:

"JELLY ROLL BLUES"	GRANDPA SPELLS
WOLVERINE BLUES	KING PORTER STOMP
LONDON BLUES	THE PEARL STOMP
MR. JELLY LORD	KANSAS CITY STOMP
MILLENBURG JOYS	NEW ORLEANS BLUES
BIG FOOT HAM	AND MANY OTHERS

RECORDING ARTISTS
FOR GENNETT OKEH & PARAMOUNT RECORDS

Jelly Roll Morton (Top, L) achieved immortality with the carefully produced records he made for Victor in 1926–27. Shortly after settling in Chicago in 1922, Morton began making player-piano rolls and records, the best of which were a dozen-odd piano solos for Gennett Records. When Morton's music publisher, Walter Melrose, got him a contract with Victor in 1926, he brought all his resources and creative skills to bear and produced some of the finest jazz records of all time with players of his own choosing. These include *Black Bottom Stomp, The Chant,* and *Doctor Jazz.* Unsuccessful with partner Jimmy Thompson (Middle, R) in vaudeville, Morton offended most people, including many of his musical peers, by boasting of his musical talent (Top, R). Fortunately, history has borne him out, and his Red Hot Peppers recording group of 1926—(Bottom, L to R) Omer Simeon, clarinet; Andrew Hilaire, drums; Johnny Lindsay, bass; Johnny St. Cyr, banjo; Kid Ory, trombone; and cornetist George Mitchell—all did exactly as he asked and recorded more than a dozen masterpieces. Despite all this, Jelly played dates *outside* Chicago until going to New York in 1928.

Throughout the 1920s clubs boomed, from the small Kelly's Stables on Rush Street downtown, where Johnny and Baby Dodds worked for years after they left King Oliver, to the big, brassy Sunset with its lavish, well-produced shows directed by actor Clarence Muse. The Sunset (Top, L) had Carroll Dickerson's big band, one of the best in Chicago for years, although he never achieved national acclaim. The Vendome Theatre (Top, M) presented Erskine Tate through 1927 with an array of fine soloists (and one great recording, *Stomp Off, Let's Go,* on Vocalion in 1926), but then surrendered its position to the Regal and theaters in other areas. Pianist and composer Richard M. Jones (Middle, L, on L) was noted mostly for his composition *Trouble in Mind,* for signing black artists and managing Okeh's "race" department and later Decca's, and for recording superior sides with his Jazz Wizards on Vocalion (Johnny St. Cyr, banjo, and Albert Nicholas, clarinet). Okeh, Victor, Vocalion, Columbia, Paramount, and Gennett cataloged and sold their jazz and blues records as "race"—i.e., black (Middle, M)—separately from their other popular and classical releases. Catalogs often featured ugly racial stereotypes, but this didn't prevent knowing white customers from buying them in black neighborhoods or having them specially ordered, much to the chagrin of their own neighborhood store owners. All the companies maintained the practice of race lists until the end of World War II. (Bottom) The Doc Cheatham Orchestra, Dreamland Café, 1926. Trumpeter Cheatham led this band with Gerald Reeves, trombone, and Jerry Blake, alto sax, for a brief period, and then the bottom seemed to drop out. The reasons were various: owners weren't paying off, and something called an "Amplivox" (an early form of jukebox) began playing Armstrong's and Morton's records in restaurants and buffet flats. Dave Peyton, in his *Chicago Defender* column, saw the handwriting on the wall: "They're getting ready for the gray-haired days." Chicago was slowing down. Cheatham and Blake jumped down to Philadelphia to join Bobby Lee's Cottonpickers.

Erskine Tate's Vendome Theatre Orchestra, 1925. Violinist Tate (seventh from L) directed pit orchestras at three of Chicago's best theaters—the Vendome, the Michigan, and the Metropolitan—from 1919 to 1932, when talking pictures brought an end to the pit band. The famous "Little Symphony" at the Vendome, featuring pianist Teddy Weatherford (L) and trumpeter Reuben Reeves (fifth from R), accompanied silent films and played a one-hour jazz concert between shows. The concerts became a sublime experience when Louis Armstrong replaced Reeves in late 1925. After 1932 Tate fronted out-of-town bands, played walkathons, taught music, had his own music school, and ended up working in the post office.

King Oliver's Dixie Syncopators, spring 1926. Oliver's new big band featured Bob Shoffner (third from R) on second trumpet and a reed section with Darnell Howard (sixth from R); Albert Nicholas (fourth from R), who played clarinet solos; and Barney Bigard (second from R), who by his own admission was the "slappingest and poppingest sax man in all New Orleans." Bigard's tenor, even though he claimed he hated the instrument, rated on a par with Coleman Hawkins's. Oliver joined Dave Peyton at the Plantation Café, befriended the management, and soon eased Peyton out and brought in his own band. Oliver's Brunswick and Vocalion recordings reflect the increasingly commercial leanings of management but are redeemed on *Sugarfoot Stomp, Farewell Blues,* and *Wa Wa Wa.* His biggest sellers were *Someday Sweetheart,* notable for Bert Cobb's tuba solo, and *Snag It.* The arrangements held Oliver back, but he always managed a note of almost unbearable poignancy, as if he had a premonition that Chicago's and his great days were past.

The Sammy Stewart Band, Michigan Theatre, November 1929. Pianist-organist Stewart (in raccoon coat), from Columbus, Ohio, brought Chicago the first band that played special arrangements in 1923. He worked the Entertainer's Café, the Sunset, and the Metropolitan, Grand, and Michigan theaters until he went to New York in 1930 to play the Savoy and Arcadia ballrooms. His fine lineup included George Dixon and Walter Fuller, trumpets (L and fourth from R); Alex Hill, piano (third from L); Banjo Ikey Robinson (second from L); and Big Sid Catlett, drums (top). After 1933 his career went steadily downhill, and he died in 1960.

Louis Armstrong's Stompers, Sunset Café, 1927. In 1926 Louis Armstrong was in Carroll Dickerson's band at the Sunset and doubling with Erskine Tate at the Vendome Theatre. In early 1927 Sunset manager Joe Glaser fired Dickerson because of his supposed unsolicited attentions to silent-screen star Bebe Daniels, who was in the audience, and named Armstrong (seated) leader and pianist Earl Hines (standing, third from L) musical director. Good players like Fred "Tubby" Hall (L), trombonist Honoré Dutrey (second from L), and saxist Boyd Atkins (third from R), composer of one of Armstrong's biggest hits, *Heebie Jeebies,* helped make this a strong unit, but despite repeated entreaties, Okeh made only one side by this group, *Chicago Breakdown,* which went unreleased until Columbia's first jazz re-issue program in 1940.

Chicago's romance with hot jazz seemed short-lived. When George Brunies's older brother Merritt (Middle, L, arms folded) replaced the New Orleans Rhythm Kings at the Friars Inn in 1925, he still had a good unit with himself on trumpet, another brother, Henry, on trombone, and sometimes Volly De Faut, clarinet, or Danny Polo (Top, R). But the band now included violin and three saxes, and they had to play floor shows. They didn't last very long. Saxist-violinist Johnny Provenzano's Band (Bottom, L) was working in Ralph Capone's Hawthorne Inn in suburban Cicero in 1926, also backing up acts, but still allowing room for hot trumpeters Charles "Nosey" Altiere (standing, L) and Phil Dooley and pianist Art Gronwall to solo. Pianist Charley Straight (Bottom, R) led large reading dance bands at swank hotels but liked hot music, and he occasionally hired players like Wingy Manone and Bix Beiderbecke to play in his band. (Top, L) The Mound City Blue Blowers, 1925: (L to R) Dick Slevin, Jack Bland, Eddie Lang, and Red McKenzie. This sensational novelty group, led by McKenzie, a former St. Louis jockey, had a million-seller for Brunswick Records in *Arkansaw Blues*. Vocalist and kazoo player McKenzie was the equal of Jack Teagarden as a white jazz singer, of which there were few.

BACK TO THE
OLD HOME TOWN

(Top, L) Eddie Condon, 1926. Wisecracking banjo player Condon (referring to Red Nichols: "He thought he played like Bix, but the similarity stopped when he opened his case") drifted into Chicago from Goodland, Indiana. He got acquainted early with Bix Beiderbecke and played jobs with a dozen leaders, including Louis Panico, Charles Pierce (the cornet-playing butcher), and pianist Jack Gardner. Condon recorded with Red McKenzie and moved to New York in 1928, where he played occasional jobs with anyone who would hire him. (Top, R) Benny Goodman, 1926. Goodman began playing clarinet at Hull House in World War I, joined the union at thirteen, and after gaining experience joined Ben Pollack's new band in 1925 when he was sixteen. Except for a few months with Isham Jones in 1927, he stayed with Pollack, making all his Victor records, and went to New York with him in 1928. (Bottom, L, L to R) Pianist Jess Stacy, clarinetist-saxist Frank Teschmacher, and drummer George Wettling were among the best young players. They worked together whenever possible with sympathetic leaders like Floyd Towne, Sig Meyers, Charlie Straight, and Art Kassel, who wasn't always easy to please. Wettling went to New York in 1936, Stacy joined Benny Goodman in 1935, and Teschmacher was killed in an auto accident in 1932 while riding in Wild Bill Davison's Packard. (Bottom, R) White City Amusement Park, 1929. (L to R) Milton "Mezz" Mezzrow; Josh Billings, drums; Frank Vernier, friend; and Frank Teschmacher. Mezzrow played clarinet and saxes, sometimes with the Austin High Gang, although he wasn't in their class musically. He got jobs, always hired jazzmen, and talked. Finding work scarce, he moved to New York in 1929 and learned to augment his income in other ways.

(Top, L) Frankie Lehman and Dave Tough, 1925. Banjoist Lehman (L) was one of many leaders who liked jazz well enough to give work to gifted young players like drummer Dave Tough. An Oak Park, Illinois, member of the Austin High Gang, and according to McPartland its "idea" man, Tough sailed for Europe in 1927 with Danny Polo, played with Mezzrow in Paris, recorded in Berlin, and returned home in 1929, playing aboard the *Ile de France*. (Top, R) Gene Krupa, his brother, and friends, ca. 1926. Drummer Krupa (third from L, looking eerily like young Sal Mineo, who starred in *The Gene Krupa Story*) started off a bit later than Dave Tough and some of the Austin High crowd, with leaders like Joe Kayser, bassist Thelma Terry, Mezz Mezzrow, the Benson Orchestra, and the Seattle Harmony Kings before moving to New York in 1928.

Husk O'Hare's Wolverines, Riverview Park, Des Moines, 1926. This unit comprised most of the jazz players who came out of Austin High School in the early twenties, followers of the New Orleans Rhythm Kings and the Original Wolverines. All the men in this group, led by cornetist Jimmy McPartland (standing, M), read music well, and all were jazzmen: (L to R) Frank Teschmacher, Jim Lannigan, Bud Freeman, Jimmy McPartland, Dave Tough, Floyd O'Brien, Dave North, Dick McPartland. Back home playing at White City Amusement Park later in the summer of 1926, McPartland remembered: "Pee Wee, Bix, and Frankie Trumbauer were working down at Hudson Lake [Opposite Page, M].... every Monday, their night off, they'd come and hear us. When we got finished, we would all go off together and catch Louis or Jimmie Noone at the Apex."

(Top) Ray Miller was a former drummer from San Francisco who had been very successful in the East with a group called the Black & White Melody Boys and then formed a larger band. He liked jazz and played it as often as he could after settling in Chicago in 1927. He hired cornetist Muggsy Spanier not long after this 1928 photo was taken and, with some fine arrangements by pianist Art Gronwall, made some very good Brunswick records, the most notable being *Angry.* After Ben Pollack left the Blackhawk Restaurant for New York, Miller had the best band in Chicago, operating out of the College Inn, the basement club in the Hotel Sherman. He left the city one night in 1929 and never returned; some say he owed large gambling debts. (Middle) Roadhouses like the Hudson Lake Casino, near South Bend, Indiana, were a post–World War I development that lasted until World War II. Some, like this one, were seasonal, for summer and early fall; others operated year round and gave jobs to good territory bands from all over the country. Jean Goldkette built at least two of these ballrooms under the Blue Lantern name (Bottom, R), one outside Detroit, the other in Hudson Lake, Indiana (Middle), where Frankie Trumbauer led an all-star Goldkette unit featuring Bix Beiderbecke and Pee Wee Russell in the summer of 1926. (Bottom) Ben Pollack's Californians, Chicago, 1926. Drummer Pollack worked as a sideman in Art Kassel's band and then formed this working and recording group out of the Southmoor Hotel and, later, the Blackhawk Restaurant: (L to R) Glenn Miller, trombone; Benny Goodman, clarinet; Gil Rodin, alto sax; Harry Greenberg, cornet; Ben Pollack, drums; Fud Livingston, tenor sax; Al Harris, cornet; Harry Goodman, bass; Vic Breidis, piano; Lou Kessler, banjo. On December 17, 1926, "that kid in short pants who plays the clarinet," a not-much-over-seventeen Benny Goodman, cut his first solo on Pollack's *He's the Last Word.* The Pollack band worked steadily but had no great success until they went to New York and opened at the Little Club on Broadway in 1928.

Eddie South's Alabamians (Top) were organized by the violinist-leader (R) in 1927 after he directed Jimmy Wade's orchestra for several years. South, the first to make the violin a viable jazz instrument, recorded for Victor that year with drummer Jerome Burke, banjoist Mike McKendrick, and pianist Henry Crowder (British steamship heiress Nancy Cunard's lover in Europe) before touring the Continent for three years, 1928–30. South's music was suitable for smaller clubs like the downtown Club Alabam (Top, R) and contrasted with that of Walter Barnes's Royal Creolians (Middle), who opened the lavish Capone-owned Cotton Club in Cicero in 1928. Natty Barnes (holding one of his Brunswick recordings) featured trombonist Ed Burke (second from L) and William ("Hot Papa") "Bullet" Bradley (fourth from L), trumpeter Lawrence "Cicero" Thomas (fifth from R), and a good drummer, Bill Winston (fifth from L). None of the men in Barnes's band were from New Orleans, despite the Creolian billing. François Mosley's Louisianians (Bottom) claimed at least three players from that state: leader-drummer Mosley (L), the great trumpeter Ernest "Punch" Miller (third from R), and guitarist Charles Ducasting (R). They worked steadily at the Golden Lily Tavern, a Chinese restaurant at 55th and Garfield, for nearly five years, 1929–34. Under the name of Frankie Franko and His Louisianians they made one great recording—*Somebody Stole My Gal*—featuring Punch Miller. Miller got his nickname from having a twin sister, Ernestine Judy. For all his obvious ability, he spent a harried career barnstorming with carnival and circus bands all over the country in the 1930s and with early rhythm and blues revues in the 1940s and 1950s. He returned to New Orleans in the late 1950s in time for the revival, toured with George Lewis in the 1960s, and died there in 1971.

Some of Chicago's outstanding prewar players included trumpeters Eddie Mallory, Punch Miller, and Lee Collins (Top, L to R) and Jabbo Smith (Middle, M). Mallory played with a warm tone; he worked with the Alabamians and Tiny Parham before leading a fine band at the Villa Venice and the Granada Café. He directed the Mills Blue Rhythm Band, married Ethel Waters, and led a big band for her throughout the middle and late 1930s. Miller and Collins were gifted New Orleanians of Armstrong's generation who never rose above small-club work. Jabbo Smith had all the star qualities: exceptional musicianship, tone, technique, ideas, and personality. Brunswick Records recorded his bravura style throughout 1929 in an unsuccessful effort to attract some of Louis Armstrong's audience. Trombonist Preston Jackson, who was with Jabbo Smith in Carroll Dickerson's all-star band at the Sunset, reminisced: "Man that band, Jabbo would play a few tunes and then go down in the basement and sleep. He was always that way. Jabbo was always hard to handle. You had to let him have his way, play what and when he wanted to play. . . . Jabbo was a hot man, he was explosive." His casual attitude cost him his chances, and by the time he changed, newcomers like Roy Eldridge had taken over the spotlight. Pianist Cleo Brown (Middle, L) could play any style well (e.g., *Pelican Stomp* for Decca, 1935) and was a successful entertainer in clubs and on records for a decade. Johnny Dodds (Middle, R) played small South Side clubs all his life, saved his money, and owned an apartment building long before he died in 1940. Banjo Ikey Robinson (Bottom, L) played intricate single-string solos but became better known as an entertainer, leading small groups in and out of Chicago. Paul "Stumpy" Evans (Bottom, M) was Chicago's most promising saxophonist until tuberculosis killed him in 1928. Bassist Thelma Terry (Bottom, R) hired jazzmen like Gene Krupa and Bob Zurke whenever she had the chance.

Pianist Earl Hines made an immediate impression when he arrived in Chicago from Pittsburgh in 1925. Soon he was considered better than established players like Teddy Weatherford and Cassino Simpson. He worked with Carroll Dickerson, Louis Armstrong, and Jimmie Noone, making outstanding records, particularly with Armstrong and Noone, as well as some solos on Okeh and Q.R.S. By 1928 all the upcoming young players were imitating him, and his driving, jagged, and dazzling style remained the most influential until one of his young followers, Teddy Wilson, became famous with Benny Goodman's swing band after 1936. He organized a big band (Bottom) with the help of trumpeter Bob Shoffner and opened at the brand-new, mob-run Grand Terrace Café on his birthday, December 28, 1928, for what would be the longest association with one club, other than Duke Ellington's, in jazz. Hines's big band began recording for Victor in 1929, featuring trombonist Billy Franklin (L), trumpeter Shirley Clay (fifth from L), and the arrangements and tenor sax of Cecil Irwin (second from R). Hines had little trouble riding out the Depression with the Terrace as a base and acquired regular network broadcasts and a new long-term recording contract with Brunswick in 1932. By then he had strengthened his band considerably.

My Best wishes
"Lavere"
from
Louis Armstrong
5/22/31

Gibson
CHICAGO

Johnny Collins
PRESENTS
The International Star
Louis Armstrong

Despite having made dozens of history-making records like *Fireworks, Muggles, West End Blue, Knee Drops,* and *Weatherbird* in 1925–28, and his growing importance as an artist, Louis Armstrong found jobs few and far between after 1928. After selling a book of trumpet exercises to the Melrose firm, he took off for New York, where he soon starred at Connie's Inn in Harlem and doubled in *Connie's Hot Chocolates* at the Hudson Theatre on West 44th Street. He introduced the hit song *Ain't Misbehavin',* which he recorded for Okeh; his audience was greatly enlarged as a result of his turning to quality pop songs of the day. He returned to Chicago in 1931 with a new manager, Johnny Collins, who had him organize a new band to play the Showboat on North Clark Street. Louis had lost weight, he had special arrangements and a band he was happy with, and his records were selling well, despite Okeh's near bankruptcy. When gangsters tried to muscle in and take over his contract, manager Collins booked him down South on one-nighters; he wound up at the new Suburban Gardens outside New Orleans for an entire summer. He was earning nearly $1,000 a week, and his recordings of *I Surrender Dear, When Your Lover Has Gone, All of Me, Georgia on My Mind,* and his theme, *When It's Sleepy-Time Down South,* made him a national name, leading the way to his first trip abroad in 1932.

McKinney's Cotton Pickers were a semi-jazz band before becoming a national attraction under Jean Goldkette's management. Goldkette hired arranger, alto saxist, and vocalist Don Redman (Top, sixth from R) at $300 a week to direct the band in 1927. After constant drilling, they began recording for Victor in 1928, showing the results of Redman's work with good ensembles and intelligent use of the vocal talents of banjoist Dave Wilborn and saxist George Thomas (fourth and second from L). Solos were done by trumpeter-arranger John Nesbitt (third from R), trombonist Claude Jones, and tenor and clarinet star Prince Robinson (third from L). Records like *Cherry, Shim-Me-Sha-Wabble, There's a Rainbow Round My Shoulder,* and *Four or Five Times* made them immediately popular on a national scale, and their dances at the Graystone Ballroom on Woodward Avenue in Detroit and broadcasts over WJR radio drew such crowds that management refused to allow the entire band to go to New York for new recordings in 1929. Redman, Claude Jones, and Joe Smith (fourth from R) did go, and Redman assembled all-star orchestras that included Coleman Hawkins, Fats Waller, Sidney DeParis, Benny Carter, and Kaiser Marshall to make masterpieces like *Gee, Baby Ain't I Good to You, Miss Hannah, Peggy, The Way I Feel Today, Plain Dirt,* and others. Thereafter management relented and allowed the whole band (Top, in 1930) to travel and to record. McKinney's Cotton Pickers was the first band to feature pop vocalists intelligently and to present its music as an ensemble with star soloists. Unfortunately, Goldkette management was overextended with proposed renovations of the Graystone Ballroom, so Redman left to start his own band in 1931. Despite fine newcomers like Roy Eldridge (Bottom, second from L), director Billy Bowen (kneeling), and Joe Eldridge (extreme R) in 1933, McKinney's name meant little after 1935.

Chicago may not have seemed so bright after 1930, but the city hadn't dried up musically by any means. Pianist Cassino Simpson's Band (Top) had been Jabbo Smith's in 1931, but Jabbo neglected business so often that the brilliant pianist was asked to take over. He had fine players like Ed Burke (second from L), Guy Kelly (fifth from L), Milt Hinton (fourth from R), Franz Jackson (third from R), and Scoville Browne (R). "Guy Kelly was on the order of Joe Oliver and Little Mitch [George Mitchell], in the middle register he'd damn near run you crazy," said Preston Jackson. "Guy could play more changes...you put Guy on the blues and slower tunes." When Cass deteriorated mentally the band dispersed; he was institutionalized in 1935 after trying to kill entertainer Frankie "Half-Pint" Jaxon. Three-hundred-pound arranger-pianist Hartzell "Tiny" Parham (Second, with baton) became popular around 1928 and recorded for Victor until 1930. He played many leading nightclubs, theaters, and ballrooms and led one of the groups that replaced Earl Hines at the Grand Terrace around 1931. He hired top sidemen, including Al Wynn (third from L), Guy Kelly (fourth from L), and Willie Randall (second from R). By the end of the decade, Tiny was playing organ at the Savoy when it was converted into a skating rink. He died in 1943. Arranger-composer Jesse Stone (in white suit) organized his Cyclones (Third) to back dancer Sunshine Sammy in 1934 and went on location at the new El Morocco in the fall. Many musicians thought it was the best band in Chicago while it lasted. The new club, located at 55th and Garfield, had a strong show and drew a lot of business away from the Grand Terrace. Players like Doc Wheeler (fourth from L), Bobby Hicks (third from L), Al Wynn (fourth from L), Gideon Honore (sixth from L), Willie Randall (fourth from R), and Budd Johnson (R) made this a great band. Jabbo Smith liked it so much he sat in on rehearsals, wrote out his own parts, and eventually joined it on two different occasions in 1934–35, but the band never had proper management and broke up after only a year. Earl Hines's band (Bottom, Hines holding mike) remained the dominant force in Chicago music for more than a decade. By 1932 he had added good sidemen like George Dixon (second from L), who played trumpet, alto, and baritone saxes, all exceptionally well; Omer Simeon (fifth from L), who was a fine lead sax and clarinet soloist; drummer Wallace Bishop (standing behind Hines); Darnell Howard (fourth from R), a gifted clarinetist and violin soloist; and trumpeter-vocalist Walter Fuller (R). Hines, tenor man Cecil Irwin (fifth from R), and bassist Quinn Wilson (third from R) all arranged, and their Brunswick records of 1932–34 vintage are vastly superior musically (if not in sound) to those done by his first group in 1929. *Cavernism, Swingin' Down, Blue Drag,* and *That's a Plenty* showed how skilled arrangers could successfully adapt Dixieland favorites for a big band. Hines had the Terrace, road tours in the East and South (this photo, Pearl Theatre, Philadelphia, 1932), and nightly network broadcasts (an announcer dubbed him "Fatha"), which made his orchestra as well known as Cab Calloway's and Duke Ellington's.

The Grand Terrace was the best-known place to see and hear jazzmen, but it wasn't the only one. Smaller clubs like the short-lived Zeppelin Inn (Top) presented Frankie "Half-Pint" Jaxon with a combo of five and, as an added guest attraction, Freddie Keppard's band, the last group to play Bert Kelly's Stables before it burned down. Keppard was still strong and powerful, but drinking had slowed him and within three years he would be dead of tuberculosis, not knowing who he was. Jaxon went into radio (Bottom, R) in the early 1930s, toured, played many hotel dates from 1937 to 1941, and went to work for the Pentagon during World War II. His composition and signature theme, *Fan It,* was recorded by Woody Herman's Second Herd in 1946. The Sunset Café sometimes tried out two bands, such as Erskine Tate's and Carroll Dickerson's (Bottom), in an effort to attract customers in 1934. Dickerson's band was in a class with Earl Hines's at this time and appeared at the Savoy Ballroom, where this photo was taken in 1935, with Guy Kelly (L), Ed Burke (sixth from L), Zinky Cohn (seventh from L), and three outstanding saxes in Del Bright (third from R), Scoops Carry (second from R), and Leon Washington (R). Jabbo Smith, Banjo Ikey Robinson, and Zutty Singleton were all in Dickerson's band at the Sunset, but their temperaments clashed and none stayed very long. Dickerson's band should have gone places, but it lasted only a year. The Savoy Ballroom (Middle) had been the last ballroom built, in 1928, and was responsible for shifting the center of black night life from State Street to South Parkway and 47th Street (now Martin Luther King Drive). All the leading Chicago bands, as well as the best territory bands like Bernie Young's and Don Albert's, played long stands there. For a while King Kolax had what amounted to a house band on weekends in the late 1930s. It became a skating rink during World War II.

Joe "Wingy" Manone lost his right arm in a streetcar accident in his hometown, New Orleans, played kazoo, sang in kids' bands, learned enough trumpet to play on the riverboats, barnstormed all through the South and Midwest, and wound up in Chicago. "Wingy had such personality," recalled Art Hodes, "could be so funny, and above all, could really play then. He had a beat you couldn't get away from. If we had two blocks to walk, we'd walk it in time. Those couple of years I lived with Wingy, we lived with a beat. Our mistress was music; we worshiped her as a god." That association produced a 1928 jazz masterpiece on Vocalion, *Isn't There a Little Love*. A few years later, Wingy was a star on 52nd Street.

Cornetist Wild Bill Davison (Top, R, extreme R) spent the years 1927–32 playing with the Seattle Harmony Kings, Charlie Dornberger, Ray Miller, and Benny Meroff's large stage orchestra (Bottom) before forming his own big band in 1931. Meroff was a classy dancer (center) and showman and featured Davison (second from L, front row) and alto man Boyce Brown (fifth from L, top row) on his 1928 Okeh recording *Smiling Skies*. Meroff's road tours took the band as far as Mitchell, South Dakota, where they played the famed Corn Palace Ballroom in 1931 (Above). Davison's own band (Top, R) had a hard time finding work, despite having blown out Tiny Parham in a battle of bands, but with tenor man Bill Dohler (second from L), guitarist Jack Goss (extreme L), and bassist Ralph Hancock (second from R) they did strolling music in downtown Chicago hotels. When star alto and clarinet man Frank Teschmacher was killed in Davison's Packard in 1932, it was the end of Davison's sojourn in Chicago. He spent the next seven years leading his own groups based in Milwaukee or on the road in territory bands. He relocated to New York in 1941.

Survival during the Depression sometimes meant taking jobs, as did pianist Jess Stacy and drummer George Wettling with the fine dance team of Norman and Arlene Selby (Top, L) in 1932. Selby's stamina allowed him to play trumpet while dancing, but the act broke up before either jazzman made much of a living. Pianist Frank Melrose (Top, R) was the younger brother of the music-publishing Melroses and the nearest thing to a barrel-house pianist a white man could be. He worked mostly with small groups, out of town more than in, and billed himself "Kansas City Frank" or "Broadway Rastus" when he recorded *Whoopee Stomp, Jelly Roll Blues*, and *Pass the Jug* for race-labels Paramount and Brunswick in 1929. Some thought it was Jelly Roll Morton. He was murdered after playing a job in Hammond, Indiana, in 1941, under circumstances never satisfactorily explained. (Middle) Drummer Frank Snyder (standing) had been a New Orleans Rhythm King in 1921 and got the job at the Subway Cafe (open twenty-four hours) on North Wabash in 1934. He hired first-rate jazzmen like Oro "Tut" Soper, piano (L); Bud Jacobson, clarinet and sax (center); and trombonist George Lugg (R). They stayed on this job with only one or two changes in personnel well into 1935. Drummer Ben Pollack replaced Snyder in the New Orleans Rhythm Kings and later started his own big band in Chicago. He eventually became one of the finest bandleaders of the late 1920s and Depression years. After his original band broke up in Hollywood in late 1934 (most of the members became the nucleus of the first Bob Crosby band), Pollack reorganized and with another strong band came east to play the suburban Lincoln Tavern in the summer of 1935. (Bottom, L to R) Ben Pollack, leader and drums; Bruce Squires, trombone; Freddie Slack, piano; George Hill, clarinet and sax; Bob Goodrich, trumpet; Opie Cates, clarinet and sax; Stan Loy, alto sax; and Dick Morgan, guitar and vocals; (front) Tripod, Dick Morgan's dog. When trumpeter Bob Goodrich got homesick, Harry James replaced him in 1936. That was one of the last good bands Pollack put together in his long quest for musical superiority while dealing with commercialism.

Small clubs continued to offer good music throughout the Depression. Ray Nance's Rhythm Barons (Top, R) worked together on two jobs from 1933 until 1937, when Ray decided to join Earl Hines's band. Nance (seated) played trumpet and violin, sang, and tap-danced and was so popular that his band was able to work as a unit at Dave's Café and the Midnight Club. Albert Ammons's Rhythm Kings (Top, L) worked at the Club De Lisa for two years, starting in 1935. Ammons was a protégé of rent-party pianists Jimmy Yancey and Pine Top Smith, but learned to play all styles well. This unit recorded *Boogie Woogie Stomp, Early Morning Blues,* and *Mile-or-Mo Bird Rag* for Decca in 1936, after Guy Kelly replaced Bobby Hicks (L) and bassist Israel Crosby replaced Mickey Sims (R). Drummer Jimmy Hoskins and clarinet and sax player Del Bright (third from L) made this one of Chicago's most swinging little bands. Two years later John Hammond brought Ammons to New York, where he succeeded during the boogie-woogie craze after 1938. (Middle) Banjo Ikey Robinson formed this group after leaving Carroll Dickerson in 1935, to work with a road revue called *The Passing Show.* Sidemen were Ed Fant, trombone; Zilner T. Randolph, trumpet and arranger; Jack Oglesby, alto sax; Robinson, banjo and guitar; and Leonard Bibbs, bass. When the group split up, Robinson began playing small clubs in the East with occasional trips to Chicago until well after World War II. (Bottom) Drummer Little Joe Lindsay (standing, R rear) had the band at Tony's Tavern in 1934–35 with trumpeter Herb Morand (standing, L rear), guitarist Isadore Langlois, and pianist William Barbee. They hosted a party on February 14, 1935, to celebrate Louis Armstrong's homecoming after eighteen months in Europe and tied it in with Duke Ellington's stand at the Congress Hotel downtown. Friendly trumpet rival Punch Miller sits at the table (L rear, under Morand's trumpet); Ellington's bassist Wellman Braud is across the table from Duke and Louis. Alpha Smith, Louis's girl friend, is next to him. Louis was resting a sore lip and, after years of managerial difficulties, was about to align himself with manager Joe Glaser. That fall he opened at Connie's Inn in New York and began a brand-new career.

Lil Armstrong's Swing Shack

COME OUT AND BEAT YOUR CHOPS ON OUR SWING FOOD.
OUR MEALS ARE A SOLID SENDER RIGHT IN THE GROOVE.

Flat-Foot Floogie (pig feet)   Boogie-Woogie Stew
Rug Cutter's Roast and Dipsy Doodle Noodles
Hamburg Swingaroo.   Bob-cat Fish.   Jam Session Pies
Tutti-Frutti Inner tubes (chitterlings)   Down Beat Beans (red)

BREAKFAST SPECIALS
Tisket Biscuits and Tasket Hash — Killer Diller Waffles
With Divine Swine— Ham or Bacon

We mug lightly, politely and nightly
We'll swing your crumb-crushers right in the groove.   3406 S. State St.

(Top, L) Lil Armstrong, 1935. Lil led all-male big bands and all-girl orchestras under the name of Mrs. "Louie" Armstrong. She recorded for Decca in 1936 and, while there, became house "pianiste." She returned to Chicago in 1940 and opened her Swing Shack Restaurant (Inset) with its "Tisket" biscuits and "Killer Diller" waffles two years too late. (Top, R) Zutty Singleton returned to Chicago in 1933, worked on and off with Carroll Dickerson, and led his own band at the New Deal Club, the Flagship, and finally at Sam Beers's Three Deuces on North State Street. In 1935 he recorded for Decca and a year later was drumming for Roy Eldridge at the same location. He moved back to New York in late 1937.

Fletcher Henderson revitalized his career when he took his final great band into the Grand Terrace Café, newly located at 35th and Calumet (the site of the old Sunset Café) in November 1935. He featured Roy Eldridge (the object of Fletcher's baton), Buster Bailey (eighth from R), and tenor man Chu Berry (L), whose tune *Christopher Columbus* became a hit recording on the Vocalion label in 1936. Unbusinesslike as ever, Fletcher lost his new stars within a year. Much of the time he was writing arrangements for Benny Goodman or plugging current pop tunes for music publishers while broadcasting. By 1939 he gave up and began playing piano in Benny Goodman's band.

SWING FANS WELCOME TO BRONZEVILLE

THE BRONZEVILLE GazettE

Swing Convention Special

National Edition

VOLUME 2   JUNE 22, 1937   Number 6

PUBLISHED BY THE BRONZEVILLE BOOSTER'S CLUB, 543 E., 47th STREET, CHICAGO, ILL.   PHONE DREXEL 6339

BENNY GOODMAN & ROY ELDRIDGE "SWING OUT" IN CHICAGO JUNE 22

—The Swing Master

BENNY GOODMAN:

"Swing Convention" Biggest Event In Dance History

Teddy Wilson, Lionel Hampton, Gene Krupa and Peg La Centra Starred With Swingmaster

ELDRIDGE IS BANKING ON CLEO BROWN AND ZUTTY

With the 8th Regiment Armory 'specially decorated and air-cooled . . . with Benny Goodman and his clarinet all ready to go . . . Teddy Wilson's fingers a-twisting . . . Lionel Hampton ready for action . . . Gene Krupa all beat out . . . Peg La Centra all loaded down with songs . . . Roy Eldridge and his trumpet all oiled up . . . Cleo Brown all set for action and "Zutty" Singleton cryin', "Bring On the Swing" . . . the Nation is about to witness the biggest, hottest and greatest Swing and Jam session in dance history . . . Many other celebrities will also be there to share honors . . . It's the Swing Convention, Tuesday, June 22, 1937, at the 8th Regiment Armory in Chicago.

Celebs From All Over Globe To Be There

Headed by The Harlem Express, Jimmie Lunceford who just captivated Europe, there will be Celebrities there from throughout the globe to join in the biggest "SWING" and JAMMIN' Session ever attempted. Jimmie Lunceford upon his last visit to Bronzeville, advised the Committee that he would fly here from New York, where he will be playing Nightly at the popular Larchmont Casino to witness the SWING

—Pride of Bronzeville

ROY ELDRIDGE

Bronzeville Boosters Club Welcomes You To The Greatest "Swing" Session In Dance History

543 E. 47th St.
Suite 14,
Chicago, Ill.

DEAR SWING FANS:

We are indeed proud to bring together the greatest array of stars ever to perform under one roof. In offering you the music of the Swingmaster, Benny Goodman and his famous Band with Teddy Wilson, Lionel Hampton, Gene

LAST MINUTE FLASHES:

New York, June 1—Benny Goodman and Ork will leave here June 15 playing one night stands en route to Chicago where he will head the Swing Convention on June 22.

Chicago, June 5—Roy Eldridge told reporters this week that with Cleo Brown at the Baby Grand, Zutty Singleton on the hides and he and his trumpet hitting a few of those high ones fans will soon learn why he was chosen to play the Swing Convention along with Benny Goodman.

Hollywood, June 2—Movie colonies will be in a panic for at least a week as many of the stars have

things at the Swing Convention in Chicago on June 22nd.

Chicago, June 10 — Officials of the Bronzeville Boosters Club declares this Swing Convention will be the biggest affair in dance history as requests for tickets have come in from as far as Japan.

Chicago, June 1—Officials of the Music Corporation of America offered to lay ten to two that never before in History has there ever been as many stars on the same dance program as it is at the Swing Convention. No one has accepted this bet to date.

New York City, June 5—When advance tickets for the Swing Con-

ROY ELDRIDGE TRUMPET WIZARD ON HIS Martin TRUMPET

To my Lou
marde

By 1936 Roy Eldridge was the new king of jazz trumpeters (Louis Armstrong was already beyond categorizing). Not since the Jabbo Smith of 1929 had any brass man been so excessive but, unlike Jabbo, also so disciplined. For the next decade Eldridge's ideas, range, drive, endurance, and unbelievable speed dazzled all other brass players. That year his band opened the Three Deuces and began weekly broadcasts that quickly became the talk of the jazz world. In 1937 they recorded six classic sides for Vocalion with a lineup of (Bottom, L to R) Scoops Carry, Zutty Singleton, Dave Young, Teddy Cole, Roy, John Collins, and Truck Parham. *Wabash Stomp, Florida Stomp, Heckler's Hop,* and especially *After You've Gone* were fingered and memorized much the way Louis Armstrong's *Cornet Chop Suey* had been more than a decade earlier. In 1938 Roy went to New York with an augmented band and began a long run at the Arcadia Ballroom.

Walter Barnes

Drummer Red Saunders had played for walk-athons and Tiny Parham before going into the Club De Lisa in 1937 for what became an eighteen-year run. By 1938 (Top) he and tenor man Leon Washington (R) were the stars. Trumpeter King Kolax (né Bill Little, Bottom, R) started his own band in 1936, which toured with singers and dancer Bill Robinson and by the end of the decade was house band at the Savoy Ballroom. Kolax played lead in Billy Eckstine's band and then led small groups, eventually becoming a fine modern soloist. Lil Armstrong played one of Johnny and Baby Dodds's last jobs at the Hotel Hayes, April 1939 (Middle), with Natty Dominique, trumpet; Sudie Reynaud, bass; and singer Lonnie Johnson on guitar. Johnson had returned to music with new Decca and Bluebird releases in 1937 after a long layoff and often worked with traditional groups like this one. A year later Johnny Dodds died, at forty-eight. The Walter Barnes Band (Bottom) worked steadily because they had built up a big following all over the South and had played the Savoy Ballroom before going back south for their annual spring tour. Some of the sidemen, like Preston Jackson (third from L) and tenor man Johnny Hartzfield (second from R), stayed in Chicago, but Barnes was used to comings and goings in his band and usually had little difficulty finding replacements among younger players eager for road experience. On April 24, 1940, he played the Rhythm Club in Natchez, Mississippi, an old church remade into a nightclub whose windows and rear door had been sealed off to prevent people from getting in free. A fire broke out suddenly and raged out of control, while the patrons stampeded to get out the front door. Barnes's band kept playing, trying to maintain calm, but it was too late; he and all his men but two (bassist Art Edwards and drummer Oscar Brown, shown in photo) were trapped. A total of 198 persons lost their lives. Several blues singers recorded the story of the Natchez fire, which forty-two years later remains one of the ten worst fire-related tragedies in U.S. history. Barnes was three months short of his thirty-fifth birthday.

Earl Hines and the Grand Terrace Chorus, 1939. After a generally lackluster year, Earl Hines reorganized his band in 1939 and signed with RCA to record for Bluebird. The Grand Terrace, pride of the city's black-and-tan clubs, shut down in 1940, and Earl broke his ties with manager Ed Fox. He went back again briefly in 1941 and four years later realized a long-cherished dream. He opened his own lavish supper club, the El Grotto, with another fine band, but the time was wrong, and after a year of trying he gave it up. Two years later he was with Louis Armstrong's All-Stars.

Jimmie Noone and "girls," Cabin Inn, 35th and South State Street, 1939. Jimmie Noone formed a big band after one of the South Side pimps opened a nightclub, the Platinum Lounge, at 36th and Vincennes for him in 1937. He played New Orleans with it for the first time in twenty years. He liked his band and it was popular, working at Benny Skoller's Swingland and then the infamous Cabin Inn (the old Dreamland), which billed itself as the oddest nightclub in town (it was). It had a transvestite chorus line, allowed homosexual and interracial dancing, and even put in a radio wire, but Noone was unable to interest anyone in recording his band, which featured Al Wynn, trombone; Moses Gant, tenor sax; Dalton Nickerson, trumpet; Gideon Honore, piano; and an outstanding young ballad singer, Joe Williams. The club was closed in 1940, and Noone led combos until he left for Hollywood in 1943.

Staged jam sessions (Top, R) organized by Harry Lim featured Roy Eldridge, Bud Freeman, and Jimmy McPartland, and the Panther Room at the Hotel Sherman brought in Fats Waller in 1939 (Top, L) to appear opposite the new Muggsy Spanier Ragtime Band, which recorded some marvelous sides for Bluebird in its short existence. Spanier was born in Chicago in 1906, made his first records with the Stomp Six on Autograph in the Marsh Building in 1924, and later appeared with Ray Miller's fine band to record *Angry*. He spent the Depression touring with Ted Lewis and Ben Pollack and after a long illness formed the Ragtime Band, which made its debut at the Hotel Sherman on April 29, 1939, in both the Old Town and Panther rooms four nights (and afternoon sessions as well) a week. *Relaxin' at the Touro* and *Big Butter and Egg Man* are among the masterpieces this band (Middle, R) produced with fine interplay between Spanier and his clarinetist, Rod Cless, and trombonist George Brunis. Six months later the band broke up in New York when no further work was available. The playing of nearsighted alto man Boyce Brown (Middle, L), heard on location discs, was original, timeless, and avant garde at the same time; his trio work at the Liberty Inn is the basis of this assessment. He never attracted attention and in the fifties entered a Catholic mission, took vows, and became known as Brother Matthew. (Bottom, L) Members of Paul Whiteman's band paid a visit to Bix Beiderbecke's grave site in Davenport, Iowa, in 1940: (L to R) Harry Goldfield, George Wettling, Mike Pingitore, Miff Mole, and Charlie Teagarden. Teagarden and Mole were Whiteman's soloists that year but soon left, Mole to cure his ulcers and return to studio work and teaching, and Teagarden to start his own big band, which he kept throughout 1941.

Horace Henderson (Top, L, second from L) organized outstanding bands faster than anyone else in the business, and some musicians liked his arrangements better than his brother's. From 1937 to 1942 he had long stands at Benny Skoller's Swingland, the Savoy, the Grand Terrace, and the 5100 Club. (L to R) Ed Fant, Ray Nance, (Horace), Viola Jefferson, Nat Atkins, and Pee Wee Jackson were in his 1940 band, which made *Shufflin' Joe, Kitty on Toast, When Dreams Come True,* and others for Okeh. To give him a send-off, his first Okehs bore the label "Fletcher Henderson conducts Horace Henderson's orchestra." It didn't help; Horace never broke through. He joined the army in 1942 and led small groups after the war, away from Chicago.

(Top, R, second from R) Wingy Manone returned to Chicago as an established name with a long string of recordings when he played the Brass Rail in 1941 with Floyd Bean, piano; Bob McCracken, clarinet; and Warren Smith, trombone. He had the benefit of starring in a Bing Crosby–Mary Martin film, *Rhythm on the River,* for Paramount, had a brief coast tour with a big band, and then opened the Rail over New Year's. (Above) Roy Eldridge's band at the Capitol Lounge, January 1941, was the hardest-swinging band in Chicago, with John Simmons, bass; Kansas Fields, drums; Rozelle Claxton, piano; and Dave Young, tenor sax. Eldridge didn't record with it, but took Gene Krupa's offer to become a featured soloist with his big band in April.

(Opposite Page) In the shadows of the South Side, men like Lee Collins, Punch Miller, and Herb Morand, all veteran New Orleans men, eked out a small living, their musicianship intact, but their ability was vastly overshadowed by the Roy Eldridges and by newcomers like King Kolax. (Top, R) Trumpeter Lee Collins was at the Ship, North Clark Street near Ontario, in 1939–40, with a small band and a group of singers and dancers. He had been forgotten as a jazzman. By 1940 even Erskine Tate found the band business unrewarding and opened his own music school (Top, L) with some degree of success in 1945, but with the advent of modern jazz he found himself in the post office. Downtown in the Loop area, name bands played the large theaters, and a New York star, Red Allen, became one of Chicago's hottest names at the Downbeat Club and Joe Sherman's Garrick Lounge on Randolph Street (Middle, R) with J. C. Higginbotham, trombone, and Don Stovall, alto sax, from 1942 to 1946. In the summer of 1942, Billie Holiday had a long engagement at the Downbeat accompanied by Allen's band. Club owner Joe Sherman tried branching out with jazz concerts (Middle, L) but without the success they were having in New York. Popular newcomers included former Kansas City star trumpeter Bill Martin, whose band, with tenor man Moses Gant, recorded for small companies like Hy-Tone. A former favorite, Jabbo Smith (Bottom, L), went back, not to Chicago, but to Milwaukee in 1945, after working in obscurity at the Alcazar in Newark. Jabbo could still play well, but soon there was little opportunity or incentive to do so, and eventually he stopped trying. (Above) Fats Waller's Orchestra, on tour, stopped to attend the Musicians' Annual Picnic (Top, L) with all the local names on hand. The Chicago Theatre (Top, R) was just one of the many Loop theaters that featured stage shows with name bands and top acts in 1938–45. (Bottom) Pianist Max Miller (L) was a local radio favorite before the war and was flexible enough on piano and vibraphone to adapt to modern jazz. His 1948 combo at the Stage Door in Milwaukee featured trumpeter Tommy Allison and ex-Krupa trombonist Jay Kelliher. Miller remained only a local favorite.

Postwar jazz centered around lounges like the Circle Inn (Top, R), where jam sessions featuring Red Allen (R) and Roy Eldridge (L) augmented music played by ex-Hines trumpet star George Dixon's band (Dixon, R of Allen). The Bee Hive (Top, L) opened in 1948 and kept veterans like Chippie Hill, Art Hodes (billed, ironically, as New York's favorite, after a decade and a half in his hometown), and Minneapolis cornetist Doc Evans busy. The booming club scene could not save great old Chicago landmarks like the Vendome Theatre (Bottom, torn down in 1949), where Erskine Tate held sway from 1919 through early 1928 with stars like Louis Armstrong, Reuben Reeves, Stump Evans, and Teddy Weatherford. The Chicago of Big Bill Thompson, Hecht and MacArthur, and even Nelson Algren was beginning to disappear.

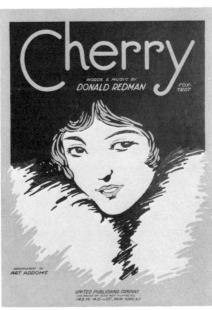

Gennett
5102-A   11357
Wolverine Blues
(Spikes-Morton-Spikes)
New Orleans Rhythm Kings
Formerly Friar's Society Orch.
DIVISION OF
THE STARR PIANO CO.
RICHMOND
IND.

Gennett
5133-B   11384
Canal Street Blues
(Oliver-Armstrong)
King Oliver's Creole
Jazz Band
DIVISION OF
THE STARR PIANO CO.
RICHMOND
IND.

VE
VICTOR
Orthophonic Recording   Orchestra
Steamboat Stomp—Fox Trot
(Vaivén del Buque)
(Morton)
Jelly Roll Morton's Red Hot Peppers
20296-B
VICTOR TALKING MACHINE CO.
Camden, N.J.
VE

VE
VICTOR
Orthophonic Recording   Orchestra
Sunday—Fox Trot
(Domingo)
(Miller-Cohn-Stein-Kreuger)
Jean Goldkette and His Orchestra
Vocal refrain by Keller Sisters and Lynch
20273-B
VICTOR TALKING MACHINE CO.
Camden, N.J.
VE

Brunswick
Fox Trot
WILD MAN BLUES
Las tristezas de un bohemio
JOHNNY DODDS' BLACK BOTTOM
STOMPERS
3567—A
THE BRUNSWICK-BALKE-COLLENDER COMPANY
MADE IN U.S.A.
REG. U.S. PAT. OFFICE. M. de F. MARCA INDUSTRIAL REGISTRADA

OKeh
ELECTRIC
FOR BEST RESULTS
USE OKeh NEEDLES
41001   Fox Trot
SORRY
(Quicksell)
BIX BEIDERBECKE
AND HIS GANG
(81569)
MADE AND PATD IN U.S.A. JAN. 21, '13 AND RE 16685
OKEH PHONOGRAPH CORPORATION NEW YORK

OKeh
ELECTRIC
FOR BEST RESULTS
USE OKeh NEEDLES
40971   Fox Trot
NOBODY'S SWEETHEART
(Kahn-Erdman-Meyers-Schoebel)
McKENZIE AND
CONDON'S CHICAGOANS
(82082)
MADE AND PATD IN U.S.A. JAN. 21, '13 AND MAY 22-23
OKEH PHONOGRAPH CORPORATION NEW YORK

Vocalion
U.S. PAT. 1.637.544
Not Licensed for   Radio Broadcast
7185
Four or Five Times—Fox Trot
Quatro o cinco veces   —Hellman - Gay—
Jimmie Noones' Apex Club Orchestra
With Vocal Chorus
BRUNSWICK RECORD CORPORATION

Brunswick
U.S. PAT. 1.637.544
Fox Trot
With
Vocal Scat
DECATUR STREET TUTTI
—Smith— JABBO SMITH and His
RHYTHM ACES   (Four Aces
and the Joker)
Vocal Scat by Jabbo Smith
7078
THE BRUNSWICK-BALKE-COLLENDER COMPANY
MADE IN U.S.A.
REC. U.S. PAT. OFFICE. M. de F. MARCA INDUSTRIAL REGISTRADA

VE
Orthophonic Recording
VICTOR
For best results
use Victor Needles
V—38118-B
ZONKY—Fox Trot
(Andy Razaf-Thos. Waller)
McKinney's Cotton Pickers
RCA Victor Company, Inc.
Camden, N.J.
VE

Brunswick
MADE IN U.S.A. U.S. PAT. 1.637.544
Not Licensed For Radio Broadcast
Fox Trot
Vocal Chorus by
Walter Fuller
ROSETTA
—Hines—
EARL HINES
and His Orchestra
6541
BRUNSWICK RECORD CORPORATION
U.S. PAT. OFFICE. M. de F. MARCA INDUSTRIAL REGISTRADA

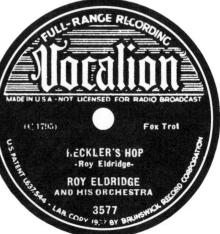

FULL-RANGE RECORDING
Vocalion
MADE IN U.S.A.—NOT LICENSED FOR RADIO BROADCAST
(C 1795)   Fox Trot
HECKLER'S HOP
—Roy Eldridge—
ROY ELDRIDGE
AND HIS ORCHESTRA
3577
U.S. PATENT 1.637.544 — LAB. COPY 1937 BY BRUNSWICK RECORD CORPORATION

Good Old New York
1917-1950

"American music is not jazz. Jazz is not music. Jazz remains a striking indigenous product, a small sounding folk-chaos, counterpart of other national developments...The chief excitement in it proceeds from a series of jerks, systematic anticipations and retardations of the arbitrary, regular, unfailing beat...We have here to do with an extraordinarily popular drug-like use of the materials of sound...It is smart; superficially alert, good humoured, and cynical. Essentially, nonetheless, it is just another means of escape...

—Paul Rosenfeld, *An Hour with American Music*, 1929

Riverboat bandleader Fate Marable once stated, "I can tell a New Orleans band from a Chicago band or a St. Louis type anytime, but New York, of course, doesn't have any particular style—it has everybody's way of playing."

New York assimilated everything, homogenized it, smoothed it out, repackaged it, and then sent it out as its own. It took the carefully played music of the Original Dixieland Jazz Band, five men from New Orleans, and capitalized on the barnyard noises they made on their horns on tunes like *Livery Stable Blues* at Reisenweber's to create "the first sensational amusement novelty of 1917." The ODJB's records sold in the millions and spawned dozens of imitators.

Harlem's post-1920 emergence was due in part to the overnight success of vaudeville singer Mamie Smith's Okeh record of *Crazy Blues*. It sold 75,000 copies the first month and began a rush to record any possibly talented female singer over the next four years, few of whom were real blues singers. (Bessie Smith, despite her popularity and high income, was never New York's ideal; she was never slick enough to be homogenized.) New York preferred tall, handsome Ethel Waters, who sang ballads and jazz tunes better than anyone else, and would later be a Broadway star.

The success of Sissle and Blake's musical *Shuffle Along* in 1921 brought scores of Broadway stage directors, stars, and bandleaders rushing up to Harlem trying to unearth its gold. Park Avenue socialites fought over choice black maids who knew how to do the Charleston, and clubs like Barron's Exclusive Club, Connie's Inn, and the Cotton Club offered torrid floor shows competing for the downtown carriage and tourist trade and big-time Broadway spenders.

Harlem's first jazz star was Memphis trumpeter Johnny Dunn, who accompanied Mamie Smith on records. His hard, bright tone, use of mutes and wa-wa effects, double-time breaks, and other devices on *Dunn's Cornet Blues* made him famous and widely imitated. Six foot five, a dandy in his box-back coat, Dunn had an ego that knew no bounds after the Prince of Wales presented him with a five-foot-long English coach horn for his show-stopping solos in the Plantation Revue in London in 1923.

Much more advanced music was being played by solo pianists like James P. Johnson, Lucky Roberts, Willie Gant, and Willie "The Lion" Smith, who evolved an intricate, stride-bass style out of ragtime in intense competi-
tions in small clubs in Harlem and on San Juan Hill in the West Sixties. Black was beautiful, but Paul Whiteman, whose orchestra was hugely successful with fiddles and saxophones at the Palais Royal on Broadway, made "a lady out of jazz," playing George Gershwin's *Rhapsody In Blue* with the composer at the piano, at Aeolian Hall in 1924.

That year Fletcher Henderson's orchestra began its long stand at Roseland Ballroom on Broadway at Fifty-first Street and added Louis Armstrong on trumpet. At the same time cornetist Bix Beiderbecke's playing with the Original Wolverine band was overwhelming musicians at the Cinderella Ballroom three blocks away. Musicians witnessed Armstrong's destruction of Johnny Dunn as a role model and would later refer to the period as "Before Louis and Bix" and "After Louis and Bix."

Despite Armstrong's and Beiderbecke's impact, cool and businesslike cornetist Red Nichols and his Five Pennies, with trombonist Miff Mole, recording on a dozen labels from 1925 through 1931, were the public's favorite, and Nichols hired out at huge sums to any leader willing to pay.

New York's two hundred-plus ballrooms brought in bands from all over the country, and some, like the Roseland and its archrival, the Arcadia, held five thousand dancers. In Harlem the Savoy Ballroom, equally large, opened in 1926 and used the hottest bands it could find, inspiring brilliant dance steps, from the Lindy Hop to the Shag, for the next decade. The "Track" as it became known, featured breakfast dances lasting until noon, with continuous music by Chick Webb, Jimmie Lunceford, Teddy Hill, and Erskine Hawkins, and a relief band, the relentlessly swinging Savoy Sultans. All for forty cents.

Jam sessions in Harlem ranged from the Nest and the Rhythm Club to Clark Monroe's Uptown House and Minton's Playhouse. Fifty-second Street's dozens of clubs, from 1933 to the late forties, were a perpetual carnival of jazz and entertainment, with everyone from soloists like Art Tatum and Billie Holiday to big bands like Count Basie's.

New York had become the vortex of the entertainment industry: recording, music publishing, and radio were centered here. It was the proving ground, necessary for individual players as well as bands of all sizes. Reputations meant little away from New York. One had to be seen and heard here, in the Apple, and then it was possible to join a name band, to challenge the giants in jam sessions, as Lester Young, Charlie Christian, and Charlie Parker did, even though they had done it already in Kansas City and the Southwest. Only then did you become a star. It is still true.

Duke Ellington's career was unstructured before he went to the Cotton Club on Lenox Avenue in 1927. At that time Irving Mills became his manager and his music publisher, and in an unusual contract arrangement, Mills worked out these percentages: Duke Ellington, 45 percent; Irving Mills, 45 percent; and lawyer Sam Buzzell, 10 percent—a closed corporation. The relationship bore fruit, for however great his band and his ideas, Ellington was still a black man in a white society; in 1927 and for many years thereafter, Mills was the only man capable of getting him maximum money and a steady job with no layoffs (he was at the Cotton Club through 1933). Ellington made more than three hundred recordings for half a dozen labels through 1934, made four motion pictures, and took a highly successful tour of Great Britain (1933). Duke performed his "Jungle Nights in Harlem" at the Cotton Club: all-white clientele, all-black show; Broadway sports, high public officials, foreign royalty. And gangsters: Jack "Legs" Diamond, with girl friend Kiki Roberts, to Ellington: "Play *St. Louis Blues.*" He played it. Diamond danced by the bandstand, repeating his request all night. Ellington continued to play *St. Louis Blues.* Diamond gave Duke a $1,000 bill—"Buy yourself a cigar!"—then another $1,000 bill, and he walked off into the dawn. It was that kind of time.

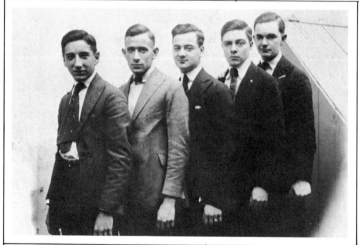

(Top, L) The Original Dixieland Jazz Band's success as a Novelty Event, 1917–18, at Reisenweber's Restaurant, Eighth Avenue at 58th Street, and their million-seller Victor records *Livery Stable Blues* (replete with barnyard noises from the front line), *Dixie Jass Band One-Step, Margie,* and *Palesteena* inspired dozens of similar bands. The best of them, the Original Memphis Five (Bottom, L), with organizer-trumpeter Phil Napoleon (third from L) and trombonist Miff Mole (extreme R and Middle, L), produced more than two hundred recordings, including *Aunt Hagar's Children's Blues,* which composer Darius Milhaud, entranced with jazz, took back to Paris with him in 1922. Mole, from Roosevelt, Long Island, adapted his childhood violin training to the trombone and became the most widely copied player of the twenties, famous for his fast, clean staccato style. Mole's and Napoleon's services were sought by commercial leaders such as Sam Lanin (Middle, R), who paid them large salaries to jazz up his band at Roseland Ballroom. Known as "$22.50 Sam" (sideman's recording scale then), Lanin recorded often, hiring men like the Dorsey brothers and Red Nichols for their jazz skills. Violinist Paul Specht's orchestra (Bottom, R), with its hot unit, the Georgians, led by trumpeter Frank Guarente (fourth from L) and featuring Russ Morgan (fourth from R) and pianist Arthur Schutt (fifth from L, with sax), were admired for their musicianship and Columbia recordings like *Snake Hips, Way Down Yonder in New Orleans,* and *I Wish I Could Shimmy Like My Sister Kate.*

Fletcher Henderson (Top, L) at twenty-six looked every inch a leader—tall, well dressed, and college educated. His band (Top, R) played special arrangements written by multi-instrumentalist Don Redman (fourth from R) at the Club Alabam on West 44th Street. After six months at the Alabam, they replaced A. J. Piron's New Orleans band at Roseland Ballroom on Broadway at 51st Street in July 1924, beginning a relationship that lasted off and on for seventeen years. Until Louis Armstrong (Bottom, third from L) and Buster Bailey (fifth from R) joined in October, trombonist Charlie Green (third from R) was the only inspired soloist. Armstrong's playing on *Shanghai Shuffle, Naughty Man,* and sides that were otherwise horrors such as *I Miss My Swiss* helped pull the entire band out of its Whiteman-oriented playing and inspired Don Redman (extreme R) to write imaginative arrangements on *Copenhagen, Sugar Foot Stomp, Money Blues,* and *What-Cha-Call 'Em Blues,* which put Henderson in a class by himself. Despite the prestige of working with Fletcher Henderson, Armstrong felt confined, unable to sing (he did one vocal, the first take of *Everybody Loves My Baby* on Regal), and returned to Chicago in November 1925. Henderson replaced him with Russell Smith, then added Rex Stewart; but it was slim, handsome Joe Smith—whose playing was the closest possible thing to the human voice—whom some fans like young John Hammond preferred to Armstrong. Henderson broadcast regularly from Roseland over radio station WHN, as he had done from the Club Alabam. He was the "Colored King of Jazz."

Public Theatre   Second Avenue at Fourth Street

Directions: Lexington Avenue Subway to Astor Place

Gala Opening Friday, April 15th
F L E T C H E R   ?
HENDERSON
AND HIS ORCHESTRA in
"Harlem Highsteppers"
W I T H
GREENLEE & ROGERS   DOC STRAINE & VIOLA McCOY
CONWAY & PARKS   16 DANCING GIRLS
IN STAGE SENSATION Produced by
ADDISON CAREY and CHARLES DAVIS
PLUS RECENT TALKING PICTURES
Astonishingly Low Prices

Matinee		Evening	
15c—Balcony	25c—Orchestra	25c—Balcony	35c—Orchestra

(Weekends—Ten Cents Increase)
NEW SHOW EVERY FRIDAY—Continuous 11:30 A. M. - 11:30 P. M.
SPECIAL SATURDAY MIDNIGHT SHOW

Fletcher Henderson, at his peak in 1927 (Top, R) with trumpeters Joe Smith and Tommy Ladnier (second and third from R), trombonists Jimmy Harrison and Benny Morton (third and fifth from L), and Coleman Hawkins (fifth from R), recorded *Rocky Mountain Blues* and *Hop Off*. But Don Redman's departure and an auto accident in 1928 that resulted in dismissal from Vincent Youman's *Great Day* show in 1929 sent Henderson's star earthward. Casual and carefree, seated in his Packard convertible (Middle, L), Fletcher Henderson relaxed with cast members: composer Harold Arlen (second from L), Lois Deppe (waving), orquestrator Will Marion Cook (white pants), and trumpeters Bobby Stark (fourth from R) and Rex Stewart (extreme R). His lack of concern (and management) cost Henderson his position at Roseland Ballroom, although he got the job at Connie's Inn in 1931 instead. In 1932 John Hammond (Middle, R) booked him into his theater and brought him back on records. His band in 1932: (Bottom, L to R) Russell Procope, Coleman Hawkins, Edgar Sampson, Clarence Holiday, Walter Johnson, John Kirby, (Henderson), Russell Smith, Bobby Stark, Rex Stewart, J. C. Higginbotham, and Sandy Williams. A year later Hammond recorded such masterpieces as *Happy Feet, Nagasaki,* and the Coleman Hawkins vehicle *It's the Talk of the Town* for English Columbia.

Duke Ellington arrived in New York in 1923 as pianist in banjoist Elmer Snowden's Washingtonians. They played several months at Barron Wilkins's club in Harlem and then began a four-year run at the Hollywood, later Kentucky, Club on West 49th Street near Broadway. After Snowden quit to join Broadway Jones, Ellington became leader. In 1925: (L to R) Sonny Greer, Charlie Irvis, Otto Hardwicke, Snowden (who returned briefly), and Bubber Miley. Ellington there met his future manager, Irving Mills, who groomed him by having him play two downtown nightclubs with a larger band in preparation for the job that would bring him fame.

James Wesley "Bubber" Miley (L) co-authored *East St. Louis Toodle-oo* and *Black and Tan Fantasy,* two of Duke Ellington's most important songs. Ellington acknowledged his debt when he wrote: "Our band changed its character when Bubber came in. That's when we forgot all about sweet music." Miley left him at the Cotton Club in 1929 to free-lance here and abroad, including a spot with dancer and later dance and jazz critic Roger Pryor Dodge (R) in Billy Rose's *Third Little Show* in 1931. Later that year Ellington's manager, Irving Mills, built a show and band around him called *Harlem Scandals,* but tuberculosis set in after only a short time on the road. He died in May 1932 at twenty-nine.

The California Ramblers (Top, R) featured Adrian Rollini, bass sax and xylophone (sixth from R), and Fud Livingston and Bobby Davis (fourth and third from R), saxophones, at their Rambler's Inn on Pelham Parkway in the Bronx. Their best recordings, like *Vo Do-Do-Do-Do-De-O Blues* on Okeh, were by the Little Ramblers or Goofus Five. Detroit's Jean Goldkette band (Bottom) had Bill Challis's advanced arrangements and all-star personnel—Bix Beiderbecke (Top, L, and Bottom, fourth from L); Don Murray, clarinet (fifth from L); Frankie Trumbauer, C-melody sax (second from R); Steve Brown, bass (with water pistol); and Chauncey Morehouse, drums (seventh from R). Victor's rigid dictates inhibited them; only *Sunday, Clementine*, and a few other recordings capture their thrilling sounds. Last-minute ballyhoo at the Bronx Zoo (Middle, L) failed to stop their breakup in 1927. Adrian Rollini took the soloists (Middle, R) plus Eddie Lang (second from L) and Joe Venuti (second from R) to the Club New Yorker for three weeks; that brief association is fortunately preserved on Trumbauer's Okeh records of *Baltimore* and *Krazy Kat* and on Beiderbecke's own *At the Jazz Band Ball* and *Jazz me Blues*.

In 1929 Nichols toured with some of the wild and woolly, undisciplined, hard-drinking Chicagoans: (L to R) Max Kaminsky, Mezz Mezzrow, Bud Freeman, Joe Sullivan, Dave Tough, Pee Wee Russell, (Nichols), Eddie Condon, Herb Taylor. Nichols used some of these men on his Brunswick records, but they never got along personally, much as he admired their playing. Nichols was really a conservative, whereas the Chicagoans were left-wingers by that day's standards.

The musicians raved about Bix, but the public preferred cornetist Red Nichols, whose recordings, many made in partnership with Miff Mole, dominated the industry, 1925–31. Nichols's playing was clean and precise, and he had worked with everyone from Sam Lanin to Paul Whiteman by his twenty-second birthday. Hundreds of his records, made under names like the Five Pennies, Red and Miff's Stompers, Arkansas Travellers, the Red Heads, Charleston Chasers, and Miff Mole & His Little Molers, display Nichols's pure tone and concern for form. He once stated: "Every man in the band had the opportunity for individual expression, but it's disciplined freedom, so the result has an overall pattern." No Nichols recording is less than interesting, and some, like *Shimme Sha Wabble, One Step to Heaven,* and *Farewell Blues,* are extraordinary. Nichols was a role model for many black brass men in the twenties. Yet, despite his eminence, after his band played the Park Central Hotel in 1931, Nichols disbanded and relocated in the Midwest using unknown players. His World Famous Pennies spent most of the thirties on the road. He came back once, 1935–36, to conduct on radio as Loring Nichols, for Bob Hope and Ruth Etting. His turn came again after the war when combos were again in fashion.

Ray Miller's band (Middle, L) played the rival Arcadia Ballroom on Broadway at 53rd Street and made it tough on Sam Lanin at Roseland by hiring away Miff Mole (kneeling, M) to join Frankie Trumbauer (fifth from R) and Andy Sannella (second from R), alto sax. Roger Wolfe Kahn's multimillionaire father, art patron and banker Otto Kahn, bankrolled his son's superb orchestra (Top, R), which played the Biltmore Hotel in 1925, and then, digging even deeper, built the lavish Perroquet de Paris at 146 West 57th Street for the band. It had a lighted glass dance floor, the Williams Sisters, and a $5 cover charge. Even with fine Victor records like *Jersey Walk, Delilah,* and *Crazy Rhythm,* which featured Arthur Schutt (L), Vic Berton (fourth from L), Joe Venuti (seventh from L), and the much sought-after Miff Mole (third from R), Kahn couldn't make it. He tried a last stand at the Hotel Pennsylvania in 1932–33 and then left the business. Later he became a test pilot for Grumman Aircraft on Long Island. The last great band of the era was Ben Pollack's (Bottom), which delighted New Yorkers at the Little Club, at the Silver Slipper, in two musical comedies, and over a nine-month run at the Park Central Hotel, 1928–29. Jimmy McPartland on cornet (fifth from L), Benny Goodman (sixth from L), and Jack Teagarden (fourth from R and Top, L) played arrangements by Teagarden's predecessor, Glenn Miller; *My Kinda Love* on Victor stands out.

In 1928 Jelly Roll Morton (Bottom) moved to New York after burning his bridges in the Midwest. His new business card said "Originator of Jazz—Stomp—Swing. Victor artist—nothing too large—nothing too small." Still a major Victor artist, he quickly made some important new masterpieces, including *Georgia Swing* (one of the first uses of the term in jazz), *Kansas City Stomps, Shoe Shiner's Drag, Boogaboo,* and *Mournful Serenade*. New players like trumpeter Ward Pinkett and trombonist Geechie Fields were joined by his favorite clarinetist, Omer Simeon, working in Luis Russell's band at the Nest Club. Pinkett and Fields also worked on the only regular job Morton ever held in New York, at Rose Danceland on West 125th Street, a second-floor dance hall above the Harlem Opera House, in 1928. A year later he found it difficult to get jobs and to assemble enough sympathetic players who would play what he wanted. In RCA Victor's Camden studios in July 1929 (Top, R) he had only two New Orleans players, clarinetist George Baquet (who worked in Philadelphia) and alto man Paul Barnes (R); Walter "Foots" Thomas (fifth from L) and his brother Joe (third from R), who had been on tour with him in 1927; and ex-Ellington trombonist Charlie Irvis (fifth from R). They produced *Tank Town Bump* and *Burning the Iceberg,* two good but not memorable recordings. Booker Harry Moss kept Morton (Top, L) working mostly out of town, whenever possible, but jobs were few and far between after 1930. And there were to be no more recordings for eight long years.

When few good jobs were available in 1930, one way to succeed was to be outrageously handsome, dress superbly in white tie and tails, play light, flashy, stride piano, and lead a soft, smoothly swinging band with a fine rhythm section. It didn't hurt twenty-seven-year-old Claude Hopkins (Top, L) that he had a high tenor named Orlando Robeson to swing *Marie* (years before Tommy Dorsey) and sing ballads like *Trees,* or a personable trumpeter-vocalist named Ovie Alston (Top, R) to sing the Hopkins theme, *I Would Do Anything for You*, and a fine acid-toned New Orleans clarinetist in Edmond Hall (L). They were very successful at Roseland Ballroom and on Columbia, Brunswick, and Decca records; made both features and short films; and played at the Cotton Club. But it didn't last. When swing came into vogue, Claude Hopkins seemed an anomaly, and even after adding stronger players like Jabbo Smith and Vic Dickenson, he had to declare bankruptcy in 1938. Although he resumed his career in 1939, he never again rose to the top. Cornetist Rex Stewart organized his band (Bottom) after he left Fletcher Henderson in 1933. He followed Henderson into the Empire Ballroom at 48th and Broadway. Edgar Sampson wrote many good scores, including tunes that Chick Webb would later make famous, and Stewart featured Ward Pinkett (third from L), trumpet; Ram Ramirez (fifth from R), piano; Rudy Powell (R), saxes; and Tommy Benford (second from R), drums. A year later he and his singer, Sonny Woods, joined Luis Russell at the same ballroom for several months and then went with Duke Ellington, who really knew how to display his talent.

Eccentric Indiana trumpeter-trombonist Jack Purvis (Middle, L) had played and recorded with Hal Kemp and the California Ramblers in 1929–31, set fire to hotel rooms, flown as a mercenary in South America, written suites for 110-piece orchestra, and returned to New York to play 52nd Street briefly in 1935. Three years later he made headlines when he was discovered leading a prison band in Texas. His bravura trumpet style is heard on *Mental Strain at Dawn* on Okeh. Puerto Rican trumpeter Louis "King" Garcia (Top, R) was more dependable and played society jobs for years, amazing jazzmen in after-hours battles with his solo work and power; but he never hesitated to let anyone know how good he was and as a result made few friends and fewer records. *Swing Mr. Charlie* on Bluebird is a good example of his playing in 1935. Percussionist Vic Berton (Top, L) was very advanced musically, a dabbler in the occult who often greeted his students in flowing black robes. In 1935 he led a big band that recorded, but he failed to get work and departed for the Hollywood studios. Joe Venuti (Top, M) played *everything* on violin; he was well loved, but irresponsible and a practical joker. He led some good bands but never seemed to go anywhere because he wouldn't take his work seriously. Ray Noble's debut at the Rainbow Room (Middle, R) was highly publicized; trombonist-arranger Glenn Miller (seventh from R) had put together an all-star unit with Claude Thornhill, piano, and Charlie Spivak, trumpet (fifth and eighth from L); Pee Wee Erwin, trumpet; and Bud Freeman, tenor (fourth and sixth from R). Mildred Bailey (Bottom) came out of enforced retirement to resume her recording and radio career in 1935. Husband Red Norvo (R) took a fine sextet into the Famous Door late that year.

Sidney Bechet revived his career in 1938 and was soon recording for several labels and playing at Nick's (Top, R). Musicians and critics regarded Bobby Hackett (Top, R) so highly that he began working as soon as he arrived from Boston in 1937. In 1938 he was at Nick's opposite Sharkey Bonano's band and was recording for Vocalion. His fine 1939 big band (Bottom) had more than its share of heavy drinkers but made beautiful records like *Embraceable You*. They were set for a major hotel job and a commercial radio show, if they could pull themselves together for the audition. They never made it; Sammy Kaye got the job, and Hackett wound up working for Horace Heidt, deeply in debt. Muggsy Spanier (Middle, R) left Bob Crosby's band in 1941 and started a similar big band with Dean Kincaide arrangements that featured Vernon Brown (sixth from L), George Wettling (sixth from R), and the gorgeous and talented Linda Keene (R). They set a house record at the Arcadia Ballroom that year and made some good records for Decca, but the draft took too many good players and Spanier was forced to disband in 1943.

For twenty years, in nearly thirty different clubs, one kind of jazz or another was being played in a two-block area from Fifth to Seventh avenues on West 52nd Street. The first may have been Elmer Snowden's band at the Furnace Club, west of Broadway, and the Mound City Blue Blowers at John Perona's Bath Club at 35 West 53rd Street, in 1930. Art Tatum or Willie "The Lion" Smith or both may have played Joe Helbock's Onyx Club at 35 West 52nd Street around this time, and it can be proved that Joe Sullivan and Tatum did play there after Repeal in 1933 with the Spirits of Rhythm. A year later the Hickory House, Famous Door, and others began competing with groups led by Bunny Berigan (Middle, R) with singer Red McKenzie (M). A 1936 montage shot (Top, L) shows the Onyx and Jack White's Club 18, where Berigan worked briefly after leaving Benny Goodman. With Berigan's group were Joe Bushkin and Eddie Condon (second and third from R); they made his first record of *I Can't Get Started with You* on Vocalion that year. Joe Marsala (Bottom) led a mixed group with Red Allen on trumpet at the Hickory House in April 1936, when Allen was on a layoff from the Blue Rhythm Band. It went without incident. Condon and Bushkin were also on this job. Fats Waller (Top, R) played the Yacht Club at length in 1938 at the height of his career.

There was something for everyone on 52nd Street, from the novelty jazz of *Music Goes Round and Round* (Decca, 1935) by Mike Riley and Eddie Farley (Top, L, R and L) to Count Basie's band at the Famous Door (Bottom, R). Wingy Manone's quartet (Bottom, L) opened the Hickory House in 1934 with Joe Marsala (L); Sid Weiss, bass; and Carmen Mastren (R). Manone's Vocalion record *The Isle of Capri* was such a big hit in 1935–36 that he had to go on the road with a big band to ride on its publicity. Stuff Smith (Middle, L) hit with *I'se A-Muggin'* on Vocalion in 1936, and its success took him to Hollywood to seek a film career that never materialized. John Kirby's band (Middle, R)—with Charlie Shavers, trumpet; Buster Bailey, clarinet; and Russell Procope, alto sax—played intricate arrangements of classical tunes like *Anitra's Dance* on Vocalion. Immaculately attired, they played the best clubs and hotels until the war, when key personnel left and Kirby could not maintain the group's sound quality. Joe Marsala's band at the Hickory House in 1937 (Top, R) featured brother Marty on trumpet and Joe's wife, Adele Girard, on harp, which gave their Variety record of *Jazz Me Blues* an ethereal quality. Count Basie's band (Bottom, R) with Buck Clayton on trumpet initiated the Famous Door's big-band policy in July 1938; they also recorded classics like *Jumpin' at the Woodside* for Decca. (Opposite Page, Third row R, L to R) The Scarsdale Wildcats, the youngest revival group, 1946: (L to R) Eddie Phyfe, Johnny Glasel, Bob Wilbur, Dick Wellstood, and Charlie Traeger. (Opposite Page, Top, L and R) Coleman Hawkins's debut at Kelly's Stables in 1939 resulted in a jazz classic, his Bluebird record of *Body and Soul*, his theme song, a last-minute substitution. The Spirits of Rhythm featured gifted pianist Marlowe Morris (Middle, R, extreme L) at Kelly's Stables in 1940, the year Jimmy Ryan's (Middle, L) opened with traditional jazz. Milt Gabler had weekly jam sessions there in 1941 with everyone from Red Allen (Bottom, R, fourth from L), Hot Lips Page, Pete Brown, Marty Marsala, and Earl Hines (fifth through second from R), whose big band was playing a block away at Roseland Ballroom. (Bottom, L) Veteran Harlem pianist Don Frye (his name is misspelled in Ryan's side wall ad) became intermission pianist in 1943 and stayed until Ryan's closed in 1962.

The Downbeat (Top, L) opened during the war on the site of the Yacht Club and presented Art Tatum's new trio (Middle, L) with Slam Stewart, bass, and Tiny Grimes, guitar. Their interplay was the talk of the jazz world, yet their only recordings were made by struggling independents Comet and Asch. Hot Lips Page (Middle, R) led many groups on 52nd Street from 1939 until the fifties. This 1945 group worked at Kelly's Stables after they had moved to the street in 1940. Drummer Jack Parker, Don Byas on sax, Billy Taylor on bass, and pianist Cyril Haynes rounded out the band, which did not record. The Downbeat Club, 66 West 52nd, featured Billie Holiday, Coleman Hawkins, and the Tiny Grimes group. (Top, R) Hailing a cab at closing, swing guitarist Teddy Bunn (one of the street's originals, as far back as 1933) returned from a lengthy stay in California to play an engagement at the Downbeat in 1946. His group did not make any records. (Bottom) The street as it appeared in its twilight, ca. 1947, with just a handful of jazz clubs remaining. The Onyx with Billy Eckstine after his big band broke up, Jimmy Ryan's with Jack Teagarden after his band broke up; crew cuts, pipes, and sports jackets were giving way to bald spots, cigars, and paunches. Sherry Britton, Lili St. Cyr, and Winnie Garrett were bumping and grinding to the sounds of a Lester Young–inspired sexophonist.

Greenwich Village had little jazz groups at the Pirate's Den, the Cowboy, and the Starlight Room on Christopher Street in the twenties. The Hot Feet Club on West Houston Street featured Otto Hardwicke's band with Fats Waller in 1931; the Village Nut Club had Joe Haymes's big band with Pee Wee Erwin and Johnny Mince in 1932–33; the Black Cat on West Broadway had bands throughout the thirties, led by Lonnie Simmons or Skeets Tolbert, and in 1937 Clarence Profit began a long run at George's Tavern on Grove Street. The real boom came with the opening of Nick's in 1937, and later with Café Society and the Village Vanguard, with well-publicized and regular jazz bills. Billie Holiday with Frankie Newton's band (Middle, R) opened Café Society in 1939 with the Boogie Woogie Boys (Bottom, L), Albert Ammons and Meade Lux Lewis (R), plus Pete Johnson and Joe Turner. Red Allen's band (Top, R) with Kenny Kersey (L), J. C. Higginbotham (second from L), and Edmond Hall (third from R) played Café Society in 1940 and worked steadily for a decade. Eddie Heywood (Bottom, R) played relief piano at Nick's, worked with Leonard Ware (a fine guitarist) at George's Tavern and with Zutty Singleton and his own trio at the Vanguard, and in 1944 formed his own sextet. The sextet featured Vic Dickenson and Doc Cheatham (second and third from R) but mainly Heywood's own highly individualistic and stylized piano, most notable on Cole Porter's *Begin the Beguine*, which made him a national attraction in theaters, cafés, and motion pictures. He had to stop playing in 1947, at the peak of his career, because of paralysis, but he resumed his career successfully after 1950.

Nick Rongetti (Top, L), Fordham Law School 1927, preferred playing piano in Greenwich Village nightclubs. By 1936 he was able to open his own place at 140 Seventh Avenue South, later moving to Seventh Avenue and 10th Street. He loved jazz and jazz musicians and kept Sidney Bechet, Sharkey Bonano, Bobby Hackett, Bud Freeman's Summa Cum Laude Band (Bottom), and Jimmy McPartland (Top, R) working. His was the first of the name jazz clubs in the Village, and it continued after his death. Nick kept a grand piano on stage and two uprights for intermission pianists like Willie "The Lion" Smith, Mel Powell, Eddie Heywood, Cliff Jackson, and others; he used the other to play duets. Sometimes he played more often than the jazzmen wanted, but they liked working for him. Eddie Condon was more or less his house man, working with most of the bands that played there. George Brunis and Pee Wee Russell filled that role as well. Freeman's band with (L to R) Dave Bowman, Condon, Pee Wee, Stan King, Max Kaminsky, Clyde Newcomb, (Freeman), and Brad Gowans made wonderful records for Bluebird, Decca, and Columbia in its year of existence. McPartland's band (Top, R, L to R) had Joe Sullivan, Hank Isaacs, Brunis, (the leader), Condon, and Pee Wee Russell; they did not record.

I'LL BE SEEING YOU AFTER THE SHOW IN ANOTHER GREAT HIT "THE COTTON CLUB PARADE"

ME TOO!

WALTER WINCHELL said:

"I've been around for more than a decade and I want to go on record as saying that the show with those star performers, BILL ROBINSON and CAB CALLOWAY, is the GREATEST COTTON CLUB SHOW OF THEM ALL"

BROADWAY at 48th ST.   CI 7-1000

AFTER THE SHOW the Scene Shifts to the COTTON CLUB

DUKE ELLINGTON PETERS SISTERS PegLeg BATES Mae JOHNSON

CHOCOLATEERS AIDA WARD ALAND & ANISE 50 COPPER-COLORED GALS 50 SEPIAN STARS

3 SHOWS NIGHTLY: 7-12-2

NEVER A LOCATION OR COVER CHARGE MINIMUM AFTER 10 DINNER $1.50 6 TO 9:30 SAT.-SUN.-HOLIDAYS $2.

COTTON CLUB B'WAY at 48th ST. • Circle 7-1000

THE WORLD FAMOUS

COTTON CLUB
BROADWAY & 48th ST., N.Y.C.   LAck 4-7300
HERMAN STARK, DIRECTOR

FIRE NOTICE: Look around now and choose the nearest exit to your seat. In case of fire, walk (not run) to that exit. Do not try to beat your neighbor to the street.   JOHN J. McELLIGOTT, Fire Chief and Commissioner.

THE COTTON CLUB

Presents

COTTON CLUB PARADE
SECOND EDITION

Book By IRVING MILLS

Lyrics and Music By
DUKE ELLINGTON, REGINALD FORSYTHE, ANDY RAZAF, JOHN REDMOND
LEE DAVID, LEE WAINER, LUPIN FIEN

Orchestral Arrangements by   Production Conceived and Staged by
WILL H. VODERY   CLARENCE ROBINSON

FEATURING

ETHEL WATERS + DUKE ELLINGTON
NICHOLAS BROS.

GEORGE DEWEY WASHINGTON

BILL BAILEY   MAY DIGGS   3 GIANTS OF RHYTHM
ANISE & ALAND   BESSIE DUDLEY   IVY ANDERSON
RENEE & ESTELA   MARDO BROWN   TALBERT'S CHOIR

"KALOAH"

DUKE ELLINGTON AND HIS FAMOUS ORCHESTRA
IVY ANDERSON, Vocalist

EDDIE MALLORY and his CALIFORNIANS

ENTIRE ROOM CONCEIVED AND DECORATED
BY
JULIAN HARRISON

PROGRAM ON LAST PAGE

The Cotton Club reopened downtown in September 1936 on the site of the Palais Royale, 48th and Broadway, which for a year had been Connie's Inn downtown. Irving Mills handled the talent, usually Duke Ellington's and Cab Calloway's bands plus headliners Ethel Waters and Bill Robinson. Ellington began writing for the show (Bottom, R), which starred Ethel Waters in 1937. The bands had to play for dancing (Middle, R) as well. Ellington wrote the entire score for the 1938 show (Bottom, M), including the hit *I Let a Song Go Out of My Heart.* When he decided not to return, Louis Armstrong and Maxine Sullivan did the 1939 shows with Cab and Bill Robinson. Troubles loomed when the club was cited for income-tax violations. Don Redman's and Andy Kirk's bands played the remainder of 1939 and until June 1940, when the club closed without warning, leaving Kirk unpaid. It was the end of an era; two other major Broadway nightclubs, the Paradise and the Hollywood, both closed around the same time. During the war, the Hurricane, Café Zanzibar, and one or two other clubs staged black shows and used black bands.

CABARET NIGHT
AT THE MUSIC BOX 1211 U St., N. W.
Friday, June 3rd, 1938, 9 P. M.
FEATURED ENTERTAINMENT
"JELLY ROLL MORTON"
Number One Swing Pianist of America Presents
THE BIRTH OF SWING
DINE—WINE—DANCE
Subscription 50c
Under Auspices of Laundry Workers Organization Committee

After running a small nightclub near Howard University in Washington, D.C., for two years, Jelly Roll Morton (Top, L) burst into the news again by attacking W. C. Handy's place in jazz history in the pages of a 1938 *Down Beat* magazine. The publicity encouraged him, and he decided to tackle Good Old New York one more time in 1939. Roseland Ballroom continued to use top-ranked black bands like Count Basie's, Earl Hines's, and Ella Fitzgerald's (Middle, L), with guest artist Erskine Hawkins on trumpet. The Arcadia featured Roy Eldridge's fiery trumpet, vocals, and red-hot band for a good part of 1939. Besides Roy's solos, all three reed men were featured at length, and miraculously, all of it went over the full Mutual network! Their records, however, were poorly made by Varsity. Clarence Profit's trio (Bottom, L) worked the Village, 52nd Street, and the Hotel Times Square and made some marvelous records for Brunswick, Columbia, and Decca. Teddy Wilson called him a true original who had complete knowledge of chords but was too wrapped up in his music to care for himself; he died in 1944 at the age of thirty-two. The Café Zanzibar (Bottom, R) was one of several (Hurricane, Bandbox, etc.) that kept big bands and black shows working during and after the war.

A new group of historians, fans, and record collectors built a cult around sixty-four-year-old New Orleans trumpeter Bunk Johnson, whose band's triumphal debut at the Stuyvesant Casino (Top, L and R) on the Lower East Side commanded media space from none other than composer-critic Virgil Thomson of the *Herald Tribune*. Johnson was still capable of playing inspired music at an age when the elder statesmen of jazz, Duke Ellington and Louis Armstrong, were in their mid-forties, and Victor and Decca snapped him up. Aside from Johnson, many focused on the passionate, sweeping clarinet of George Lewis (Top, R), whose playing was later slavishly copied by impressionable young white players the world over. Master publicist Ernie Anderson built a market for Eddie Condon's persona with concerts, broadcasts, jam sessions, and a constant stream of articles in magazines and newspapers, so that late in 1945 Condon was able to open his own nightclub (Bottom) on East 3rd Street, featuring the same men he had been associated with for the past decade. Condon's, Nick's, and Jimmy Ryan's catered pretty much to a Dixieland format of trumpet-trombone-clarinet (Bud Freeman and Ernie Caceres were exceptions), and when 52nd Street and Harlem dried up after the war, hundreds of fine players, once welcome everywhere, were faced with no outlet for their brand of jazz. Stuyvesant Casino and Central Plaza (a windy catering hall) began presenting weekend jam-session-style combos—men from this floating pool of talent—and making them play in this Dixieland format, with very mixed results. Swing, in particular the saxophone, was dead....

5¢ in our Automatic Phonograph

BRINGS YOU THE SWINGING RHYTHM OF

RED (HENRY) ALLEN
and his ORCHESTRA

★ EXCLUSIVE VOCALION RECORD ARTISTS

imagine if Beethoven had recorded

ninety - twelve inch record sides of his playing, his personal memoirs, his thoughts and feelings about music. Would there be a more priceless living document in all classical music? Unfortunately this did not happen.

but it did happen in the American music called jazz. On May 21, 1938,

Ferdinand Jelly Roll Morton sat at the piano in the Coolidge

Auditorium at the Library of Congress. This historic day marked the beginning of five weeks of recording, from which emerged

a living history of jazz colorful, fascinating, importantly factual, as only Morton, greatest creative personality of jazz, could play, sing, and tell it.

inaccessible for nine years these records remained in the Library Archives while music lovers the world over clamored for them.

now they will be issued The enterprise and prestige of CIRCLE SOUND, Inc., documentors of pure Afro-American music, have secured the rights to release this American documentary.

More jazz records were made in New York than anywhere else, and few made better ones from 1934 to 1937 than Red Allen (Top, L). But they did not make him a star, and he joined Louis Armstrong's band as a sideman at the same time Louis (Middle, L) was signing for a series of Fleischmann's Yeast programs in 1937. Joe Glaser (L) and agency head Cork O'Keefe look on. Shortly after this February 1934 Columbia Records date (Top, R), Benny Goodman started a swing band and by the end of the year was broadcasting on NBC's new "Let's Dance" program, which built him a national audience that later helped make him the "King of Swing." Jelly Roll Morton (Bottom) renewed his ties with Victor in 1939 and recorded a series of old New Orleans tunes. He hired Sidney Bechet (L), Zutty Singleton (third from L), and Albert Nicholas (fourth from R) to assist in making it New Orleans music and produced the masterpiece *I Thought I Heard Buddy Bolden Say*. Eight years after his death, in 1948, Rudi Blesh and Circle Records secured the rights to release his historic 1938 Library of Congress recordings (Middle, R), which opened an entire new field of study.

Recording supervisors (artists and repertoire men now) often went unnoticed by the public because their names never appeared on records before long-play. Ed Kirkeby, Frank Walker, Harry Grey, and Morty Palitz at Columbia; Tommy Rockwell, Bob Stephens, and Richard M. Jones at Okeh; Dick Voynow, Milt Gabler, and Bob Stephens at Decca and Brunswick; and Ralph Peer, Eli Oberstein, Harry Meyerson, and Steve Sholes at Victor were among many who made major recordings in jazz history. But one man in particular, a tall dropout named John Hammond, seemed to be everywhere at once and did more than just about anyone else to make the thirties a golden decade in jazz. Hammond (Top, L) recorded and helped make stars out of dozens of artists. The careers of older ones like Bessie Smith and Fletcher Henderson were briefly renewed, and those of new ones like Billie Holiday (Top, R, and Middle), Teddy Wilson, and Count Basie (Bottom) flourished. Holiday's 1940 Vocalion date—with Roy Eldridge, trumpet; Sonny White, piano; and Kermit Scott, tenor sax—produced *Ghost of Yesterday* and *Body and Soul.* Count Basie's March 1940 Columbia session with Lester Young (fourth from L), Buck Clayton (sixth from R), Harry Edison (R), and Dickie Wells (fifth from R), joined by newcomers Al Killian and Vic Dickenson (second and eighth from R), resulted in *Louisiana* and *Tickle Toe.*

Radio and recordings were more accessible in New York than elsewhere. Ohioan Wild Bill Davison (Top, M) was almost unknown and unrecorded before he moved to New York and affiliated with Eddie Condon and Commodore Records. Critic-composer Leonard Feather produced sessions free-lance for many labels, including a 1947 Coleman Hawkins session with Budd Johnson (Top, L) for Victor and Helen Humes's first date as a soloist at Decca in 1942 (Middle, R) with Dizzy Gillespie (second from L), Pete Brown (L), Sammy Price (fourth from L), and Jimmy Hamilton (R). Lionel Hampton's Victor sessions (Middle, L), 1937–41, were among the many delights of the swing era, often rivaling the Teddy Wilson dates for superb jazz. The 1939 date that produced *Hot Mallets*, a classic, featured four of the greatest saxophone players in jazz: (L to R) Ben Webster, Benny Carter, Chu Berry, and Coleman Hawkins. Mary Lou Williams's trio (Bottom, L) with trumpeter Bill Coleman and Al Hall made *Blue Skies* and *Persian Rug* for Moses Asch in 1944. Rudi Blesh's WOR radio series "This Is Jazz" ran for several months in 1947 and featured players like Muggsy Spanier and Danny Barker (Bottom, R). A major breakthrough in race relations occurred when Raymond Scott's ABC house orchestra (Top, R) hired black jazzmen Charlie Shavers (third from R), Ben Webster (third from L), Benny Morton (fourth from L), Israel Crosby (second from R), and Specs Powell (fifth from R). It didn't last, and after some devious politicking they were all dismissed in 1945, amid great bitterness.

A NEW CATALOGUE
OF RECENT
RECORDINGS AND
RARE, OUT-OF-PRINT,
OLD TIME GOOD ONES
BY OUTSTANDING
SWING VIRTUOSI

COMMODORE
CLASSICS
IN
SWING

In the late thirties jazz records were bought mainly at the Commodore Music Shop on 42nd Street east of Lexington Avenue (Top, M) and at the H.R.S. Record Shop (Bottom, L) at 853 Seventh Avenue. Both produced their own recordings of small-band traditional jazz and swing and sold the catalogs of Bluenote, Jazz Man, Jazz Information, Solo-Art, and others that began at that time. Lee Wiley (Top, R) was favored by Commodore, as well as Liberty, Rabson's, and Schirmer's, all local stores that released their own records, when Victor, Decca, and Columbia would have nothing to do with her. (Middle, R) Label owners Steve Smith and Dan Qualey (L and third from L) stroll on a summer day with Sid Stiber (second from L), Art Hodes (second from R), and man-about-jazz, knowledgeable Herman Rosenberg (R), 1940. (Bottom, R, L to R) *Metronome* editors George Simon and Barry Ulanov confer with record supervisor Morty Palitz and Columbia executive Manny Sacks prior to making the first *Metronome* All-Star session in 1939.

The Finest in Hot Jazz

BLUE NOTE

The modern record store

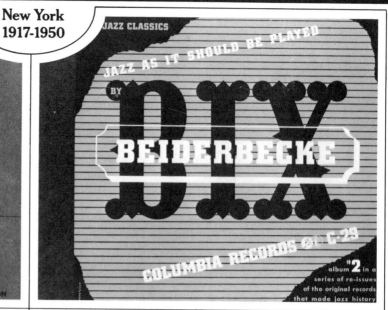

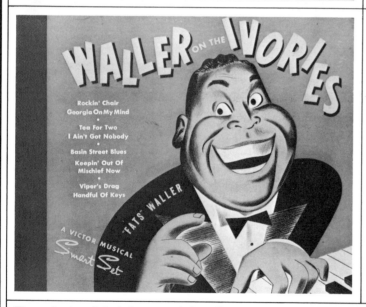

The packaging of single jazz records into albums began in 1938 with the Bessie Smith Memorial Album (Top, L). John Hammond, with much help from George Avakian, produced all of Columbia's Hot Jazz Classics re-issue albums in 1940–41. Decca released albums by Count Basie, Art Tatum, and others under contract, and Victor's Musical Smart Sets encompassed Fats Waller and Duke Ellington in the same period. During and after the war, numerous smaller firms began releasing albums like Philo's Norman Granz–produced Lester Young trio sides of 1942 (not even board-backed). Albums made it possible to work out and plan concepts like Asch's marvelous James P. Johnson New York Jazz set and Circle's Marching Jazz, all newly recorded records documenting an idea or a style. Packaging became valid and necessary when *Esquire*'s Jazz Concerts (Opposite Page, Bottom, R) were recorded, in part, by Victor. These records would have been unthinkable released as singles but made sense jacketed in three- or four-pocket albums. Many of these, as well as many others, were in most of the major jazz record collections, assembled in the days before long-playing records made them obsolete.

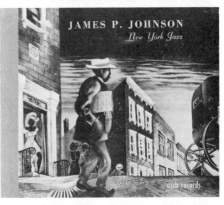

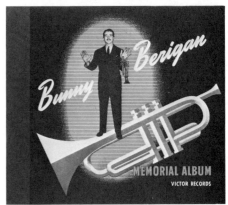

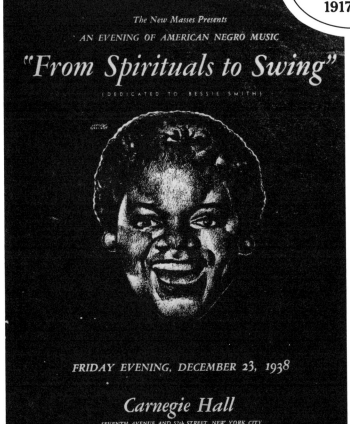

The New Masses Presents

AN EVENING OF AMERICAN NEGRO MUSIC

"From Spirituals to Swing"

(DEDICATED TO BESSIE SMITH)

FRIDAY EVENING, DECEMBER 23, 1938

Carnegie Hall

SEVENTH AVENUE AND 57th STREET, NEW YORK CITY

BILLIE HOLIDAY

TOWN HALL · SATURDAY, FEBRUARY 16 · 5:30 p.m.

Ernest Anderson presents
FRED ROBBINS'
ONE-NITE STAND
A Midnight Variety Concert
starring

Eleven-Thirty Saturday Night
At TOWN HALL
All Seats Reserved

Jamming was organized, packaged, and promoted on 52nd Street, in hotels, recording studios, even outdoors, by men like Ernie Anderson, Martin Block, Milt Gabler, Leonard Feather, Harry Lim, and later by Timme Rosenkrantz, Ralph Berton, Monte Kay, and others. Anderson, John Hammond, and Feather staged jams at Carnegie Hall, Town Hall, and elsewhere as jazz concerts. Anderson's Park Lane sessions (Opposite Page, Top, L) were built around the personality of Eddie Condon (extreme L), with (L to R) Pee Wee Russell, Bobby Hackett, Sterling Bose, Hot Lips Page, Bud Freeman, and Joe Marsala. Backstage at Carnegie Hall (Top, R), Count Basie (fifth from R), Don Byas (extreme L), and Buck Clayton (second from L) jammed with Red Allen (third from L), J. C. Higginbotham (fourth from R), Pete Johnson (third from R) and Lena Horne (extreme R) in 1941. (Middle, L) Chick Webb, drums; Artie Shaw, clarinet; and Duke Ellington jammed at a Broadway recording studio, 1937. WNEW radio disc jockey Martin Block staged day-long concerts at Randall's Island (Middle, R) for Local 802's Emergency Relief Fund in 1938 with as many as twenty different bands; this photo shows Lester Young with Basie's band. *Life* magazine devoted its "Life Goes to a Party" section to one of Harry Lim's (fifth from R) sessions at cartoonist Burris Jenkin's studio (Bottom) with (L to R) J. C. Higginbotham, Clyde Newcomb, Rex Stewart, Billie Holiday, (Lim), Cozy Cole, Eddie Condon, Max Kaminsky, and Hot Lips Page. (Above) Jazz concerts were the capstone of the swing years. John Hammond's "Spirituals to Swing" in 1938 (Top, L) was one of the most interesting. *Esquire*'s jazz concert at the Metropolitan Opera House in 1944 was recorded in part by V-Disc with (Middle, R, L to R) Roy Eldridge, Oscar Pettiford, Billie Holiday, and Art Tatum. Major stars like Billie Holiday (Bottom, L) and Louis Armstrong had their own concerts after the war. Jazz acceptance was complete when Armstrong, the first jazz artist thus honored, made *Time*'s cover (Bottom, R) in 1949.

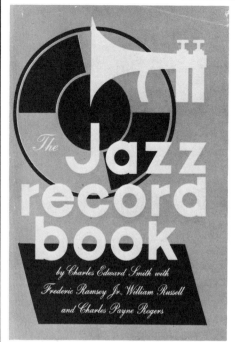

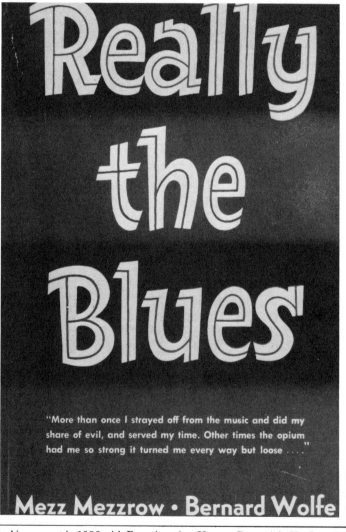

Books devoted to jazz history, biography, and studies of its recordings started in earnest in 1936 with French author Hugues Panassie's *Hot Jazz* (a translation from the French of his 1934 work) and Louis Armstrong's autobiography *Swing That Music*. Dorothy Baker's 1938 *Young Man with a Horn* made fiction of jazz. Thereafter, jazz books were published every other year or so. A biography of Benny Goodman (1939), *The Kingdom of Swing*, Eddie Condon's *We Called It Music* (1946), Mezz Mezzrow's *Really the Blues* (1947), and Jelly Roll Morton's *Mister Jelly Roll* (1950) vied with attempts at formal history like *Jazzmen* (1939), *Jazz from the Congo to the Metropolitan* (1944), *Jazz Cavalcade* (1946), and *Shining Trumpets* (1946). Discussions of recordings and criticism and dissection of styles started with Panassie's *Hot Jazz*, much of which he refuted in his 1942 *The Real Jazz*. The *Jazz Record Book* (1942) was a sober analysis of then-available recordings (all 78 rpm), some of which, amazingly, are still unavailable forty years later! *Esquire* magazine's annual *Jazz Books*, which ran from 1944 to 1947 (Page 123, Bottom, R), covered the year's activities and recordings; they devoted considerable space to the early history of New Orleans and Chicago with photographs and valuable street maps of the cities' nightclubs, theaters, and cafés in their heyday. All offered valuable insights and facts (some later disputed).

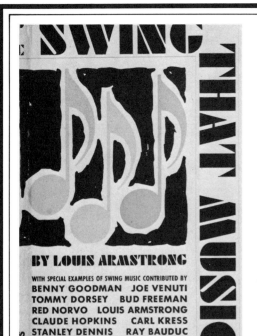

SWING THAT MUSIC

BY LOUIS ARMSTRONG

WITH SPECIAL EXAMPLES OF SWING MUSIC CONTRIBUTED BY
BENNY GOODMAN   JOE VENUTI
TOMMY DORSEY   BUD FREEMAN
RED NORVO   LOUIS ARMSTRONG
CLAUDE HOPKINS   CARL KRESS
STANLEY DENNIS   RAY BAUDUC
INTRODUCTION BY RUDY VALLEE

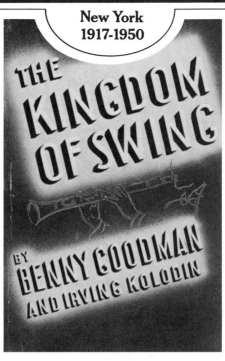

THE KINGDOM OF SWING

BY BENNY GOODMAN AND IRVING KOLODIN

JAZZ
FROM THE CONGO TO THE METROPOLITAN

ROBERT GOFFIN
With an Introduction by ARNOLD GINGRICH, Editor of Esquire

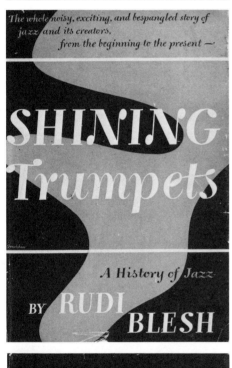

The whole noisy, exciting, and bespangled story of jazz and its creators, from the beginning to the present —

SHINING Trumpets

A History of Jazz

BY RUDI BLESH

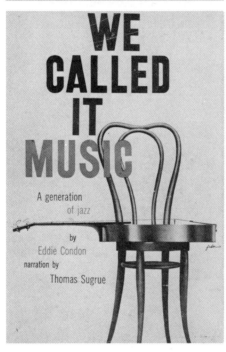

WE CALLED IT MUSIC

A generation of jazz

by Eddie Condon
narration by Thomas Sugrue

Mister JELLY ROLL

By Alan Lomax
Drawings by David Stone Martin

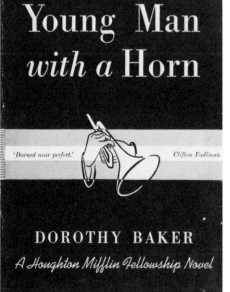

Young Man with a Horn

'Darned near perfect.' Clifton Fadiman

DOROTHY BAKER
A Houghton Mifflin Fellowship Novel

DAVE DEXTER, JR.
with foreword by ORSON WELLES

JAZZ CAVALCADE

The inside story of Jazz written by one of America's foremost authorities. The former editor of DOWN BEAT and correspondent for METRONOME takes you behind the scenes in the first book of its kind on modern American music.

"Dave Dexter's Jazz Cavalcade is just about the best stuff I have ever read on the subject. Of all the writer-editors, Dexter is the most accurate, unprejudiced, and blessed with background."
— BENNY GOODMAN

Esquire's 1945 Jazz book

Edited by PAUL EDUARD MILLER
Introduction by ARNOLD GINGRICH

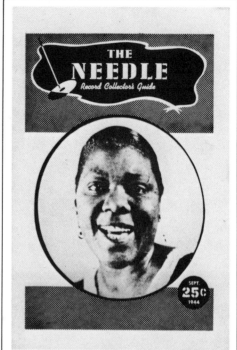

The little jazz-appreciation magazines began appearing in the late thirties as a reaction to the commercial, swing-oriented publications like *Down Beat, Metronome,* and *Tempo,* all of which had originated as musicians' magazines. *H.R.S. Rag* (named after the Hot Record Society), edited by Heywood Hale Broun and Russell Sanjek (Top, M), led the way in 1938. These magazines were edited by young men of intellectual bent and sometimes included poetry and abstract musical analyses of aspects of jazz that were unpublishable elsewhere. Probably the best was *Jazz Information* (Top, L), edited by Gene Williams and Ralph Gleason. Having started as an eight-page offset digest of news and record reviews in 1939, it grew to a digest-size magazine in 1940 (when *H.R.S. Rag* was discontinued) and published news, information, and feature articles not found in *Down Beat* or *Metronome* (*Tempo* had folded in 1940). Its acid record reviews also covered blues, still released then as "race" records. Its final number, a huge double issue devoted to James P. Johnson, was published in November 1941. *The Record Changer* (Bottom, M) appeared as a record-trading magazine, digest-size in 1942, edited by Gordon Gullickson, and included Roy Carew's invaluable "New Orleans Memoirs" of 1913. Later it grew to standard-size format with pictures under the editorship of Bill Grauer with Orrin Keepnews; it ran well into the 1950s. Robert Reynold's *The Needle* (Top, R) debuted in 1944, a year after Art Hodes's *Jazz Record* (Bottom, L); both contained features, news, and record reviews. *The Needle* finished a year later; *Jazz Record* lasted until late 1947. Others appeared for a year or more, like Bob Thiele's *Jazz* in 1943–45, both digest- and standard-size with slick format and good paper, and Orin Blackstone's *Playback* and *Jazzfinder,* which was published in New Orleans in 1948–50. *Esquire*'s 1947 *Jazz Book* (Bottom, R) was published only in oversize magazine format, unlike its three predecessors, which were published in hardback editions as well. The reason for this, and for *Esquire*'s dropping out of jazz for many years thereafter: the large panel of experts, including every prominent authority in jazz—George Avakian, E. Simms Campbell, Robert Goffin, Leonard Feather, John Hammond, Harry Lim, Dan Burley, Bucklin Moon, Dave Dexter, Timme Rosenkrantz, George Hoefer, Charles Edward Smith, George Simon, Barry Ulanov, and editor (of the 1944–46 books) Paul Eduard Miller—who in the previous three years had selected *Esquire*'s award winners charged that editor Ernie Anderson loaded the 1947 book with features on his favorite, Eddie Condon, and Condon's musical associates. Anderson accomplished his goal, but the rest of the panel resigned en masse in protest, and *Esquire* discontinued its yearbooks.

New York never accepted blues the way Chicago and most southern cities did, but the blues recording industry started there in 1920 with Mamie Smith's Jazz Hounds (Bottom). Her Okeh recording of *Crazy Blues* was so successful that dozens of talented black vaudeville entertainers were signed to make blues recordings. Mamie used jazzmen like Willie "The Lion" Smith (third from R) and Ernest Elliott (L). Katie Krippen (Top, R) was less successful, but smart enough to use young Bill Basie (L) and Elmer Williams (second from L) in her act. Bessie Smith (Top, L) got off to a slow start on records and never found much of an audience in New York.

Columbia Records signed Mary Stafford, Edith Wilson, and Leona Williams to capture a share of the blues audience. Edith Wilson (Top) was one of the most versatile women in show business, with a powerful voice well suited to blues, although she didn't think so. Her Jazz Hounds included Johnny Dunn (third from R) and Garvin Bushell (second from L), who were among Mamie Smith's sidemen. Her *What Do You Care (What I Do)* is a classic. Clarinet wizard Wilbur Sweatman (Middle) straddled ragtime, vaudeville, and jazz; he usually finished his show playing three clarinets simultaneously. His March 1923 appearance at the Lafayette Theatre in Harlem included Duke Ellington on piano and Sonny Greer, drums. Perhaps the greatest singer of them all was a tall, slender, Pennsylvania-born beauty named Ethel Waters (Bottom, R). She was the star of Harry Pace's Black Swan Records, the first black-owned company, until it went bankrupt in 1924. A year later she was one of Columbia's biggest stars, with best-selling records of *Dinah, Sweet Georgia Brown,* and others, alternating on Columbia's main popular series (sold everywhere) and the "race" lists with Bessie and Clara Smith. She later became a nightclub, Broadway, and film star. Duke Ellington expanded his orchestra (Bottom) for theater dates at the Lafayette in 1927 and to play larger nightclubs like Ciro's and the Club Richman downtown, before taking the Cotton Club job uptown. (L to R) Joe Nanton, Sonny Greer, Bubber Miley, Harry Carney, Wellman Braud, Rudy Jackson, Fred Guy, Nelson Kincaid (depping for Otto Hardwicke), Ellsworth Reynolds. Reynolds was hired to conduct the show but left after a month when Ellington felt comfortable enough to do it himself.

From the more formal, written ragtime, sophisticated and technically formidable pianists like James P. Johnson (Top, L) and Luckey Roberts (Middle, L) developed the "stride" style, named for the swiftly striding syncopated left hand hitting single bass notes and their related chords an octave or more down the keyboard against a mix of chords, single notes, and runs improvised in the right hand. Both players later wrote show and popular music, but it was their competition pieces, such as Johnson's *Carolina Shout* and Roberts's *Ripples of the Nile,* that younger men like Willie "The Lion" Smith (Bottom, L), the "Beetle," Stephen Henderson (Middle, R), Bobby Henderson (Bottom, M), and Art Tatum (Bottom, R) were required to learn before their peers could rate them. Pianist Cliff Jackson led competitive bands like the Krazy Kats (Top, R) at Newark's Cotton Club and Harlem's Lenox Club well into the Depression before going downtown to Nick's. Midwesterner Alex Hill (Middle, M) worked in duos with Fats Waller and became known as one of Harlem's best arrangers before he died of tuberculosis in 1937. John Hammond and other record executives gnashed their teeth in vain trying to persuade the two Hendersons to record. The "Beetle," known for his perfect left hand, often accepted advances and then just disappeared. Bobby Henderson moved upstate and had to wait thirty years for Hammond to find and record him. The piano style perfected by these men and others largely disappeared after the war.

Harlem's talents were many and varied. Violinist Ralph "Shrimp" Jones was an active leader and good soloist throughout the Harlem era until the war. The Royal Flush Orchestra (Top, R), a hot Victor recording band led by Fess Williams with his diamond-studded tuxedo and eccentric showmanship, opened the fabled Savoy Ballroom in 1926 and was its main attraction well into the thirties. Jazzmen seeking jobs went to the Rhythm Club (Middle, L), which for a time put out its own newsletter. Pianist Luis Russell's band (Middle, R) had the best job in Harlem, 1929–31, working at numbers king Casper Holstein's Saratoga Club. Holstein made so much money that he didn't care if he had customers or not; he let the band play anything they wanted. That gave jazzmen Red Allen (L), Greely Walton (second from L), Paul Barbarin (third from L), Charlie Holmes (fourth from L), Albert Nicholas (fifth from R), Pops Foster (third from R), and J. C. Higginbotham (second from R) a competitive edge that shows on their Okeh records of *Panama, Feeling the Spirit, Louisiana Swing, Jersey Lightning,* and *Saratoga Shout.* Walton stated emphatically, "We had the hottest band in Harlem, man, we blew 'em all out." In contrast, Benny Carter's Savoy Playboys (Bottom) stressed his superlative arrangements and ensemble, since he was his only outstanding soloist. By 1930 he was back in Fletcher Henderson's band.

Hello Luis Russell from your friend Henry Allen Jr. Jan 31, 1935 N.Y. city

Henry "Red" Allen looked like a bloodhound, but he played with a relentless drive and a stabbing, angular style that often went over the heads of his peers. He drove the Luis Russell band to new heights with his fiery solos and was signed by Victor in 1929 as competition for Louis Armstrong. That association produced the superb *Biffly Blues*, *Swing Out*, and *Pleasin' Paul*, among others. Although a devoted family man, Allen found time to jam after hours at the Rhythm Club and Smalls's. In fellow Russell sideman Greely Walton's opinion, "There were only two around here then who could blow him out, Ward Pinkett and Cootie Williams, and then not all the time." Allen joined Fletcher Henderson in 1933 and, when Henderson's band broke up, the Mills Blue Rhythm Band (Inset). He recorded, with all-star lineups, such masterpieces as *Body and Soul*, *There's a House in Harlem for Sale*, *Midnight Blue*, and *Chloe* for Vocalion and the American Record Company labels, 1934–37, but they failed to make him a star. He spent the rest of the thirties as a member of Louis Armstrong's big band and made no more records. After he formed his own band in 1940, which played 52nd Street, Café Society, and other prominant clubs, he concentrated more on showmanship.

Cab Calloway (L and R) became Harlem's newest sensation and Irving Mills's biggest box-office attraction when he took over the Missourians (R) and replaced Duke Ellington at the Cotton Club in 1930. His acrobatic, head-shaking performance on his own *Minnie the Moocher* with its "hi-de-ho" choruses made him a household word in the thirties. Occasionally he let talented sidemen Foots Thomas (second from L), Thorton Blue (sixth from L), and R. Q. Dickerson (fourth from R) solo on records like *Hot Toddy, Bugle Call Rag,* and others, but it wasn't until later that Chu Berry, Tyree Glenn, Jonah Jones, Dizzy Gillespie, and other players made the band important.

Chick Webb (L, with snare drum) and Vernon Andrade (R, with baton) sought different goals. Andrade had the house band at the Renaissance Ballroom for a decade and rarely traveled; he was content to play lucrative private parties. In 1930 he had a fine band with George Washington (L), Louis Metcalfe (third from L), Al Morgan (fourth from L), Zutty Singleton (fourth from R), Gene Mikell (third from R), and Happy Caldwell (R). Webb was unable to hold onto players like Johnny Hodges and Cootie Williams, who were hired by Duke Ellington and Fletcher Henderson, until he got the house band at the Savoy in 1934. Then came the fine Edgar Sampson arrangements of *Stompin' at the Savoy* and *Don't Be That Way* and players like Taft Jordan, Sandy Williams, Bobby Stark, and, above all, Ella Fitzgerald.

King Oliver (standing L) went to New York in 1927 to play the Savoy and turned down the Cotton Club job. He felt the money was too little, unmindful that his Chicago heyday was over. Although he made more than fifty records for Brunswick and Victor over the next four years, they were all with pickup bands, since he held no steady job in the city during that time. He left New York to play the Middle West in 1931, featuring Clyde Bernhardt (L), Freddie Moore (fifth from L), Hank Duncan (fifth from R), and Paul Barnes (fourth from R). Later, after the band members went home, he settled there, using territory bands, and kept working, moving farther and farther south. He died, sick and forgotten, in Georgia in 1938. His nephew, Dave Nelson (R, with baton), got most of his recording bands for him and led some of his own without notable success, despite having players like veteran Charlie Elgar, Danny Barker, and Thorton Blue (fifth, sixth, and fourth from R). Nelson died in 1946.

Don Redman's debut at Connie's Inn (L) was a major event in 1931. His and pianist Horace Henderson's arrangements featured Sidney DeParis (L), Benny Morton (second from L), Shirley Clay (third from L), Claude Jones (seventh from L), Ed Inge (fifth from R), and Bob Carroll (third from R) and a superb rhythm section. *Chant of the Weed* and *I Got Rhythm* were among their many memorable Brunswick recordings. The Mills Blue Rhythm Band (R) had five leaders in its seven-year existence. Edgar Hayes (L) was the musical director, while Carroll Dickerson (second from L) fronted in 1931. The arrangements of Harry White (R) featured Cass McCord and Ed Anderson (sixth and fourth from R). They were Irving Mills's backup band at the Cotton Club whenever Duke Ellington and Cab Calloway were on the road.

Ralph Cooper's Congo Knights (L) was a good but short-lived band in 1932–33. Ex-dancer Cooper (fifth from L) directed players like Henry Goodwin (third from L), Zutty Singleton (sixth from L), and Booker Pittman (sixth from R) but couldn't find enough work and later became master of ceremonies at the Apollo Theatre and a disc jockey. The Original Shim Sham Band (R) was a novelty group with a front line of kazoo players who imitated big-band sounds. They were highly popular at Dickie Wells's at 169 West 133rd Street, the former Nest Club, which he opened in 1933. Pianist Kenny Watts (third from R) led and was fortunate to have a fine drummer in Eddie Dougherty. Years later they appeared at Kelly's Stables as Kenny Watts and the Kilowatts opposite Bud Freeman.

Former dancer Willie Bryant (L, standing L) did fairly well with his band in the thirties. With sidemen like Teddy Wilson (L), Edgar Battle (third from L), Cozy Cole (sixth from L), Glyn Paque (fifth from R), and Johnny Russell (R), and augmented by Benny Carter (on trumpet!) and Ben Webster in 1935, they made some good Victor records like *Chimes at the Meeting, Sheik of Araby,* and *Steak and Potatoes* and had a long run at the Savoy Ballroom. Bryant led other bands off and on until 1948, interspersed with emcee roles at the Apollo and jobs as an actor and disc jockey. The Mills Blue Rhythm Band (R) was improved considerably by 1936 with Red Allen (third from R), J. C. Higginbotham (fifth from L), Buster Bailey (sixth from R), superb drumming by O'Neil Spencer, strong arrangements by Joe Garland (fourth from R), and the high-voltage showmanship of Lucky Millinder (L). *Harlem Heat* and *Ride, Red, Ride* are among their better recordings.

The Savoy Sultans (Top, L) outswung so many name bands at the Savoy after 1937 that many refused to play against them. Soloists Sam Massenberg (second from R) and Rudy Williams (third from L) were driven hard by Grachan Moncur (L) and Alex "Razz" Mitchell (second from L). *Frenzy, Stitches,* and *Little Sally Water* are some of the fine Decca recordings they made before they broke up in 1946. Teddy Hill's 1937 band (Top, R) featured Russell Procope (third from L), Dickie Wells (fourth from L), Cecil Scott (seventh from L), and Frankie Newton (sixth from R). Chappie Willetts's arrangements of *Blue Rhythm Fantasy* on Vocalion and *King Porter Stomp* on Bluebird were among their finest recordings. Hill managed Minton's Playhouse after he gave up the band in 1940. Dancing, singing, demon showman Tiny Bradshaw (Middle, L) was billed as "Super Cab Calloway" in 1934 but did not succeed until years later in the rhythm-and-blues field. Lester Young (Middle, R) changed the way a generation of saxophonists played. Chick Webb's band (Bottom, L) was fronted by Ella Fitzgerald after his death with either Eddie Barefield (sixth from L) or Teddy McRae (second from R) as musical director. Without Webb, though, it had no musical personality. (Bottom, R) Pianist Dan Burley explained the language of musicians and showpeople in this wartime booklet. He was then the editor of the *Amsterdam News.*

Harlem became world famous in the twenties for its nightclubs, their shows, and the many fine hot bands that played in them. Barron's (Bottom, L) at 2259 Seventh Avenue was one of the first big uptown clubs, featuring pianists like Luckey Roberts, James P. Johnson, and then bands like the Washingtonians, who went downtown in 1923. Barron Wilkins was stabbed to death in 1924. The Nest Club (Bottom, R) was celebrated in a famous Don Redman record, *Shakin' the African,* as a place for relief from the more dicty clubs. Charlie Johnson's band (Middle), with the superb George Stafford on drums, opened it in 1925, followed by Elmer Snowden and Luis Russell, among others. In 1933 it became Dickie Wells's Shim Sham Club. Ed Smalls's Paradise (Top, L) at 2294½ Seventh Avenue was one of the hottest clubs for a decade. It outlasted all the rest, remaining open well after World War II and the Harlem era had ended. Before that Smalls had had the Sugar Cane Club on Fifth Avenue, where June Clark's Jazz Band (Top, R), featuring the leader on trumpet and Jimmy Harrison on trombone, worked. Bill Basie played piano in this group at Connor's on West 135th Street for a while. Few men were more important in Harlem's recording history than composer Perry Bradford (third from L), who sold Mamie Smith to Okeh Records in 1920 and continued to play an important role in recording throughout the twenties.

DUKE
ELLINGTON
AND HIS
FAMOUS Cotton Club
Orchestra
Management
IRVING MILLS
150 WEST 46th ST.
NEW YORK CITY

(Opposite Page, Inset) During the Depression Duke Ellington was Harlem's brightest star. He had the most prestigious job in Harlem, and with his music and the lavish stage shows and nightly broadcasts heard over the CBS network from the Cotton Club, he was the pacesetter that Fletcher Henderson had been for the preceding decade. He was the one who created sounds and backgrounds utilizing the highly individualistic talents of Joe "Tricky Sam" Nanton (L), Cootie Williams (third from L), Arthur Whetsol (fifth from L), Harry Carney (fifth from R), Johnny Hodges (third from R), and Barney Bigard (R). The Cotton Club was a magnet for wealthy New Yorkers as well as titled foreign visitors. They may not have understood Ellington's unique music, but they certainly had little difficulty getting Cab Calloway's message (Bottom, R). Cab had fine players like Doc Cheatham (L) and Foots Thomas (third from R), but they were mainly background for the electrifying brand of Calloway showmanship. The apogee came with the 1933 Cotton Club show with Ethel Waters and the Ellington orchestra (Middle, L), which introduced an especially rich Ted Koehler–Harold Arlen score, including *Stormy Weather,* which propelled Ethel Waters to stardom on Broadway later that year. The Cotton Club's heyday was drawing to a close, despite good shows headlining Adelaide Hall, and Jimmie Lunceford's band, and the 1935 show with Claude Hopkins's band which featured *Truckin'.* Dicty people weren't coming uptown anymore (the March 1935 Harlem race riots were the final signal that the "tourist trade" days were over), and the Cotton Club closed for good in February 1936, to reopen downtown that fall.

One Week Only!

Commencing

SATURDAY
JULY 14th

★

The Incomparable

FLETCHER
HENDERSON
and his FAMOUS ORCHESTRA

playing against

Chick Webb...
... and his Sensational Band

SAVOY World's Finest Ballroom
Lenox Ave., 140-141 Sts.

By Overwhelming Popular Demand

BREAKFAST DANCE

FEATURING THE RETURN OF

CHICK
WEBB
and his Chicks

★

TEDDY
HILL
and Band

★

WILLIE
BRYANT
Newest Musical
Sensation

JIMMIE
LUNCEFORD
AND HIS
COTTON CLUB
ORCHESTRA

4
Sensational
Bands

★

Adm.
35c

5 p.m. to 8 p.m.

75c thereafter

SATURDAY, AUGUST 25th

SAVOY

LENOX AVENUE—140th-141st STREETS

A HISTORY MAKING.........BATTLE OF SWING

SUNDAY
JAN. 16'

The King
OF THE
DRUMS

The Royalist
OF THE
KEYBOARD

Chick WEBB vs Count BASIE
& AMERICA'S OUTSTANDING...SWING BAND~   & HIS ORCHESTRA
                                              The Aristocrat of Rhythm

Ella FITZGERALD   Chick Webb & HIS FAMOUS ORCHESTRA   Billie HOLLIDAY
FEATURED   WILL PLAY NIGHTLY AT THE SAVOY   FEATURED
WITH   Special Matinee 3 P.M.   WITH THE
CHICK   No Increase in Admission   COUNT....

LENOX·AVE
at 140' STREET. SAVOY THE WORLDS FINEST
                        BALLROOM

Connie's Inn (Top, R), which George and Connie Immerman opened in 1923, rivaled the Cotton Club for its shows and bands. The career of Louis Armstrong (Bottom) was shaped to an extent by his work in the 1929 show, *Connie's Hot Chocolates,* which was brought to a downtown theater that year. In it he sang Fats Waller and Andy Razaf's hit song *Ain't Misbehavin'* and soon began to record a large percentage of the day's most popular songs, thereby broadening his audience appeal and marketability enormously. Connie's and the Cotton Club were expensive, whites-only places; the Savoy Ballroom (Opposite Page), which opened a block away from the Cotton Club in 1926, soon became world famous for its hot bands and creative dance steps. From Fess Williams to Erskine Hawkins, Chick Webb, the Savoy Sultans, and Lucky Millinder, the Savoy ran without any real competition for thirty years. Dances like the Lindy Hop, the Shag, the Shim Sham, and many others were created there and went around the world. The breakfast dances (Top, R), with four outstanding bands playing nonstop from midnight to dawn, and battles of music (Top, L) became sellouts as soon as they were advertised; thousands were turned away for the famous ones like Chick Webb against Count Basie (Bottom, L) in 1938 and earlier in 1937 against Benny Goodman. The fact that the Savoy had become a multimillion-dollar business was not lost on some musicians who refused to work there because of the low salaries (rarely more than $50 a week). Bands like Duke Ellington's, Fletcher Henderson's, and Jimmie Lunceford's appeared there rarely. The reason? Moe Gale's booking agency, Gale, Inc., also booked the Savoy's regular bands like Chick Webb's, Hawkins's, and Millinder's, and for a time Don Redman and Benny Carter while they appeared there regularly in 1938–39. Bands that refused to sign with Gale, Inc., rarely if ever got to play the Savoy. The Savoy declined gradually, just as Harlem did, after World War II. The big bands began to have less and less meaning, and television and changing musical styles made dancing less important than it had been before the war. The Savoy could still draw people for certain occasions, but the bottom had dropped out by the fifties.

HARLEM'S HIGH SPOT

WORLD'S GREATEST COLORED SHOWS

APOLLO
125ᵗʰ ST. near 8ᵗʰ Ave · Tel. UNiversity 4-4490

ONE WEEK ONLY Beg. FRIDAY, DEC. 1st

The Famous Singing Star

BILLIE HOLIDAY

ONE BIG WEEK
Begin.
FRI., NOV. 6th

The Greatest Show Yet—

FLETCHER AND HIS BAND

HENDERSON

and an All-Headliner Cast

and

JACKIE

MABLEY

Funniest Woman in America

WORLD'S GREATEST COLORED SHOWS

HARLEM'S HIGH SPOT

APOLLO

125th ST. near 8th Ave. · Tel. UNiversity 4-4490

HARLEM'S HIGH SPOT

WORLD'S GREATEST COLORED SHOWS

APOLLO

125th ST. near 8th Ave. · Tel. UNiversity 4-4490

WEEK Beginning FRIDAY, FEBRUARY 6th

THE KING OF THEM ALL—

In Person!

The TRUMPET KING OF SWING

Louis ARMSTRONG

HIS ORCHESTRA AND REVUE

SONNY WOODS

ANNE BAKER

and a Great Cast of Headliners

APOLLO

ERSKINE HAWKINS AND BAND

JIMMIE MITCHELL-ACE HARRIS

SMITH SISTERS-SANDY BURNS

STAGE AMATEUR NITE TONITE

APOLLO

(Opposite Page) Frank Schiffman and Leo Brecher began presenting stage shows at the Apollo Theatre on West 125th Street in January 1934 after seeing their Lafayette Theatre lose business steadily to the Harlem Opera House a few doors west of the Apollo for several years. Bessie Smith (Top, L) was on their second bill and was seen regularly there until the end of 1936. Billie Holiday (Middle, L) first appeared there in 1935 and in 1937 as Count Basie's vocalist in his first appearance. Schiffman soon bought the Harlem Opera House and discontinued its stage policy as well as the Lafayette's in 1935, leaving Harlem with only one presentation house. Billie Holiday (Bottom, R) was a major headliner backed by the Hot Lips Page band in December 1944 (Bobby Evans was the master of ceremonies) as was Count Basie's band (Middle, R) in 1940. (Above, Top, L and R) Fletcher Henderson's and Louis Armstrong's appearances were always welcome events because they usually worked downtown. Neither Frankie Newton (Middle, L) nor Hot Lips Page (Middle, R) appeared at the Apollo more than a handful of times, but that was no measure of their abilities. The marquee changed in the forties (Bottom, R), and onstage jamming (Bottom, L, 1946, L to R: Tiny Grimes, Stuff Smith, Buster Bailey, Dizzy Gillespie, Trummy Young, Slam Stewart) sometimes took place in an impromptu manner unless done specifically for one of Harlem's many charities. The Apollo continued for many years thereafter.

(Opposite Page) Harlem's clubs and theaters often had short vogues. The Renaissance (Top, L) had Andrade's house band or, on weekends or for special events, Jimmie Lunceford, Edgar Hayes, and Al Sears, or nothing at all. The Lafayette (Top, R) closed in 1935 after Frank Schiffman's newer Apollo Theatre on 125th Street became the focal point. The Harlem Opera House (Middle, R), nearby, also closed that year, leaving the Apollo as Harlem's sole presentation house for the remainder of the decade. The Alhambra (Bottom, L) around the corner on 126th Street had shows in the twenties through 1931 but gave up as the Harlem Opera House became more successful. The Alhambra and West End theaters competed unsuccessfully against the Apollo at different times. Ex-dancer Clark Monroe opened his Uptown House (Bottom, R) on the site of the old Theatrical Grill, with shows, hot bands, and legendary after-hours jam sessions with every major player uptown and many from downtown. In 1943 he moved to 52nd Street. The Ubangi Club (Above, Top, L) was the only one to succeed in the old Connie's Inn spot on Seventh Avenue; it stayed through 1936 with Erskine Hawkins (Top, R), who followed Teddy Hill and preceded Willie Bryant. Later the Ubangi relocated downtown. Newark's Alcazar Café (Middle, R) featured some forgotten stars when Jabbo Smith (L) and Donald Lambert (second from L) settled in for a long stay in 1941; Smith was featured in the local Hot Club's concert that year as well (Middle, L). Lester Young and Billie Holiday, with Sonny White (Bottom, L), visited the short-lived Golden Gate Ballroom in 1940, and trumpeter Louis Metcalfe's Heatwave on West 145th Street (Bottom, R) featured shows and the leader's own brand of hot trumpet and showmanship until he left for Canada in 1946.

Harlem snapshots and street scenes. (Opposite Page, Top, L) Henry "Red" Allen and wife, Pearlie May, Lenox Avenue, 1935. (Top, R) Louis Armstrong, Zutty Singleton, Louis's chauffeur, "Too Sweet," and Dick Curry, amusement arcade, 1929. (Middle, L) Fats Waller and Willie "The Lion" Smith, May 1936. Jelly Roll Morton (Middle, R) signifies to nonbeliever Freddie Moore outside the Rhythm Club, summer 1939. Rex Stewart (Bottom, L) displays some of the daytime style for which Harlem was famous, 1938. Jimmie Lunceford and Teddy Hill (Bottom, R) sport boaters on 126th Street, 1935. (Above, Top, L, L to R) Roy Eldridge, Russell Procope, Chu Berry, and Dickie Wells, in front of the Savoy, summer, 1935. Billie Holiday relaxing with Willie Bryant bandsmen between shows at the Apollo: (Top, R) Ben Webster (L), Ram Ramirez (bottom), and Johnny Russell (R), August 1935. Teddy Bunn and Jimmy Phipps (Middle, L) with three of the era's best brass men, Ed Lewis (M), Hot Lips Page (second from L), and Bobby Moore (L), 125th Street, summer 1939. Moore was committed the following year for the rest of his life. (Middle, R) A bedraggled Lucky Millinder stands in sharp contrast to the suave elegance of Joe Garland (M) and Red Allen (R), Cotton Club, 1935. Garland, Greely Walton, Walter Johnson, Henderson, Ellington, Claude Hopkins, and others bought their suits from London tailors who made their band uniforms until they could afford to go downtown to Leighton's at 48th and Broadway. Fats Waller (Bottom) greets Jackie Mabley (much later, Moms Mabley), May 1936.

Slim, elegant bandleader Willie Bryant (Top, L) with ribald song-and-dance star Gladys Bentley, headliners at the Ubangi Club, pose against a Harlem billboard advertising their August 1936 show at the Apollo Theatre. Cab Calloway guitarist Danny Barker (Top, R) stands symbolically in front of the railroad yards. Trains had brought him to New York seeking fame and fortune, and nine years later, after he found it in the highest-paid band in the land, would keep him on the road forty to fifty weeks a year, but he had arrived. Jimmy Blanton (Bottom, L) served a brief apprenticeship in St. Louis before joining Duke Ellington in 1939 and revolutionizing the way bass was played. Unable to reap what he sowed, he fell ill with tuberculosis in 1941 and died in 1942, at age twenty-three. Dizzy Gillespie, 1940 (Bottom, R), was featured in the bands of Teddy Hill, Claude Hopkins, Cab Calloway, Lucky Millinder, and Earl Hines before he formulated a new way of playing jazz that was rhythmically and technically advanced and that few others understood or could play. It became known as bebop.

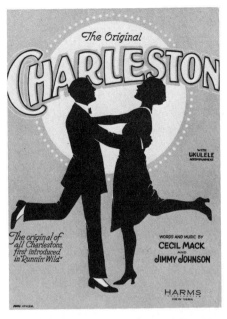

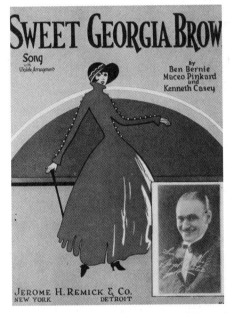

OKeh

4738-A · Fox Trot

SOME OF THESE DAYS
(Shelton Brooks)
ORIGINAL DIXIELAND
JAZZ BAND

GENERAL PHONOGRAPH CORPORATION NEW YORK

Brunswick
Fox Trot

THE JAPANESE SANDMAN
Duendecillo Japonés
—Egan—Whiting—
RED NICHOLS and his
FIVE PENNIES
3855-A

THE BRUNSWICK-BALKE-COLLENDER COMPANY
MADE IN U.S.A.

OKeh
ELECTRIC

41350 · Fox Trot with Vocal Refrain

FOR BEST RESULTS
USE OKeh NEEDLES

AFTER YOU'VE GONE
(Creamer-Layton)
LOUIS ARMSTRONG & HIS
ORCHESTRA
(403454)

OKeh PHONOGRAPH CORPORATION, NEW YORK

OKeh
ELECTRIC

41403 · Fox Trot

FOR BEST RESULTS
USE OKeh NEEDLES

SAN SUE STRUT
(El Andar De San Sue)
(Mannone)
CASA LOMA ORCH.
(403756)

OKeh PHONOGRAPH CORPORATION, NEW YORK

OKeh
ELECTRIC

NOT LICENSED FOR RADIO BROADCAST

41565 · Fox Trot

NEW KING PORTER STOMP
(Henderson)
FLETCHER HENDERSON AND
HIS ORCHESTRA
(152325)

OKeh PHONOGRAPH CORPORATION, NEW YORK

Vocalion
U S PAT 1,63?,544

Not Licensed for   Radio Broadcast

2913-B
(17005) · Fox Trot

THE ISLE OF CAPRI
—Kennedy-Grosz—
WINGY MANNONE & his Orchestra

BRUNSWICK RECORD CORPORATION

DECCA
TRADE MARK REGISTERED

NOT LICENSED FOR RADIO BROADCAST

Fox Trot
Vocal Chorus by
Mike Reilly

THE MUSIC GOES AROUND
AND AROUND
(REILLY-FARLEY)
EDDY-REILLY and their
"ONYX CLUB BOYS"
578 A

MANUFACTURED IN U.S.A. BY DECCA RECORDS, INC.

VICTOR

Not Licensed for
Radio Broadcast

25295-A

US ON A BUS—Fox Trot
(From the musical production "Summer Wives")
(Tot Seymour-Vee Lawnhurst)
"Fats" Waller and his Rhythm
Vocal refrain and piano by "Fats" Waller

RCA Manufacturing Co., Inc.
Camden, N.J., U.S.A.

Vocalion
FULL-RANGE RECORDING
MADE IN U.S.A. · NOT LICENSED FOR RADIO BROADCAST

Fox Trot
(21249) · Vocal by
Billie Holiday

ME, MYSELF AND I
(Are All In Love With You)
-Gordon-Roberts-Kaufman-
BILLIE HOLIDAY
AND HER ORCHESTRA
James Sherman-Jo Jones-Freddie Green
Walter Page-Edmund Hall-Lester Young
Buck Clayton
3593

LAB. COPY 1937 BY BRUNSWICK RECORD CORPORATION

COMMODORE
CLASSICS IN SWING
505 A
22831-1
Eddie Condon & his Windy City Seven

Meet Me Tonight in Dreamland
(Friedman-Whitson)
Jackson Teagarden, Trombone—Bud Freeman,
Tenor Saxophone—Pee Wee Russell, Clarinet
Jess Stacy, Piano—Bobby Hackett,
Cornet—Eddie Condon, Guitar
George Wettling, Drums
Artie Shapiro, Bass

Not Licensed for Radio Broadcast—Electrically Recorded April, 1938
Published by Commodore Music Shop, 144 East 42nd Street, New York City

HOT RECORD SOCIETY
Originals
HRS 1001

THERE'LL BE SOME CHANGES MADE
(Higgins-Overstreet)
PEE-WEE RUSSELL'S RHYTHMAKERS
Pee-Wee Russell, Clarinet; Max Kaminsky, Trumpet; Dicky
Wells, Trombone; Al Gold, Tenor Sax; Jimmy Johnson,
Piano; Freddie Green, Guitar; Zutty Singleton,
Drums; Wellman Braud, Bass
(P 23392)

MFD. BY AMERICAN RECORD CORP.

VICTOR
SWING CLASSIC

For best results
use Victor Needles

26640-A

SHAKE IT AND BREAK IT—Fox Trot
(H. Qualli Clark-Signor Friscoe Louchiha)
Sidney Bechet and his New Orleans Feetwarmers
(Sidney Bechet, Soprano Sax-Sidney DeParis,
Trumpet-Sandy Williams, Trombone-Cliff
Jackson, Piano-Bernard Addison,
Guitar-Wellman Braud, Bass-
Sidney Catlett, Drums)

RCA MANUFACTURING CO., INC., CAMDEN, N.J., U.S.A.

Kaycee Territory
Piney Brown's Town and Pendergast's Too!
1922-1948

"Well, I've been to Kansas City, Girls and everything is really all-right,
Yes, I've been to Kansas City, Girls and everything is really all-right.
Say, the boys jump and swing until broad daylight.
Yes, I dreamed last night I was standing on 18th and Vine,
Yes, I dreamed last night I was standing on 18th and Vine,
I shook hands with Piney Brown, and I could hardly keep from crying."

—*Piney Brown Blues*, Joe Turner/Pete Johnson

"If you want to see some sin, forget about Paris and go to Kansas City," wrote Edward Morrow in the Omaha *World-Herald*. Westbrook Pegler called it "The Paris of the Plains" and novelist Edward Dahlberg called it "a wild and concupiscient city."

Boss Tom Pendergast gave Kansas City to Johnny Lazia just as Big Bill Thompson gave Chicago to Al Capone. The renowned style of the town lasted until 1938, when Pendergast was indicted for income-tax fraud. In between, Lazia was murdered in the best gangland style, and the Union Station Massacre got headlines for Pretty Boy Floyd. Reform elements inevitably took over, the cabarets and clubs were shut. The good times ended, and "The Paris of the Plains" was no more.

The good times were good indeed! At its peak in the Depression, when the whole country seemed to be shutting down, nearly a hundred clubs, dance halls, and restaurants on Twelfth and Eighteenth streets intersected by Vine and spreading out into the county and downtown, featured everything from pianists like Pete Johnson to big bands led by Andy Kirk, Tommy Douglas, and Clarence Love (whose smoothly well-disciplined band played the tired businessmen's lunch at the Chesterfield Club at Ninth and Oak, where the waitresses wore only cellophane skirts in 1933). Twelfth and Paseo had the clubs—Sunset, Boulevard Lounge, Cherry Blossom, and Lone Star. Eighteenth and Paseo had the Panama, Subway, Lucille's Band Box, Elk's Rest, and Old Kentucky Bar-B-Cue. Twelfth and Cherry had the Reno, Amos and Andy, Greenleaf Gardens, and the Hey Hey Club. The general downtown area and environs had the College Inn, Bar Le Duc, Hole in the Wall, Hi Hat, Elmer's Bean Club, Novelty Club, Vanity Fair, Wolfe's Buffet, The Spinning Wheel, Hawaiian Gardens, Yellow Front Saloon, Playhouse, Martin's On-The-Plaza, the Antlers, and Tootie Clarkin's Mayfair.

The Vanity Fair, Club Harlem, and the Cherry Blossom had stage shows that rivaled Chicago's and New York's, and while few of the owners paid much money, none allowed their performers or musicians to go hungry. Drummer Jo Jones, who came there in 1933 after three years in Omaha and on the road, said, "I had been to New Orleans and to Chicago, but I never heard music that had the kind of feeling in jazz that I most admire until I went to Kansas City."

Bennie Moten and singer-saxist George E. Lee built large stable bands without having to leave town. Touring road shows often got stranded in Kansas City, and one left pianist Bill Basie from Red Bank, New Jersey, who fell in love with the atmosphere. Even after landing a job with one of the region's best territory bands, Walter Page's Blue Devils with Lips Page, Buster Smith, and Jimmy Rushing, Basie stayed only a few months before coming back to the night life in Kansas City.

Jamming in Kansas City was a serious proposition, and jammed onto tiny stages that were meant for two or three pieces would be half a dozen trumpeters, saxists, or pianists, all waiting their turn to play. They were fond of laying a trap for name players with out-of-town bands who came to sit in. Depending on the style, either Ben Webster or Dick Wilson would start the battle, and Herschel Evans and Lester Young would hide in the wings and then step out and blow the visitor off the stand. Hot Lips Page did the same on trumpet, and pianists like Basie, Mary Lou Williams, Vivian Jones, Countess Johnson, or Sleepy Hickox had all bases covered. These sessions ruined many a national reputation, however briefly, and brought offers from name bands after all-night action on the stage of the Sunset or Reno clubs.

Every city throughout the Midwest, Southwest, and Southeast had fine players and outstanding territory bands, and all of them sent scores of talented sidemen into the big time, including men like Jack and Charlie Teagarden, Harry James, Tex Beneke, Jimmy Blanton, Tab Smith, Jimmy Forrest, and many others. Most of the people who idolized them in the big bands didn't know they came from anywhere.

From Dallas to Omaha, from Baton Rouge to Little Rock, Milwaukee to Des Moines, Miami to Charleston, territory bands crisscrossed the major part of the country on constant one-nighters, with few favored summer resort jobs lasting two months or more at a time. No place, no matter how rich its jazz history or great its individual players, gave so many players and bands into the mainstream of jazz as Kansas City. And probably no place kept so many first quality players, despite the outflux; Kansas City was so rich, so overflowing, that the depletion of its ranks seemed to produce two for one—somewhat like the Hydra, or the *Sorcerer's Apprentice*.

Every true jazz fan has dreamt of standing with Charlie Parker at the fabled Reno Club, listening to Lester Young, Buster Smith, and Lips Page play some of the most exciting music in America for three dollars a night and a share of the kitty. And has also dreamt of standing with Joe Turner on the corner of Eighteenth and Vine, shaking hands with Piney Brown.

Count Basie learned, in a few weeks with Walter Page's Blue Devils in 1928, how string bass and rhythm guitar could lift and drive a band as no tuba or banjo could. Later, with trombonist and arranger Eddie Durham, he quietly modernized the Bennie Moten band. On *New Vine Street Blues* his soft chords lead the sections and cue the soloists, whose work is more deeply felt and relaxed. The transition was completed in 1932 when Moten hired Ben Webster, Eddie Barefield, and the greatest bass player in jazz, Walter Page. Without concern for the future, Basie took destiny in his hands and helped produce jazz classics like *Moten Swing, Toby, Prince of Wales,* and *Milenberg Joys.* These records show the integrated rhythm section walking behind the reeds on *Milenberg Joys* and Webster's chorus on *Prince of Wales;* The lightning-fast execution of reed and brass call-and-response figures; Basie lightening his left hand while Page's bass line flowed steadily on. They are the essence of swing. As a member of a rival Kansas City band remarked, "They were the kind of guys who had their own thing at heart and that was all they were going to do. They were not going to compromise." Clearly, Basie had achieved something that surpassed even what Fletcher Henderson's, Don Redman's, and Earl Hines's bands were doing. This is what he would give to the world six years later at the Famous Door on 52nd Street.

Bennie Moten's band played a synthesis of ragtime and imitation New Orleans jazz in 1923. (Top, L to R) Willie Hall, Lamar Wright, Bennie Moten, Thamon Hayes, Woodie Walder. This group made fourteen Okeh records, 1923–25, including *Kater Street Rag, Vine Street Blues,* and *South,* on which Moten's piano and Wright's trumpet are outstanding. They had added five men by the time they switched to Victor in 1926 (Middle): saxophonists Harlan Leonard and LaForest Dent (fourth and fifth from L); Sam Tall, banjo; Vernon Page, tuba; and a better drummer, Willie McWashington (fourth, third, and second from R). Their records evolved gradually from the vo-do-de-o saxes and staccato trumpet of *Kansas City Shuffle* (1926); through trumpet-trombone chase choruses in *Pass Out Lightly,* with Ed Lewis added on trumpet and Jack Washington in for Dent on alto and baritone sax; to the powerful ensemble climaxes of *Moten Stomp* (1927), the tune that decided many a battle of bands in their favor at the annual spring musicians' ball. *Get Low Down Blues* (1928) has an expressive solo by Ed Lewis and, over boogie-woogie bass figures, the cavernous sound of Jack Washington's baritone sax. Moten's band laid down a warm, thick carpet of sound that was perfectly suited to the needs of dancers. Moten banjoist Buster Berry explained: "Bennie had that old Boston beat which young and old alike had no trouble with. We never played too fast or too slow. We tried to study what the public wanted and we gave it to them." Moten was a master at setting tempos. His devotion to detail brought the band long stands at the lavish new El Torreon Ballroom on 31st and Gillham, and their records attracted important jobs in resorts in upstate New York in 1928–29. Two significant newcomers joined in 1929: pianist Bill Basie and arranger and trombonist Eddie Durham, who together and separately began modernizing the Moten band. They got the sections to work together better; made good use of Bus Moten's accordion and Jimmy Rushing's powerful ballad style; and they recorded one prophetic blues, *That Too, Do,* from which *Good Morning Blues* and *Sent for You Yesterday* evolved later in the Basie band years. At Fairyland Park in 1931 (Bottom), Moten was at his peak with Hot Lips Page, Ed Lewis, Basie, Durham (third, fourth, second, and seventh from L), Bus Moten (dark suit), Jimmy Rushing (top, R), and Jack Washington (extreme R). A year later, Lips Page, Basie, Durham, Jack Washington, banjo, and drums were joined by Ben Webster, Eddie Barefield, and younger brass men, a change that overnight boosted their musical standard to the level of Henderson, Hines, and Don Redman. Neither midwestern nor eastern audiences appreciated the stylistic change, however. The band's last records, *Moten Swing, Toby,* and the others, were jazz masterpieces, but Moten nearly lost his band. Just before his death in April 1935 he was on his way back, negotiating for a shot at the Grand Terrace in Chicago and new recordings. In the band now were Lester Young, Herschel Evans, Buster Smith, Jack Washington, saxes; Jo Jones, drums; and Basie, directing from the keyboard as only he could do. They went ahead to the Rainbow Ballroom in Denver, while Moten remained behind for a tonsillectomy. He died on the operating table; it was over.

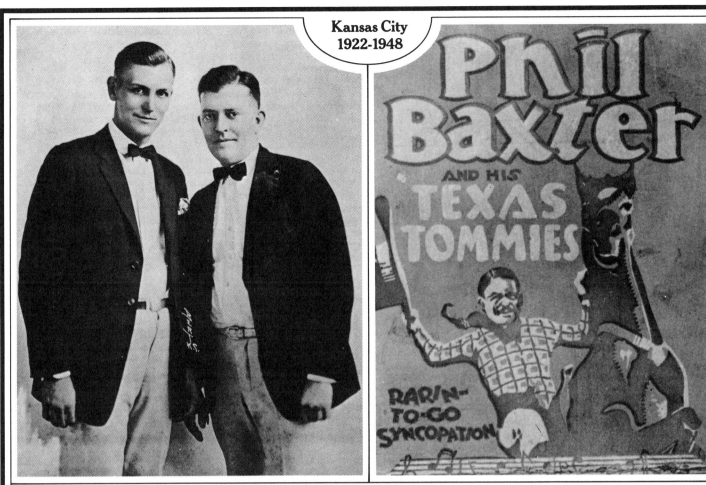

Pianist Joe Sanders (Top, L) and drummer Carlton Coon (R) brought their Nighthawks Orchestra into the Muehlebach Hotel in 1921. Their brash humor and jazz-tinged dance music made them national favorites at the Blackhawk in Chicago after 1924. Sanders's tunes and arrangements and his vocals with Coon on their best-selling Victor records of *Sluefoot, Blazin', Roodles,* and *Here Comes My Ball and Chain* won them legions of fans. It all ended a year after Coon's death in 1932. Texas pianist and composer *(Ding Dong Daddy, Piccolo Pete,* etc.) Phil Baxter's Texas Tommies opened the El Torreon Ballroom and became its house band. Their Victor record of *Down Where the Blue Bonnets Grow* features Al Jennings on trombone. Severe arthritis forced Baxter to give up the band in 1929. Later he wrote many hit songs.

Kansas City's oldest active bandleader was pianist Paul Banks (third from R), who kept playing steadily from the ragtime era until 1934, when he turned over his band interests to younger brother Clifton (extreme L). Banks usually played stock arrangements, but hired promising young players like trumpeter Ed Lewis and tuba player Jap Allen. Lewis joined Moten in 1927, and two years later Allen took most of Banks's band to start his own Cotton Pickers. Banks was well liked because he split fees down the middle, paid off promptly, and showed his contracts to his sidemen. He never gave up his daytime job at the Armour company.

George E. Lee (Bottom, fourth from L) had just begun his career when Charlie Parker (Top, L) was born in 1920. Lee and his sister, pianist Julia (Top, R, and Bottom), were Bennie Moten's archrivals throughout the twenties. Lee's powerful voice and showmanship usually overshadowed his soloists, clarinetist Bob Garner and trombonist Thurston "Sox" Moppins (third from L). Soon after pianist-arranger Jesse Stone and other younger players joined his band in 1929, Lee's musicianship rivaled Moten's, especially the adroit section work and integrated solos on their Brunswick records *Ruff Scuffling* and *Paseo Strut*. Julia Lee made *Won't You Come Over to My House, Baby* at the same time as a showcase for her spirited barrelhouse piano and singing. Lee's name meant big business in a dozen states until 1933, when the union merged his and Bennie Moten's bands. The new group went to the new Cherry Blossom nightclub (the old Eblon Theatre) and then the equally new Harlem Club (the old Paseo Hall). Lee's star was fading fast when that arrangement came to an end in 1934, and he began holding out on his sidemen. Julia wisely elected to work as a single with various drummers at half a dozen 12th Street clubs over the next decade, until former Kansas City reporter Dave Dexter, then with Capitol Records, signed her. Her hits, such as *King Size Papa* and *Snatch It and Grab It,* took her to Harry Truman's White House in 1949.

BENNIE MOTEN Musical Crew in DANGER

Jesse Stone Defies Bennie For Orchestra Contest

$500 Side Bet— Bennie Posts $250.00 Stone's Money is Up.

Bennie Accepts Challenge

THURS. NIGHT FEB. 3

15th & Paseo RECREATION HALL

Who Will Win?

Come
O u t
a n d
S e e!

Bennie Moten's bands combined the strength of his ensembles, the showmanship of Jimmy Rushing (Page 153, Bottom, R), the powerful, preaching trumpet style of Ed Lewis (Page 153, Bottom, L), and Moten's built-in popularity to win most of the battles of bands against sometimes musically superior bands like Jesse Stone's, which was the first to play specially written arrangements in the Kansas City area in 1928. Moten maintained his popularity with his old-fashioned music, but after he hired Bill Basie and Bus Moten (Page 153, Top, R, L and R) in 1929, and trombonist and arranger-guitarist Eddie Durham (Page 154, Top, L), their thinking influenced him to the point where he let go all of his senior bandsmen, the ones who made his old style. Jimmy Rushing's powerful voice helped offset rival George E. Lee's. Bus Moten's accordion playing was shrewdly blended with the brass and reeds ("Who's that kid? Better keep him; hell, he's forty percent of the band!"), and he was a good conductor as well. The change, even though it brought in fine players like Eddie Barefield (Page 154, Bottom, L) and Ben Webster, cost Moten his audience. Booker T. Pittman (Page 154, Top, R), grandson of Booker T. Washington, was rated highly in Jap Allen's Cotton Pickers, but left town and settled in Europe in 1933. (Page 154, Bottom, R) Bassist Joe Durham (L) and drummer Kenny McVey with Artis Gilmore, owner of Street's Hotel, were with the Moten and Lee band at the Harlem Club, one of the low points in both careers. Moten was on his way back in 1935; Lee was sinking further.

Andy Kirk (Top, L, extreme R) became leader of T. Holder's band in Dallas in 1929 after Holder failed to meet the payroll. He took the renamed Clouds of Joy to Spring Lake Park in Oklahoma City that summer (Bottom). There he met George E. Lee, whose connections enabled Kirk to work Kansas City's best ballrooms and nightclubs. When Brunswick Records' Jack Kapp recorded Kirk in November, he did more than he planned. Nineteen-year-old Mary Lou Williams (Top, R), wife of Kirk's alto and baritone soloist, John Williams (Bottom, third from R), substituted at piano because Kirk's pianist did not show up; Kapp was entranced with her playing and insisted that she make all the dates or there wouldn't be any more. Her strong Hines-like attack on *Messa Stomp* shows why Kapp liked her so much. She finally joined Kirk's band full-time in 1931 and became chief arranger. They worked as often as anyone else because of their good musicianship and, by 1934, because they added a highly commercial singer, Pha Terrell (Top, L, L), and a melodic trumpet and ballad arranger, Earl Thompson. The Clouds of Joy felt the effects of the Depression less than most.

Everyone wanted tall, soft-spoken trumpeter Irving "Mouse" Randolph (Top, L) with his broad, powerful tone. He spent the Depression in Andy Kirk's band and was noted for his regular participation in the jam sessions at the Sunset and elsewhere. Kirk's solo tenor chair during that time was occupied by Ben Webster (who with Randolph joined Fletcher Henderson's band in the summer of 1934), Lester Young, and Buddy Tate before 1935, when Dick Wilson (Top, R) settled in. Wilson's smooth and silky tone graced almost all of Kirk's Decca records until his death in 1941. Prominent are *Lotta Sax Appeal, Walkin' and Swingin',* and *Bear Down,* among others. Kirk's band succeeded nationally, the first from Kansas City since Moten's heyday in the twenties to do so, on the strength of the phenomenal success of his theme song, *Until the Real Thing Comes Along,* sung by Pha Terrell in the soft tenor style of the day. The Clouds of Joy played major ballrooms and nightclubs like the Grand Terrace in Chicago and leading theaters throughout the East, South, and Middle West. Mary Lou Williams's arrangements had distinction in that they were swinging and punchy, even though Kirk used only four brass long after most bands had five or six. They relocated in New York after 1938.

"Howdy" Folks
Tommy Douglas and his Band

The finest and fastest Colored Band on the road

Showmen, Vocalists, Musicians - A Real Entertaining Attraction

KXBY — Kansas City
RADIO FAVORITES

Harlem's
ARISTOCRATS OF
RHYTHM ★ NOVELTIES
Singing Sizzling Swinging Syncopating

Park Region Orchestra Service, Battle Lake, Minn.

Printed at The KINGSLEY PRESS, Wadena, Minn.

ROSCOE HALL
18th AND PROSPECT
SUNDAY, JULY 4th
ADMISSION 50 Cents — *Including Tax* — Advance Tickets 35 cents

Hours - - - 9 Until ? ? ?

As a saxophone soloist Tommy Douglas (Top, L) had few peers. His full tone, original ideas, and conservatory-acquired technique made him much in demand, but he preferred leading his own bands. He often played music that neither ballroom operators nor most of his fellow jazzmen understood. Standoffish, he had to be begged to take part in jam sessions, but, as Curtyse Foster marveled, "when he took out that clarinet, that was the end of the session. He blew everyone out!" His playing was a source of inspiration to Charlie Parker, a sideman in his 1936 combo at the Antler's Club. His 1938 band, which featured Bill Martin, Fred Beckett, Curtyse Foster, his brothers Bill and Buck (second through sixth from L), and pianist Bill Searcy (fourth from R), was a fine one, but Douglas chiseled his sidemen and had to drive on back roads to avoid his many creditors. When his band recorded for Capitol in 1949, he refused to solo in a rhythm-and-blues format.

Count Basie and Hot Lips Page (R) worked at the Reno Club in 1936, but after Joe Glaser signed him to a management contract, Lips stayed to front Bus Moten's band after Basie's new big band went to Chicago in November. Page's playing was timeless, and aside from one hallowed cutting contest when trumpeter and tap-dancer Harry Smith made him put up his horn (Smith replaced him in the Blue Devils band), Lips was the jam-session king. Of his playing on the famed 1932 Moten records of *New Orleans, Moten Swing,* and others critic Gunther Schuller wrote, "Page's best solos reflect a minimum of activity with a maximum of expression, a lesson his colleague Lester Young would extend a few years later." Page left Kansas City for New York in 1937.

The careers of Joe Turner (L) and Pete Johnson were intertwined from the mid-thirties onward. Johnson, who was born in 1904, had played in 12th Street clubs as a single or led small bands since the twenties and had eight men at the Sunset Crystal Palace at 12th and Woodlawn, where Joe Turner was tending bar. Turner (born in 1911) stepped out to lend his powerful voice to the proceedings. When John Hammond made the rounds seeking talent, Johnson's sidemen were rarely on the bandstand, so Johnson and Turner made enough music to convince Hammond of their worth, and he arranged for their debut at Carnegie Hall at his "Spirituals to Swing" concert in December 1938 and a job at Café Society in 1939, where *Roll 'Em Pete, Cherry Red,* and *Piney Brown Blues* became favorites.

Thamon Hayes's Kansas City Skyrockets, composed of castoffs from Moten's and George Lee's bands, were molded into a sharp unit by arranger-pianist Jesse Stone (second from R). They beat Moten decisively at the annual union-sponsored battle of bands and won the coveted summer season at Fairyland Park. Stone shrewdly retained some of the old Moten-Lee down-home music and showmanship, mixing them with his own advanced ideas and new soloists like Vic Dickenson (second from L). Hayes worked steadily while Moten and Lee floundered, but, unable to crack Chicago's union barriers, in 1935 he turned the band over to Harlan Leonard, who kept it working another two years

When Harlan Leonard disbanded in 1937, Woodie and Herman Walder joined forces, using Booker Washington, trumpet; Baby Lovett, drums; and others. They played good clubs like the Spinning Wheel on Troost (L) until the war and then went their separate ways. Leonard took over Tommy Douglas's band and became Kansas City's most popular attraction at Fairyland Park in 1938. Two years later they had attracted national publicity and began recording for RCA Victor in Chicago. (R, L to R) Richmond Henderson, Jimmie Keith, Edward Johnson, James Ross, Leonard, William Smith, Darwin Jones, Winston Williams, Henry Bridges, Jesse Price, and William H. Smith.

Most of the recordings of Harlan Leonard (L) were arranged by James Ross or Tadd Dameron, whom Leonard picked up while playing Harlem's new Golden Gate Ballroom. Pitted against the superb bands of Coleman Hawkins, Claude Hopkins, Les Hite, and Teddy Wilson, the Rockets were unable to leave a strong impression. Yet on records like *Rockin' with the Rockets, Rock and Ride, A la Bridges,* and *Mistreated* (with a fine Ernie Williams vocal), they show good section work and intonation, strong rhythm, and first-rate solo work from trumpeters William Smith (third from L) and James Ross, and importantly from Henry Bridges, tenor sax (fifth from L), and Fred Beckett, trombone (L). Charlie Christian (second from L) sat in on this Lincoln Hall jam session.

The Reno Club at 12th and Cherry, scene of so many vital jam sessions, had a co-op band (Bottom) after Bus Moten left in 1937. Prince Babb (L) and Christianna Buckner (R) were part of the floor show; nickel beer and hot dogs made it an inexpensive evening. Birmingham trumpeter Bill Martin rivaled Lips Page in popularity, and tenor man Buck Douglas was once offered a job in Count Basie's band. The Reno and a dozen other clubs were shut down for tax evasion in the reform wave that had toppled the Pendergast regime in 1938. It was at the Reno that drummer Jo Jones flung a cymbal at Charlie Parker's head when he failed to bring off his solo ideas. Four years later, in 1940, Parker (Top, L) signified to a ten-cent penny-arcade photo machine that his dues were paid. He had absorbed the lessons of Tommy Douglas, Buster Smith, and Lester Young; and after a detour in 1938 to Chicago, where he studied Scoops Carry's playing, and to an after-hours club in Harlem, where he listened to Art Tatum, he was ready for all comers. Now he was the focus of Jay McShann's new big band, which impressed everyone who heard it—none more so than an avid fan named Fred Higginson, a student at the University of Kansas who had the good sense to get the soloists and rhythm section, Parker and Gene Ramey (Top, R) included, to station KFBI in town (owned by goat-gland Dr. Brinkley) to record some of their solo flights for history on acetates. *Lady Be Good, Moten Swing, I Found a New Baby,* and *Body and Soul* were thus preserved for history.

161

Muskogee pianist Jay McShann (L), one of Kansas City's most sought-after sidemen in 1937, was so popular that he organized his own sextet with Charlie Parker on alto sax and became the first leader to work at Claire Martin's exclusive club in the south-side Plaza district. By 1941 (R) his big band challenged and (many thought) eclipsed Harlan Leonard's in popularity. Key sidemen, photographed in San Antonio, were trumpeters Buddy Anderson (sixth from L) and Orville Minor (fourth from R), Charlie Parker (third from L), bassist Gene Ramey (extreme R), drummer Gus Johnson (second from R), and blues singer Walter Brown (second from L).

Fairyland Park (R) was Jay McShann's home base whenever the big band came off the road from their midwestern tours. His sidemen, like bassist Gene Ramey and trumpeter Buddy Anderson (second from R), jammed anywhere. They met in Wichita with Floyd Ray sidemen Charlie Jacobs (extreme L) and tenor man Shirley Green (R) while University of Kansas student Fred Higginson enjoyed. Anderson's playing excited Dizzy Gillespie when he went to Kansas City with Cab Calloway's band, but tuberculosis and bad habits caught up with Anderson when he was with Billy Eckstine's band in 1944, and he soon had to stop playing trumpet. Later he became a union executive.

Walter Brown (L) made the difference. The Texas-born blues singer, a onetime CCC worker who won a contest at the Sunset, upset audiences everywhere with his *Confessin' the Blues,* sung in a nasal style. McShann's band was burning up the Midwest on dates, but Decca Records cheated them and the public by recording Brown with just the rhythm section and refusing to allow McShann to use more than a small portion of originals like *Swingmatism.* The draft and the recording ban in 1942 robbed McShann of his proper place in history.

Everything came naturally to Jack Teagarden, who was born in 1905 in Vernon, Texas, where he absorbed black "holy roller" revival music right next door. In Oklahoma City, where he heard Indian tribal chants at the old fairgrounds, "...that came natural to me, too. I could embellish on that and I could play an Indian thing—just pick up my horn and play it to where you couldn't tell the difference....I don't know how that came so natural...." With his stomach or "jug" tone and phenomenal technique, acquired by playing all kinds of music, including classical, Teagarden was made welcome everywhere. Playing in Marin's Southern Trumpeters at Abel's Restaurant in Mexico City in 1924, he made a strong impression on the members of the Mexican National Opera House orchestra who were working across the street. That year (Inset) he worked with Terry Shand (L) and Pee Wee Russell (R) in Peck Kelly's Bad Boys at Sylvan Beach, a summer resort on Galveston Bay.

Houston pianist John "Peck" Kelly (Top, standing M) loved classical music and had a prodigious technique like Art Tatum's. He preferred jobs like this one at Sylvan Beach in 1924, where he could hire jazzmen like Jack Teagarden (fourth from L) and Pee Wee Russell (fourth from R). He constantly shunned offers from Paul Whiteman, Ben Bernie, and leaders of other "name" bands and refused to make records. Drummer E. V. "Doc" Ross's Jazz Bandits (Middle, L) featured players such as Jack Teagarden (extreme R), Bob McCracken (kneeling), and Wingy Manone (second from R) for jobs at the Paso del Norte Hotel in El Paso in 1926. Introverted Louisiana guitarist Eddie "Snoozer" Quinn (Middle, R) combined single-string and chord solos, amazing everyone who heard him. He spent his career in nightclubs until illness forced him out of music. He died in 1949. Clarinetist Jimmy Maloney's Joys (Bottom) turned professional right out of the University of Texas, and Maloney had a long career as a bandleader. Pianist Charlie Bob Ballew and Collis Bradt (R) were featured in 1921. Their 1924–25 Okeh records of *Wild Jazz* and *Stomp It Mr. Kelly* caused a sensation.

Ken "Goof" Moyer (L) from Oklahoma City specialized in hot mellophone solos and made two scarce records, *Echoes of Oklahoma* and *Mellophone Stomp,* for Banner while working in New York in 1926. Back in Oklahoma, he led semicommercial bands throughout the thirties. The Louisiana Ramblers (R) were organized by Pat (second from R) and Bobby DeCuir (extreme R) and Rome Landry (extreme L) in Alexandria in 1920. They built a big following throughout Louisiana, Texas, and Oklahoma, but never played New Orleans; they disbanded in 1927. Pianist Bob Canfield and clarinetist Tim Kelly were important soloists of that period.

Clarinetist Marshall Van Pool's orchestra was the best in Oklahoma City for a decade. They played fine hotels like the Skirvin, where Van Pool (seated R) featured pianist Stan Wrightsman, saxist Chuck Gentry (second and fourth from L), and trombonist King Jackson (extreme R). A later Van Pool band featured Harry James. Much later he enjoyed a successful career in real estate. Saxist Ben Young (extreme R) from Winn Parish, Louisiana, had one of Texas's best swing bands in the Depression and played major hotels and ballrooms with sidemen like Tex Beneke (extreme L), Dalton Rizzotto (third from L), Dave Schultze (fifth from L), Claude Lakey (fifth from R), and Tommy Gonsoulin (fourth from R), who left him to join Glenn Miller's, Gene Krupa's, and Harry James's bands at different times.

Despite national publicity after a 1940 *Collier's* magazine story, Peck Kelly continued working in Houston's Southern Dinner Club for $50 a week, resolutely refusing all offers to record or travel. His last job was at the Dixie Bar in 1949; then he just stopped playing. Had similar publicity been given the swinging little jazz unit at Jake's College Club on 23rd Avenue in Oklahoma City in 1941, the piano playing of Norma Teagarden (extreme R), Smith Sutley's tenor sax, Woodie Wood's clarinet, and Alex Brashear's cornet might have gained the exposure that they richly deserved. This group, with minor changes and four different leaders (whoever got the job), worked there from 1939 to 1941, here under guitarist Al Gilbo.

TRENT'S ADOLPHUS HOTEL ORCHESTRA

Alphonso Trent AND HIS Orchestra ··
·· 12-Brown Skin Marvels-12 ··

RECORDING
VICTOR AND GENNETT

BROADCASTING
KDKF═WDAF═WFI
WETF═WCCO═JLW═WMAK
═WJR═KRLB
WTKM══WGR═
WEBR═WGR═
KTRC═WKY═WOAI═KLRA═
ONE YEAR
OVER
WFAA-

COMPOSERS OF-
"GILDED KISSES"
"BLUE MEMORIES"
"I'M CRAZY ABOUT YOU"
"SHOUT, SISTER, SHOUT"

ANDERSON LACY
DIRECTOR
VIOLINIST, VOCALIST

ALEXANDER HILL
PIANIST

A·G GODLEY
ECCENTRIC DRUMMER
ORIGINATOR OF THE
DRUM SOLO

LEO MOSELY
TROMBONIST
COMPOSER AND
MASTER OF THE SLIDE
SAXAPHONE, A VERY

NOTABLE ENGAGEMENTS
ONE YEAR AT EXCLUSIVE
HOTEL ADOLPHUS, DALLAS, TEXAS

SIX MONTHS AT THE
GUNTER HOTEL, SAN ANTONIO, TEXAS

FOUR MONTHS AT THE
PALAIS ROYALE NITE CLUB
BUFFALO, N.Y.

THREE MONTHS AT THE
HOLLYWOOD CAFE
CLEVELAND, OHIO

FOUR MONTHS AT THE
GREYSTONE BALLROOM
CINCINNATI, O

O PRACTICALLY ALL
DING BALLROOMS, CAFES
THEATERS AND HOTELS

Arkansas pianist Alphonso Trent (Top, L) played Dallas's famed Adolphus Hotel, broadcasting regularly over WFAA, for a year, 1924–25. (Top, R, L to R) A. G. Godley, drums; T. Holder, Chester Clark, trumpets; Snub Mosley, trombone; Gene Crook, banjo; Trent; James Jeter, alto sax; John Fielding, vocals; Brent Sparks, tuba; Wendell Holloway, tenor sax. They played in tune, dressed well, and had fervent admirers in Paul Whiteman and Fletcher Henderson, who urged them to go to New York. Fearful of losing his best men, Trent chose Cleveland's Plantation Club, where they lost their instruments and scores when the club burned down in 1930. Trent's Gennett records of *Black and Blue Rhapsody, Nightmare, After You've Gone,* and a stomp version of *St. James Infirmary* display their ensemble precision and solos by Stuff Smith, violin; Peanuts Holland, trumpet; Hayes Pillars, tenor sax; and Snub Mosley, trombone. Compromised incessantly by mismanagement, Trent's band declined steadily, and outward appearances of prosperity in 1932 (Middle) could not hide the fact that the end was near. (L to R in Memphis) Chester Clark, Hayes Pillars, John Fielding, A. G. Godley, George Hudson, Dan Minor, Peanuts Holland, Anderson Lacy, Gene Crook, Trent, Jim Jeter, Snub Mosley, Lewis Pitts, Brent Sparks, Eppi Jackson. Trent's last recordings, for Champion in March 1933, of *Clementine* and *I Found a New Baby* were made only months ahead of the band's demise.

Creole trumpeter Don Albert (Top, L) was the star of Troy Floyd's Band on Okeh Records *(Shadowland Blues)* and at San Antonio's famed Shadowland nightclub outside town (Middle). A year later his own Ten Happy Pals headlined the same club. His swing band (Top, R) with Ellington-style arrangements drew crowds all over the South and Midwest. Staffed with New Orleans players—Alvin Alcorn on trumpet, ex-Buddy Bolden bassist Jimmy Johnson, Fats Martin on drums (second, fourth, and fifth from L); Louis Cottrell on clarinet and tenor sax; and lead alto and baritone sax soloist Herb Hall (sixth and second from R)—and talented southwestern players Lloyd Glenn (third from L), piano-arranger; Dink Taylor, alto sax; and New Haven trumpet star Billy Douglas (missing), the band made the fine 1936 Vocalion records *Rockin' and Swingin', Deep Blue Melody, Liza,* and *Sunny Side of the Street,* which reveal a well-honed mix of southwestern swing and fine solos by Douglas, Cottrell, Taylor, and Hall and rich-sounding ensembles. (Bottom, L) Showstopping Ernestine "Annisteen" Allen from Springfield, Ohio, was one of Don Albert's outstanding talents in the late 1930s. Albert's refusal of job offers at the French Casino in New York and the Savoy in Harlem and Joe Glaser's management ultimately cost him his band, which he dismantled in Houston in 1940. He later opened the South's first integrated nightclub, the Keyhole in San Antonio, and booked bands. Milt Larkin's orchestra was stiff competition for traveling bands like Jimmie Lunceford's at Houston's Harlem Grill in the late thirties with players like Eddie "Cleanhead" Vinson (Bottom, R, second from R), Arnett Cobb (extreme R), Cedric Haywood on piano, and arranger Bill Davis (fourth from R). Larkin (third from L, front row) and his group in 1942 became house band at the Rhumboogie in Chicago, where they stayed nine months. Larkin was drafted in 1943. After the war he relocated in New York and moved into the rhythm-and-blues and club-date field. His band did not record.

White bands in the Southwest and Middle West were rarely allowed to play much jazz. Dallas-based pianist Ligon Smith (eighth from the L, seated) led bands since the early twenties and mixed sweet and swing, cutting up stocks, and playing the best hotels in Texas without having to travel extensively. He liked having fine players like Harry James (second from R) and Warren Smith, trombone (sixth from L), who got a chance to blow on the handful of "specials" that Smith would pull out when they had a younger crowd to play for. Here they're shown relaxing at the Texas auto show in San Antonio, 1934, with popular bandleader Carl "Deacon" Moore (fourth from R), a onetime Texas Tommies drummer. James and Smith between them apprenticed in a dozen territory bands like this before joining Ben Pollack's, Benny Goodman's, and Bob Crosby's bands.

Atlanta-based guitarist and bandleader Marty Britt (extreme L) is best known for two hot Victor records, *Goose Creek* (Stomp) and *Sadness Will Be Gladness*, recorded a day apart in 1928 and released on Victor's national and regional labels. Their personnel have yet to be confirmed, but *Goose Creek* is really the jazz standard *Weary Blues* with a fine rambling piano solo by Terry Shand (second from L); he and guitarist Eddie "Snoozer" Quinn (third from R) were two of the region's most sought-after players in the twenties and thirties. Britt's band played the summer season at Sylvan Beach in 1928, but this lineup did not make the records. Britt's career as a bandleader seemed to founder during the Depression, and Shand joined Freddy Martin.

Sunday   Hallowe'en

October 28   Wed. Oct. 31

Syncopation Kings of the Southwest

Blue Devil Orchestra

After Alphonso Trent moved north in 1927, Walter Page's Blue Devils (Top L and Bottom) became the most advanced band in the Southwest. Page was taught by Major N. Clark Smith at Lincoln High School in Kansas City. He played with Bennie Moten and Dave Lewis until he went on the road with Billy King. Stranded in Oklahoma City in 1926, Page persuaded local businessmen to build a band around him. Shown at radio station KFJE in 1928 are Hot Lips Page (extreme L), trumpet; Buster Smith, alto sax and clarinet (second from L); Willie Lewis, piano; and blues-singing drummer Ernie Williams (second from R), surrounding Walter Page (fourth from L), who played tuba, string bass, and baritone sax. Page seemed to hold his band together by telepathy; "for some reason or other," he remarked, "they all used to watch me.... I'd have the piano and the guitar and the drums all around me, and I'd never give any signals, but they all knew when to come in." For a short while in 1928 Bill Basie (Top L, second from L) played piano. "The first time I heard Basie," Page recalled, "I thought he was the greatest thing I ever heard in my life." The impression was mutual; in 1929, when Basie was with Bennie Moten, he played piano on Page's Vocalion record of *Blue Devil Blues* and *Squabblin'*. Page and Lips Page later joined Moten's band and made recorded history in 1932. The Blue Devils (Top, R), reorganized by Buster Smith and Ernie Williams (L), lasted another year with George Hudson and Lester Young (R).

Despite having a band some ranked as good as or better than Andy Kirk's, Kansas City saxophonist Clarence Love (M) enjoyed only a few years of commercial success before disbanding on the road. Built around the playing and arranging of pianist Eddie Heywood (second from L), guitarist Jim "Daddy" Walker (fourth from R), and trumpeter Clarence Trice (extreme R), the band played leading spots like Oklahoma City's Blossom Heath in 1936 before joining forces with successful singer Orlando Robeson in what promised to be his ticket to national success. The tour ended disastrously. Love formed other bands, but none with the promise of this unit.

After an apprenticeship on tuba and piano with Alphonso Trent, Ernie Fields, and local groups, Leslie Sheffield (fifth from R) took his Rhythmaires to Oklahoma City's Ritz Ballroom for a long stay in 1936. Featured were Charles "Little Dog" Johnson, Nat "Monk" McFay, Abe Bolar, and Charlie Christian (second, third, sixth, and seventh from L). The director, Charlie Waterford (standing), became known as the "Crown Prince of the Blues" in the postwar years. Many of these men later joined the bands of Harlan Leonard, Lucky Millinder, and others. Christian left Sheffield's combo in 1939 to join Benny Goodman.

On a boiling-hot August day in 1939, twenty-three-year-old Charlie Christian (second from R) said good-bye to trumpeter James Simpson and older brother Eddie (extreme R) before taking the Super Chief to Los Angeles to join Benny Goodman's band at the Victor Hugo Restaurant in Beverly Hills. Arriving on the bandstand, Goodman noted Christian's purple shirt and yellow shoes and, with obvious distaste, called out *Rose Room,* a tune he figured the newcomer didn't know. Forty-five minutes later, Christian's inspired solos lifted Goodman and the Sextet to new heights as the number came to an end amid some of the most tumultuous applause of Goodman's career.

His classical ambitions unfulfilled despite praise from Fritz Kreisler, violinist George Morrison (L, second from L) went on to become Denver's most popular society leader for over two decades. In 1922 he toured the Pantages Circuit featuring singer Hattie McDaniel (the Academy Award–winning actress), who recorded *Boo Hoo Blues* and others for Okeh. He also started a young Denver mailman named Andy Kirk (extreme R) on his musical career. Two former Morrison sidemen, saxist Kimble Dial and pianist Clyde Hart (R, L and R), formed their own Ginger Blue Orchestra for territory work out of Silver City, New Mexico, in 1927. Dial played with a dozen territory outfits before settling in St. Louis to work with Fate Marable and George Hudson. Hart wound up years later on 52nd Street.

Trombonist Bert Johnson's Sharps and Flats (L) were highly regarded in 1933 when they appeared at the El Fidel Hotel in Albuquerque. Johnson (third from L) featured trumpeter-pianist Dewey Lamont (extreme L), tenor man Merrill Anderson (fourth from R), and younger brother Cee Pee Johnson's Calloway-style showmanship and tom-toms. Both Johnsons settled in Los Angeles, where the latter became a name in the war years. Pianist Eddie Carson's Hot-Ten-Tots (R, extreme L) were organized in Albuquerque in 1931 and became well known over a wide area by 1937. Their arrangements offered a great deal of color because several of the men doubled on brass and reed instruments. Contributing an arrangement as well as doubling on piano was seventeen-year-old John Lewis (second from R). Trumpeter-trombonist Earl Broussard and Roscoe Robinson (sixth and fifth from L) were among the soloists. The war broke up the band in San Diego.

Kenny "Sticks" McVey (L, on drums) worked with George Morrison, Clarence Love, and the Bennie Moten–George E. Lee band before returning to Denver to lead the house band at Hymie Hirschorn's Tivoli Terrace at West 32nd and Shoshone from 1934 to 1940. This was Denver's best job. They broadcast regularly from the club and enjoyed a wide reputation for their smooth swing. His stars were pianist John Reagor (extreme L) and tenor man Merrill Anderson (extreme R), whose all-night battles with Lester Young are still remembered. Jamming in the Five Points section took place in Benny Hooper's basement in the 2600 block on Welton, where one might easily find Charlie Christian and Andy Kirk tenor man Dick Wilson (R) playing all night with local alto man Sam Hughes. This photo was actually made at Ruby's Grill in Oklahoma City, where Christian worked with pianist Leslie Sheffield before joining Benny Goodman.

Pianist-bandleader Eddie Heywood, Sr. (Top, L, L), and Jodie "Butterbeans" Edwards double-signify in front of Atlanta's 81 Theatre, where Heywood led the band for Butterbeans and Susie as well as making some of their many Okeh records like *Deal Yourself Another Hand.* Later Heywood led the band for Irvin C. Miller's *Brown Skin Models* revues before retiring to Atlanta. He died in 1942 just as his son Eddie, Jr., was on his way to nationwide success with his own combo. St. Louis trumpeter Charlie Creath (Top, R, R) evoked mass emotional response with his room-filling sound until he contracted tuberculosis in 1928. New Orleans drummer Zutty Singleton (L) married Creath's sister Marge, a pianist, and played in Creath's Jazz-o-Maniacs, who had made the first recording, on Okeh, of Jelly Roll Morton's *Grandpa's Spells.* Creath later became co-leader with Fate Marable on the riverboats until he left for Chicago to start a nightclub and other ventures, all of which failed. He died in 1951. Fate Marable's orchestras (Bottom) were the Streckfus Line's mainstay for over twenty years. Marable became leader in 1917 after ten years on the boats and made only one recording, *Frankie and Johnnie,* with this 1924 band, cleanly played but notable only for Sidney Desvignes's stop-time chorus. (L to R) Zutty Singleton, Norman Mason, Bert Bailey, Marable, Walter Thomas, Willie Foster, Desvignes, Amos White, Henry Kimball, Harvey Lankford, Garnet Bradley. Marable left the river in 1940 and played small clubs until his death in 1947.

Trumpeter Dewey Jackson recorded *Capitol Blues* and *Go Won to Town* for Vocalion in 1926, which show some of the power and feeling he put into his solos. His star rose after Charlie Creath had to stop playing in 1928. He played the Castle Ballroom, and his 1941 big band was the last to play the riverboats out of St. Louis. James Jeter and Hayes Pillars (R, L and R) had the house band at the Club Plantation, 1934–42, and made *Lazy Rhythm* for Vocalion in 1937, which introduced guitarist Floyd Smith. They later did USO work.

Pianist Eddie Johnson's Crackerjacks (R) made one great record for Victor in 1932, *Good Old Bosom Bread,* which features Ernest "Chink" Franklin's booting tenor sax and the brilliant tone of eighteen-year-old trumpeter Harold "Shorty" Baker (extreme R). Trumpeter Ed Lewis thought that "...around St. Louis the best territory band was Johnson's Crackerjacks. That's just what the name meant—crackerjack! Talk about playing; you never heard such music in your life. Every time we went down to St. Louis to play, they'd wash us right down the drain. As great as Bennie Moten was in those days, it was something terrible when they got through playing. After they finished, there wasn't anything left for us to play." Johnson kept good bands, one featuring Clark Terry and Jimmy Forrest, until the late fifties.

Two of St. Louis's successful bands were George Hudson's (L) and Eddie Randle's Blue Devils (R). Trumpeter Randle started with seven pieces in 1932 and worked steadily for the next thirty years, by balancing good music with what his public wanted to hear. His 1938 band featured Al Guichard (extreme L) and Elbert Claybrooks (second from L) on alto and tenor saxes and pianist Robert "Bonky" Parker. Later bands included Ernie Wilkins and Miles Davis. Trumpeter George Hudson worked with Alphonso Trent, the Blue Devils, Bennie Moten, Jeter-Pillars, and Dewey Jackson before starting his own big band in 1941 with arrangements given him by Count Basie and Stan Kenton, among others. For the next thirty years or so he toured with Dinah Washington, the Ink Spots, and other popular acts.

ZACK WHYTE & HIS CHOCOLATE BEAU BRUMMELS

Jan. 22, 24 & 27, Tue., Thur., Sun. Mat.
CRYSTAL DANSANT

Zack Whyte's 11 Chocolate Beau Brummels
of Cincinnati

Featuring

MELVIN OLIVER

Cornetist and Director

Come and See Our Home Boy Go.

Zach Whyte's Cincinnati-based band was well known from 1925 to 1940 and reached a peak with the 1929 band (Top). They made *West End Blues, Mandy,* and others with arrangements by Sy Oliver (third from L) and featured Henry Savage (second from L), Al Sears (extreme L), and Herman Chittison (sixth from L), piano. The Vocalion records made in 1931 by Grant Moore's New Orleans Black Devils (Middle) of *Original Dixieland One Step* and *Mama Don't Allow* featured trumpeter Bob Russell (fourth from L), altoist Earl Keith, and tenor man Willard Brown (fourth and third from R). Moore (extreme R) retired after the 1936 season to run a restaurant in Milwaukee. Bernie Young's Creole Roof Orchestra (Bottom) was affiliated with the Wisconsin Roof at 6th and Vermont avenues in Milwaukee from the late twenties until after World War II. (L to R, 1929) Preston Jackson, Young, Sylvester Rice, Z. T. Randolph, Mike McKendrick, Burroughs Lovingood, Gilbert Mundy, Ed Inge, Winston Walker, Bert Bailey. Despite WPA backing later on, Young never rose above territorial status.

Lawrence "Speed" Webb's Hollywood Blue Devils started in Toledo in 1926. They made several films—*Riley the Cop, Sables and Furs, On with the Show*—from 1927 to 1929 while playing Los Angeles ballrooms. As a result, Webb aspired to compete with Henderson and McKinney and built his best band in 1929: (L to R) Leonard Gay, Teddy Wilson, Smoke Richardson, Chuck Wallace, Melvin Bowles, William Warfield, (Webb), Sammy Scott, Roy Eldridge, Vic Dickenson, Reunald Jones, Gus Wilson, and Steve Dunn. They played major jobs in ten states before dispersing in 1931. Teddy Wilson compared the Webb group to Basie's. Other Webb bands had less success.

Eli Rice (R, third from L) was forty-six when he started his Dixie Cotton Pickers band in 1925 after a career as singer-dancer in minstrel companies, shoeshine boy, and "megaphonist" in Oshkosh, Wisconsin. Unrecorded, his big bands played the Midwest to California and back until 1942. His 1931 band, shown at the Coliseum Ballroom in Davenport, Iowa: (L to R) Joe Thomas; (Rice) Keg Johnson; Eddie Tompkins; Bernard Wright, alto; Sylvester Rice, drums; Charlie Oden, bass; Victoria Layne, piano; Boyd Atkins, alto; Sanford Beatty, banjo; Bert Bailey, tenor sax. (L) The "Imperial Brass Section" of Keg Johnson, trombone, and Joe Thomas and Eddie Tompkins, trumpets.

Indianapolis trumpeter Raymond "Syd" Valentine (L) and his Patent Leather Kids, with James Helms, piano (M), and Paul George, banjo, made eight red-hot Gennett records, including *Patent Leather Stomp* and *Jelly Bean Drag,* all for $20. Valentine played with Bernie Young, Tiny Bradshaw, Horace Henderson, and others until the war. Tulsa trombonist Ernie Fields (R) attained national repute when John Hammond recorded *Lard Stomp, T Town Blues,* and *High Jivin'* for Vocalion in 1939. They featured Amos Woodruff (fourth from L), Luther "Lard" West (third from R), and Buck Douglas (second from R). Fields later had some success in rhythm-and-blues.

Easygoing Omaha trumpeter Lloyd Hunter's Serenaders (Top) made one record, *Sensational Mood*, for Vocalion while they were touring with singer Victoria Spivey in 1931. Five years later Hunter (in white suit) featured pianist Sir Charles Thompson (second from R) and drummer Debo Mills (extreme R). Hunter's and five other Omaha bands were displaced when Nat Towles (Middle, extreme R) moved his crack band there in 1936. Towles's polished outfit featured Buddy Tate (seventh from R) and Henry Coker (sixth from L), but he was unable to record until he was past his prime in 1943, for a small firm, Tower in Chicago. He led combos after breaking up his big band in 1950. The Original Sunset Royal Serenaders (Bottom) rivaled the best territory bands. From West Palm Beach, Florida, their showmanship and arrangements like *Marie*, which became one of Tommy Dorsey's biggest hits, made them extremely popular. Their 1937 Vocalion records of *Who, Rhythm About Town,* and *Hurly Burly* show good section work. Prominent among their sidemen in 1935 were pianist Ace Harris (extreme L), saxist-arranger Bobby Smith (fifth from L), lead trumpet E. V. Perry (fifth from R), bassist Al Lucas, and multi-instrumentalist Steve Washington (third from R), who sang and arranged; he died in Boston in 1936. Doc Wheeler later led the band.

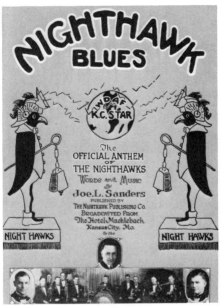

OKeh

Creath Record No. 1-B

Fox Trot
Vocal Chorus by Floyd Campbell

MARKET STREET BLUES
(Chas. Creath)

CHAS. CREATH'S JAZZ-O-MANIACS
Recorded in St. Louis

GENERAL PHONOGRAPH CORPORATION NEW YORK

OKeh
ELECTRIC

FOR BEST RESULTS USE OKeh NEEDLES

8571

Fox Trot
With Vocal Refrain

SHADOWLAND BLUES (PART 1)

TROY FLOYD & HIS PLAZA HOTEL ORCH.
(400507)

MADE AND PAT'D IN U.S.A. JAN 21, '13 AND RE 16583
OKEH PHONOGRAPH CORPORATION, NEW YORK

New Electrobeam
Gennett

6710-B

Fox Trot
2-29

BLACK AND BLUE RHAPSODY
(Madison)

Alphonso Trent and His Orch.

GENNETT RECORDS
RICHMOND, IND.

New Electrobeam
Gennett

6781-A

Race Record—Dance
4-29

MANDY
(From "Shufflin' Along")

Zack Whyte's Chocolate Beau Brummels

GENNETT RECORDS
RICHMOND, IND.

Brunswick

Fox Trot

PASEO STREET
Calle del Paseo
— Stone —

GEORGE E. LEE and HIS ORCHESTRA
7132

THE BRUNSWICK-BALKE-COLLENDER COMPANY
MADE IN U.S.A

VE
Orthophonic Recording

HIS MASTER'S VOICE

VICTOR

For best results use Victor Needles

23329–A

THE DUCK'S YAS YAS YAS—Fox Trot
(Jas. Stomp Johnson)
Eddie Johnson and his Cracker-Jacks
with vocal refrains

RCA Victor Company Inc
Camden N.J.

VE

BLUEBIRD
Electrically Recorded
PHONOGRAPH RECORDS

Not Licensed for Radio Broadcast

ROSE ROOM—Fox Trot
(Harry Williams-Art Hickman)
Boots and his Buddies
B 6063 B

RCA Manufacturing Co., Inc., Camden, N.J., U.S.A.

DECCA
TRADE MARK REGISTERED

NOT LICENSED FOR RADIO BROADCAST

(60852)

FOX TROT

WALKIN' AND SWINGIN'
(Mary Williams)

ANDY KIRK and his TWELVE CLOUDS OF JOY
809 B

Vocalion

Not Licensed for Radio Broadcast
(SA 2525)

Fox Trot

ROCKIN' AND SWINGIN'
-Don Albert-
DON ALBERT and his ORCHESTRA
3401

U.S.PAT. 1637544 BRUNSWICK RECORD CORPORATION

OKeh

Licensed by Mfr. under U.S. Patent Nos. 1625705 and/or 1708348 (and other patents pending) only for non-commercial use on phonographs in homes.

Use Columbia or Okeh Needles

6692
(H 849)

LET'S RIDE WITH BOB
(Theme Song)   Instrumental
-Wills-

BOB WILLS & his TEXAS PLAYBOYS

HIS MASTER'S VOICE
REG. U.S. PAT. OFF.   MARCA REGISTRADA

BLUEBIRD

For best results use Victor Needles

B-10883-A

ROCK AND RIDE—Fox Trot
(Tad Dameron-Harlan Leonard)

Harlan Leonard and his Rockets

RCA MANUFACTURING CO., INC., CAMDEN, N.J., U.S.A.

DECCA
Sepia SERIES

MANUFACTURED IN U.S.A. • BY DECCA RECORDS, INC.

(93731)

Blues Dance
with Singing by
WALTER BROWN

HOOTIE BLUES
(Jay McShann-Charles Parker)

JAY McSHANN
And His Orchestra

8559 B

West Coasting
Avalon, Treasure Island, and Central Avenue
1918-1949

"Now I'll relate a few incidents from the West Coast in California when Vic Berton and I got busted together. It was during our intermission…while Vic and I were blasting this joint…that two big healthy Dicks (detectives) came from behind a car and said to us, we'll take the roach boys. (Hmm)"
—*Louis*, Max Jones and John Chilton

There was no "there" there, and there was no jazz there, either. It had to be imported. Charlie Barnet summed up the situation in 1932: "California was a total musical desert. L.A. was just one Hawaiian band after another. I did get to meet Lionel Hampton and Lawrence Brown. I sat in with them at Sebastian's, the only jazz-oriented place in town. I also heard the Dixie Rhythm Kings, who had Buck Clayton. I was on a real jazz kick. I got several jobs but was fired for having too much of a jazz approach."

The Original Creole Band's tour of the Pantages Circuit inspired many West Coast musicians, including a teenaged saxophonist from Steubenville, Ohio, Paul Howard, who had been content with German beer-garden music. Dallas-born Reb Spikes, billed as "the greatest saxophonist in the world" in 1915, was featured with the Original So Different Orchestra at the So Different Club on San Francisco's Barbary Coast. Trombonist Harry Southard's Original Black and Tan Orchestra came from Texas around 1916 and later featured Howard and another fine player from Kansas City, a music teacher named Leon Herriford.

Papa Mutt Carey and Kid Ory came from New Orleans and enjoyed such popularity from 1919 on that they had to send back to New Orleans or to Chicago to bring musicians out to take jobs because there wasn't enough local talent to go around. King Oliver's Creole Band answered the call, coming from Chicago to play Los Angeles and San Francisco.

The early and middle twenties were dominated by the Black and Tan Orchestra, Reb Spikes's band, and the Sunnyland Jazz Orchestra with "King" Porter, trumpet, Ashford Hardee, trombone, Buster Wilson, piano, and alto man Charlie Lawrence, the only native Californian in the band. Their hegemony was upset by the increasingly popular new bands led by Paul Howard, drummer Curtis Mosby from Kansas City (he had run a music store in Oakland earlier), and pianist Sonny Clay.

The white bands mixed jazz and hotel music and were led by Chicago-born drummer Abe Lyman, who featured New Orleans cornetist Ray Lopez, clarinetist Gus Mueller and pianist Gus Arnheim. Suave, handsome violinist Henry Halstead featured Indiana drummer Phil Harris and hired Red Nichols at a huge salary one season to keep ahead of such hot bands as trumpeter Herb Wiedoeft's at the Cinderella Roof, pianist Eddie Frazier's with saxist Ted Mack at the Plantation Cafe, and Carlisle Stevenson's house band at the El Patio ballroom, Vermont and Third. These

bands recorded for Brunswick and Victor and a short-lived local firm, Hollywood. Lyman and Halstead turned commercial after the lush hotel successes of Anson Weeks, Jimmie Grier, and Gus Arnheim during the Depression.

Howard, Clay, and Mosby disbanded in the thirties, and former Illinois saxist Les Hite emerged as the name in Los Angeles when he became Frank Sebastian's house bandleader at the Cotton Club in Culver City, a job he held until 1939. The job didn't pay any more than any other, but it was steady, seven nights a week (he had to punch a time clock).

Ambitious young leaders like showman-trumpeter Charlie Echols, who employed everyone from Kid Ory and Benn-o Kennedy to Buck Clayton, Don Byas, and Jack McVea; and pianist-arranger Lorenzo Flennoy, whose Club Alabam group featured Teddy Buckner, Red Mack, and Oliver "Big Six" Reeves at different times, were forever disbanding for lack of steady work.

It wasn't any easier for white leaders who tried to play jazz: Everett Hoagland, who featured Vido Musso and Stan Kenton in 1933; Gil Evans from Stockton; Seger Ellis's Choirs of Brass (eight brass, one clarinet, and rhythm), which made dozens of transcriptions and a handful of sides for Decca in 1937; several Vido Musso–led big bands; arranger Spud Murphy's band, featuring Nate Kazebier, which recorded for Decca in 1938—all dispersed, went east, or turned commercial.

The best white musicians aimed for studio work, while black players could from time to time pick up twenty-five dollars a day appearing in nightclub scenes. When *King Kong* was filming at RKO in 1933, every out-of-work black musician, singer, actor, and dancer rushed to that lot for work on "Skull Island." Buck Clayton made that rush with his last money, only to be turned away because he was too light. He had to walk six miles home. A year later it was an easy decision to go to China on a two-year contract when no other jobs were available.

The Coast's status was assured when Lionel Hampton's and Stan Kenton's bands made it nationally during the war, while in Los Angeles Central Avenue clubs like the Club Alabam drew in swing and jump bands and rhythm-and-blues groups and displayed young players like Dexter Gordon, Wardell Gray, Sonny Criss, and Hampton Hawes, all maturing in the wake of Charlie Parker and Dizzy Gillespie.

By World War II California had found its "there"—the Central Avenue hipster (precursor of New York's?), Billy Berg's, and the Dawn Club on Annie Street in San Francisco, where Lu Watters's Yerba Buena Jazz Band birthed the New Orleans traditional jazz revival in 1941-42.

Lionel Hampton learned about drums and xylophone from Snags Jones and Jimmy Bertrand when he played in the *Chicago Defender*'s Newsboys Band and with local groups before going to Los Angeles in 1927. An integral part of Frank Sebastian's Cotton Club floor shows in the Depression, Hampton's drums and vibes backed headliner Louis Armstrong on his famous Okeh recordings *I'm Confessin', Body and Soul, Memories of You,* and *Shine.* In 1936 he led his own band at the Paradise, a Main Street nightclub where John Hammond took Benny Goodman to hear him. Goodman wrote: "I knew something about his reputation as a good drummer, but for about three years he had been specializing in vibes—and what he got out of that instrument was unlike anything I ever heard in my life before. The next night I came down with Teddy and Gene, and when the last customer had cleared out, they locked up the joint and we started to play. How long it went on I can't remember, but it was pretty near daylight when we quit. It was the story of the trio all over again—one of those natural things that was just meant to be." Hampton's all-star Victor dates, 1937–41, showed his drums, two-finger piano (*Piano Stomp*), and vibes on ninety-two sides. He was a star, the first to make it from California.

Jelly Roll Morton moved to California around 1917, after appearing in vaudeville as Morton and Morton (Top, L); his partner is remembered now only as Rose. He found plenty of good bands, like Mississippian Dink Johnson's Jazz Band (Top, R) with (L to R) Claude "Benno" Kennedy; Buster Wilson; Johnson on clarinet and banjo; Ashford Hardee, trombone; and Ben Borders, drums. Kennedy, Hardee, and Borders were from Texas; Wilson, who became one of Jelly's followers, from Atlanta. Jelly, according to one source, made most of his money from "the Pacific Coast line," a group of girls he pimped for. He also played a lot of pool and ran shows at the Cadillac Café in Watts (Bottom), on Central Avenue between 6th and 7th streets, where Ada "Bricktop" Smith (third from R, Jelly behind her) appeared. Jelly was happy-go-lucky then, as Shep Allen, then touring with the Panama Trio, recalled: "Anyway it would come it was all right with Jelly Roll. It was all right if it broke good and it was all right if it broke bad, he just took it in his stride. He had the diamond in his tooth and a lot of money in his hands or in his pockets, all the time, every day."

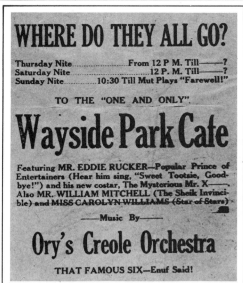

Trombonist Kid Ory's doctor advised him to seek a drier climate, so in 1919 he went to California, where he formed his Creole Jazz Band with (L to R) Papa Mutt Carey, trumpet; Alton Redd, drums; Ed "Montudi" Garland, bass (at piano); and Wade Whaley, clarinet. Ory was so popular that he could hardly keep up with the demand for his services, and in 1921 he recommended King Oliver (Bottom) for one of his regular jobs. A year later he made the first jazz record in California, *Ory's Creole Trombone,* for Sunshine.

Henderson's Oak Leaf Jazz Band (L) and Curtis Mosby's Dixieland Blue Blowers (R) were competitors in the twenties. J. M. Henderson's band came from Texas with (L to R) William Payne, Russell Massengale, (Henderson), Ashford Hardee, and Henry "Tin Can" Allen. Drummer Mosby (R, extreme R) featured pianist Henry Starr (extreme L), saxist Herschel Brassfield (third from L), trumpeter Harry Barker, and trombonist Lloyd "Country" Allen in 1923. Later Mosby units with Les Hite and Ashford Hardee recorded *Hardee Stomp, Blue Blowers Blues,* and *Louisiana Bo Bo* for Columbia. Mosby later ran his own Apex nightclubs in Los Angeles and San Francisco.

King Oliver's Creole Jazz Band opened at the Pergola Dancing Pavilion, 949 Market Street, San Francisco, on June 12, 1921, with (L to R) Minor "Ram" Hall, Honoré Dutrey, (Oliver), Lil Hardin (piano), David Jones, Johnny Dodds, Jimmy Palao, and Ed Garland. After Hall joined Ory across the bay in Oakland, Baby Dodds came in on drums, and the band played a variety of jobs in Los Angeles that fall. At one point Oliver reputedly joined Jelly Roll Morton's ten-piece big band at the Grand Hotel in Los Angeles. Oliver rejected "all kinds of inducements" to stay in California and went back to Chicago in April 1922.

ABE LYMAN And HIS CALIFORNIA BRUNSWICK ORCHESTRA

When Art Hickman's and other bands failed to please the dancers at the Ambassador Hotel's Coconut Grove ballroom in Los Angeles, drummer Abe Lyman (Bottom, seated) was hired and became an immediate hit. His enlarged band featured cornetist Ray Lopez (extreme L), clarinetist Gus Mueller (second from L), and string bassist Jake Garcia (second from R) in 1924. They packed the Grove nightly, and their Brunswick records, especially *Shake That Thing, San,* and *Too Bad,* confused many collectors who thought they had to be King Oliver and his band using a pseudonym. Lyman's ego caused a rift with the hotel, however, and he left for the East in 1927. Paul Howard's Quality Serenaders (Top) were the most musical band in Los Angeles in the late 1920s. Howard (extreme L) came from Steubenville, Ohio, and formed his own quartet at the Quality Café on 12th and Central Avenue in 1924. Three years later the Quality Serenaders were playing the Cotton Club: (L to R) George Orendorff, Lewis Taylor, Henry "Tin Can" Allen, Thomas Valentine, Harvey Brooks (piano, holding sax), and Leon Herriford. In 1929 their style was formed by saxist Charlie Lawrence, William Grant Still's nephew, whose arrangements featured a new trombonist, Lawrence Brown. Their Victor recordings, driven by Lionel Hampton's drums, showed off their poise, smart ensembles, and soloists on *The Ramble, Stuff, Quality Shout,* and *Moonlight Blues.* They left the Kentucky Club on Central Avenue, augmented by trumpeter Earl Thompson and saxophonist Lloyd Reese, for Eddie Brandstatter's swank Montmartre Café on Hollywood Boulevard. Their last records, *California Swing, Harlem,* and *Cuttin' Up,* failed to keep the band from breaking up late in summer 1930. Orendorff, Hampton, and Brown joined the Cotton Club house band. Paul Howard, unable to keep his band working, finally gave up and joined Ed Garland's band, working at the 111 Dance Hall on Main Street.

The bands of Henry Halstead (Top), Fred Elizalde (Middle), and Ben Pollack (Bottom) had varying degrees of success. Suave, handsome Halstead (not shown) maneuvered his semi-hot band into all the best hotels and ballrooms in Los Angeles and made a series of Victor records from 1924 to 1929, including *Panama*. Shown in front of Coulter's department store on Main Street, spring 1926, are (from L) Red Nichols, trumpeter Ted Shilling, and drummer Phil Harris. Pianist Fred Elizalde, a student at Stanford University, was the son of a well-to-do Philippine sugar planter who was willing to underwrite his band between college terms. In 1926 he hired Dick Morgan (extreme L), Fran

Baker (fifth from L), arranger Leo Kronman (third from R), and Fred Stoddard (extreme R) and got breaks in jobs on the beach before replacing Herb Wiedoeft's band at the Cinderella Roof for the summer season. The band recorded hot sides, featuring Ted Shilling, trumpet, for the Hollywood label; *Boneyard Shuffle* was one. They disbanded after the season, and Elizalde went to England in 1927. Drummer Ben Pollack's band started at Venice Beach in 1924. Back in Los Angeles in 1927 when no other work was available around Chicago, they played private parties (here at MGM) with sidemen Benny Goodman (second from L) and Glenn Miller (extreme R).

Reb Spikes (L, with baton) wrote and produced shows and songs like *Someday Sweetheart,* operated his own Sunshine Record Company *(Ory's Creole Trombone),* ran a music store at 12th and Central as a clearinghouse for jazz jobs in the area, and led bands into the mid-1930s. The Majors and Minors (L) at the Main Street Theatre recorded *Fight That Thing* and *My Mammy's Blues* for Columbia in 1927, featuring William Woodman (fourth from L), George Bryant (fifth from L), Adam Mitchell (third from R), and Fitz Weston (second from R). Later Spikes became wealthy from real estate. (R) Leon Rene's Southern Syncopators, 1928. Louisana composer-pianist Leon Rene (M, holding music) wrote hits like *When It's Sleepy-Time Down South* and *I Like a Guy What Takes His Time* with brother Otis; produced a hit show, *Lucky Day;* and played piano in and directed bands like this one with (L to R) Russell Jones, dancer; Ben Borders, drums; Charlie Jones, tenor sax; Marvin Johnson, alto sax; (Rene); S. H. Phillips, bass; Andrew Blakeney, trumpet; Ceele Burke, banjo; and Leon White, trombone. His songs for Mae West and wartime hits *(When the Swallows Come Back to Capistrano,* for example) enabled him to form a successful record company, Exclusive, which launched the careers of Johnny Moore's Three Blazers, Deacon Joe Liggins, Herb Jeffries, and others after World War II.

William Rogers Campbell "Sonny" Clay started out on drums in Phoenix, Arizona, in 1911 and later moved to California, where he switched to piano after playing drums with the Spikes Brothers orchestra. In the twenties his band recorded more often than Mosby's, Hite's, and Howard's, for Vocalion, Sunset, and finally Champion. His 1927 band: (L to R) (Clay); Luther "Sonny" Craven, trombone; David "Baby" Lewis, drums; Archie Lancaster, trumpet; Louis Dodd, sax and banjo; Ernest "Nenny" Coycault, trumpet; William Griffin, alto sax; Rupert Jordan, banjo; Leo Davis, tenor sax and clarinet; and Herman Hoy, tuba. This unit recorded *Devil's Serenade* for Vocalion before leaving for Australia in 1928. The Australian venture ended badly (see Page 239), but Clay, unperturbed, resumed his career. His last recordings, made in 1929 for Brunswick but somehow sold to Gennett for their Champion label, were *Cho-King* and *St. Louis Blues,* plus two other titles. Clay kept a band together until 1933 and then did solo work, but he drank more and more until he had to stop playing altogether. Clay claimed his band appeared in sixty-five films in his heyday. After conducting a Special Services band in the army, he worked again around Riverside until his health failed. He took a job at the post office and tuned pianos on the side.

Texas drummer Rhythm Ben Borders (L) played with the Sunnyland Jazz Orchestra and many other good Los Angeles bands before forming his own band in 1931. He retired in 1935 and died a few years later. Trumpeter Teddy Buckner (M) worked with everyone from Sonny Clay and Curtis Mosby to Buck Clayton and Lorenzo Flennoy, and later with Gerald Wilson, Johnny Otis, the Blenders, and Kid Ory. While in Lionel Hampton's 1948 bebop band, Buckner always had a solo spot for a tribute to Louis Armstrong.

Louis Armstrong (third from R) was on the verge of stardom when he traveled to Hollywood to star as a soloist at Sebastian's Cotton Club in July 1930. He found time to record *Blue Yodel #9* with wife Lil (Top, R) for country singer Jimmie Rodgers on Victor and to make his first film, *Ex-Flame,* starring Neal Hamilton, for Liberty Films. More important, he made some of his greatest Okeh recordings with the Les Hite house band, including *Ding Dong Daddy, I'm in the Market for You, I'm Confessin',* and *Just a Gigolo,* all popular songs or tied in with current movies. The recordings on this tour (he stayed nine months) helped widen his audience considerably. He and studio drummer Vic Berton got busted for marijuana and spent ten days in jail, so a hurry-up call went out to Red Mack Morris, one of the best local trumpeters, who played Louis's solos and sang his vocals. Only the musicians knew the difference. Louis had enjoyed himself so much the year before that he returned to Sebastian's for three more months in 1932.

The three Erwing brothers—James (third from L), Dorchester (fourth from L), and Harris (fourth from R)—were active around Los Angeles from 1927 through 1935, when they left music for religion. Their hard-swinging band made one rare Vocalion record in 1933, *The Erwing Blues* and *Rhythm,* while appearing at the Main Street or 111 Dance Hall. The other members were (L to R) Calvin Temple, Carl "Fats" Dozier, Horace Moore, Charles Wright, Wesley Prince, and Babe Carter. Bassist Prince later joined Nat "King" Cole, and Harris Erwing came back with Ceele Burke's band in 1940. They gave talented youngsters like Buck Clayton experience.

Pianist Edythe Turnham (M) and her husband, Floyd, drums, were popular during the late twenties and well into the thirties. Their Dixie Aces band worked many of the finest clubs in the city as well as in San Diego and farther north. At the Club Alabam around 1932: (L to R) George "Trombone Happy" Johnson, Floyd Turnham, Sr., Teddy Buckner, Frank Pasley, Charles Saunders, Edythe Turnham, William Griffin, Floyd Turnham, Jr., S. H. Phillips, and "Fats" Eddie Wilson. Floyd Turnham, Jr., a source of considerable parental pride, later led his own bands and played all the saxophones and clarinet well. His band in 1939 became the nucleus of the one Les Hite took on the road in 1940 to play the Golden Gate Ballroom in New York.

Les Hite (Top, L) worked with Curtis Mosby's, Paul Howard's, and half a dozen other bands before taking over as house leader at Sebastian's Cotton Club over the summer of 1930. He held that job through 1939 when the club closed, leaving only for summer tours as far north as Vancouver and south to San Diego. His band made appearances at City Hall in 1933 (Middle, L) and backed up stars like Fats Waller in 1935 (Top, R). Because he worked steadily, Hite could hire the best men, like trombonist-arranger Parker Berry (extreme R); saxophonist and arranger Lloyd Reese (fifth from L, standing); drummer Peppy Prince, who replaced Lionel Hampton in 1934 (standing behind Waller); and Marshall Royal, alto sax (fifth from R, standing). Hite reorganized in 1939 and made an extensive eastern tour (Bottom) with (L to R) Nat Walker, Al Morgan, Bob Love, Oscar Bradley, Frank Pasley, Walter Williams, Paul Campbell, Qudellis Martyn, Forrest Powell, Floyd Turnham, Britt Woodman, (Hite), Sol Moore, Allen Durham, and Rodgers Hurd. This group recorded *T-Bone Blues* and *Board Meeting* for Varsity and Bluebird and in 1942, with Dizzy Gillespie, Joe Wilder, and Gerald Wiggins, *Jersey Bounce* and *Idaho* for Hit. Les Hite's bands made sixty-five films while in Hollywood. He disbanded in 1943 and became an agent; he died in 1962.

Leon Herriford (Top, standing) led his own bands until his death in the late thirties. At the Cotton Club in 1934 his key sidemen were Buster Wilson (extreme L), Andy Blakeney (fifth from L), Lionel Hampton (sixth from L), and Ceele Burke (second from R). When Frank Sebastian wanted showman trumpeter Charlie Echols (Middle, R, kneeling) to lead the band Herriford quit, but most of his sidemen stayed, security being uppermost in their minds. Paul Howard (fifth from L) and Red Mack (fifth from R) joined Echols, who, unable to play the difficult Greely and Broomfield floor shows, was fired. Lionel Hampton then became leader and took the band on the road to Sweets' Ballroom in Oakland in July 1935: (Bottom, L to R) Buster Wilson, two dancers, Charles Rousseau, Johnny Miller, Herman Grimes, (Hampton), Bob Barefield, Paul King, Paul Howard, Alton Grant, Don Byas, Lloyd "Country" Allen, David Booker, two dancers. Hampton worked up to Vancouver and down to San Diego, but he had no more than a West Coast reputation and was unable to get beyond that part of the country after a year of trying.

Pianist-arranger Lorenzo Flennoy (kneeling, dark suit) had a nice personality and piano style that he developed after working with the bands of Atwell Rose, Charlie Echols, and Jim Wynn. He started a big band around 1935 and finally got a plum job, at the Club Alabam, in 1937 with (L to R) Ceele Burke, guitar; James Beard, trumpet; Vernon Gower, bass; Baron Willie Moorehead, trombone; Oliver "Big Six" Reeves, tenor sax; Raymond Tate, trumpet; Wallace Boviland, alto and tenor sax; William Griffin, alto sax; Oscar Bradley, drums; and Paul Campbell, trumpet. Campbell and Beard came from St.

Louis with Irvin C. Miller's *Brown Skin Models,* the show that moved so many musicians throughout the country. This band made no recordings and appeared in no films, but Flennoy, a slim six-footer who played organ later in his career, stated, "We had the best band you ever wanted to hear. I had different musicians from New York wanting to come and join my band. I had a *good* band. Boy, I had some good musicians. I had that basic left hand, a heavy left hand, and everyone knew me. When I took my solo, I rocked the band." Flennoy worked with combos and made movies in the forties.

Saxist-arranger Eddie Barefield (with baton) left Cab Calloway's band in Los Angeles in 1936. Noting a dearth of first-rate bands, he organized one, with the help of Paul Howard, which played the Club Alabam in 1936–37 and the Cotton Club, Arrowhead Inn, and other spots. (L to R) Ned Standfield, Al Morgan, Barefield, Lee Young, Buddy Harper, Country Allen, Tyree Glenn, Red Mack, Jack McVea, Herschel Douglas, Hugo Dandridge, Pee Wee Brice, Paul Howard, Don Byas. Recordings made privately by Glenn Wallichs and Al Jarvis have never been found. Barefield joined Les Hite and then left California to return east with Fletcher Henderson in 1938.

Floyd Ray's Harlem Dictators (Ray, extreme L) went to Los Angeles in 1936 with a Miller and Slayter show, having been organized in Scranton, Pennsylvania, in 1934. They became popular playing weekend dances at the Warner Brothers lot and, unlike most local bands, were willing to travel, enabling them to get national exposure. In 1937: (L to R) Ray; Cappy Oliver, trumpet; Sol Moore, sax; Kenny Bryant, piano; Clayton Smith, trombone; George Ward, drums; Eddie Vanderveer, trumpet; Iverne Whittaker; Willie Lee Floyd; Ivy Jones; Johnny Alston, tenor sax; Chippie Outcalt, trumpet-arranger; Gilbert Kelly, trombone; George Fauntleroy, sax; Gene Brown, guitar; Benny Booker, bass; Carroll "Stretch" Ridley, tenor sax. They recorded *Firefly Stomp* for Decca in 1939 and disbanded in 1941.

Guitarist Ceele Burke (L, second from L), a Los Angeles native, often worked in Hawaii in the twenties. When he had his own band at the Bal Tabarin in Gardena—with George Orendorff, trumpet; Harris Erwing, alto sax (M, front); and Charlie Jones, tenor sax—he mixed Hawaiian numbers with ballads and swing and stayed on the job four years. Trumpeter Red Mack (R, real name: McClure Morris) led his own bands after playing with everyone else's around Los Angeles. At the Streets of Paris club in 1939 he featured Lady Will Carr on piano. Mack went east as hot man in Will Osborne's big band in 1941 and later switched to drums and vibes, and even later to piano and organ. He recorded tunes like *The Joint Is Jumpin'*, for Gold Seal, Atlas, and Mercury.

Paul Howard (L, third from R) took a combo into Bill and Virginia's in Eagle Rock in 1940 and stayed there fourteen years. (L to R) Richard Bates, piano; Ted Brinson, bass and guitar; Buddy Harper, guitar; Eleanor Williams; Howard, clarinet, tenor, and baritone saxes; Dorothy Webster; Willis McDaniel, drums. Floyd Turnham, Jr.'s, band—with (R, L to R) John Anderson, trumpet; Coney Woodman, piano; unidentified bass; Turnham, alto sax and clarinet; Oscar Bradley, drums; and Britt Woodman, trombone—became the nucleus of Les Hite's revamped band, which went to New York to play the Golden Gate Ballroom in Harlem and record for Varsity and Bluebird records in 1940-41.

Arkansas trombonist George "Trombone Happy" Johnson arrived in Los Angeles in 1927 and later worked with Buck Clayton, with whom he went to China; he took his own band to China a year later. When he returned, he organized this big band to play the Vogue Ballroom at 9th and Grand Avenue in 1938, which featured Red Callendar (third from L); Rabon Tarrant, drums; Bob Dorsey (tenth from L); Streamline John Ewing (fifth from R); and Forrest Powell (second from R). Most of these players came from the Midwest or Southwest. Johnson later led popular jump bands which recorded *Barbecued Hot Dog* for Columbia in 1947 with Hampton Hawes on piano.

Clarinetist Kenny Baker (L) led a Benny Goodman–style band that enjoyed popularity on the West Coast before and during the war, but made no recordings other than transcriptions. Bobby Sherwood (R) had been a studio musician since 1934, when he accompanied the Boswell Sisters on guitar on radio, and Bing Crosby on records and in films. In 1942 he organized a big band that was greeted with great enthusiasm for its original Capitol recordings like *The Elks Parade, Swingin' at the Semloh,* and, later, *Sherwood's Forest.* Young and mostly unknown players like Zoot Sims gained experience traveling cross-country with this band. A constant experimenter, Sherwood, who played trombone and piano as well as trumpet and guitar, broke up the band to star in the play *Young Man with a Horn* in 1946, just as *Sherwood's Forest* was beginning to sell well.

Nat "King" Cole (L, second from R) was stranded in Los Angeles with a revival of *Shuffle Along* in 1937 when he began playing in Central Avenue clubs with a trio. One day a club owner told him to start singing or lose the job. Slowly his trio evolved, and his subtle Hines-style piano gradually receded into the background as his singing became more and more popular. At Capitol's studios in 1944 Cole is shown with guitarist Oscar Moore, bassist Johnnie Miller, and co-owner of the company, singer-songwriter Johnny Mercer (extreme R). *Straighten Up and Fly Right* was typical of his work at that time. San Francisco singer and guitarist Saunders King (R, extreme L) was so popular in the Bay Area in 1939 that MCA was willing to build a big band and send him on national tour; only King, careless to a fault, never showed up to sign the contract. (L to R) With Eddie Taylor, Johnny Cooper, Sammy Deane, and rhythm he made *S. K. Blues* for the local Rhythm label in 1942.

Cee Pee Johnson's frantic tom-tom playing (L) hid the fact that he had a jumping band at Billy Berg's Swing Club in 1942 with Teddy Buckner and Karl George, trumpets; Ed "Popeye" Hale (third from L), alto sax; Buddy Banks (fifth from R), tenor sax; and Joe Liggins (third from R) on piano. *Hour After Hour* was a hit for him on Apollo in 1945. Tulsa drummer and dancer Roy Milton (R, extreme L) made $2 a night singing on Central Avenue until the war brought him big audiences at Marco's Café with sidemen Luke Jones, alto sax; Betty Hall Jones, piano; and Forrest Powell, trumpet. A few years later *Rhythm Cocktail* and *R. M. Blues* were hits.

The dynamic personality of Stan Kenton (Bottom, third from L) and his absolute belief in his music won him either intense admiration or utter scorn. His first band, which sounded like Jimmie Lunceford's, featured tenor man Red Dorris (Middle, L). His early hits for Capitol included *Eager Beaver, Intermission Riff,* and *Artistry Jumps,* the last-named one of many theme ideas he used over the years. As his music grew more complex, his popularity rose with Anita O'Day's *And Her Tears Flowed Like Wine* and *Tampico* with June Christy (Top, R). By the time he had gotten Shelly Manne (Bottom, third from L), Eddie Safranski (second from L), Boots Mussulli on alto sax (tenth from L), and Bob Cooper (extreme R), Kenton was moving away from dance music to create elaborate compositions like *Concerto to End All Concertos* in 1946. Dance patrons enjoyed Kenton's music at Catalina Island (Middle, R), where the band could relax in the bay (Top, L). Kenton won the 1946 *Metronome* poll and the *Down Beat* poll in 1947; he broke up his band later that year.

California
1918-1949

Lu Watters
and his Yerba Buena JAZZ BAND

ANNIE ST.

BASTIAN STUDIO

Returns FRIDAY MARCH 1, 1946
DAWN CLUB
San Francisco.

A group of disgruntled Bay Area musicians started rehearsing, learning, and playing ragtime and the music of King Oliver and Jelly Roll Morton at the Big Bear Tavern in 1936–37. Trumpeter Lu Watters (third from L) formed his own band in 1937, and Turk Murphy (second from L) and Bob Helm (third from R) formed another. Neither group was successful, but they knew what they wanted to play. By 1941 Watters had gotten them all together at the Dawn Club on Annie Street as the Yerba Buena Jazz Band and built an enthusiastic audience for their stomps, blues, and rags, recorded on the Jazz Man label. *Smoky Mokes* and *Terrible Blues* display their devotion to the sound and ensemble of the old King Oliver band. The war broke them up, but the die was cast, and San Francisco audiences, obviously in love with traditions, were ready and waiting for them to regroup in 1946 (Top, R) at the Dawn Club. Watters and second trumpeter Bob Scobey, pianist Wally Rose, and drummer Bill Dart had all learned more about ensemble work, and their new well-made records on the West Coast label, like *Working Man Blues* and *Chattanooga Stomp,* reveal them much more at ease. In 1947 they moved to Hambone Kelly's in El Cerrito. Turk Murphy left in 1949 to start his own band, and in 1950 Bob Scobey to start his. Watters had achieved his goal and retired from music to become a chef.

Mutt Carey (Top, L), Kid Ory (Top, R), and Bunk Johnson (Bottom, extreme R) had all stopped playing music in 1933. After farming on his brother's chicken ranch, Kid Ory returned to music as a bass player with Barney Bigard's band and later added alto sax before getting back on trombone. Bunk Johnson played a concert a week at the Geary Theatre (Bottom) in San Francisco, starting in May 1943, and recruited from Los Angeles players who were sympathetic to his aims: (L to R) Everett Walsh, drums; Buster Wilson; Ed Garland; Bertha Gonsoulin, pianist, who replaced Lil Hardin in King Oliver's band in 1921; guitarist Frank Pasley, late of Les Hite's band; and Kid Ory. When producer Adrian Michaelis wanted an authentic New Orleans band for the Standard Oil broadcasts in 1944–45, he asked Marili Morden of the Jazz Man Record Shop for help. She rounded up Mutt Carey; Kid Ory; Jimmie Noone, clarinet, who had just come to town from Chicago; Bud Scott; Buster Wilson; Ed Garland; and Zutty Singleton, whose own group was working around town. Orson Welles narrated those landmark programs. Ory reorganized his old band with Mutt Carey and recorded for Crescent, Exner, Decca, and Columbia such old favorites as *Muskrat Ramble* and *Savoy Blues*. Mutt, who left to start his own band, died in 1948. Ory rode the revival boom.

Big bands swelled during the war years to eighteen men, as the jazz intellectuals—the arrangers—kept asking for larger and larger vehicles for their new spread chords and voicings. The 25 percent wartime amusement tax was still in effect, but all looked well in 1946 when pianist Ike Carpenter (Top, L) and Bob Crosby (Bottom) started their new bands. Carpenter did a long stint at Horace Heidt's Trianon Ballroom, on Firestone Boulevard in South Gate, with players like Lucky Thompson on tenor sax. On tour in 1945 (Top, R), Carpenter featured eighteen-year-old Gerry Mulligan (second from R) on baritone sax. His 1947–48 recordings of *Jeeps Blues* and *Day Dream* on Modern and Victor reflect his love of Duke Ellington's music. Bob Crosby was discharged from the Marine Corps in December 1945 and started a new big band, this time a straight-ahead, four-four swing band without any particular stylistic distinction—just good, hard blowing from trumpeter Dick Cathcart, trombonists Dick Noel and Phil Washburne, and tenor man Dave Pell, and arrangements by pianist Tommy Todd. They recorded for a new California company, ARA, but only one title, *Java Jive,* gives any indication of the strength of the band, which leaned more or less in the Count Basie direction. (L to R) Bob Lawson, Washburne, Frank Myers, Noel, Dale Pierce, Murray McEachern, Wilbur Schwartz, Earl Collier, Billy Hearn, Jack Mootz, Gus Bivona, Cathcart, Ralph Collier, Pell, Jimmy Stutz, Crosby, Todd, Bob Bain. Even engagements at the Hollywood Palladium, Elitch's Gardens (a change from their prewar hotel-style policy), and a sponsored radio program, "Ford's Out Front," could not keep them going after 1947, when Crosby gave up the band and turned to radio and television work.

Texas tenor man Ulysses "Buddy" Banks (Top, L, M) had worked in all the best bands since 1935 and led his own successful jump band throughout the forties with (L to R) Wallace Huff, trombone; William "Basie" Day, bass; Fluffy Hunter, vocals; (Banks); Frosty Pyles, guitar; Nat "Monk" McFay; and Earl Knight, piano. *Banks Boogie* and *Goin' for the Okey Doke* were two of their sides for Melodisc and Excelsior. Master eccentric showman Slim Gaillard (Top, R), shown with bassist Tiny Brown (L), worked at length in Hollywood clubs during the forties and recorded at least one session for nearly every label in town, including Bee Bee, Four Star, Cadet, Atomic, and Beltone. Usually he worked with Brown and drummer Zutty Singleton in clubs. He cut such record classics as *Ding Dong Oreeney, Yeproc Heresi,* and the famous *Cement Mixer.*

Zutty Singleton went to Hollywood in 1943 to make the film *Stormy Weather*. He enjoyed it, but he was eager to return to New York until Billy Berg, owner of the Swing Club, offered him a job. Zutty sent to New York for Joe Eldridge (second from R) and Bass Hill (extreme R) and hired pianist Kenny Bryant (sixth from L), Kid Ory (fourth from R), and trumpeter Norman Bowden (third from R) for a long run at the Swing Club starting in May. Later that year he worked with Paul Howard and T-Bone Walker; the following year he met Orson Welles and made appearances on the Standard Oil radio series on jazz.

Los Angeles–born tenor man Jack McVea (Bottom, second from R) played banjo in his father Satchel McVea's band in the twenties, and alto and baritone with Charlie Echols, Eddie Barefield, and in Lionel Hampton's first successful band, before striking out on his own in 1943. By 1944 he added his showmanship to a hard-swinging little band at Jack's Tavern with Cappy Oliver, trumpet; Bob Mosley, piano; and Frank Clarke, bass. McVea's reputation soared when he went with "Jazz at the Philharmonic" and recorded *Open the Door Richard*, a hit, and *Silver Symphony* on Black and White and Melodisc.

Pianist Joe Liggins (L, second from L) played every joint on Central Avenue through the thirties and with Cee Pee Johnson's band (Page 193) before developing his own audience for his soulful blues and ballads. He had a national hit with *The Honeydripper* on Exclusive, featuring his funky two-horn front line and veteran Frank Pasley's blues guitar. His *Blue Champagne* and other records did well for years. Trumpeter Gerald Wilson (R, extreme R) emerged from the Lunceford, Carter, and Les Hite bands to start his own in 1944: (L to R) Henry Tucker Green, Jimmy Bunn, Chuck Waller, Art Edwards, Jose Sanchez, Odell West, Teddy Buckner, Floyd Turnham, Melba Liston, Jack Trainor, Ed "Popeye" Hale, Miles Davis, Jose Huerta, Hobart Dotson, Maurice Simon. *Moon Rise* and *Synthetic Joe* are examples of Wilson's as well as trombonist Melba Liston's modern arranging. The band played every spot available to big bands in 1945–47, but Wilson was unable to find enough work to keep them going beyond then. He organized other bands as jobs became available.

His dream realized, drummer-vibist Johnny Otis (M), born in Vallejo, California, in 1922, celebrated his twenty-third birthday in Los Angeles, surrounded by his all-black band. Otis chose to work only with black musicians and played drums with George Morrison, Lloyd Hunter, and Harlan Leonard before starting his own band. He staffed it with experienced veterans like trumpeters Bobby Jones (fifth from R) and Teddy Buckner (standing, R) and guitarist Burney Cobb (extreme R), and with good young players like tenor man Jim Von Streeter (third from L) and bassist Curtis Counce (fifth from L). Otis's closest friend, Preston Love (sixth from L), joined the party. from Count Basie's band, which was working at the Trianon Ballroom. Despite strong initial buildup with broadcasts, a cross-country tour, and recordings on Excelsior like *Omaha Flash, Sgt. Barksdale* and *Harlem Nocturne*, Otis's band, as well as those of Gerald Wilson, Ike Carpenter, and others better known and managed, could not find enough work after 1947. Otis later became very successful in rhythm-and-blues.

(Opposite Page) Jazz concerts became a source of high income and good work for musicians when film editor Norman Granz began having them locally at Music Town in 1944 and then at the Civic Auditorium in Pasadena. His first "Jazz at the Philharmonic" (JATP) concert featured (Top, L to R) Barney Kessel, Corky Concoran, Illinois Jacquet, Jack McVea, Al Killian, and Sammy Yates. (Middle, L to R) Jean Sherock, Nat "King" Cole, Norman Granz, Arleen Thompson, Shorty Sherock, and Ruth, a secretary at Disney Studios; Cole and Sherock were in a 1945 concert. (Bottom) A rival concert promotion was local disc jockey Gene Norman's "Just Jazz" series, which started in 1947 with (L to R) Irving Ashby, Charlie Drayton, Wardell Gray, Benny Carter, and Howard McGhee. (Above) The scene on Central Avenue (Top, L) in front of the Club Alabam on 42nd Street, where Roy Milton's hot little band was appearing in the late forties. (Top, R) The saxophone section, including a very young Eric Dolphy (third from R), of the new eighteen-piece Roy Porter's Seventeen BeBoppers, which recorded *Little Wig* for Savoy in 1948. A road accident a year later, in which leader-drummer Porter and trumpeter Art Farmer were injured, finished this exciting new band. (Bottom) When Lionel Hampton's band of Californians met with Count Basie's in Chicago in 1940, sparks flew. (Standing, L to R) unidentified, Karl George, Ernie Royal, Buddy Tate, (Hampton), Charlie Carpenter, Jack Trainor, and Jack McVea. (Seated, L to R, and foreground) Harry Edison, Marshall Royal, Irving Ashby, Evelyn Meyers, Don Byas, Illinois Jacquet, and Shadow Wilson.

California was privy to all styles for a time in the postwar years. Cornetist Red Nichols formed a new Five Pennies group (Top, L) in 1945 and signed with Capitol, using Rollie Culver, Paul Leu on piano, Herbie Haymer, Heinie Beau, and Thurman Teague for *Can't Help Lovin' Dat Man.* Both Coleman Hawkins and Benny Carter (Top, R, L and R) recorded for Capitol with their own bands, but this was a Capitol All-Stars date in 1945 with (L to R) John Kirby, Oscar Moore, Bill Coleman, Max Roach, and Buster Bailey. Central Avenue clubs jumped with T-Bone Walker's earthy blues guitar and acrobatic splits (Middle, L) and recordings like *Call It Stormy Monday* and the great blue ballad *That's Better for Me.* Guitarist Teddy Bunn (Middle, M) didn't sing, but he played great guitar, and his jump band with Red Mack on trumpet made a swinging *Seven Come Eleven* for Gilt Edge. Guitarist Johnny Moore's Three Blazers (Middle, R), with the gifted soulful pianist Charles Brown, made one of the great postwar blues, *Drifting Blues,* on Aladdin in 1945. This was a crooning blues, rich in feeling with Brown's exquisite piano. Moore was King Cole guitarist Oscar's brother. A modern experiment was bassist Red Callendar's short-lived 1948 band (Bottom, R) with (L to R) Jimmy Bunn, (Callendar), Charlie Mingus, Kenny Bright, Bill Douglas, and Teddy Edwards. They made no records; the group worked during the recording ban that year. Kansas City pianist Jay McShann (Bottom, L) worked mostly on the West Coast with his blues and jump band, 1947–50. Shown at the Suzi-Q in 1949 are blues vocalist Jimmy Witherspoon, trumpeter Benny Bailey, bassist Addison Farmer, and Jay's cousin, drummer Pete McShann. Both McShann and Witherspoon recorded extensively during this time for Downbeat, Swingtime, Aladdin, and Modern. They had a big hit with *'Tain't Nobody's Business If I Do.*

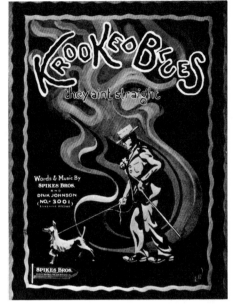

SUNSHINE

MANUF. BY SPIKES BROS. PHONOGRAPH CO. INC LOS ANGELES

Vocal Blues — 3001-A

Krooked Blues
(Spikes Bros. and Dink Johnson)
Roberta Dudley
And Ory's Sunshine Orchestra

Columbia

Viva-tonal — Recording

ELECTRICAL PROCESS — Fox Trot

LOUISIANA BOBO
(EL BOBO DE LUISIANA)
(Nixon)
CURTIS MOSBY AND HIS
DIXIELAND BLUE BLOWERS
40001-D
(147818)
MADE AND PAT'D IN U.S.A. JAN. 21, '13 AND RE. 16588
COLUMBIA PHONOGRAPH COMPANY, INC. NEW YORK

VE
Orthophonic Recording
"HIS MASTER'S VOICE"

VICTOR

For best results use Victor Needles — V–38122–B

STUFF—Stomp
(Costa)
(Harvey O. Brooks)
Paul Howard's Quality Serenaders
Vocal refrain by Lionel Hampton
VICTOR TALKING MACHINE Co.
Camden, N.J.
VE

OKeh
ELECTRIC

FOR BEST RESULTS USE OKeh NEEDLES

41468 — Fox Trot with Vocal Refrain

BODY AND SOUL
(Cuerpo y Alma)
(From "Three's A Crowd")
(Green, Heyman & Sour)
LOUIS ARMSTRONG & HIS
SEBASTIAN NEW COTTON
CLUB ORCHESTRA
(404411)
MADE AND PAT'D IN U.S.A. RE. 16588 AND 1703564
OKeh PHONOGRAPH CORPORATION NEW YORK

VARSITY
REG. U S PAT OFFICE
MADE IN U.S.A.
UNITED STATES RECORD CORPORATION
NEW YORK

(US 1852) — 8391

T-BONE BLUES—F. T.
(Walker-Hite)
LES HITE and his ORCHESTRA
Vocal by T-Bone Walker
(Frank Pasley at the Guitar)

No. 14 (124)

LU WATTERS'
YERBA BUENA JAZZ BAND

Jazz Man

SUNSET CAFE STOMP
by Venable
Lu Watters, Bob Scobey, *Cornets*; Ellis Horne,
Clarinet; Turk Murphy, *Trombone*; Walter Rose,
Piano; Clarence Hayes, Russ Bennett, *Banjos*;
Squire Girsback, *Bass*; Bill Dart, *Drums*.
Recorded March
1942
FOR HOME USE ONLY
RELEASED BY Jazz Man Record Shop, 1221 N. VINE ST., HOLLYWOOD 38, CALIFORNIA

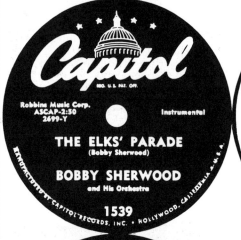

Capitol
REG. U.S. PAT. OFF.

Robbins Music Corp.
ASCAP-2:50 — Instrumental
2699-Y

THE ELKS' PARADE
(Bobby Sherwood)

BOBBY SHERWOOD
and His Orchestra

1539
MANUFACTURED BY CAPITOL RECORDS, INC. • HOLLYWOOD, CALIFORNIA, U.S.A.

Rhythm
RECORDINGS

NOT LICENSED FOR RADIO BROADCAST

SAUNDERS KING RHYTHM

SAUNDERS KING, Guitar;
SAMMY DEANE, Trumpet;
EDDIE TAYLOR, Tenor Sax;
JOHNNY COOPER, Piano;
JOE HOLDER, Bass;
BUNNY PETERS, Drums.

MFG. IN U.S.A.
APS 386
3-A

S.K. BLUES—Part I
(Saunders King)
Vocal: Saunders King

RECORDED IN
SAN FRANCISCO
JUNE, 1942

Released by
Rhythm Recordings Inc
1317 Grove Street
San Francisco

Capitol

MANUFACTURED BY CAPITOL RECORDS, INC., U.S.A.

(778) — Instrumental

ARTISTRY JUMPS
(Stan Kenton)
STAN KENTON
and his Orchestra
Piano Solo—Stan Kenton
Tenor Saxophone Solo—
Vido Musso
229

SPECIALTY RECORDS, INC. • 311 VENICE BOULEVARD • LOS ANGELES 5, CALIF.

S

Specialty
PRICE
79¢
TAX INCL.
Instrumental

RHYTHM COCKTAIL
(R. Milton)

ROY MILTON
And His Solid Senders

SP 504 B
ONLY FOR NON COMMERCIAL USE FOR PHONOGRAPHS IN HOMES

Excelsior
RECORDS

EXCELSIOR RECORD C NY - HOLLYWOOD, U.S.A.
DELUXE SERIES
JO 141B — Instrumental

"PRESTON LOVE'S MANSION"
(Johnny Otis)
JOHNNY OTIS his Drums & his Orchestra
Trumpets; Teddy Buckner, Billy Jones, Loyal Walker, Par
Jones; Trombones, Lorenzo Cocker, Eli Robinson, John
Pettigrew; Jap Jones; Saxophones, Rene Block,
James Von Streeter, Paul Quinechelte, Bob
Harris, Leon Beck; Bass, Curtis Counce;
Guitar, Bernie Cobbs; Piano,
Bill Dogett.
ONLY FOR NON-COMMERCIAL USE ON PHONOGRAPHS IN HOMES. MFR. & ORIGINAL PURCHASER HAVE AGREED
THIS RECORD SHALL NOT BE RESOLD, OR USED FOR ANY OTHER PURPOSE

REX
HOLLYWOOD

25056-A — MR 5

BIRD LEGS
(T. Edwards)
Tenor Sax, Teddy Edwards; Trumpet,
Bailey; Piano, Duke Brooks;
Drums, Roy Porter; Bass,
Addison Farmer.
MADE IN U.S.A.
LICENSED FOR RADIO BROADCAST

Crow Jim Europe
Hangin' Around Montmartre and Shanghai Gestures
1919-1950

"Chez Boudon!" There's Nothing more wonderful than to see a Negro handling a white woman carelessly. It thrills me. If only they were American Women—Southerners? I'd pay money to see it. And for all their carelessness these Negro boys are a lot more gentle than your chivalrous white Southern men."

—Henry Miller to Anaïs Nin, May 3, 1934

Jean Cocteau, poet, scenarist, soon-to-be dramatist, and occasional drummer, recorded his impression of one of the first black musicians in Paris, Louis Mitchell— "King of Noise"—in 1919: "The American band accompanied them [Harry Pilcer and Gaby Deslys] on banjos and big nickel-plated horns. On the right of the small black-clad group was a barman of noise behind a gilded stand laden with bells, rods, boards, and motorcycle horns. He poured these into cocktails, putting in a dash of cymbals every now and then, getting up, strutting, and smiling to the angels."

Mitchell's success and that of the Original Dixieland Jazz Band's London stay, 1919-20, had been well paved by everyone from the Fisk Jubilee Singers and Williams and Walker, to ragtime pianist Joe Jordan's Memphis Students. Former Clef Club drummer Mitchell could hardly be called a jazzman, but he was successful because he was black, personable, and knew how to entertain.

Outstanding American jazzmen overseas in the 1920s included Sidney Bechet, Tommy Ladnier, Frank Guarente, Teddy Weatherford, Adrian Rollini, and black Canadian trumpeter Arthur Briggs. Bechet was praised by conductor Ernest Ansermet in 1919 when he was featured with Will Marion Cook's forty-piece Southern Syncopated Orchestra in London. Although Bechet spent nearly eight years in Europe on two tours, no one saw fit to record him.

Tommy Ladnier was one of several stars in Sam Wooding's big band, which toured Germany with the revue *Chocolate Kiddies* in 1925-26. Wooding played and recorded semi-symphonic pieces and stomps like *Shanghai Shuffle* with a tremendous chorus by Ladnier on trumpet, which compares favorably with Fletcher Henderson's recording. Ladnier returned to Europe with Wooding in 1928 and later joined Noble Sissle in 1930, where cornetist Muggsy Spanier, on tour with Ted Lewis, found him. Said Muggsy: "We spent a lot of time together, that is, when Tommy wasn't hobnobbing with the upper crust. I've never seen a more popular guy with the higher ups, the dukes and counts and things." Hobnobbing notwithstanding, Ladnier returned to New York later that year unrecorded.

The steady release of American jazz records throughout Europe and their reviews in the *Melody Maker* (which began publishing in 1926) and elsewhere inspired players like Nat Gonella, Ted Heath, George Chisholm, and Gerry Moore in England; Philippe Brun, Stephane Grappelly, Andre Ekyan, Alix Combelle, and Django Reinhardt in France; Louis DeVries in Holland; Fritz Schultz-Reichel ("Crazy Otto") in Germany; and countless others.

During the thirties, the formation of "hot" clubs in France and Belgium (which presented jazz concerts), the growth of rhythm clubs in England, visits by Louis Armstrong, Duke Ellington, and Joe Venuti, and lengthy stays by Coleman Hawkins and Benny Carter lifted the quality of European jazz considerably. It was requited love. That same mutuality of affection and respect led to the founding of the first jazz label, Swing. Started in 1937 in Paris by Hugues Panassie and Charles Delaunay, it made stars of Bill Coleman, Herman Chittison, Joe Turner, and other Americans not well known back home.

Farther east, the huge figure of Teddy Weatherford cast a long shadow over Asia. Immaculate in his white sharkskin suit, the "King of Shanghai" spread his enormous hands to play set pieces like *Rhapsody In Blue* twice nightly at the Canidrome, a Chinese-owned nightclub and gambling casino. Then he turned the elaborate bandstand over to Buck Clayton's 14 Gentlemen of Harlem, who proceeded to blow their hot stomps without restriction, to the bewilderment of the wealthy European patrons. For Clayton and his band members from California, fifty dollars a week American bought a lot of good times thousands of miles away from home in 1934-35.

World War II finished this way of life. Freddy Johnson and Valaida Snow lost their health in concentration camps, and leaders like Benny Peyton and Willie Lewis never played again after returning home.

After the war, modern jazz became popular in Europe, bringing in Dizzy Gillespie and Charlie Parker on concert tours. Veterans like Bill Coleman and Sidney Bechet realized that Europe still offered them a better way of life and went there to live in the late 1940s (Kenny Clarke, Dexter Gordon, and Bud Powell would follow much later). Back home many of Coleman's contemporaries were going into the post office or driving cabs after 1950. Europe offered Coleman and the others honor and respect, and wisely they took it.

Malcolm Lowry's novella *Lunar Caustic* (written in 1934) expressed his perceptions of the transatlantic jazz traffic: "Perhaps it was America I was in love with. You know, you people get sentimental over England from time to time with your guff about sweetest Shakespeare. Well, this was the other way around. Only it was Eddie Lang and Joe Venuti and the death of Bix. . . . What about a drink? And I wanted to see where Melville lived."

Bill Coleman's playing came as a complete surprise to the French; despite the fact that he had recorded with Luis Russell (where he was in the shadow of Red Allen), and later with Fats Waller *(Dream Man, I'm Growing Fonder of You, Baby Brown)* and Teddy Hill (where Roy Eldridge was the star), few of his solos were known in France. He went to Europe with Lucky Millinder in 1933 to play Paris and the Riviera. Also in the show was a slim, handsome dancer named Freddy Taylor, who was a great admirer of Louis Armstrong. Coleman gave him a trumpet and some pointers on how to play it; two years later Taylor, well established as a personality in Paris, hired Coleman to play in his band. Only a few months later Bill Coleman was a genuine star, something he had not been able to achieve back home—a valid star who would make dozens of fine recordings, 1935–38, that assured him a place in the trumpet players' pantheon.

The Original Dixieland Jazz Band (L) was as successful in London—at the Martan Club and the Hammersmith Palais de Danse, with Emile Christian, trombone, and Londoner Billy Jones, piano—as it had been in New York. The band recorded twelve-inch versions of *Tiger Rag, Ostrich Walk,* and *Sensation Rag* for Columbia before going home in 1920. Will Marion Cook's Southern Syncopated Orchestra, thirty-six men in all, gave concerts at Philharmonic Hall and performed for King George V at Buckingham Palace. Swiss conductor Ernest Ansermet wrote in *Revue Romande,* "There is an extraordinary clarinet player, who is, so it seems, the first of his race to have composed perfectly formed blues on the clarinet. I wish to set down the name of this artist of genius; as for myself I shall never forget it—it is Sidney Bechet!" He was featured with Benny Peyton's Jazz Kings (R, extreme R) in 1920.

Mitchell's Jazz Kings (L) started right after World War I in Belgium and France. Drummer Louis Mitchell, a star in London before the war, earned 7,000 francs a week, recorded fifty tunes for Pathé, and influenced young Frenchmen like trombonist Leo Vauchant, who recalled: "They knew about chords. At least the trombone player, Frank Withers, did, and Cricket Smith [trumpet] certainly did. When he improvised, it was right on the nose. It was a little out of tune. They never tuned. They just started to play." Mitchell, "the toast of Paris," later ran the Grand Duc nightclub in Montmartre, gambled away his fortune, and returned home before the crash. Canadian trumpeter Arthur Briggs (R) formed his band in Liège, Belgium, in 1922 and by 1925, at the Weinberg Bar in Vienna, was one of the most popular players in Europe. He had a strong, clear tone and recorded several dozen tunes, including *Hallelujah,* in Germany in 1927.

Jazz reached Russia in the mid-twenties when Sam Wooding's and Frank Withers's bands played Moscow, Leningrad, and other cities. Garvin Bushell (L) was Wooding's clarinet and multi-reed star in 1926. Sidney Bechet (R, middle, seventh from L), the star of Withers's band, joined members of Wooding's band and the cast from the *Chocolate Kiddies* show at the Artists Club in Moscow. The music, incidentally, met with a warmer reception than the show, which folded not long after the Russian tour. Wooding's band then began working steadily on its own. Bechet later formed another band and rejoined *Revue Nègre.*

Buddy Gilmore (Top, L), drummer with the Southern Syncopated Orchestra, personified jazz for most Europeans after World War I. He went out of his way to show youngsters how to play. The *Revue Nègre* (Top, R) starred Josephine Baker (third from L) and had a jazz band led by Claude Hopkins (second from R). Duke Ellington wrote the music for the *Chocolate Kiddies* show (Middle, R) in New York, but the show, with Sam Wooding's band, ran only in Europe. Wooding sidemen Tommy Ladnier and Herb Flemming (Middle, L, standing and seated, L) enjoyed an outing in Berlin with chorus members, June 1925. They recorded *Shanghai Shuffle* and *Alabamy Bound* in ten- and twelve-inch versions for Vox, comparable to Fletcher Henderson's recordings. Wooding went to South America in 1927 and returned to Europe in 1928, at the UFA Palast Theatre, Berlin, with Edith Wilson (Bottom, extreme L) and some new sidemen, including pianist-arranger Freddy Johnson (third from L), saxist Jerry Blake (second from L), drummer Ted Fields (sixth from R), and trumpeter Doc Cheatham (second from R), who joined veterans Gene Sedric on tenor sax (fourth from L) and Tommy Ladnier (fourth from R) in Hamburg, 1928. New recordings for Pathé and Parlophone in Paris and Barcelona, 1929, included *Bull Foot Stomp, Downcast Blues, Carrie,* and *Tiger Rag.* Wooding's European sojourn ended in 1931.

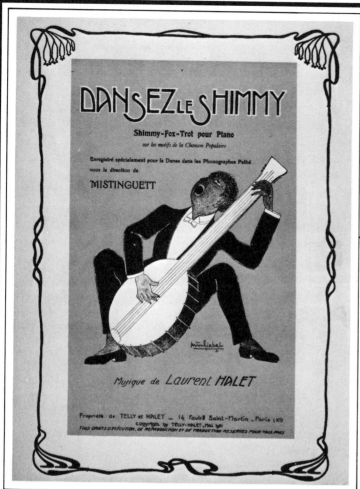

Mediocre players who were black were in demand in Europe, and suave entertainer Jocelyn "Frisco" Bingham kept many working at his Chez Frisco (Middle, R) on rue Notre Dame de Lorette, where he catered to the carriage trade. Trumpeter Johnny Dunn (Top, R, extreme L), whose style was passé back home, joined the cast of *Blackbirds of 1928*, left the show in Paris in 1929, and spent the rest of his life working in France, Holland, and Belgium, where his New Yorkers appeared at the Gaieté Dancing on rue Fosse-aux-Loups in Brussels, 1932. He died in Paris in 1937. Few Montmartre nightclubs were better known than Joe Zelli's Royal Box (Bottom) at 16 rue Fontaine. For years, cigar-chomping ragtime veteran J. Glover Compton led the house band at the piano. The players included trumpeter Cricket Smith and Frank "Big Boy" Goudie, tenor sax and clarinet, who played the jazz while the others, such as ex-boxer and Lafayette Escadrille flyer Gene Bullard, who played drums, stayed discreetly in the background. Proprietor Zelli (third from L) drew many of the big spenders in 1927; after consuming twenty bottles of vintage champagne, they inscribed the photo: "Paris will never forget Patty—the party still going strong when the sun came up the next day. . . ."

White American jazzmen were also in demand. Emile Christian (Top, L, top) worked with half a dozen bands, including pianist Tommy Waltham's (L, with glasses) Ad-Libs. The world-famous Georgians (Top, R), featuring trumpeter Frank Guarente (extreme L) and trombonist Ben Pickering (fourth from L), later with Dorsey and Savitt, toured Europe, 1924–27; they recorded *Georgian Blues* and *Boneyard Shuffle* in Zurich for Kalophon in 1926 after spending the summer at Scheveningen, Holland. The New Yorkers (Bottom, L) stayed for a summer at Ostend, Belgium, and then played the Barbarina Cabaret in Berlin, where leader George Carhart (second from L) signed a recording contract with Tri-Ergon and produced *Ostrich Walk* and *Clarinet Marmalade,* featuring Jack O'Brien, piano (third from R); Danny Polo, clarinet (second from R); and Dave Tough, drums (extreme R). Wealthy pianist Fred Elizalde (Middle, R) formed a band at Cambridge University, where he had gone to keep his younger brother company. Its success playing jazz led to a contract at the Savoy Hotel in London in 1927. He hired Adrian Rollini (fourth from L), Chelsea Quealey (third from R), and Bobby Davis (extreme R) from the California Ramblers. The Americans performed with the full band on *Sugar, Coquette,* and *Crazy Rhythm* and with the Hot Music unit on *Tiger Rag* and *Darktown Strutter's Ball.* Additional help came from (Middle, L, L to R) Adrian Rollini, Max Farley, Harold Fillis (Fred Elizalde's manager), Fud Livingston, and Art Rollini in 1929, but the Savoy canceled after the stock-market crash. Elizalde began writing longer works and later became Franco's musical director in Spain.

Comfortably ensconced in the best hotels, onetime pit drummer Lud Gluskin (Top, L, bald), the "Paul Whiteman of Europe," played hot dance music, featuring soloists like pianist Paulie Freed (second from L); Gene Prendergast, alto sax (fourth from L); trombonist Emile Christian (fourth from L); and Spencer Clark, bass sax (fourth from R and Page 211, Bottom, R). As required by French law, one-quarter of his band were French—fine players such as trombonist-arranger Leo Vauchant, seen with his replacement, Emile Christian, in Le Touquet, 1929 (Middle, L, R and L). The American players included trumpeter Eddie Ritten, drummer Jim Kelly, and guitarist Howard Kennedy at the Haus Gurmenia in Berlin in 1929 (Middle, R, second from L, fifth and sixth from R). Extensively recorded in Paris and Berlin, Gluskin's band produced *That's a Plenty*, *Milenberg Joys*, and *St. Louis Blues*, among others, for Pathé, Tri-Ergon, and half a dozen other labels, 1927–34. One of Gluskin's best arrangers was Prix de Rome winner Russ Goudey (Top, R, extreme L), who sent his scores by train every week, until Gluskin asked him to take Spencer Clark's place on bass sax in 1931. The following year Goudey, who was an ardent Coleman Hawkins admirer, joined pianist and later leading film composer Paul Misraki (second from L) in Ray Ventura's orchestra. An early participant in Montmartre jam sessions with Arthur Briggs, Big Boy Goudie, and others, Goudey visited South America in 1934 and stayed six years. Ted Lewis (Bottom) imported Muggsy Spanier, Jimmy Dorsey, and George Brunis (extreme L, fourth from L, and third from R) to Europe in 1930, enabling Jimmy Dorsey to record *Tiger Rag* and *After You've Gone* with Spike Hughes in London.

Drummer Benny Peyton's letterhead read "Blue Ribbon Orchestra—colored American musicians and entertainers playing refined syncopation." From his office on rue Chevalier de la Barre he booked leading hotels, restaurants, and casinos until the war broke out in 1939. At the Palais de la Méditerranée in Nice he had (L to R) John Forrester, June Cole, Tommy Ladnier, Henri Saparo, Will Tyler, (Peyton), Horace Eubanks, Lou Henley, Lonnie Williams, and Fred Coxito. Peyton never recorded, but by mixing jazz soloists like Ladnier and Eubanks with reading players, he was able to enjoy a high standard of living for twenty years.

Violinist Leon Abbey (standing, fourth from R) worked with J. Rosamond Johnson and directed the Savoy Bearcats when the Savoy Ballroom opened in Harlem in 1926. A year later he was in South America (Page 227, Top, R) and then in 1928 took a new band to London to play the Olympia Ballroom. Their HMV recordings were never released. His special arrangements were possibly too strong; the ballroom manager told him, "The uniforms were beautiful. . . but that screaming of the horns isn't done heah!" Thereafter Abbey played stocks. At Deauville, 1928: (L to R) Harry Cooper, tp; Ollie Tines, dms; Ralph James, as; Bill Caines, p; John Warren, tba; Peter DuCongé, as-clt; Abbey; Charlie Johnson, tp; Jake Green, tb; Fletcher Allen, ts-arr; and Don Perico, bjo.

Composer-singer Noble Sissle (Top, R, with baton) did a solo act with pianist-composer Harry Revel (fourth from R) in 1928 and then formed his band at Les Ambassadeurs in Paris, featuring Johnny Dunn (extreme L), Thorton Blue, Sidney Bechet, and Otto Hardwicke (third and second from R and extreme R). Bechet (Top, L) left to join another group and in 1930 went to the Haus Vaterland in Berlin (Middle, L), where his Berliners band was hired for the UFA film *Einbrechers* ("The Burglars"). Later he rejoined Sissle; both returned to New York in 1931. The Hayman-Swayze Plantation Orchestra (Middle, R) came out of the *Blackbirds* show in 1929 to play the Abbaye Thélème in Montmartre. Joe Hayman (second from L), trumpeter Ed Swayze (fourth from R), and trombonist Herb Flemming (fourth from L) were the key players. Bricktop's (Bottom) on rue Pigalle was the watering hole for Cole Porter, Elsa Maxwell, Tallulah Bankhead, and the Prince of Wales. Arthur Briggs recalled: "She had a very select clientele. We had to play all the musical-comedy numbers. We played them our way, with swing, but never noisily. It was just society music, you know. We'd take solos but with a mute—softly, so as not to disturb our guests. Freddy Johnson was a very, very good piano player—a really fine accompanist. He played for the audience and not for himself. We worked together like clockwork. We just felt it—we didn't have to say a word. In that band we had Big Boy Goudie on sax, Peter DuCongé on clarinet, Billy Taylor on drums, Herb Flemming on trombone, and Juan Fernandez, bass. It was a very good band." Fats Waller (third from R) is shown with Spencer Williams and Ada "Bricktop" Smith, 1932.

Louis Armstrong posed in a Le Corbusier chair in 1932 for Princess Ava, famed London theatrical photographer, on his first visit to Europe, while at the peak of his technical powers. Only a handful of musicians and British jazz fans understood what he was doing. "Monday at the Palladium was a sensation," Robert Goffin wrote. "Never have I experienced such an emotion...the place was rocking like a steamship in heavy weather." Armstrong himself later said: "A lot of the musicians asked me if it wasn't true that when I hit my high C's on the record I had a clarinet take the notes. They had not thought it was really my trumpet getting up there on C...and they weren't satisfied until they handed me a trumpet they had with them and had me swing it." Brothers Nat and Bruts Gonella, two of England's best trumpeters, remembered tripping people up in the darkness as they left the theater; people were leaving, muttering, "This hell music."

LONDON PALLADIUM
ADJOINING OXFORD CIRCUS TUBE STATION

TWICE NIGHTLY AT 6.30 AND 9.0 P.M.	COMMENCING MONDAY, JULY 18TH, 1932	MATINEES AT 2.30 WEDNESDAY & THURSDAY

VAUDEVILLE'S BIGGEST BILL!!!

JACK HYLTON INTRODUCES FOR THE FIRST TIME IN ENGLAND

LOUIS ARMSTRONG
KING OF THE TRUMPET AND CREATOR OF HIS OWN SONG STYLE

WITH HIS NEW RHYTHM BAND AND "SNAKE-HIPS" DANCERS TAYLOR AND ALLMAN
PRESENTED BY JOHNNY COLLINS

HUGH WAKEFIELD
with ZILLAH BATEMAN AND CO.
IN A CONVULSION OF LAUGHTER IN ONE ACT BY J. GORDON BOSTOCK
"WEDNESDAY AT THE RITZ"

PATTI MOORE RETURN OF THE GREAT COMEDY TAP DANCERS SAMMY AND LEWIS

THE WORLD'S GREATEST CLUB JUGGLERS THREE SWIFTS

THE FAMOUS SINGER OF 'LA REVE PASSE' ROBERT CHISHOLM

THE ROYAL HINDUSTANS "VALENCIA" TRIO

JOE BROWNING FIRST TIME HERE
WIERE BROTHERS
EDWIN STYLES
MAX MILLER

SHEFFIELD EMPIRE
Proprietors: MOSS' EMPIRES LTD.
Managing Directors: R. H. GILLESPIE, W. EVANS and F. GULLIVER
Manager: *Phone No. 22082. F. NEATE

6-40	MONDAY, SEPT. 26th, 1932 And during the Week. TWICE NIGHTLY	8-50

FIRST TIME IN SHEFFIELD
JOHNNY COLLINS presents
THE SENSATIONAL

LOUIS ARMSTRONG
King of the Trumpet—Creator of his own song style and his
NEW RHYTHM BAND

LOU RADFORD THE POPULAR XYLOPHONIST	JIMMY CAMPBELL A BURDEN ON THE RATES

NICOL & MARTIN
INTERNATIONAL CYCLING COMEDIANS

AMBROSE BARKER & PEGGY WYNNE
"SMILEAGE"

KLIFTON KABARET KIDS	HENGLER BROTHERS STRONG SILENT MEN

MURRAY & MOONEY
A COUPLE OF COMICS

LOUIS ARMSTRONG
F.S.M.
LIP-SALVE
MADE BY
FRANZ SCHÜRITZ
MANNHEIM
GERMANY

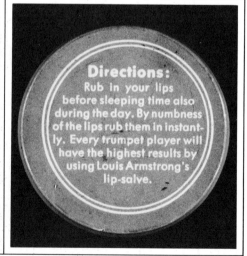

Directions: Rub in your lips before sleeping time also during the day. By numbness of the lips rub them in instantly. Every trumpet player will have the highest results by using Louis Armstrong's lip-salve.

To jazz fan Max Jones he was "... a lithe, smallish but power-packed figure prowling the stage restlessly, menacingly almost, and growling and gesticulating when he was not playing, singing or talking into the microphone. He addressed his trumpet as though it had life of its own ('Speak to 'em Satchel-mouth'), and controlled the band with faintly alien instructions like 'Way down, way down,' 'Keep muggin'... lightly, lightly and politely,' and 'Swing, swing, swing you cats,'" The *Melody Maker* critic "Mike" wrote, "This is something for the moment that will not be believed in years to come when you tell your grandchildren of the good old days at the Palladium in 1932." When he returned a year later, Armstrong toured the country with girl friend Alpha Smith (Top, M) and with trumpeter Jack Hamilton (Top, L) and read the paper that proclaimed his stature (Top, R). Years later (Bottom, M and R), special lip salve was made under his name in Germany for a recurring embouchure problem (Bottom, L).

Louis, with his pianist, Justo Barretto, England, 1933, decked out in plus fours with his dog. Nat Gonella, Armstrong admirer and one of England's best jazzmen, noted, "Louis was always a sharp dresser, smart and a bit loud." For a good part of the time he spent in England in 1933 he rested his overworked lips, while his sidemen, all resident in Paris, had to scramble to find any jobs they could. A *Melody Maker* headline in August after his Holborn Empire appearance ran "Amazing Reception for Armstrong—Frenzied Applause for Meaningless Performance." The seventy high C's and the high F at the end of *Shine* were soon toned down.

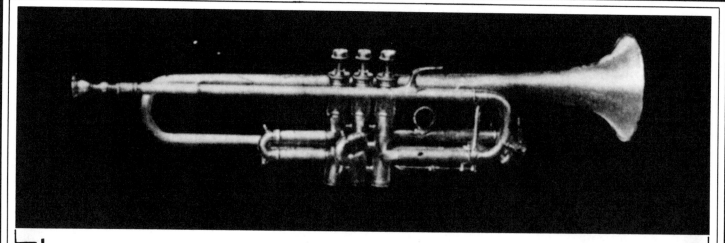

Modèle **ARMSTRONG 1934**
H. SELMER & C° - 4, Place Dancourt - PARIS

Louis Armstrong made two side trips to Copenhagen and Amsterdam, where (Bottom) he played the Carlton Hotel and broadcast to England. He was still experiencing problems with his lip, and a proposed concert sponsored by Jack Hylton, to feature Coleman Hawkins who was due in England in March 1934, never came off. Louis's band: (L to R) Fletcher Allen, Justo Barretto, Henry Tyree, Pete DuCongé, (Louis), Ollie Tines, Jack Hamilton, German Arago, Charlie Johnson, and Lionel Guimaraes. Louis and Alpha (Middle, L) "lazied around Paris for three or four months, had lots of fun with musicians from the States—French cats too." With some reorganizing, with Herman Chittison on piano and Cass McCord (R) on tenor sax, he recorded six titles for Brunswick on November 7. A two-part *Sunny Side of the Street* and a lovely (and quickly withdrawn) *Song of the Vipers* were the highlights. (Top) The Selmer Company took advantage of Armstrong's presence to market an Armstrong-model trumpet. Arthur Briggs was one of the first to try it out.

LONDON PALLADIUM
ADJOINING OXFORD CIRCUS TUBE STATION

TWICE NIGHTLY AT 6.30 AND 9.0 P.M.	COMMENCING MONDAY, JUNE 12TH, 1933	MATINEES AT 2.30 WEDNESDAY & THURSDAY

JACK HYLTON PRESENTS (By Arrangement with MILLS-ROCKWELL Inc.)

DUKE ELLINGTON

FIRST TIME IN ENGLAND **AND HIS** CREATOR OF A NEW VOGUE IN DANCE MUSIC

FAMOUS ORCHESTRA

BESSIE [Original Snake-Hips Girl] **DUDLEY** | **THREE** World's Most Sensational Acrobatic Roller Skaters **WHIRLWINDS** SIXTEEN PALLADIUM GIRLS | **BAILEY AND** [Rhapsody in Taps] **DERBY**

SEVEN ROYAL HINDUSTANS | **MURRAY & MOONEY** | **FRANK & BETTY BOSTON**

RANDOLPH SUTTON | **LASSITER BROTHERS** One of America's Biggest Laughing Acts | CHEEKY CHAPPIE **MAX MILLER** | **DE WOLF METCALF** [What! No Rumba?] **& FORD**

PRICES: 9d. to 5/- (Tax extra). Saturdays and Holidays, slight increase

Duke Ellington's first trip to England in June 1933 was even more significant than Louis Armstrong's. The British press took notice of Australian composer Percy Grainger's comparison of Ellington to their own Frederick Delius. Ironically, Ellington had difficulty securing a hotel room, let alone a first-rate hotel. (He was finally booked into the Dorchester—"He is not very black. He is a master of harmony. He wears a brown suit and a yellow tie that harmonize with his skin.") The rest of the band and artists were housed in Bloomsbury hotels or rooming houses. The serious-minded jazz fans and writers felt there was "perfection in every note that he played." A *Melody Maker*–sponsored concert at the Trocadero Cinema started off with the best Ellington music, but midway through, Ellington sensed the crowd was not interested in his slower, introspective works, and "I went back and gave a vaudeville show...."At the next *Melody Maker* concert, three weeks later, Spike Hughes issued instructions to the audience: not to applaud during solos or to laugh at Tricky Sam Nanton's trombone. Hughes's careful planning paid off; the audience sat in apparent reverence. Composer Constant Lambert summarized the Ellington experience: "...after hearing what Ellington can do with fourteen players in pieces like *Jive Stomp* and *Mood Indigo,* the average modern composer who splashes about with eighty players in the Respighi manner must feel a little chastened."

"I am of little value without my band," Duke Ellington explained to his sponsor, Jack Hylton, on a BBC radio program. (Bottom) At the Palladium: (L to R) Freddy Jenkins, tp; Duke Ellington, p; Cootie Williams, tp; Arthur Whetsol, tp; Joe Nanton, tb; Juan Tizol, vtb; Lawrence Brown, tb; Otto Hardwicke, as; Fred Guy, gtr-bjo; Harry Carney, bar sax; Sonny Greer, dms-vo; Johnny Hodges, as. His Palladium concerts (Above) were geared more to the public than to the critics, of whom Spike Hughes was the most vocal. Hughes (Ellington called him "The Hot Dictator") thought Ellington's programs unworthy of him. (Top, R) Ellington and Ivie Anderson, who was overcome with the reception given her work in England and in France. While in London the band recorded four tunes for Decca—*Hyde Park (Every Tub), Harlem Speaks, Ain't Misbehavin',* and *Chicago*— and released an interview by P. Mathison Brooks, editor of *Melody Maker,* on Oriole. After this tour English writers in *Melody Maker* and other publications no longer spent as much time writing about white jazz players.

DUKE ELLINGTON & HIS ORCHESTRA

By kind permission of JACK HYLTON   *By arrangement with* IRVING MILLS

Programme

SELECTIONS FROM THE FOLLOWING:

1. OLD MAN BLUES — *Ellington*
2. ECHOES OF THE JUNGLE — *Ellington*
3. THE DUKE STEPS OUT — *Ellington*
4. THE MOOCHE — *Ellington*
5. LIGHTNIN' — *Ellington*
6. MOOD INDIGO — *Ellington*
7. EV'RY TUB — *Ellington*
8. LAZY RHAPSODY — *Ellington*
9. BLUE TUNE — *Ellington*
10. MERRY-GO ROUND — *Ellington*
11. THE MYSTERY SONG — *Ellington*
12. RING DEM BELLS — *Ellington*
13. CREOLE RHAPSODY (In two Parts) — *Ellington*
14. SIROCCO — *Spike Hughes*
15. SWING LOW — *Ellington*
16. BLACK AND TAN FANTASY — *Ellington*
17. TWELFTH STREET RAG — *Bowman, arr. Ellington*
18. ROCKIN' IN RHYTHM — *Ellington*
19. ST. LOUIS BLUES — *W. C. Handy, arr. Ellington*
20. BLACK BEAUTY — *Ellington*
21. BUGLE CALL RAG — *Schoebel, arr. Ellington*
22. BLUE RAMBLE — *Ellington*
23. DOUBLE CHECK STOMP — *Ellington*
24. BABY, WHEN YOU AIN'T THERE — *Ellington*
25. OLD MAN RIVER — *Kern, arr. Ellington*
26. DUCKY WUCKY — *Ellington*
27. JIVE STOMP — *Ellington*
28. DROP ME OFF IN HARLEM — *Ellington*
29. PARADISE — *Brown, arr. Benny Carter*
30. IT DON'T MEAN A THING — *Ellington*
31. CREOLE LOVE CALL — *Ellington*
32. THE MONKEY — *Ellington*
33. TIGER RAG — *La Rocca, arr. Ellington*

If understanding of Ellington's music was less than complete in the British press at the time of his 1933 tour, it was still light-years ahead of what it was back home: almost nonexistent. There were no jazz concerts in America in 1933, let alone one that was sponsored by a major music periodical. Critic Spike Hughes, who wrote under the nom de plume "Mike," had only recently concluded his own recording career in New York with the magnificent Benny Carter band; only a year or two earlier he had begun moving away from the prevailing attitude that white jazzmen with correct tuning and highly developed reading skills more than compensated for their lack of swing as compared to black jazzmen. In Ellington's band and music, both form and swing united in one piece. (Bottom) Broadcasting for the BBC were (L to R) Freddy Jenkins, trumpet; Lawrence Brown, trombone; Cootie Williams, trumpet; Juan Tizol, valve trombone; and (hidden) Arthur Whetsol, trumpet. Ellington was performing, perhaps on the advice of Irving Mills or some other wise person, Spike Hughes's own composition *Sirocco* and, as a sop to the masses, a Benny Carter arrangement of the then-new popular Bing Crosby tune *Paradise*.

As a soloist, Coleman Hawkins was second in stature only to Louis Armstrong. Noting Fletcher Henderson's obvious decline, he telegraphed Jack Hylton for a job in England. Hylton agreed, and Hawkins arrived the end of March 1934. A proposed tour with Armstrong (Bottom, L), with critic Spike Hughes (extreme L) overseeing, never took place, even though Hylton handled both. Hawkins saw the sights with Ben Davis of Selmer and P. Mathison Brooks, editor of *Melody Maker* (Top, L, L to R); took tea (Middle, L); and demonstrated his mastery of the tenor sax for the patrons of Leicester's Palais de Danse in July (Bottom, R). Most of his dates were with Mrs. Jack Hylton's orchestra, and in November he made his first recordings, for Parlophone, with Stanley Black on piano and a rhythm section, including *Lost in a Fog, Honeysuckle Rose,* and *Lady Be Good.* In December he played for the last time with Mrs. Hylton's band and moved to the Continent. In January he recorded his first date with the Ramblers in Holland (Opposite Page, Bottom) for Decca, including *Some of These Days* and *After You've Gone.* Later in the year he made *Chicago* and *Netcha's Dream.* An honored concert artist in Paris (Middle, L), Hawkins recorded *Avalon, Blue Moon,* and *What a Difference a Day Made* for HMV with an all-star band. These solos show him at the height of his romantic ballad period. Hawkins roved the Continent: in Geneva, with singer Annie Xofleer (Top, L); peak-lapeled on the streets of Copenhagen (Top, R); at the Tabarin in Zurich, 1938 (Middle, R, Top); and at the Palace in Amsterdam with Freddy Johnson, piano, and Maurice Van Kleef, drums, 1937 (Middle, R, Bottom). Hawkins felt at home in Europe, possibly more so than any of the other major players who went over. It was the best time of his life. Arthur Briggs summed up Hawkins's five-year sojourn: "He didn't gamble. He'd just be at the bar . . . I never knew him to practice. . . . He didn't talk much. But he had wonderful taste. I remember him paying twenty dollars for a pair of socks. He was crazy about beautiful shirts in silk and things like that. He would dress like a prince. I think Europe was a rest cure for him. . . ."

SALLE RAMEAU
(Ex-Pleyel)
252, rue du Faubourg Saint-Honoré

LE HOT CLUB DE FRANCE
annonce pour la 1ʳᵉ fois à Paris
sous le Patronnage de la Revue 'Jazz-Hot'
Le plus célèbre Saxophoniste du Monde

Samedi 23 Février 1935
en Soirée
— à 21 heures —

COLEMAN HAWKINS

avec la participation de
ARTHUR BRIGGS
et son orchestre
renforcé de plusieurs vedettes
actuellement en EUROPE.

et avec le concours de
DJANGO REINHARDT
et son Quintette du HOT CLUB DE FRANCE
avec Stéphane **GRAPPELLY**

avec **FREDDY TAYLOR**
avec **GARLAND WILSON**

PRIX DES PLACES : *Deuxième Balcon*... 10 et 15 fr.
Premier Balcon..... 15 et 20 fr.
Loge de 1ᵉʳ Balcon, la place 20 fr.
Parterre............. 15 fr.
Orchestre.......... 20-30-40 fr.
Orchestre réservé.... 40 et 20 fr.
Loge réservée, la place.... 50 fr.

LOCATION : à la SALLE RAMEAU, 252, Faubourg
Saint-Honoré; chez MM. DURAND, 4, Place de la
Madeleine; à l'ECOLE NORMALE DE MUSIQUE, 114 *bis*,
Boulevard Malesherbes; à la BOITE A MUSIQUE, 133,
Boulevard Raspail; dans toutes les AGENCES et à
l'Administration de Concerts A. et M. DANDELOT, 83,
Rue d'Amsterdam. Tri. 31-94.

ROBERT GOFFIN

AUX FRONTIÈRES DU JAZZ

Préface de Pierre Mac Orlan

PREMIÈRE ÉDITION
illustrée de 60 photographies.

" LES DOCUMENTAIRES "
EDITIONS DU SAGITTAIRE
(ANCIENNES ÉDITIONS KRA)
20, Rue Henri-Regnault, 20
—— PARIS-XIV• ——

HUGUES PANASSIÉ

LE JAZZ HOT

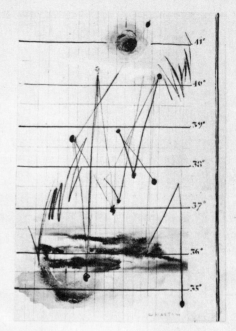

Présenté par Louis ARMSTRONG
Préfacé par Eugène MARSAN
Dessins de Roger CHASTEL

ÉDITIONS R.-A. CORRÊA - PARIS

RHYTHM ON RECORD

Who's Who and Register of
Recorded Dance Music, 1906/1936

—— by ——
Hilton R.
Schleman

21 YEARS of SWING MUSIC on *Brunswick* RECORDS

- A complete survey of Swing Music from 1916 to 1937 contained in two albums of Brunswick records.

- With notes on the history and development.

- Including a selected list of the best swing music on Brunswick, Decca and Vocalion records—WITH PERSONNELS.

- Compiled by LEONARD HIBBS
  (Editor of "Swing Music").

PRICE 1/6

HUGUES PANASSIÉ

LA VÉRITABLE
MUSIQUE
DE
JAZZ

ROBERT LAFFONT
MCMXLVI
12ᵉ édition

The first important book on jazz was Belgian attorney Robert Goffin's *Aux Frontières de Jazz* (published in Paris, 1932), which began as a series of articles in the Belgian *Music* in 1930. Goffin had been affected by the music of Louis Mitchell and Arthur Briggs, from whom he learned a lot about music in general. Frenchman Hugues Panassie's *Le Jazz Hot* was published in 1934 and, unlike Goffin's book, was translated and published in New York in 1936. Both men were then heavily in favor of white jazz, but Panassie later refuted much of what he had written in *La Véritable Musique de Jazz,* which was translated and first published in New York in 1942 as *The Real Jazz* and published after the war in France. Hilton R. Schleman's *Rhythm on Record,* published by *Melody Maker* in 1936, was a primitive attempt to compile an encyclopedia of jazz and popular music. Sample entries: "Eddie Condon, white American banjoist, was born in Chicago where he was discovered by Jimmie Noone. Eddie was with Noone for some considerable time...." Another on Andy Kirk: "Very little is known of Kirk in this country...." *21 Years of Swing Music* was a booklet accompanying two albums of re-issues in 1936, an initial attempt at a history of jazz up to that time.

PRIX: 3frs   NUMERO ■

REVUE INTERNATIONALE DE LA MUSIQUE DE JAZZ

PRIX: 3 frs   N° 6

BENNIE GOODMAN

REVUE INTERNATIONALE DE LA MUSIQUE DE JAZZ

INTERNATIONAL REVIEW OF JAZZ-MUSIC

PRIX: 3 frs   NUMÉRO 7

LOUIS ARMSTRONG

REVUE INTERNATIONALE DE LA MUSIQUE DE JAZZ

INTERNATIONAL REVIEW OF JAZZ MUSIC

AVRIL 1936

3ª ANNÉE   PRIX: 20 Frs

REVUE DU JAZZ CLUB DE FRANCE

DUKE ELLINGTON

OCTOBRE 1945   N° 1 (Nouvelle Série)

THE MAGAZINE OF TRUE JAZZ

THE WORLD'S BEST CONTRIBUTORS :

Misses Helen Oakley (U.S.A.), Madeleine Gautier (France) and Messrs Bernard Addison (U.S.A.) ; Jeff R. Aldam (England) ; Michel G. Andico (Roumania) ; Louis Armstrong (U.S.A.) ; P.-E. Beha (Switzerland) ; Henri Bernard (France°; Bennie Carter, Garnet Clark (U.S.A.) ; Charles Delaunay (France) ; Stanley F. Dance (England) ; André Ekyan (France) ; George F. Frazier (U.S.A.) ; Pierre Gzères (France) ; Ad. de Haas, John Hamond Jr (U.S.A.) ; Georges Herment, Georges Hilaire (France) ; Wilder Hobson, Preston Jackson (U.S.A.) ; Alexander Landau (Poland) ; Ezio Levi (Italy) ; Jean Malrieu, Sétphane Mougin (France-U.S.A.) ; Henk Niesen (Holland) ; Hugues Panassié (France) ; Joost Van Praag (Holland) ; Maxwell Philpott (Spain) ; M. Prunières (France) ; Dietrich Schulz (Germany) ; Jan Sima (Tchecoslovaquia) ; Marschell W. Stearns, Perrin Strikes (U.S.A.) ; N. Suris (Spain) ; Léon Vauchant (France-U.S.A.) ; Edgar Wiggins (U.S.A.-France) ; Spencer Williams (U.S.A.), etc..., etc...

Jazz Hot fulfilled a special need in France, a need for a real jazz magazine. Before its publication in March 1935, there had been *La Revue de Jazz* (1929–30) and *Jazz Tango Dancing* (Page 229), both carrying articles by Hugues Panassie and the musicians Michel Emer and Stephane Mougin. Around 1933 there was also a newsletter from America written by John Hammond and George Frazier, printed in both French and English; but it contained more non-jazz news, reviews of records and activities of tango orchestras as well as other kinds of music. So Charles Delaunay (Middle, R), Hugues Panassie (Middle, M, L), and Pierre Nourry put together *Jazz Hot*, the first magazine devoted exclusively to jazz and carrying newsletters or articles from Helen Oakley (Bottom, M) and Marshall Stearns (Bottom, L) from Chicago and New York respectively. John Hammond (Middle, M, R) wrote for *Jazz Hot* as well. The magazine ran bilingually until the German occupation in 1940, then went underground. In 1945 it resumed publication in French only.

The Melody Maker, November 21, 1936

THE PETER MAURICE "FAMOUSTYLE"
Series of Solos by famous instrumentalists.
'Valse Elegance,' 'Such is life,' 'Ups & downs.'
B flat : Cornet solo by Sid. Phillips,
"CLARINET STRUT"
Trombone Solo by Lew Davis,
"TRICKY TROMBONE," "DOWN THE SLIDE"
In preparation, solos by Carroll Gibbons, Bert Read, Benny Carter, etc.
Published at 1 - each title.
Increase your style by playing the "Famoustyle" way.
Titles for all instruments by world-famous exponents. *Write for list.*
The PETER MAURICE ORCHESTRAL SUPPLY
21 Denmark St., W.C.2. Phone: Tem. Bar 3856

"VOTE FOR THE VOCALISTS" COMPETITION—See p. 11

Melody Maker

Vol. XII. No. 183   NOVEMBER 21, 1936   THREEPENCE

JIMMIE LUNCEFORD'S BAND FOR EUROPE BUT NOT FOR ENGLAND

"M.M." SWING MUSIC CONCERT

ALTHOUGH the Benny Carter Swing Music concert for musicians was only announced in last week's "M.M.," within the space of five days four hundred tickets have already been sold, half at 2 6 and half at 5/-.

JIMMIE LUNCEFORD and his Orchestra, the great American coloured band attraction originally built up by Irving Mills, and now under the personal direction of Harold Oxley, sail for Europe on January 27 for a tour which will take them all over Norway, Sweden, Denmark, Holland, Belgium and France, following an opening at Oslo.

This itinerary, as will be seen, omits England entirely and so points to the ridiculous situation which exists between America and England resulting in both countries locking out each other's bands.

ENTER DENNY DENNIS' RIVAL!

The Melody Maker, December 25, 1937.

You've heard AMBROSE broadcast
IDA
SWEET AS APPLE CIDER
It's a Peter Maurice Hot Series Publication arranged by JIMMY DALE
Price 2/9 per single orch.; by post 2/11.
THE PETER MAURICE MUSIC CO., LTD.,
21, Denmark Street, London, W.C.2.
TURN TO P. 2 & get particulars of the New P. M. Club Terms.

CHRISTMAS ROUND THE PROVINCES—See p. 3

Melody Maker

Vol. XIII. No. 240   DECEMBER 25, 1937   THREEPENCE

To Our Readers
ALL YOU WISH YOURSELVES THIS CHRISTMASTIDE

FIERCE RUSH FOR TICKETS FOR GRAPPELLY - REINHARDT CONCERT COMMENCES

Two Hundred Seats Ordered By First Post

HENDERSON'S UPS AND DOWNS

HOW FLETCHER'S NOW-FAMOUS BAND WAS NEARLY EXTINGUISHED

by John Hammond
"The Melody Maker's" New York Correspondent

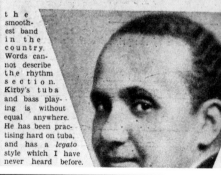

MANY years ago, long before the name of Duke Ellington had been coined, Fletcher Henderson's Orchestra was the leading bunch of coloured music-makers. For seven years straight this band played at Broadway's Roseland Ballroom, and their fame became international. Here it was that Louis Armstrong made his New York debut. And Bennie Carter, Buster Bailey, as well as countless other renowned folk, first saw the Broadway limelight while working here.

Fletcher acquired a reputation—and also a manager. For a few years the band toured the country. making considerable money. Then the leader and the manager had the inevitable argu-

the smoothest band in the country. Words cannot describe the rhythm section. Kirby's tuba and bass playing is without equal anywhere. He has been practising hard on tuba, and has a *legato* style which I have never heard before.

composer. The band makes hot music in the true sense of the word.

There may be other orchestras in this country, but I haven't been thinking much about them lately. Of course, you probably know by now that what I meant by

Pollack is in town looking for a new group. May I humbly suggest that he take over Joe Haymes' *in toto*, which is doing nothing at the moment except Columbia recording.

It was Herbie Spencer, and not Glenn Miller, who made that ace arrangement of *Harlem Lullaby* for Mildred Bailey and the Dorseys on Brunswick (release August 1). My apologies. Miller did the reverse side—*Is That Religion?*

Tother day I was down at the Columbia record studios and heard the English pressings of Ellington's *Down a Carolina Lane* and *I've Got the World on a String-a* (as Ivie Anderson would say). Both are so bad that I dread reading "Mike's" reviews.

Lennie Hayton's Orchestra made its vaudeville debut at the Loew's State Theatre last week. After its air reputation most of us were expecting great

---

Melody Maker debuted in 1926 as a musicians' newspaper. It encouraged the formation of Rhythm Clubs (a page was devoted to their activities), which in turn helped stimulate sales of jazz records and a better understanding of jazz. Composer-arranger and bassist Spike Hughes's articles and criticism were printed under the nom de plume "Mike." In its back pages were "engagements wanted" ads—"Pianist—young, semi-pro, wants to join band, modern swing style, own library, willing to rehearse—Phone Liberty 5065." Columns and articles by Edgar Jackson, Reginald Forsythe, Roy Fox, and other leading and lesser lights of British dance bands ran side by side with columns by John Hammond and later Leonard Feather. Heavy coverage was given to American players active in England and on the Continent.

South Americans had been receptive to jazz since the very early twenties, when violinist and pool shark Paul Wyer settled in Buenos Aires. Sam Wooding and Leon Abbey descended on Argentina in mid-1927 (Top, R). Shown are Willie Lewis (extreme L, with Wooding), Abbey (fifth from R), Joe Garland (fourth from R), and Demas Dean (extreme R). Wooding spent three months in Buenos Aires and two smaller cities, while Abbey's band also played Uruguay and Brazil. West Indian showman-dancer Harry Flemming (Top, L) roamed the world between the wars, went to South America in 1929, picked up the guitar team Les Loups (one of whom was Oscar Aleman), and took them back to Europe. Ex-Wooding trombonist Herb Flemming (Bottom, L) and his International Rhythm Aces, which included Cricket Smith (above Flemming) and saxists Cle Saddler (extreme L) and Roy Butler (extreme R), played the Novelty Club in Buenos Aires for six months in 1933. Clarinet and alto man Booker Pittman visited Brazil in 1935. A year later he was featured with guitarist David Washington's Swing Stars (Middle, R) at La Chaumière in Buenos Aires. Jack Bragg, trumpet, and Lovey Price, drums, were also Americans. Pittman inspired young Argentine jazzmen (Bottom, R) when he had his own big band in Buenos Aires, 1939–42. His career came to a end with the advent of Juan Peron's regime.

WILLIE LEWIS
AND HIS
ENTERTAINERS

Willie Lewis (Top, L) and four former Wooding sidemen—Johnny Mitchell, guitar; June Cole, bass; Ted Fields, drums; and Bobby Martin, trumpet—and leading Belgian musicians took over Wooding's old job at the Merry Grill on Place du Samedi in Brussels in late November 1931 and spent the next years in Belgium. Lewis moved to Paris, played the Chez Florence on rue Blanche, and improved his band considerably by 1935; (Top, R, top row, L to R) June Cole, bass; Bobby Martin, trumpet; Ted Fields, drums; Benny Carter, alto, trumpet, and arranger; Herman Chittison, piano. (Bottom row, L to R) Johnny Mitchell, guitar; Willie Lewis, alto sax and vocals; Joe Hayman, alto and tenor saxes. Carter's original arrangements and playing made the Lewis band the best in Europe. Their Pathé records included *Stardust, All of Me,* and *Just a Mood* (Lewis used this as his theme song on Poste Parisien radio broadcasts to London). Keith Stowell remembered: "It was in the happy days when for 10 francs, 120 francs to the pound, you could sit at the bar with a glass filled with scotch and just replenish it with water and sit the whole evening. No cover charge or anything, so literally for just a few cents you could hear the best music in Europe for a whole evening." Lewis's band peaked in 1937 with (Bottom, L to R) Ted Fields, Jack Butler, Billy Burns, Herman Chittison, Big Boy Goudie, Willie Lewis, Bill Coleman, George Johnson, Wilson Myers, Joe Hayman, and Johnny Mitchell. This unit made *Christopher Columbus, Stompin' at the Savoy, Swingtime,* and *Swingin' for a Swiss Miss* on Pathé. Lewis reorganized in 1939 with Freddy Johnson, Louis Bacon, and Tommy Benford; played Holland and Switzerland; and recorded twenty-four titles for Elite, including *Bacon's Blues* and *Happy Feet,* before setting off for the band's last stand in Estoril, Portugal, in the summer of 1941. They left for New York in September, the last American band to play in Europe. It was the end of *their* "Belle Epoque."

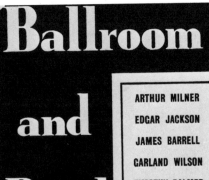

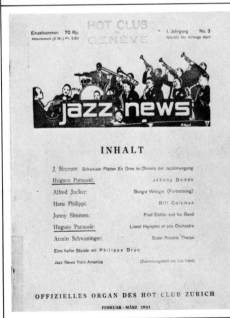

European magazines devoted space to jazz, reviewing records and appearances by American and local jazz groups, years before the United States paid attention to its own music in *Down Beat* and *Metronome*. *Music*, which was first published in 1924, ran until 1940. England's *Ballroom and Band* combined articles on dancing and jazz and ran a year, 1934–35. The Dutch *De Jazz Wereld* printed some articles in English; it ran from 1932 to 1940 and resumed after the war. Duke Ellington's photograph appeared on all its covers until 1940. *Jazz Tango Dancing*, published in Paris from 1930 to 1940, lost most of its audience to *Jazz Hot* after 1935. Baron Timme Rosenkrantz's *Jazz Revy*, published in Copenhagen, 1935–36, was useful because of the editor's personal visits to New York. *Orkester Journalen* began in Stockholm in 1933 but it didn't cover jazz until 1935; it is still published monthly today. *Syncopa y Ritmo* from Buenos Aires, 1934–44, contained good coverage of visiting jazz bands from America. *Jazz News,* based in Zurich in 1941, carried Hugues Panassie's writing; he spent much of the war there. The Italian *Jazz* ran a year, 1945–46, and included a story on Louis Armstrong's final concert in Turin, January 1935. From the time *Music* started until the war, nearly thirty magazines were published in England, France, Germany, the Low Countries, Scandinavia, Czechoslovakia, Poland, and Spain.

Le **HOT CLUB** DE **FRANCE**
ET **JAZZ HOT** PRÉSENTENT:

LE 11 AVRIL 1935, à 20 h. 45
A L'ÉCOLE NORMALE DE MUSIQUE
94, RUE CARDINET, PARIS

Arthur Briggs
Le fameux trompette qui vient de remporter
un triomphe à la Salle Rameau

Jerry Blake
Un des plus extraordinaires clarinettistes
du Monde

FRANK 'BIG BOY' GOODIE
"Dont la ligne mélodique est très purement hot.
Peu de musiciens jouent avec tant de "swing"
Panassié

ACCOMPAGNÉS PAR UNE SECTION RYTHMIQUE DE GRANDE VALEUR

DANS UNE IMPROVISATION ABSOLUE, INDIVIDUELLE ET COLLECTIVE, A PLUSIEURS PARTIES MÉLODIQUES

PRIX DES PLACES : **5, 10 et 15 francs**
Location : Boîte à Musique, 133, Boulevard Raspail et
à la Salle de l'École Normale de Musique.

Canadian trumpeter Arthur Briggs was head and shoulders above any other player living in Europe until Bill Coleman went abroad. Extremely popular and personable, the short, dapper Briggs was an original member of the Hot Club of France (Inset) when it was founded in 1932. Said Doc Cheatham: "Arthur Briggs impressed me more than the other trumpet players I heard there. He had originality and style. He was a stylist. He had lots of technique—very clean and a good jazz swing man." With pianist Freddy Johnson, Briggs worked at Bricktop's on rue Pigalle: "I think we were the first orchestra to play *Night and Day.* Cole Porter played the piano with us for that.... The Prince of Wales used to come in all the time. There was one tune he asked for all the time. It was *Don't Put All Your Eggs in One Basket."* Luckily, Brunswick recorded Briggs and Johnson on *Grabbin' Blues* and *Japanese Sandman* and, with a large all-star band, *I Got Rhythm,* which Freddy directed for the first concerts of the Hot Club of France. When Coleman Hawkins began recording, Briggs played magnificent solos on *What a Difference a Day Made, Avalon,* and *Blue Moon.* Most of his jobs, except for jazz concerts, were society-oriented. He was imprisoned throughout the war, came back after being repatriated, played Chez Florence for six years, and then began teaching.

"I am a Negro musician," wrote Bill Coleman in 1941. "I spent nearly five years abroad. Two of them I lived in Paris. It was a mellow, cultured city where you were accepted for what you were without regard to color. If you were a musician, you were a musician. Nothing else mattered.... In Bombay and Alexandria people liked jazz music, just as they did in Paris and Ostend. We played exactly the same type of music we play here [New York]." His life in Paris began in September 1935 with Freddy Taylor's band at the Villa d'Este at 4 rue Arsène-Houssaye, at a salary of $5 a night. Two months later he was recording with pianist Garnet Clark, on Disque Gramophone, *Rosetta* and *The Object of My Affection* (with a Coleman vocal). In January 1936 he made his first solo record on the same label, *After You've Gone,* with Herman Chittison, piano. His superb tone in middle and upper registers made him the star of many Hot Club concerts; he was welcome sitting in (Bottom) with the Quintette of the Hot Club of France at Nuits Bleues on the rue Fromentin jand was well recorded on *Bill Coleman Blues, Rose Room,* and *Bugle Call Rag* (with Dickie Wells).

No single musician abroad was more widely admired than the gypsy guitarist Django Reinhardt (Top, L). An accidental fire limited the use of the fingers of his left hand, so he played every note and chord with unusual clarity. He had no formal education and was unable to read music, but he grasped harmony intuitively and became the greatest guitar player in jazz history. The Quintette of the Hot Club of France (Bottom, L to R: Stephane Grappelly, Joseph Reinhardt, Django Reinhardt, Louis Vola, and Pierre Ferret) got much of its work in society because it played softly, with no drums or piano. Bricktop helped promote them, using the group in her club and recommending them for private parties. Their records began with Ultraphone in 1934 with *Dinah, Tiger Rag, Lady Be Good, I Saw Stars,* and *Swanee River*. Reinhardt's guitar was heard on over two hundred recordings until his partner, violinist Stephane Grappelly, stayed in London after war broke out in 1939. (Top, R) At the Casanova Club on rue Fromentin they played for high society. When trumpeter Doc Cheatham heard them on a visit to Paris in 1939, he was amazed: "The quintet knocked me out. It was a different style [from] what I heard over here. He wasn't playing American jazz, but he was swinging. It was upsetting to hear a man who was a foreigner swing like that."

UN CONCERT SENSATION

SALLE DE L'ÉCOLE NORMALE DE MUSIQUE
78, RUE CARDINET, 78
(MÉTRO MALESHERBES)

LE VENDREDI 17 DÉCEMBRE 1937, à 20 heures 45

Le **HOT CLUB DE FRANCE**
ET LA REVUE **JAZZ HOT** PRÉSENTENT

BENNIE CARTER

et les meilleurs solistes
actuellement à Paris
avec le concours de

GARLAND WILSON

PRIX DES PLACES : 10 A 30 FRANCS (RÉDUCTIONS AUX MEMBRES DU HOT CLUB)

Unable to find work for his own superb orchestra, Benny Carter (Top, R) succumbed to Willie Lewis's blandishments and joined him at the Chez Florence on rue Blanche in 1935. (Middle, R) On the Riviera that summer: (L to R) June Cole, Alix Combelle, Ted Fields, and Carter. In 1936 he became a staff arranger for Henry Hall's BBC orchestra in London and, through Leonard Feather, recorded with an all-star British band (Bottom) a series of his own tunes and arrangements for Vocalion, including *Swingin' at Maida Vale, Swingin' the Blues,* and *Scandal in A Flat.* The first date in April also produced a magnificent tenorsax solo by Carter on *Nightfall.* Shown are Tommy McQuater (extreme L), Duncan Whyte (fourth from L), Buddy Featherstonhaugh (seventh from L), and Ted Heath (fifth from R). (Middle, L) Carter (seated with Danish jazz fan Baron Timme Rosenkrantz above him) played concert dates in Copenhagen and Stockholm and led an international band at Scheveningen, Holland, for the summer of 1937; they recorded *Skip It, Lazy Afternoon,* and *Blues in My Heart* and, with Coleman Hawkins added, in a smaller group, *My Buddy* and *Pardon Me Pretty Baby.* Leonard Feather also supervised these dates. After playing at the Boeuf sur le Toit in Paris in 1938 and recording *Blue Light Blues* and *I'm Comin' Virginia* for Swing, he went home. In a little over three years he had recorded fifty sides—more than three times his entire output in America.

CHARLES DELAUNAY

DISCOGRAPHY

EDITED BY

JAZZ

CHARLES DELAUNAY

HOT DISCOGRAPHY

FOREWORDS BY

HUGUES & LUCIENNE PANASSIÉ

AND

HENRI BERNARD

Translated into English
by IAN MUNRO SMYTH

1936

Edited by

15, Rue du Conservatoire, 15
PARIS-9e

CHARLES DELAUNAY

HOT DISCOGRAPHY

1938
EDITION

ÉDITÉE PAR

JAZZ

All the jazz magazines, fans, and budding critics who wrote for them were curious to find out who was on the recordings. It wasn't especially difficult to learn the personnel of those being made currently, but the lineups from the early years could only be guessed, so Leonard Feather, Hilton Schleman, Jeff Aldam, and other early writers pestered visiting musicians, playing old records for them and building, in the course of learning, a "discography"—a new word in 1936 when Charles Delaunay (Bottom, R), son of Cubist painter Robert Delaunay and artist-designer Sonia Delaunay, published his first *Hot Discography* (Top, L and M). Delaunay recalled: "Each musician who was coming to Paris, I was asking him, 'What was the first record you did? Do you know who played there? What was the personnel?' Because in those days no record company was taking down the names of the musicians." The second edition was published in 1938 (Top, R), followed by a reprint in 1943, published and distributed in the United States by the Commodore Music Shop. A final edition, the *New Hot Discography,* was published in 1948 in New York. Django Reinhardt (Bottom, L) "liked great things," remembered Stephane Grappelly, "and I believe that he experienced them in a way that they should be experienced. To see his expression in the glorious church at St. Eustache in Paris, hearing for the first time the Berlioz *Requiem,* was to see a person in ecstasy."

Slick and handsome, dancer, singer, and occasional trumpeter Freddy Taylor (Top, L) arrived in Paris with Lucky Millinder in 1933 and built a following with his easy singing style on early Quintet records and for his several stands at Sacha De Horn's La Villa d'Este near the Champs Elysées, beginning in 1935. Taylor hired (Bottom, L to R) (Taylor), Charlie "Crip" Johnson, Jean Ferrier, Art Lanier, Billy Taylor, Juan Fernandez, and Fletcher Allen. This group made the fine Ultraphone recordings *Blue Drag* and *Viper's Dream.* Taylor led combos like this until 1940. Trombonist Dickie Wells (Top, R) played in Harlem's best bands, but it took a Spike Hughes (who featured him in his 1933 recordings) or a Panassie or a Charles Delaunay to feature him properly. In Paris with the Teddy Hill band in 1937, Wells recorded, with Bill Coleman, Django Reinhardt, and Hill sidemen Howard Johnson, Bill Dillard, Sam Allen, and Shad Collins, *Between the Devil and the Deep Blue Sea, Lady Be Good, Dickie Wells Blues,* and *Hangin' Around Boudon* (Chez Boudon, rue Fontaine and rue Mansart, the site of Wells's photo, 1937), recordings that were to make jazz history. The following year Wells joined Count Basie's rising band and assumed his rightful place in the jazz hierarchy.

Drummer Benny Peyton accompanied Adelaide Hall in Zurich, 1935: (Top, R, L to R) Joe Turner; (Hall); (Peyton); Frank Ethridge, p-gtr; Harry Cooper, tp; and Peter DuCongé, clt-as. At the Grand Hotel, Budapest, 1938, Peyton featured (Middle, R) Cass McCord, ts; Tommy Chase (fourth from R), p; Cle Saddler (fifth from L); and Albert Barnes (extreme R). Chase and Barnes, from Washington, D.C., worked earlier with eccentric dancer Levy Wine (Top, L, extreme L) from Tunisia to Morocco. "He called me his Minister of Music," Chase recalled, "because he couldn't read a note...or read or write. He never interfered and paid me well. He claimed Ethiopian nobility or Indian aristocracy as it suited him. He used to try all that cultural crap on me about his kinship with Haile Selassie, the Lion of Judah. But when he opened his mouth, you could tell he was from the land of rice, down in Texas." A suave and polished entertainer, Alberta Hunter (Middle, L) shuttled back and forth from New York to Europe from 1929 until 1940. In Copenhagen she broadcast with Eli Donde's band, 1935. (Bottom, L) Pianist Ram Ramirez (R) and drummer Kaiser Marshall worked with Bobby Martin's band (Page 241); when he went home, they worked with saxist Glyn Paque's Cotton Pickers. Drummer Ollie Tines (Bottom, R) died in Europe in 1937 after working a decade with Leon Abbey.

LEON ABBEY & HIS RHYTHMETICIANS

FROM
LE BOEUF SUR LE TOIT
&
THE AMBASSADORS
PARIS

FORMERLY AT
THE CAFE DE PARIS
&
THE SPORTING CLUB
MONTE CARLO

AND
THE SILVER SLIPPER
LONDON

AMONG
OTHERS

WITH
MYRTLE
WATKINGS
the
COLOURED CROONER

OPENING GALA NIGHT — FRIDAY, SEPTEMBER 27TH

Violinist Leon Abbey (Middle, L) took two six-month tours to India, 1935–37. He played the Taj Mahal Hotel (Top, L) with entertainer Opal Cooper, shown with Mrs. Cooper and Abbey arranger Fletcher Allen (extreme R), and his glee club: (Top, R, L to R) Charlie Johnson, Fletcher Allen, and Art Lanier. The hotel printed a card (Middle, R) advertising the opening on September 27, 1935. The following year some personnel changes were made: (Bottom, L to R) C. Creighton Thompson, Art Lanier, Cricket Smith, Sterling Conaway, Charlie Johnson, Roy Butler, Cass McCord, Rudy Jackson, and Abbey. They replaced Cricket Smith's Symphonians at the Taj Mahal and augmented by hiring Smith and Jackson in addition to trumpeter Bill Coleman. Pianist Teddy Weatherford (Top, M) had been in Cricket Smith's band, which recorded for the Indian Rex label. Hotel publicity announced, "We have been able to secure the services of Teddy Weatherford for the next season. He will divide the honours of the Harbour Bar with a charming young lady named Mabel Scott—and—who knows?—perhaps Aimee again." On the hotel menu was "Poires Glacées Weatherford."

237

HARLEM RHYTHM MAKERS

ARTHUR BRIGGS
AND HIS
AMERICAN - CUBANO BOYS

Robert "Juice" Wilson (Top, L) went to Europe with Noble Sissle, with whom he made *Kansas City Kitty* in 1929. He worked with Leon Abbey and with Tommy Chase (Page 237) in Spain and throughout North Africa until settling in Malta, where he played piano, clarinet, trumpet, and saxophone as well as violin from 1939 until 1954. Arthur Briggs (Bottom, L and R) led his American-Cubano boys with arrangements and sax solos by Fletcher Allen (extreme R, top) for a season in 1937 in Alexandria and Cairo. Allen and Bill Coleman formed the Harlem Rhythm Makers (Top, R), which played both cities throughout 1939: (L to R) Herman Chittison, (Coleman), Joe Hayman, Arthur Pay, (Allen), Billy Burns, and Spider Courance. They went sightseeing (Middle, L, L to R: Courance, Coleman, Chittison, Hayman, and Allen) and played for the wedding of King Farouk's sister. Teddy Weatherford's Plantation Quartet (Middle, R, L to R) of Cricket Smith, (Weatherford), Rudy Jackson, and Roy Butler entertained wealthy British and Indians at the Galle Face Hotel in Colombo, Ceylon, 1939.

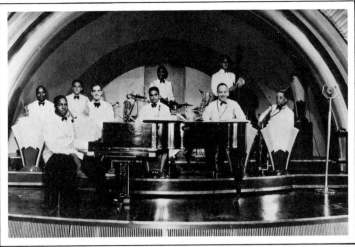

Black jazzmen lost few jobs overseas because of racial bias until Sonny Clay's band and show (Top, L) traveled to Australia in 1928. Black vaudeville troupes had appeared there at the turn of the century, but a "White Australia Policy" specifically excluded any colored race from living there. Just before Clay's arrival in January, the American musicians union banned the Australian Commonwealth Band from touring, and Wells College turned down an Australian violin teacher. Melbourne headlines screamed, "Nude girls in Melbourne flat orgy; Negro comedians as partners; raid by police." Clay's bitter comment: "From the time the boys and I landed we were chased by women who popped up no matter where we hid." Shanghai, China, proved most receptive to black bands, which had played there since 1922. Teddy Weatherford led the band at the fancy Canidrome nightclub near the racetrack since 1929 and hired Buck Clayton's 14 Gentlemen of Harlem (Bottom) for the 1934–35 season. Clayton's band played original arrangements and featured, besides the leader, trumpeter Teddy Buckner (extreme L), trombonist Happy Johnson (sixth from L), guitarist Frank Pasley (sixth from L), Bumps Myers on tenor sax (sixth from R), and Caughey Roberts on alto sax (fifth from R). A racial incident cost Clayton the job after six months and some of the men went home, but he and the others went to the Casanova Club until they earned enough money to go home in 1936. (Middle) Earl Whaley's orchestra, out of Seattle, went to Shanghai in 1937 and picked up ex-Clayton bassist and tuba player Reginald Jones (second from L). Teddy Weatherford (Top, R) played Singapore and Java before settling down in India at the Taj Mahal Hotel with Cricket Smith (extreme L), Roy Butler (third from R), and Rudy Jackson (extreme R) in 1938. He moved to the Grand Hotel in Calcutta late in 1941 and died there of cholera in April 1945.

Valaida Snow (Top, L, and Middle, L) was a remarkably gifted singer, dancer, conductor, show producer, and trumpet player; she made all her records in Europe, 1935–40, on Parlophone, Sonora, and Tono in London, Stockholm, and Copenhagen, including *Whisper Sweet, High Hat, Trumpet and Rhythm, I Must Have That Man, Sweet Heartache,* and *The Mood That I'm In.* She was imprisoned by the Germans in Denmark in 1940. Violinist Eddie South (Bottom) toured Europe, 1928–30 and 1937–38, recording *Doin' the Raccoon* on the first trip and *Lady Be Good* (with Stephane Grappelly and Michel Warlop) and *Fiddle Blues* for Swing. His 1938 band in Amsterdam featured pianist Dave Martin (second from L), drummer Tommy Benford (fourth from L), and singer Mabel Mercer. This unit made *Fiddleditty* for Brunswick in Hilversum in March. South appeared at Hot Club concerts in Paris (Top, R) with singer Una Mae Carlisle, a Fats Waller protégée, who made her first records under Leonard Feather's supervision for Vocalion in London, including *Hangover Blues* and *Don't Try Your Jive on Me* in 1938.

Pianists Freddy Johnson, Garnet Clark, Joe Turner (Top, L, M, and R), and Garland Wilson (Bottom, L) became stars in Europe. Johnson was a major figure in France and Holland in the thirties, an original member of the Hot Club of France whose records *Sweet Georgia Brown, I Got Rhythm* (with Arthur Briggs), and *Way Down Yonder in New Orleans* (with Coleman Hawkins) are all classics. Washingtonian Garnet Clark burned himself out with fast living, recording only three sides with Bill Coleman and Django Reinhardt before his death in 1939. Joe Turner and Garland Wilson accompanied, respectively, Adelaide Hall and Nina Mae McKinney to Europe. Turner made *Joe Turner Stomp* in Czechoslovakia in 1936 and *Loncy* and *The Ladder* for Swing in 1939 in a powerful stride style. Wilson stayed mostly in London and Paris, recording *Shim Sham Drag* for Brunswick and *The Blues I Love to Play* for Swing. Bobby Martin's band (Middle, L) played the Boeuf sur le Toit and the National Scala in Copenhagen in 1937–38: (L to R) Ram Ramirez, Glyn Paque, Thelma Minor, Ernest Purce, Kaiser Marshall, (Martin), Johnny Russell, and Bass Hill. They made a film and one record, *Crazy Rhythm* (with Bill Coleman added as soloist). Martin came home in 1939. Guitarist Oscar Aleman (Middle, R), with Javanese critic Harry Lim, recorded *Whispering* for HMV and *Russian Lullaby* for Swing. Relaxing at a sidewalk café in Paris, 1937: (Bottom, R, L to R) Russell Procope, Sam Allen, and Ralph James.

3 & 4 AVRIL 1939
PALAIS DE CHAILLOT

DUKE ELLINGTON
ET SON ORCHESTRE

After losing money playing jazz, bandleader Ray Ventura (Bottom, L, with pipe) started playing French songs and doing stage shows, and he featured clarinetist Danny Polo (eighth from L), 1938–39. His Chez Ventura nightclub featured Willie Lewis's band, 1937. Fats Waller's (Bottom, R, with wife, Anita) 1938 tour resulted in half a dozen new recordings for HMV and a *London Suite* which was lost until after his death in 1943. (Top, R, L to R) Isadore Langlois, George Johnson, and Tommy Benford played under Johnson's leadership on the Riviera and at the Boeuf sur le Toit in 1938. Johnson returned to Europe to stay in 1946. Duke Ellington's April-May 1939 concerts in France (Top, L) and the Low Countries won him many new admirers. (Middle, L) Cornetist Rex Stewart (extreme L) and clarinetist Barney Bigard recorded *Night Wind* and *Finesse* with Django Reinhardt for Swing after jamming at the Hot Club inauguration on rue Chaptal. Ellington was later quoted on the vast differences he found in Europe: "...You can go anywhere and talk to anybody and do anything you like.... When you've eaten hot dogs all your life and you're suddenly offered caviar, it's hard to believe it's true."

DOUZE ANNÉES

DE JAZZ

HUGUES PANASSIÉ

(1927-1938)

SOUVENIRS

corRêa

INTRODUCTION
A LA MUSIQUE
DE

JAZZ

par

ANDRÉ HODEIR

FORMES · ECOLES ET ŒUVRES MUSICALES

JAZZ

FESTIVAL

INTERNATIONAL

1949

CH. DELAUNAY

OUVERTURE DU FESTIVAL

❋

SYDNEY BECHET

❋

PETE JOHNSON

❋

Oran « **HOT LIPS** » **PAGE** · « **Big Chief** » **RUSSEL MOORE DON BYAS, GEORGE JOHNSON**, etc...

❋

MILES DAVIS, TAD DAMERON
Quintet,
featuring : James **MOODY**,
Kenny **CLARKE** · « bass » **SPIELER**

❋

CHARLIE PARKER'S Quintet
featuring : Kenny **DORHAM, AL. HAIG,**
Tommy **POTTER** et Max **ROACH**

CE QUE VOUS N'ENTENDREZ PAS A NICE

| VENDREDI **20** FÉVRIER à 20 h. 45 | A PLEYEL LE **HOT CLUB DE PARIS** PRÉSENTERA | DIMANCHE **22** FÉVRIER à 14 h. 30 |

UN FESTIVAL DE JAZZ BE-BOP

avec

DIZZY
GILLESPIE

ET LE PLUS SENSATIONNEL ORCHESTRE NOIR
(17 MUSICIENS)
D'AMERIQUE DEPUIS DUKE ELLINGTON

Blind British pianist George Shearing's star rose rapidly after the outbreak of the war. He recorded with Adelaide Hall (Top, M), was famous for his boogie-woogie solos, and during the buzz-bomb attacks in 1944 entranced many listeners with his new ideas on *Five Flat Flurry* and *Riff Up Them Stairs* on Decca. Brought to New York by Leonard Feather, Shearing became a major name, with his help. (Top, L) The year 1946 saw the publication of Hugues Panassie's memoir *Douze Années de Jazz, 1927–38,* a memoir of what he saw and heard during those hectic years of discovery. That year also brought forth the first work by André Hodeir (Top, R), the first of many academically trained critics. Also in 1946, Don Redman's big band with Don Byas, Tyree Glenn, Billy Taylor, and Peanuts Holland arrived in Europe, playing the first American music heard live since 1940. When Dizzy Gillespie's band played a concert at the Salle Pleyel in 1948 (Middle, R, and Bottom, R) bop was in full flower, and it caused a complete break between Hugues Panassie and Charles Delaunay, the two men who had worked so hard to make a place for jazz in France before the war. Delaunay listened with open ears; Panassie retreated to the south of France, secure in his own beliefs. The First International Jazz Festival held in Paris in 1949 (Middle, L and M) featured veteran Sidney Bechet (Bottom, L) with the young French revival soprano Claude Luter (second from L) with Hot Lips Page and others (Middle, M) versus the bands of Charlie Parker and Miles Davis.

The new sounds of Miles Davis (Top, L, L to R) with Barney Spieler, James Moody, and Kenny Clarke, and of Charlie Parker's group (Top, R) with Kenny Dorham, trumpet, drew an elite crowd. Fans began to divide into fanatical camps on both sides of the Atlantic. (Bottom) Three outstanding jazz trumpeters: Hot Lips Page (L), age thirty-one; Miles Davis (M), twenty-three; and Kenny Dorham (R), twenty-four. Page's career ran downhill after 1950, despite his showmanship and unique style. The trend of the day favored Miles Davis and most of the other players in modern jazz. Sidney Bechet's career, which was never that successful back home, took off when he began touring and recording with Claude Luter (Page 243, Bottom, L, second from L) and other traditional groups in France. He recorded, for Charles Delaunay's new label, Vogue, *Les Oignons, Riverboat Shuffle,* and, with some prewar favorites like Bill Coleman and Big Boy Goudie (with Kenny Clarke, who had once worked with Bechet in New York, on drums), *Mon Homme* and *Out of Nowhere.* Bechet settled in France and lived to see a street, rue Bechet, named after him. Along with prewar stars such as Coleman, George Johnson, Joe Turner, and Arthur Briggs came younger men like Don Byas and Peanuts Holland. Other returnees were Harry Cooper, Garland Wilson, trumpeter Jack Butler, and tenor man Benny Waters. The reason was simple: even in a world that had changed so drastically, there were more jobs in Europe for these men than there were back home.

Parlophone

(E 2404.)
(Speed 78)
R 1201

Dance

NOBODY'S SWEETHEART, FOX TROT
(Kahn--Erdman--Meyer--Schoebel)
FRED ELIZALDE AND HIS MUSIC

PARLOPHON
Electric

76.520

TIGER RAG - Fox
(Tigre fox)
(L. Schielda y D. la Rocca)
Maestro Sam Wooding
y sus Chocolate Kiddies
B. 25.420 - 1

"HIS MASTER'S VOICE"

KANSAS CITY KITTY—Fox-Trot
(LESLIE & DONALDSON)
NOBLE SISSLE AND HIS ORCHESTRA
(with Vocal Refrain)
DANCE
ORCHESTRA
(30-1027)
SPEED 78
Cat. No.
B
5731

Brunswick

(6434)
Disque N°
A 500263
instrumental

JAPANESE SANDMAN
(Whiting-Egan)
Freddy JOHNSON, piano
et Arthur BRIGGS, trompette
B.I.E.M.

POLYDOR
MUSICA
TRADE MARK

Enregistrement
Allemand
2 a
Electro-Polyfar
Chanson

WO IST DER MANN ?
(P. Kreuder-Max Kolpe)
Marlène DIETRICH,
accompagnée par Freddy JOHNSON et son Jazzi
sous la direction de P. KREUDER
B
B.I.E.M.
DISQUE N°
530002

Brunswick
Broadcasting Rights Strictly Reserved

BIEM
Cat. No.
1481

ON THE SUNNY SIDE
OF THE STREET
part 1 — Fields-Hugh
Louis Armstrong and His Dance Orchestra
A 500.491 - A

ULTRAPHONE
U

78 TOURS
FOX-TROT

I'VE FOUND A NEW BABY
Jack PALMER et SPENCER WILLIAMS
Soliste (trompette, saxo, clarinette)
FRANK "BIG BOY" GOODIE
Section rythmique avec
S. GRAPPELLY et D. REINHARDT
Matrice N°
77468
N°du Cat.
AP 1527

Vocalion
SWING SERIES
MANUFACTURED IN ENGLAND

SWINGIN' AT MAIDA VALE
(Benny Carter)
(Featuring BENNY CARTER
Clar.: Alto Sax.:—Arranger)
BENNY CARTER AND HIS ORCHESTRA
4-A

Pathé

PA 898
CPT 2631

CHRISTOPHER COLUMBUS
A Rhythm Cocktail
(Mus. de Léon Berry - arrang. Fletcher Henderson)
Fox-trot interprété par
WILLIE LEWIS & SON ORCHESTRE
COPYRIGHT
à la disposition
des Ayants droit

Panachord
REGD. TRADE MARK
NEDERL. FABRIKAAT

AM 491
B.I.E.M.

Opgenomen in het Casino "Hamdorff" te Laren
I KNOW THAT YOU KNOW
(Youmans, Caldwell)
COLEMAN HAWKINS TRIO
(Coleman Hawkins-tenor saxophone,
Freddy Johnson-piano,
Maurice van Kleef-drums)
H 1048

DECCA
THE SUPREME RECORD
THE DECCA RECORD CO. LTD

N.C.B.

CHINA BOY
(Winfree, Boutelje)
DANNY POLO (Clarinet) AND HIS SWING
STARS
P. Brun, tpt ; A. Combelle, tenor ;
Una Mae Carlisle, pno ; O. Aleman,
guit ; J. Mengo, drums ; L. Vola, bass
4863hpp
F. 7126
A

Sonora
SWING
SERIE
GYNNA SVENSK INDUSTRI

Serie/N:r
34
4875 SE
NCB

Minnie
the Moocher
Foxtrot (Bob Calloway)
»Queen of the Trumpet»
VALAIDA
Lulle Ellboys Orkester
3577

Jazz Screened
Some Playing,
Some Singing, Mostly Talking
1928-1950

"You remember that movie, *New Orleans*, that had Louis Armstrong and Billie Holiday? Well, them people took pictures of every segment of New Orleans. They made their pictures as authentic as they could get them, but they didn't put any of it in the movie, any of the authentic stuff…they showed the leading man posing for fifteen minutes, fixing his tie…"
—Danny Barker, *Hear Me Talkin' To Ya*

"I see you like swing music—legitimate swing..." Lauren Bacall remarked to Humphrey Bogart in *Dark Passage.* The record she put on the turntable was an awful mixture of Anson Weeks and Raymond Scott. (Orchestrations for the 1947 Warner Brothers film were credited to Leonid Raab.) Scenes like this, in an otherwise excellent film, caused jazz lovers great pain, sighs of exasperation, and muttering.

Jazz has been on the periphery of film making since Wood Wilson's Syncopators, a pioneer Los Angeles black band, appeared in a 1916 short film, Morosco's *Penny Dance.* As the industry grew, so did the use of music on and off the soundtrack. Duke Ellington's was the first band given billing, in Dudley Murphy's award-winning 1929 short, *Black and Tan Fantasy,* and a year later in the Amos and Andy film *Check and Double Check.* His appearance was brief in the feature, but two of his songs were used, even though studio makeup men "blacked up" the whole band to make sure viewers knew what was what.

No one went to the movies seeking films with jazz in them, because no one knew which films they might be. Jazz fans waited for happy accidents on the bills of double features, among the cartoons and "selected" short subjects. The short subjects often featured the top-rated big bands (as well as many lesser known) and small combos in "nightclub" settings. Longer short subjects ranged from Chick Webb and Bessie Smith in 1929 to Gjon Mili's beautifully photographed and directed *Jammin' The Blues*, a pure art film, in 1944. These shorts, shot mostly in the East, and hundreds of features shot on both coasts were seen in theaters briefly, rarely shown again, and practically never aired on television.

Many black bands in California appeared in films, most notably Les Hite's. Hite claimed to have made more than sixty films, from *Taxi, Please* with James Cagney to *Greenwich Village* with Carmen Miranda; these claims have been substantiated by dedicated jazz-in-film researchers over the past twenty years.

Rarely were the scenes in nightclubs or ballrooms shown except in passing—a tantalizing glimpse, then a cutaway, sometimes jump-cutting back and forth—and only the most knowing could tell who was performing. Two examples: an electrifying performance by singer-actress Theresa Harris, known usually for her maid roles,

in the George Bancroft–Fay Wray film *Thunderbolt* (1929), singing *Daddy Won't You Please Come Home* with Curtis Mosby's Dixieland Blue Blowers, and a nightclub scene in the Bette Davis–Humphrey Bogart film *Marked Woman* (1937), where the superb but little-known trumpeter Red Mack Morris takes a hot solo.

Confusion resulted in the 1937 Marx Brothers film, *A Day At The Races,* in which Duke Ellington's vocalist Ivie Anderson does such a memorable job on *All God's Chillun Got Rhythm.* Ellington's band made the soundtrack, but it was not used. Les Hite's band was brought in to dub along with the MGM studio orchestra (including Mannie Klein, trumpet), and black actors with horns are shown cavorting on the barnyard set with Ivie and Harpo Marx.

None of the bands like Hite's were given billing in these films, but at twenty-five dollars a day (sometimes they picked up four days' work) the money was good, and equal to or better than the pay on their regular jobs. Their scenes, however brief, are worth watching.

Appearances by Duke Ellington, Louis Armstrong, Fats Waller, Benny Goodman, Tommy Dorsey, and Artie Shaw usually were given adequate publicity because they were name artists in their field, but the film story lines and acting were usually preposterous. Jazz fans were willing to suffer to hear the Goodman band roar through the classic *Sing Sing Sing* in *Hollywood Hotel* in 1937, or see Fats Waller steal any scene he was in just by raising an eyebrow in *King Of Burlesque,* a 1935 Alice Faye film.

These moments, and there were many of them, gave the jazz fan a good feeling, even if the film was poor. But often the jazz artist was made to look ridiculous, as Jack Teagarden was, standing with cap on and trombone in hand, looking like Lennie in *Of Mice and Men,* in Bing Crosby's *Birth Of The Blues* (1941), or Benny Goodman with handlebar mustache in *A Song Is Born* (a remake in color by director Howard Hawks of his far better 1941 film, *Ball Of Fire,* with Gene Krupa's band).

Eagerly anticipated were such "jazz" movies as *Syncopation* (1942), *Cabin In The Sky, Stormy Weather* (1943), and *New Orleans* (1946). In every case the jazz fan got what he feared except for some marvelous individual performances by Louis Armstrong, Fats Waller, Duke Ellington, and Billie Holiday. Not even those brief moments could save the films, which were pure Hollywood.

Movies were as aware of truth in music as they were of truth in anything else. If Gary Cooper could be Lou Gehrig, why shouldn't we expect Kirk Douglas to be Rick Martin (who was never much of a Bix to begin with)?

International star and "band boy" (as Hollywood publicists would have it) Duke Ellington went west in 1934 for Mitchell Leisen's *Murder at the Vanities,* a mystery film adapted from Earl Carroll's Broadway hit. Duke's sartorial splendor (Leighton's of Broadway heavily padded out of Savile Row) went for naught, as the film opened with Duke and his band in eighteenth-century costume for a nineteenth-century work: Liszt's Second Hungarian Rhapsody. A quick dissolve, and the band was in dinner jackets and Duke was into his (?) *Ebony Rhapsody.* In typical Hollywood fashion, the songwriting team of Sam Coslow and Arthur Johnston rewrote Liszt, and Duke *improved* on their version. Hooray for Hollywood! Hooray for Duke Ellington!

(L) Musicians played mood music for silent films on the set and sometimes in scenes. Jazz musicians were occasionally called on, and some, like Kid Ory's banjoist, Arthur "Bud" Scott (with guitar), made some extra money in Jesse Lasky's *Gasoline Gus* (Paramount, 1921). (R) Alice Boulden and Her Orchestra made this Vitaphone sound short in 1929; fortunately for Alice, someone told her to hire studio sidemen Tommy and Jimmy Dorsey for her little band so that they could play jazz. Tommy and Jimmy (top, second from L and second from R) came to Alice's aid on *Easy Come, Easy Go* and *One I Love*.

(L) Gertrude Lawrence and Charles Ruggles (facing camera) whoop it up in a typical party scene from Paramount's *Battle of Paris* (1929). The real stuff was provided by far-from-amused trombonist Miff Mole (extreme L). Vocalist and hot pianist Seger Ellis (not shown) had recorded *Sposin'*, *Ain't Misbehavin'*, and *True Blue Lou* with Louis Armstrong and sang sweetly on *How Can I Love You?* in this 1929 Vitaphone short backed by his Embassy Club Orchestra: (R, L to R) Eddie Lang, Tommy Dorsey, Fuzzy Farrar, Al Duffy, Stan King, Jimmy Dorsey, and Arthur Schutt.

Sometime in August of 1929, Ben Pollack and his Park Central Orchestra made "never seen" Vitaphone short no. 872. A soundtrack transcription, pressed by Victor, contains the selections *California, Here I Come, Memories, Sweetheart of Sigma Chi, Song of the Islands,* and *My Kinda Love* (vocal by Jack Teagarden and Ben Pollack, seventh from L and front). Benny Goodman (fifth from R) claims no knowledge of the film (he was in Chicago?), and detecting aural evidence of a clarinet is hampered by the medley style of the selections. Until the film turns up, Goodman's presence is suspect.

Ted Lewis (L, front) was a big star when he made *Is Everybody Happy?* for Warner's in 1929. This Archie Mayo–directed "émigré epic" featured Lewis's acting and playing and some hot music from band members Muggsy Spanier and George Brunis (kneeling, L and R). Clarinetist Don Murray (M) died during the filming. (R) Paul Whiteman was the press-agented *King of Jazz* in director John Murray Anderson's semi-Technicolor musical for Universal (1930). The crash had slimmed Whiteman's payroll, but there are moments of quality from remaining stars Eddie Lang (L), Frankie Trumbauer (fourth from R), and Joe Venuti (not shown) on *Happy Feet, Ragamuffin Romeo,* and *It Happened in Monterey.*

(L) *Red Nichols and His Five Pennies,* Vitaphone short, 1929. Nichols (R), at the peak of his popularity, featured a fresh-faced Pee Wee Russell (third from R) and *fresh* Eddie Condon on banjo. Condon's later comment: "My first movie. I never saw it." (R) Paramount filmed *The Happiness Remedy,* a 1931 short for Ted Lewis (with ever-present hat), on Long Island. Regular sidemen Spanier and Brunis were inexplicably replaced by Red Nichols (under hat) and patent-leather-haired trombonist Jack Teagarden. Guitarist Tony Girardi thinks he's Eddie Lang.

After Seben (1929), a Vitaphone fictional short, starred the gifted actor and snake-hipped eccentric dancer James Barton (remember *Tobacco Road?*) in a blackface role (extreme R). The plot was a series of Negro stereotypes—cheating wives, shooting dice, and so on—and the last segment featured a Harlem nightclub scene with Chick Webb's orchestra playing *Sweet Sue* for several Savoy Ballroom dancers, including George "Shorty" Snowden, the inventor of the Lindy step known as the Shorty George. Webb's front line was a "murderers row" of jazz: (L to R from John Trueheart, banjo) (Webb with top hat), Benny Morton, Ward Pinkett, Edwin Swayze, Bobby Holmes, Elmer Williams, and Hilton Jefferson. James Barton danced solo to *Tiger Rag.*

Black and Tan Fantasy, RKO, 1929. Running time: nineteen minutes. Award-winning director Dudley Murphy fused jazz and plot with an avant-garde camera technique for Duke Ellington's first appearance on film. The story line was built around Duke (Top, R, and Bottom, R) as a struggling bandleader composing and rehearsing *Mood Indigo* and *Black and Tan Fantasy* for a forthcoming opening at a club not unlike the Cotton Club. The beautiful but ailing dancer Fredi Washington (Bottom, M) is to be featured in the former number. The show opens, and Miss Washington dances but suffers a heart attack. As the band prepares to come to her aid, the cigar-chomping club owner tells the stagehands to remove the stricken dancer; the show must go on. The finale is a deathbed scene with Duke and his Cotton Club Orchestra playing *Black and Tan Fantasy*. Trumpeter Arthur Whetsol (Bottom, L), whose usual role with the band was melodic lead, displays a well-rounded growl in the film. Other Ellington numbers were *The Duke Steps Out, Cotton Club Stomp,* and an accompaniment to Fredi Washington's dance routine on *Goin' to Town.*

St. Louis Blues, RKO, 1929. Running time: seventeen minutes. Co-producer W. C. Handy and director Dudley Murphy cast Bessie Smith (her only film) in this vehicle, filmed in Astoria, Long Island, to display Handy's title song. (Bessie had made the definitive recording of *St. Louis Blues* in 1925, backed by Louis Armstrong's cornet.) Bessie (Middle and Bottom) is driven to drink by her handsome, opportunistic, man-about-town boyfriend (actor-dancer Jimmy Mordecai, Middle), who sweet-talks her while romancing any little thing that catches his eye. After Bessie catches him, she proceeds to sing and drown her sorrows at the bar while an all-star band, led by pianist James P. Johnson with cornetists Joe Smith and Thomas Morris, plays Handy's *St. Louis Blues,* accompanied by (the only ludicrous note) the J. Rosamund Johnson–directed Hall Johnson choir. The *Variety* ad (Following Page), in contrast to the racist film poster (Top, R), emphasized "whiteness" in illustration and copy and has Bessie Smith recording for Victor when Columbia was her label at that time.

BLAZING SENSATION
OVERNIGHT ON BWAY

White Hot Dramatic
Show Stopper Leaves
Em Cheering in the
Aisles! . . . . .

TWO REEL RIOT OPENING WEEK
WITH "BULLDOG DRUMMOND"
AT PUBLIX RIALTO, NEW YORK
HELD OVER INDEFINITE . . . .

ST. LOUIS
BLUES

. . . all dialog
smash . . . with most stirring musical and vocal setting at the moment of moaning to press. . . .

Radio PICTURES

From original song by W. C. Handy
Directed by Dudley Murphy.
With Bessie Smith, famous Victor
recording artist and host of negro
singing and dancing artists.

Produced by R. C. A. Gra-
mercy Studios　Distributed
by RKO Distributing Corp.

(L) *Harlem After Midnight*, Oscar Michaux, 1934. This all-black, low-budget gangster feature, shot entirely in Harlem, starred Lorenzo Tucker ("the black Valentino") and Bee Freeman ("the black Mae West") and featured Leon Gross's jumping swing band with Bernard Flood (extreme L), trumpet; Pazuza Simon (second from L), tenor sax; and fine pianist Arthur Bowie (third from R). Numbers performed at the Poodle Dog Café were *Dinah, Sweet Georgia Brown,* and *I Got Rhythm.* (R) *Smash Your Baggage* (Vitaphone, 1933) is a nine-minute short notable for being the only film of banjoist Elmer Snowden's Smalls's Paradise Orchestra: (L to R) (Snowden), Otto Hardwicke, Leonard Davis, Richard Fullbright, Al Sears, Sid Catlett, Wayman Carver, Roy Eldridge, Dickie Wells, and Harlan "Red" Matthews. Set in Grand Central Terminal, the revue also featured tap dancer Rubberlegs Williams, singer Babe Wallace, and the tunes *Tiger Rag, My Man's Gone, Bugle Call Rag,* and *Plantation Capers.*

Sing, Sinner, Sing, Majestic, 1933. This rarely seen mystery feature directed by Howard Christy, made for second-run houses, is one of sixty or more films in which Les Hite's band appeared, many with Lionel Hampton (partially obscured) on drums. Other players were Sonny Craven (third from R), George Orendorff (fourth from R), Harold Brown (Lawrence Brown's brother) on piano, and the altoist Marshall Royal (hidden by Hite). Daisy Mae Diggs is the "truckin'," vocalist.

Paramount's *The Big Broadcast* (1932), a romantic comedy directed by Frank Tuttle, was nothing more than a filmed walk-on for some of the top radio acts of the day: the Mills Brothers, the Boswell Sisters, Bing Crosby, and the Cab Calloway Orchestra. Bing Crosby (L) rehearsed the fine ballad *Please* with a rich accompaniment by his personal guitarist, Eddie Lang (real name: Salvatore Massaro). Lang died tragically in 1933 of complications following a tonsillectomy. (R) The studio "blacked-up" light-skinned Cab Calloway (with baton) so that there could be no mistaking his racial identity. Cab writhed and jived *Minnie the Moocher*, but the real surprise was *Hot Toddy*, one of the band's few instrumentals, an original composition and arrangement by Benny Carter.

Louis Armstrong was the only American bandleader whose orchestra made a feature film in Europe. The strange *Kobenhavn, Kalundborg og?* (Copenhagen, Calundborg and...), shot in Copenhagen in 1933, was a filmed revue. (Josephine Baker was to have been featured, but she bowed out at the last minute.) Armstrong's segment shows a highly animated and slim Louis (L) at peak form interpreting *Dinah, I Cover the Waterfront,* and *Tiger Rag.* Paramount's *Rhapsody in Black and Blue*, a 1932 short subject, featured Armstrong (R) as a shiftless janitor who falls asleep (to one of his own recordings), dreams he is in "Jazzmania" (jazz heaven), and wakes in leopard skin and soap bubbles to play *Shine* and *I'll Be Glad When You're Dead, You Rascal You.* Sidemen included (L to R) Big Mike McKendrick, Al Washington, John Lindsay, Zilner T. Randolph, Charlie Alexander, and Tubby Hall.

Duke Ellington had risen steadily since making *Check and Double Check* for RKO in 1930. Back in Hollywood four years later, he was a well-established figure in modern American music; he had toured Europe, had dozens of outstanding compositions in his catalog, and had been a tremendous draw, even on tour in Texas. The Ellington band and Earl "Snakehips" Tucker (Middle, L, extreme L) performed nightly at Sebastian's Cotton Club in Culver City and made two Paramount features by day: Mitchell Leisen's *Murder at the Vanities* with Jack Oakie, Carl Brisson, and Kitty Carlisle and Leo McCarey's *Belle of the Nineties* with Mae West. Duke's *Ebony Rhapsody* was introduced in the *Vanities* film (Bottom), and he did the accompaniment for Mae West on *My Old Flame* in her film. Ivie Anderson got to sing the lovely ballad *Troubled Waters*. On the *Vanities* set Ellington managed to do some mugging (Top, R) for a very young bridegroom, Buck Clayton (R), then a California bandleader about to sail to Shanghai for a steady job at a lush casino. The year before, Duke had made a one-reel short for Paramount, *Bundle of Blues,* which featured Ivie Anderson's *Stormy Weather,* Florence Mills's and Bessie Dudley's tap dancing to *Bugle Call Rag,* and the band's romping on *Rockin' in Rhythm.* (Top, L, L to R) "Posey" Freddy Jenkins, Cootie Williams, Tricky Sam Nanton, Juan Tizol, Arthur Whetsol, and Lawrence Brown.

The Music Goes 'Round (Columbia, 1936) starred Harry Richman and the Riley-Farley Onyx Club Band doing their title hit, but Les Hite's band (L) provided the real jazz with altoist Marshall Royal (second from R), leader Hite (kneeling), and zany showman, dancer, and tom-tom player Cee Pee Johnson (not shown). Oscar Michaux's *Swing* (ca. 1936) was another all-black, low-budget musical featuring Leon Gross's eight-piece unit. Leader Gross (R, leaning against piano) listens to Arthur Bowie's piano while trumpeter Bernard Flood (extreme R) waits for songstress Cora Green to finish her licks. Featured were *I Think You're Wonderful, Chinatown, My Chinatown, Dear Old Southland,* and *Bei Mir Bist du Schoen.* This film has yet to surface.

Cab Calloway was the highest-paid and most successful black entertainer of the prewar years. He always had a good band, sometimes an outstanding one. He made some shorts and a handful of features, including this Al Jolson film, *The Singing Kid,* for Warner's (1936). His sidemen were (L to R) Andy Brown, Leroy Maxey, Irving Randolph, Doc Cheatham, (Cab), Claude Jones, Ben Webster, Keg Johnson, Al Morgan, and Walter "Foots" Thomas. *Keep That Hi-De-Ho in Your Soul* was about all Warner's (and Jolson) would let Cab do in this movie.

Louis Armstrong was no stranger to Hollywood. He made a feature as early as 1930, short subjects in the early thirties, and had been seen live and in animation in Betty Boop cartoons. He was also no stranger to the roles of shiftless janitor, sanitation worker, and butler. These roles required the standard Stepin Fetchit "tomming," but Armstrong, as always, let his music do the talking. *Pennies from Heaven* (Columbia, 1936) starred Bing Crosby and Madge Evans. Armstrong's sequence (Top, R) took place in the Haunted House nightclub with Louis and the masked band (including Lionel Hampton on drums) playing *Skeleton in the Closet*. (Middle, L) *Every Day's a Holiday* (Paramount, 1937) starred Mae West in a Victorian burlesque. Armstrong, as a sanitation worker, led the cream of Los Angeles musicians in a rousing version of Hoagy Carmichael's *Jubilee*. (Bottom, L) Action director Raoul Walsh tried comedy in *Artists and Models* for Paramount in 1937. Set in the New York advertising world, it featured Jack Benny and Martha Raye (atop barrel). Louis's one number, *Public Melody Number One*, was cut from many of the release prints. (Middle, R) *Going Places* (Warner Brothers, 1938) was a racetrack farce with Anita Louise, Maxine Sullivan, and a horse named Jeepers Creepers. Armstrong plays a chicken-thieving groom who sings Johnny Mercer's hit *Jeepers Creepers* to the horse. (Middle, M, and Bottom, R) Bing Crosby's *Doctor Rhythm* (Paramount, 1938) was a natural for Louis Armstrong—or so it seemed—but despite advertising, posters, and stills depicting his scenes, Louis's music, *The Trumpet Player's Lament,* wound up on the cutting-room floor and hasn't been seen since.

Claude Hopkins (standing, L) and his band were at their peak in 1935 when they made *By Request* for Vitaphone, which featured his theme *I Would Do Anything for You; Chasin' All My Blues Away,* showcasing trumpeter Ovie Alston (sixth from R); *California, Here I Come; Shine;* and *Chinatown, My Chinatown.* Soloist Edmond Hall (front row, extreme L) was aided by the addition of Henry Wells (top row, second from L), Hilton Jefferson, and Russell Smith (third and second from L) from the Lunceford and Henderson bands. Johnny "Scat" Davis (R) serenaded Lola Lane in *Mr. Chump* (Warner's, 1937), a forgettable film that included such lines as "Swing music makes you want to live!" Davis's mellow cornet, with a sock for a mute, accompanied Penny Singleton's vocal on *As Long As You Live.* Other numbers were *Bob White, Listen to the Mocking Bird,* and *Show Me the Way to Go Home.*

Pinky Tomlin—songwriter, personality, singer, and bandleader—made several low-budget films, this one, *Thanks for Listening* (L), for Conn-Ambassador in 1937 with Maureen O'Sullivan (M). Trumpeter Jonah Jones (in car), working in Hollywood with Stuff Smith's band, livened up the proceedings. *You Can't Have Everything* was an Alice Faye film for Fox in 1937, with a story by Gregory Ratoff. Louis Prima's highly successful swing band (R), one of the few then made up entirely of New Orleans players, swung *Rhythm on the Radio* and *It's a Southern Holiday.* Trumpeter Prima, like fellow New Orleanian Wingy Manone, had a "blacker" sound on trumpet than hometown players Paul Mares and Johnny Wiggs.

(L) *Garden of the Moon* (First National, 1938) starred Pat O'Brien and John Payne (with baton) conducting Joe Venuti's orchestra. The music, when it was heard, was the film's saving grace. Venuti (extreme L), Johnny "Scat" Davis (directly behind Venuti), and mustachioed trombonist Jerry Colonna (at right of tuba) performed *The Girl Friend of the Whirling Dervish, Love Is Where You Find It,* and *The Umbrella Man.* (R) Buck and Bubbles (pianist Ford Lee "Buck" Washington and dancer John W. Sublett) were one of the great international variety acts from the twenties through the forties. Buck found time to accompany Louis Armstrong, Bessie Smith, Coleman Hawkins, and Billie Holiday on records. The duo appeared in several films, here and abroad; here they're helping out Dick Powell and Fred Waring's Pennsylvanians in a film titled *Varsity Show* for Warner's (1937).

Benny Goodman's first movie, *The Big Broadcast of 1937,* was filmed in 1936 during his second engagement at the Palomar Ballroom. It featured a young and raucous Martha Raye (alongside Benny) doing *Here Comes the Bride* with Benny and the band, who did *Cross Patch* and *Bugle Call Rag,* while competing with Leopold Stokowski and Larry Adler.

Hollywood Hotel, Warner Brothers, 1937. Director Busby Berkeley built the story line around Louella Parsons, the then-feared gossip columnist for the Hearst empire. The movie starred Dick Powell, Rosemary Lane, and Benny Goodman's band at the peak of its popularity. Goodman once again was playing at the Palomar, as he had been the year before while making *The Big Broadcast of 1937. Hollywood Hotel* is considered not only Goodman's best film, but the best band film in movie history. There was the roaring *Sing, Sing, Sing,* with the recent addition of Harry James (the omnipresent Johnny "Scat" Davis was seen in the brass section lip-synching; Goodman had threatened to quit the film if Davis's dubbed trumpet was included); a scintillating *I've Got a Heartful of Music* by the Quartet: (Bottom, L to R) Hampton, Wilson, Goodman, and Krupa; an accompaniment to Mr. Davis's vocal on *Hooray for Hollywood;* and the big band on *California, Here I Come.*

Artie Shaw (Arthur Arshawsky) was handsome *and* literate (often a ruinous combination) and a musician in the artistic sense, not just a clarinetist. His playing was lyrical and harmonically interesting; and he could swing. What he was playing in 1938–39 would be a striking influence on the modern playing of Buddy DeFranco and Tony Scott a decade later. But in July of 1938, Shaw was just another struggling swing-band leader. On July 24, 1938, he recorded *Begin the Beguine*, and within a few months he was Artie Shaw, the new boy in town, swing's latest and hottest property and its matinee idol. He went from the Lincoln Hotel in New York to the Palomar Ballroom in Los Angeles to the set of *Dancing Coed*, starring the luscious Lana Turner (Shaw's third wife) and the equally attractive Ann Rutherford (Bottom, L and R). The film, a routine college comedy, showcased four of Shaw's compositions, *Nightmare, Non-stop Flight, Traffic Jam,* and *Jungle Drums;* the latter featured new drum star Buddy Rich (top row, third from R) and tenor saxist Tony Pastor (third from L), a Buddy Hackett/Lou Costello look-alike. New addition Georgie Auld on tenor (cropped, extreme L); an incisive trumpet section of Johnny Best, Chuck Peterson, and Bernie Privin (seventh, eighth, and ninth from L); and guitarist Al Avola and pianist Bob Kitsis (second from R and R) made a lot of music on a lot of footage in this film.

Paradise in Harlem (L), an all-black gangster musical filmed uptown in 1939, starred Mamie Smith with Lucky Millinder's band. Mamie sang *Harlem Blues* (Perry Bradford's old *Crazy Blues),* Edna Mae Harris sang *Harlem Serenade,* and Millinder's band did *I Gotta Put You Down.* Millinder (with baton) featured trombonist George Stevenson (third from L), drummer Shadow Wilson, and trumpeter Freddy Webster (third from R). (R) *St. Louis Blues* (1939), a Raoul Walsh–directed Paramount vehicle for Dorothy Lamour set aboard a Mississippi showboat, featured the gifted Maxine Sullivan (hand on harp) singing the title song and her hit, *Loch Lomond,* accompanied by violinist Matty Malneck and His Boys: Mannie Klein, trumpet; Milton DeLugg, accordion; and Bobby Van Eps (third from L), piano.

(L) *Some Like It Hot* (1939) bears no resemblance to the 1959 comedy. Gene Krupa's first feature—a Bob Hope and Shirley Ross comedy—presented tenor sax star Sam Donahue (second from L) on Frank Loesser's title song and on *The Lady's in Love with You.* (R) *Sweetheart of the Campus* (1941), Columbia's low-budget college musical, starred Ruby Keeler and Harriet Hilliard with Ozzie Nelson's band. It was made memorable—if only for their all-too-brief appearance—by the Four Spirits of Rhythm, starring Teddy Bunn (R), guitar, and Leo Watson (second from L), tipple and vocals.

Murder on Lenox Avenue (L) was another Jack Goldberg cheapie made for black audiences in 1941; it starred Mamie Smith. The still depicts a typical (?) after-hours jam session—booze, broads, blues, and maybe a controlled substance? The Rockland Dictators were the accompanying group. (R) Zanies Ole Olsen and Chic Johnson adapted their Broadway hit *Hellzapoppin'* to film in 1941. Universal's publicity mill described this still: "It's rhythm time when these gates swing out." The "help"—(L to R) Elmer Fain, Rex Stewart, Happy Johnson, Cee Pee Johnson, Slam Stewart, and Slim Gaillard—played for the Lindy Hoppers. Featured tunes were *Putting on the Dog, Congeroo,* and *Conga Beso.*

(L) Fox's *Orchestra Wives* (1941) served as background for the begrudged popularity of Glenn Miller and his orchestra, featuring Tex Beneke and the Modernaires. Numbers included *At Last, Serenade in Blue, Kalamazoo, Chattanooga Choo Choo,* and *American Patrol.* Fleeting jazz interest was provided by saxists Ernie Caceres and Al Klink and guitarist and sometime cornetist Bobby Hackett. (M) *The Birth of the Blues* (Paramount, 1941) had an embarrassing "how jazz came up the river" script, but it did feature Jack Teagarden and his orchestra, when Jack, cap in hand, wasn't playing yokel to Bing Crosby (his clarinet dubbed by Danny Polo) and Brian Donlevy (his cornet dubbed by section man Pokey Carriere). Bing, Mary Martin, and Jack (M, L to R) had some fun with *The Waiter and the Porter and the Upstairs Maid.* (R) Charlie Barnet's talents were wasted on such numbers as *50,000,000 Nickels* in the 1942 *Juke Box Jenny,* a Ken Murray and Iris Adrian turkey.

(L) Paramount's *Las Vegas Nights* (1941), a comedy-musical set in the frontier domain of the notorious Wilbur Clark, featured the Tommy Dorsey orchestra with Connie Haines (clapping), Jo Stafford, the Pied Pipers, and Frank Sinatra. The hot music was provided by trumpeter Ziggy Elman (fourth from L) with his Jewish-wedding vibrato on *Song of India* (he took Bunny Berigan's famous solo) and *I Gotta Ride,* ably abetted by the paradiddle drumming of Buddy Rich (with cymbal). Sinatra, Jo Stafford, and the Pied Pipers were heard on *I'll Never Smile Again* and *Cocktails for Two.* (R) Bob Crosby cocks an ear to bassist Bob Haggart's whistling and drummer Ray Bauduc's response on *Big Noise from Winnetka,* from RKO's *Let's Make Music* (1940).

(L) *You'll Never Get Rich,* a 1941 Columbia release starring Fred Astaire and Rita Hayworth, had one memorable sequence with (L to R) Red Mack Morris, Buddy Collette, Chico Hamilton, A. Grant, and jug-playing Joe Comfort, swinging *Boogie Woogie Barcarole* and *Shooting the Works for Uncle Sam* behind bars. *Greenwich Village* (R) was uncrated in a Hollywood studio, but this 1942 Fox film, which starred Carmen Miranda and Don Ameche, had a little jump sequence led by Les Hite (on piano); Teddy Buckner, trumpet; Alton Redd, drums; Buddy Banks, clarinet; and Bam Brown, bass.

It took Benny Goodman five years to get back into the studios, this time with one of his least impressive wartime bands. (L) *The Powers Girl* (United Artists, 1942) starred George Murphy, Dennis Day, Carole Landis, and Anne Shirley. Goodman sidemen Jimmy Rowles on piano, Jimmy Maxwell (L in section) on trumpet, Lou McGarity (R in section) on trombone, and Hymie Schertzer (M in section) on alto sax helped out on *Let's Dance, Roll 'Em,* and *One O'Clock Jump;* the Quintet did *I Know That You Know.* Vocalist Peggy Lee (not shown) was *The Lady Who Didn't Believe in Love.* (R) Columbia's low-budget *Reveille with Beverly* (1943) had bubbly Ann Miller as a disc jockey dispensing records that segued into three-minute band vignettes for Duke Ellington, Bob Crosby, Frank Sinatra, Ella Mae Morse with Freddy Slack, and the Mills Brothers. Duke (with his last great band?) performed *Take the A Train.*

Hollywood's oh-so-heavy hands weighed down Tommy Dorsey's fine band with eighteenth-century costumes in MGM's Technicolor adaptation of Cole Porter's Broadway musical *Dubarry Was a Lady* (1943), filmed in late 1942 (during the recording ban) and starring Red Skelton, Lucille Ball, and Gene Kelly. Dorsey's band was under wraps, although drummer Buddy Rich, Heinie Beau on alto sax, Don Lodice on tenor sax, and trumpeters Ziggy Elman, Jimmy Blake, and Chuck Peterson (playing nightly at the Palladium) provided tasteful accompaniment on *Katie Went to Haiti* and the title tune. None of the numbers lent themselves to Dorsey's ministrations, and he recorded none of them.

Vincente Minnelli's first directorial effort, *Cabin in the Sky* (MGM, 1943), was a stylized but heavy-handed folk fable based on the Broadway musical of the 1930s by Vernon Duke, Lynn Riggs, and John Latouche. Because of its "handkerchief-head" conception of blacks, it was affectionately known as "Uncle Tom's Cabin in the Sky." Nevertheless, it had a galaxy of talent: John W. Bubbles (R) heeling-and-toeing to Duke Ellington's orchestra, Mercer Ellington's *Things Ain't What They Used to Be,* Ethel Waters singing *Happiness Is a Thing Called Joe,* and Lena Horne's rendition of *Honey in the Honeycomb.* But Louis Armstrong (L)—somewhere in the Idea Department in Hell as an assistant to Lucifer—got in only a few rapid hot licks. His *Ain't It the Truth* was grounded.

William Dieterle's *Syncopation,* made for RKO in 1942, seemed like a swing fan's dream. There was the *Saturday Evening Post*'s readers poll All-American Jazz Band with Benny Goodman, Harry James, Jack Jenney, Charlie Barnet, Joe Venuti, pianist Eddy Duchin (of all people to be named a jazz pianist; he was replaced at recording time by ex–Tommy Dorsey pianist Howard Smith), Alvino Rey, Bob Haggart, and Gene Krupa. Their all-too-short epilogue introduced Adolph Menjou, Jackie Cooper, and Bonita Granville trying to trace the history and influence of jazz. Cooper's cornet (L) was dubbed by ailing trumpeter Bunny Berigan (seen at R with conductor Leigh Stevens, L, and George Thow, R). Bonita Granville (her piano was dubbed by Stan Wrightsman) seemed to be looking beyond to her role in *Hitler's Children.* Inexplicably, former Ellington cornetist Rex Stewart was seen acting and playing on screen, but again it was Stevens's pet, Berigan, who dubbed the sounds.

Fox's *Stormy Weather* (L), a sepia-toned, all-black musical made in 1943, billed Lena Horne, Bill Robinson, Cab Calloway, Katherine Dunham, the Nicholas Brothers, *and* Fats Waller. Waller played *Ain't Misbehavin'*, lifted an eyebrow, and stole the picture. Olsen and Johnson's unsuccessful follow-up to their *Hellzapoppin'* was called *Crazy House (Funzapoppin')* (Universal, 1943). It featured Count Basie's band with Thelma Carpenter and Jimmy Rushing (M, L and R) doing something called the *Tropicana*. (R) *Radio Melodies* (Universal, 1943) was a "Name Band" short featuring Stan Kenton's orchestra doing *Reed Rapture* and *Artistry in Rhythm*. Still leading a swing band, Kenton featured trumpeter Buddy Childers and tenor saxist Red Dorris.

Producer Sol Lesser and director Frank Borzage had a big hit for Universal in 1943 with *Stage Door Canteen*. It featured lots of stars who couldn't refuse (in association with the American Theater Wing) and lots of music: the bands of Count Basie, Benny Goodman, Kay Kyser, Guy Lombardo, Xavier Cugat, and Freddy Martin. Ethel Waters (M) sang *Quicksand* with one of Count Basie's greatest bands: sax section (L to R) Tate, Powell, Warren, Washington, and Byas; trumpets (L to R) Clayton, Lewis, and Edison; and the rhythm section of Basie, Jones, Page, and Greene. Benny Goodman's band (Bottom) was a wartime mix, but he had the young and shimmering Peggy Lee to do *Why Don't You Do Right?* and such disparate members as pianist Jess Stacy, trombonist Miff Mole (fixing slide), bass saxist Joe Rushton, and drummer Louis Bellson to do *Bugle Call Rag*.

Jammin' the Blues will most likely remain the greatest film to depict jazz musicians in their natural habitat. Brilliantly photographed and directed by Gjon Mili, whose New York jam sessions were legendary during the war years, and edited by former MGM film editor Norman Granz, then just starting his "Jazz at the Philharmonic" concerts, this 1944 Warner Brothers release captured some key players at the peak of their careers. Lester Young, Harry Edison, and Illinois Jacquet all solo brilliantly, and a well-integrated dance sequence by Marie Bryant and Archie Savage, and Marie Bryant's vocal of *On the Sunny Side of the Street,* are all part of a piece—the only time Hollywood kept its hands off!

(L) Ann Miller served up another batch of big-band swing in Columbia's *Jam Session* (1944). Even Jan Garber, the idol of the airwaves, had gone into swing that year. Charlie Barnet's band was featured doing *Cherokee* (on the reservation and with teepee), but his black players on the sound-track—Al Killian, Peanuts Holland, Howard McGhee, Trummy Young, and Oscar Pettiford—were replaced by white musicians on camera, in line with the prevalent racist policy. Chubby Jackson was the other bassist, and Ralph Burns was on piano.

(Top, R and L) Astor Pictures' *Caldonia* (1945) was an all-black musical quickie turned out to cash in on saxophonist-showman Louis Jordan's hit recording. Jordan, primarily a great altoist, is seen holding a tenor (L) for some obscure reason. Other numbers featuring his Tympany Five included *Buzz Me* and *Honey Chile,* with Al Morgan on bass (extreme L) and Razz Mitchell on drums (not shown). (R) *Ovoutie O'Rooney* (Astor Pictures, 1945) displayed two of the maddest musical cutups of the 1940s—Bulee "Slim" Gaillard (L), who played piano (often with the backs of his hands!) and guitar and sang; and Sherman "Scatman" Crothers (M), who played drums, ukulele, and guitar and sang—and Bam Brown (R), a muggin' bassist.

Harry James was one of the great trumpeters of his generation, and he might have been a great jazzman if commerce and his "circus" vibrato hadn't gotten in the way. Even so, he was widely copied and at the height of his popularity when he made *Best Foot Forward* for MGM in 1943, in which June Allyson had her first leading role. James (L) answers comedienne Nancy Walker. In 1947 Astor Pictures released an all-black Stepin Fetchit feature, *I Ain't Gonna Open That Door,* with Earl Bostic's hot little band: (L to R) Danny Barker, George Jenkins, Huck King, Roger Jones, Ted Barnett (tenor man sitting in on piano), ex-Ellington songstress Joya Sherrill, and Earl, a mad alto man.

Jazz fans eagerly awaited the film *New Orleans,* which was shot in Hollywood and New Orleans in 1946 and released in 1947. This talent-loaded film, made in forty-three days, featured Louis Armstrong (Top and Bottom, L, and Middle, second from R) and Billie Holiday (Top, L, and Bottom), as well as hand-picked New Orleans veterans (Middle, L to R) Zutty Singleton, Red Callender, Kid Ory, Charlie Beal, Bud Scott, (Louis), and Barney Bigard; Woody Herman's First Herd (with Sonny Berman, Bill Harris, and Flip Phillips); and Meade Lux Lewis doing thirteen numbers, including *West End Blues, Buddy Bolden's Blues, Do You Know What It Means to Miss New Orleans?* (sung by Billie, as the maid Endie, and then with Louis), *Dippermouth Blues, Mahogany Hall Stomp, Honky Tonk Train,* and others. The trouble was the film, directed by Arthur Lubin for United Artists (his later credits would be the Francis the talking mule films) and scripted by a reputed jazz lover, novelist Elliot Paul *(The Last Time I Saw Paris). New Orleans* starred the suspect talents of Arturo De Cordova, who continually fixed his tie, and Dorothy Patrick, who constantly checked her makeup, instead of letting the music, still in full flower, tell the story. The only sequence shot in New Orleans—George Lewis and Jim Robinson with Kid Howard's Brass Band (Top, R)—was deleted. Few of the tunes were played through, and Armstrong's tantalizingly beautiful music (in the small-band setting he preferred) is shown only in part. On late-night television, most of the music is eliminated.

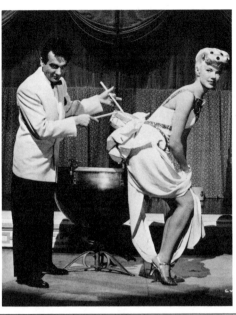

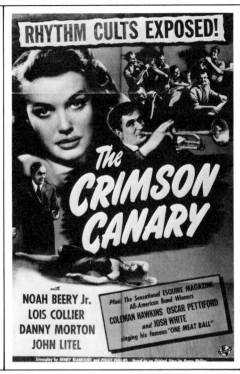

Woody Herman's band was at its peak in 1945 when he and comedian Pinky Lee (L) did a bit in *Earl Carroll's Vanities* for Republic with Dennis O'Keefe in the title role. *Apple Honey* was Woody's feature. Drummer Dave Tough and trumpeter Neal Hefti are to the left of Herman. (M) Gene Krupa snares a chorus lovely in *George White's Scandals* (RKO, 1945). Krupa's band did something called *Bolero in the Jungle* in this forgettable backstage musical. (R) *The Crimson Canary* (Universal, 1945) was a B-film mystery of jam sessions and murder. The *Esquire* magazine All-American Band winners were featured: Coleman Hawkins, Howard McGhee, Sir Charles Thompson, Oscar Pettiford, and Denzil Best. Josh White sang his hit *One Meat Ball*.

Stan Kenton's band with vocalist June Christy (second from L) and a new vocal group, the Pastels, made a two-reel short for RKO sometime before disbanding in May 1947. Saxes included Vido Musso, Boots Mussulli, and Bob Cooper (front row, extreme L, second from L, and fourth from L); Kai Winding (third from R), trombone; Eddie Safranski, bass; Shelly Manne, drums; and Buddy Childers, Ray Wetzel, and Chico Alvarez, trumpets (top row, second and third from L and extreme R).

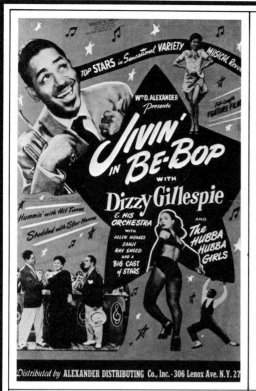

(L) Dizzy Gillespie's only feature film, *Jivin' in Bebop* (1947), was a low-budget, all-black feature made on 52nd Street with vocalist Helen Humes. It showed off Diz's fine big band on *Salt Peanuts, Shaw 'Nuff, Oop Bop Sh'Bam, Dizzy Atmosphere, One Bass Hit, Things to Come,* and other numbers. (M) Kirk Douglas as Bix Beiderbecke as played by Harry James! Michael Curtiz directed Warner's *Young Man with a Horn* (1949) from the Dorothy Baker novel. The novel was the trouble. Your friendly barroom pianist, Hoagy Carmichael, and soundtrack musicians Willie Smith, Babe Russin, Corky Corcoran, Jimmy Zito, and Nick Fatool did what they could; it wasn't enough. (R) Josh Binney's *Killer Diller* (1948) was the end of the road for black features, as well as the end for Andy Kirk, who gave up his band that year. Popular entertainers Dusty Fletcher, Butterfly McQueen, and Jackie "Moms" Mabley were joined by the King Cole Trio. Numbers included *Ain't Misbehavin'* and *Now He Tells Me.*

Republic's *Hit Parade of 1947* starred Eddie Albert, Constance Moore, Joan Edwards, Gil Lamb, William Frawley, Roy Rogers and Trigger, the Sons of the Pioneers, *and* Woody Herman's fantastic First Herd and the Woodchoppers: (L to R) Sonny Berman, Joe Mondragon, Red Norvo, Bill Harris, Chuck Wayne, Flip Phillips, (Woody).

Columbia

Paul Whiteman
AND HIS
Orchestra
Waltz Vocal refrain
by Johnny Fulton

IT HAPPENED IN MONTEREY
(*Aconteció En Monterey*)
(Wayne and Rose)
Talkie Hit from Universal Picture
"The King Of Jazz"
2163-D
(149811)

VE

VICTOR
For best results
use Victor Needles   22528-B

RING DEM BELLS—Fox Trot
(From RADIO picture, "Check and Double Check")
(Ellington-Mills)

Duke Ellington and His Orchestra
with vocal refrain

VE

VICTOR
Not Licensed for
Radio Broadcast   24622-A

EBONY RHAPSODY—Fox Trot
(From Paramount film "Murder at the Vanities")
(*Rapsodia Negra*)
(Arthur Johnston-Sam Coslow)

Duke Ellington and his Orchestra
Vocal refrain by Ivie Anderson

VICTOR
For best results
use Victor Needles   26790-B

LOVE OF MY LIFE—Fox Trot
(From the Paramount film "Second Chorus")
(*Amor de mi Vida*)
(Johnny Mercer-Artie Shaw)

Artie Shaw and his Orchestra
Vocal refrain by Anita Boyer

DECCA
REG U S PAT OFF
MANUFACTURED IN U.S.A. BY DECCA RECORDS, INC.

(DLA 2411)   Vocal
with Orchestra

THE WAITER AND THE PORTER
AND THE UPSTAIRS MAID
From Paramount Picture "Birth Of The Blues"
(Johnny Mercer)

BING CROSBY
Mary Martin and Jack Teagarden
With
Jack Teagarden and His Orchestra

3970 A

DECCA
REG U S PAT OFF
MANUFACTURED BY DECCA RECORDS, INC., NEW YORK, U.S.A.

(70028)   Fox Trot
Vocal Choruses by
Bob Eberly and
Helen O'Connell

TANGERINE
From Paramount Picture "The Fleet's In"
(Victor Schertzinger-Johnny Mercer)

JIMMY DORSEY
And His Orchestra

4123 A

DECCA
REG U S PAT OFF
MANUFACTURED BY DECCA RECORDS, INC., NEW YORK, U.S.A.

(70093)   Instrumental
Fox Trot

BLUES IN THE NIGHT—Part 1
(My Mama Done Tol' Me)
From Warner Bros. Picture "Blues In The Night"
(Harold Arlen-Johnny Mercer)

JIMMIE LUNCEFORD
And His Orchestra

4125 A

VICTOR
For best results use
RCA Victor Needles   27869-A

I'LL TAKE TALLULAH—Fox Trot
(From MGM film "Ship Ahoy")
(E. Y. Harburg-Burton Lane)

Tommy Dorsey and his Orch.
Vocal refrain by Tommy Dorsey, Frank Sinatra
and The Pied Pipers

BLUEBIRD
For best results use
RCA Victor Needles   B-11230-B

CHATTANOOGA CHOO CHOO—Fox Trot
(From the 20th Century-Fox film
"Sun Valley Serenade")
(Mack Gordon-Harry Warren)
Glenn Miller and his Orchestra
Vocal refrain by Tex Beneke and
The Four Modernaires

VICTOR
For best results use
RCA Victor Needles   27934-A

(I've Got a Gal in)
KALAMAZOO—Fox Trot
(From the 20th Century-Fox film "Orchestra Wives")
(Mack Gordon-Harry Warren)
Glenn Miller and his Orchestra
Vocal refrain by Tex Beneke, Marion Hutton
and The Modernaires

DECCA
REG U S PAT OFF
MANUFACTURED BY DECCA RECORDS, INC., NEW YORK, U.S.A.

L.3205   Fox Trot
Vocal Chorus by
Louis Jordan

IS YOU IS OR IS YOU AIN'T
(Ma' Baby)
From Universal Picture "Follow The Boys"
(Billy Austin-Louis Jordan)

LOUIS JORDAN
And His Tympany Five

8659 B

RCA VICTOR
REG U S PAT OFF MARCAS REGISTRADAS
For best results use
RCA Victor Needles   20-3064-A

A SONG WAS BORN
(from the Samuel Goldwyn picture "A Song Is Born")
(Don Raye-Gene DePaul)

Louis Armstrong and his All Stars
Vocal refrain by Louis Armstrong
and Jack Teagarden

Swing, Mr. Charlie!
1932-1948

"BENNY GOODMAN and his 'Let's Dance' band are a truly great outfit—fine arrangements and musicians who are together all the time—they phrase together, they bite together, they swing together. And there are plenty of individual stand-outs—Papa Benny's clarinet, Helen Ward's vocals, Gene Krupa's drums, Frank Froeba's piano, Jack Lacey's trombone, Pee Wee Erwin's trumpet, Arthur Rollini's tenor sax, ad infinitum...wonderful."

—George T. Simon, *Metronome*, March, 1935

"Swing is and was the way a jazz number is played, the syncopated lift a performer or ensemble gets into jazz performances" (Duke Ellington). "Swing is complete and inspired freedom on rhythmic interpretation" (Gene Krupa). "Swing is syncopated syncopation" (Jess Stacy). "Swing is a band swinging when its collective improvisation is rhythmically integrated" (John Hammond). "Swing is feeling an increase in tempo though you're still playing at the same tempo" (Wingy Manone). "Swing is something that you have to feel; a sensation that can be conveyed to others" (Glenn Miller). "Swing is my idea of how a tune should go" (Louis Armstrong).

The Swing Era began in the middle of the Great Depression. Everything in American life was changed socially and economically, including the music business. Without astute management and/or a strong affiliation with a leading nightclub, as both Duke Ellington and Cab Calloway enjoyed with Irving Mills and the Cotton Club, and as Earl Hines did with the Grand Terrace in Chicago, the jazz-oriented bands found work scarce. Fletcher Henderson lost his job at Roseland Ballroom to the softly swinging band of Claude Hopkins, who featured the high tenor vocals of Orlando Robeson on treacly ballads. Don Redman's fine new band had to feature the baritone vocals of Harlan Lattimore, the dusky Bing Crosby, to be "commercial." Jazz stalwarts like Ben Pollack and Red Nichols found their only work on the road.

Gone were the days when Luis Russell's band shouted with a barrage of fiery solos by Red Allen and J.C. Higginbotham, or sat around the Saratoga Club while its owner, Harlem numbers king Casper Holstein, regaled them with stories of his not-so-innocent past. Holstein walked away from his club, went to jail, and Russell found himself on the road playing increasingly commercial arrangements. Chick Webb and Benny Carter had to disband several times.

In the midst of this carnage, one band, the Casa Loma (formerly one of Jean Goldkette's), used precision arrangements by Gene Gifford, Clarence Hutchenrider's clarinet, and trumpeter Sonny Dunham's high notes to win the college crowd at proms. They soon found themselves at the Glen Island Casino, the Essex House, and other plush locations with radio wires.

Casa Loma's success prompted a former Ben Pollack clarinet star, Benny Goodman, to organize a new band with top musicians who wanted to play good music, not what the broadcasters or music publishers dictated. After leaving the security of his studio work, he scuffled throughout 1934, with enthusiastic backing (and some recordings) by John Hammond and a young MCA booker named Willard Alexander. But the real breakthrough was afforded by NBC's "Let's Dance" program, which enabled Goodman to buy special arrangements from Fletcher Henderson, Benny Carter, Spud Murphy, and several others. Many of these scores were good pop tunes, but few in the East heard them because NBC scheduled Goodman's segment after midnight. His one-nighters found small audiences who knew nothing about the band, until a cross-country tour revealed that audiences in California knew his music because of the broadcast time difference and were waiting for him.

The Palomar Ballroom in Los Angeles was packed, but Goodman, wary of failure, played just stocks for an hour or two. Realizing the end was near, he decided to go out in a blaze of glory and began playing the Henderson and Murphy scores to wildly enthusiastic dancers who crowded up to the bandstand. His engagement was extended several months and bookings began coming in. He was now billed by MCA as the Swing Master and an important Victor artist. The Swing Era had begun.

Magazines and newspapers wanted to know what this "swing" was all about. Musicians had been swinging for years and celebrated that fact on records by 1929 (Jelly Roll Morton's *Georgia Swing*; Duke Ellington's *Saratoga Swing*) from coast to coast. Prominent leaders were asked for definitions, none of them satisfactory (see opening quotes). Duke Ellington wrote the eventual anthem, *It Don't Mean A Thing (If It Ain't Got That Swing)* in 1932.

Jimmie Lunceford (whose highly drilled men waved their horns to and fro, fanning derbies on stage), the Dorsey Brothers, Artie Shaw, Glenn Miller, Hudson-DeLange, Harry James, Gene Krupa, and dozens of others all got on the bandwagon. Big bands were the thing. Everybody wanted some of Goodman's success.

The euphoria lasted into the war, when the draft began taking too many key soloists for the best bands to maintain their musical identity. A 20 percent amusement tax, gasoline rationing, a recording ban from 1942 to '44, and the rise of singers to stardom (Frank Sinatra, Dick Haymes, Perry Como, and others) began taking some of the money away from the bands. Arrangers didn't help; their scores became increasingly complex, demanding larger bands of up to twenty men and moving away from dance to concert-oriented music. World War II, like the Depression, changed everything. A new cycle was starting. Swing was dead.

In October 1933, with a slackening of studio work, Benny Goodman began recording for John Hammond for a sponsored series on English Columbia (also released here). Two dates featured Jack Teagarden's *I Gotta Right to Sing the Blues* and *Texas Tea Party;* there were also dates with Ethel Waters, Bessie Smith (her last), and, under Goodman's own name, Billie Holiday's first recording, *Your Mother's Son-in-Law.* A February 1934 date featured Mildred Bailey and Coleman Hawkins on *Junk Man* and *Ol' Pappy,* and another in May included Teddy Wilson, piano, on *As Long As I Live* and *Breakfast Ball.* After a decade of every possible kind of band experience in nightclubs, theaters, hotels, and ballrooms and more than four hundred recordings, Goodman's professional experience was at its peak, the right time, he felt, to form an orchestra of tip-top musicians to play specially written arrangements. After holding several auditions, he took his new band to Billy Rose's Music Hall on June 1, 1934.

Fletcher Henderson (Top, L) lost ground to Claude Hopkins's, Don Redman's, and other bands during the Depression. Despite this, the very best players wanted the honor of playing under his baton and often turned down better offers. In March 1934 the Henderson band recorded *Harlem Madness* and three other sides for Victor. (Bottom, L to R) Red Allen, Keg Johnson, Joe Thomas, Claude Jones, Russell Smith, singer Charles Holland, Horace Henderson, Walter Johnson, Fletcher Henderson, Bernard Addison, Hilton Jefferson, John Kirby, Russell Procope, Buster Bailey, Coleman Hawkins. Right after this, Coleman Hawkins left to work in Europe. His replacement, Lester Young, displeased the rest of the saxes with his unusual style and light sound and was replaced by Ben Webster. In September Decca recorded such classics as *Down South Camp Meeting, Big John Special, Happy As the Day Is Long, Rug Cutter's Swing,* and *Wrappin' It Up.* Two months later the band broke up, and Benny Goodman's new band was soon playing Henderson's scores on network radio. By 1936 Henderson had assembled another great band (Top, R), with Roy Eldridge (second from L), Chu Berry, Sid Catlett, and Buster Bailey; played at length in the Grand Terrace in Chicago; and recorded a big hit, *Christopher Columbus,* on Vocalion; but he failed to follow up by going on the road and soon lost all these men. Three years later he was playing piano for Benny Goodman.

Duke Ellington (Top, L) summed up the accomplishments of all the great black bands in the past five years when he wrote *It Don't Mean a Thing If It Ain't Got That Swing,* sung by his new singer Ivie Anderson (Top, R) in 1932. Although his position seemed unassailable, Ellington saw the difficulties black bands were experiencing—the days of the big tippers were gone, jazz was having a hard time; to an extent this was reflected in many of the excellent new recordings like *Blue Tune* and *Blue Harlem.* Bubber Miley died in 1932, and Ellington's fine band, augmented by trombonist Lawrence Brown that year, concentrated on plumbing his rich harmonies. Longer compositions like *Creole Rhapsody* and tunes like *Sophisticated Lady* and *Solitude* were being written. His last Cotton Club show was with Ethel Waters in 1933; then a successful tour of England renewed his confidence that a larger audience than he imagined was receptive to his music. Two movies in Hollywood in 1934, the cross-country train-ride echoes on *Daybreak Express,* the first Southern tour, and at years's end he was in the Oriental Theatre, Chicago: (Bottom, L to R) Wellman Braud, sb; Otto Hardwicke, as; (Ellington); Lawrence Brown, tb; Joe Nanton, tb; Rex Stewart, ct; Arthur Whetsol, tp; Sonny Greer, dms; Harry Carney, bar sax; Barney Bigard, clt; Johnny Hodges, as; Juan Tizol, vtb; Fred Guy, gtr.

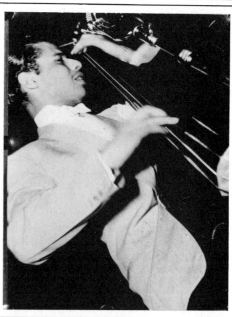

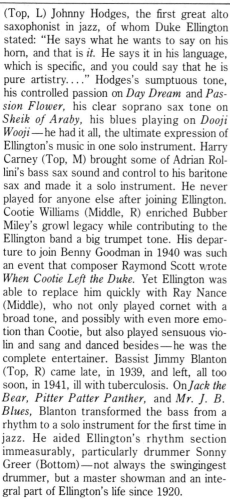

(Top, L) Johnny Hodges, the first great alto saxophonist in jazz, of whom Duke Ellington stated: "He says what he wants to say on his horn, and that is *it*. He says it in his language, which is specific, and you could say that he is pure artistry...." Hodges's sumptuous tone, his controlled passion on *Day Dream* and *Passion Flower*, his clear soprano sax tone on *Sheik of Araby*, his blues playing on *Dooji Wooji*—he had it all, the ultimate expression of Ellington's music in one solo instrument. Harry Carney (Top, M) brought some of Adrian Rollini's bass sax sound and control to his baritone sax and made it a solo instrument. He never played for anyone else after joining Ellington. Cootie Williams (Middle, R) enriched Bubber Miley's growl legacy while contributing to the Ellington band a big trumpet tone. His departure to join Benny Goodman in 1940 was such an event that composer Raymond Scott wrote *When Cootie Left the Duke*. Yet Ellington was able to replace him quickly with Ray Nance (Middle), who not only played cornet with a broad tone, and possibly with even more emotion than Cootie, but also played sensuous violin and sang and danced besides—he was the complete entertainer. Bassist Jimmy Blanton (Top, R) came late, in 1939, and left, all too soon, in 1941, ill with tuberculosis. On *Jack the Bear, Pitter Patter Panther,* and *Mr. J. B. Blues,* Blanton transformed the bass from a rhythm to a solo instrument for the first time in jazz. He aided Ellington's rhythm section immeasurably, particularly drummer Sonny Greer (Bottom)—not always the swingingest drummer, but a master showman and an integral part of Ellington's life since 1920.

When Jean Goldkette's organization was dissolving, one of his bands, the Orange Blossoms, broke away and renamed itself the Casa Loma Orchestra, after its 1927 stay at the famed Toronto castle. They played ballrooms throughout the East like Roseland in New York, where Okeh recorded their up-tempo flag-wavers *China Girl* and *San Sue Strut* in 1929. Endless rehearsals by arranger Gene Gifford and trombonist Billy Rauch polished their ensemble work, and when singer-saxist Kenny Sargent joined in 1931, their ballads *For You, Under a Blanket of Blue,* and *It's the Talk of the Town* won them a large, devoted following among college dancers. Trumpeter-trombonist Sonny Dunham (Top, L) joined in 1932 and became the first high-note player of the decade; his playing was important to such up-tempo instrumentals as *Maniac's Ball, Wild Goose Chase,* and *Black Jazz.* When CBS broadcast their playing at a Lawrenceville prom in 1933 (a first), they attracted an offer from Glen Island Casino. That was followed by a two-year run at New York's Essex House Hotel on Central Park South, 1933–34. Casa Loma had the field to itself, even after Benny Goodman, Tommy Dorsey, and Artie Shaw surpassed them, they never lost their popularity. Their brass section after Sonny Dunham left: (Top, R, L to R) Billy Rauch, Walter Smith, Grady Watts, Pee Wee Hunt, Frankie Zullo, and Fritz Hummel. (Bottom) On top of Radio City, where they were playing the Rainbow Room in 1937, the key men were Pee Wee Hunt (eighth from R), vocalist Kenny Sargent (seventh from L), and clarinetist Clarence Hutchenrider (fourth from L); leader Glen Gray (eighth from L), at six feet five inches, was an imposing leader.

cab calloway

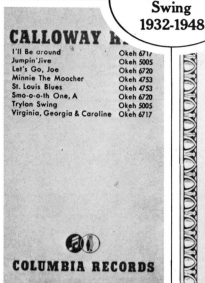

CALLOWAY H...

I'll Be around	Okeh 671?
Jumpin' Jive	Okeh 5005
Let's Go, Joe	Okeh 6720
Minnie The Moocher	Okeh 4753
St. Louis Blues	Okeh 4753
Smo-o-o-th One, A	Okeh 6720
Trylon Swing	Okeh 5005
Virginia, Georgia & Caroline	Okeh 6717

COLUMBIA RECORDS

Sampson Buttie

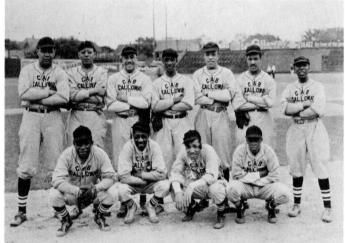

Cab Calloway was such a sensation in the thirties with his singing and showmanship that eventually he could afford to hire fine players like Chu Berry (Bottom, L) and Cozy Cole, drums (Bottom, M), and field a baseball team (Middle), complete with uniforms, mixing semipros with bandsmen like Benny Payne (extreme L), Claude Jones (third from L), Milt Hinton (fifth from L), and Garvin Bushell (fifth from R). With them his band made musical history on Okeh records: *Ghost of a Chance, Ebony Silhouette, Pickin' the Cabbage,* and *Jonah Joins the Cab,* which showed off the talents of Jonah Jones, Dizzy Gillespie, and Tyree Glenn, among others. Don Redman (Bottom, R) was crazy about baseball too. He used his own sidemen (Top, R) exclusively in 1934: (L to R) Shirley Clay, tp; (Redman); Harlan Lattimore, vo; Manzie Johnson, dms; Sidney DeParis, tp; Quentin Jackson, tb; Gene Simon, tb; Bob Carroll, ts; and Benny Morton, tb. They were responsible for Redman's fine Brunswick recordings of *Chant of the Weed, Shakin' the African* (Red Allen substituted for DeParis on this), *I Got Rhythm* with its famous trombone trio chorus, *Nagasaki,* and others. Redman gave it up in 1941, declaring: "I'd had the bright lights, the star billing; now give me the money...." He opened an arranging office on Broadway and wrote for Fred Waring, Paul Whiteman, Jimmy Dorsey, Count Basie, and others. He led other bands later.

THE NEW KING OF SYNCOPATION

Jimmie Lunceford

AND HIS ORCHESTRA

New Edition 1934-35-36

Jimmy Lunceford rose from leading a territory band in Memphis called the Chickasaw Syncopators in the late twenties to leading a highly polished, articulate, and disciplined band whose popularity after its Cotton Club debut in 1934 rivaled Cab Calloway's and Duke Ellington's. A college graduate and music teacher, Lunceford knew his band could not compete with Ellington's for originality and sound or with Fletcher Henderson's for swing, so with saxophonist Willie Smith (Middle, extreme R), trumpeter-arranger Sy Oliver (L), and pianist Eddie Wilcox, he stressed showmanship and clean, precise section work. His unusual treatment of long-forgotten pop tunes such as *Rain* (1924) and *Jealous* (1925) and originals like Oliver's *Dream of You* with its superb dynamics attracted a huge following. At the Cotton Club (Top, R) they were the favorite band and in theaters (Bottom) did turn-away business. (L to R) Sy Oliver, Paul Webster, Russell Bowles, Eddie Tompkins, Eddie Durham, Elmer Crumbley, Eddie Wilcox, Lunceford, Jimmy Crawford, Willie Smith, LaForest Dent, Al Norris, Joe Thomas, Moses Allen, and Earl Caruthers. Their Decca recordings sold so well that the company lost all interest in Fletcher Henderson, Earl Hines, and Claude Hopkins and dropped them.

Lunceford's brass were the most powerful in jazz: (Top, R, L to R) Crumbley, Bowles, Durham, Webster, Oliver, and Tompkins. Oliver and Tompkins left in 1940 and were replaced by (Top, L) Snooky Young and Gerald Wilson. Young's and Willie Smith's solos on *Uptown Blues* on Vocalion attracted so much attention that Lunceford, who had his own plane (Middle, L), used it as his theme song. His glee club— (Middle, R, L to R) Willie Smith, Trummy Young, Joe Thomas, and Gerald Wilson—sang *Ain't She Sweet* and *'Tain't What You Do (It's the Way That You Do It),* and the band made *Cheatin' on Me, Lonesome Road,* and the incredible two-part *Dinah,* but by 1942 all the key personalities but Joe Thomas had gone. Jimmy Crawford's loss was inestimable (Middle); many felt him to be the equal of Chick Webb and Jo Jones for big-band drumming. The load fell to Eddie Wilcox, who began writing crowd-pleasing arrangements like *Meditation from Thais* and *Holiday for Strings,* but it mattered little; Lunceford's day was past. There were some fine moments on records like *Moonbeams* on Manor, the year Lunceford died of a heart attack in Seaside, Oregon, but the big-band era was just about over. Thomas and Wilcox kep the band together for a year or two longer and then went their separate ways.

Tommy and Jimmy Dorsey (Top, L, R, and L) were well known for their many records, 1928–34; their past affiliations with Paul Whiteman's and other bands; and their radio work with Bing Crosby, the Boswell Sisters, and Ethel Waters (Top, R), among others. Their band, partially organized by arranger Glenn Miller, was pitched to Bing Crosby's baritone with three trombones, one trumpet, one alto and two tenor saxes, and rhythm. Its unusually deep, rich sound made its many Decca records like *Honeysuckle Rose, Tail Spin,* and *Stop, Look and Listen* sound fuller than they really were. (Bottom, L to R) Don Mattison, Ray McKinley, Skeets Herfurt, Bob Crosby, George Thow, Jack Stacy, Kay Weber, Glenn Miller, Bobby Van Eps, Jimmy Dorsey, Delmar Kaplan, Roc Hillman, Tommy Dorsey. Despite their successes at Ben Marden's Riviera, the Palais Royal (Top, L), and Glen Island Casino, the brothers did not get along. Jimmy drank heavily then, and Tommy drove the band relentlessly in his quest for musical perfection. Glenn Miller left to join Ray Noble, and Tommy walked off the bandstand when Jimmy questioned his choice of tempo. Jimmy had to take over.

BENNY GOODMAN'S
SENSATIONAL SWING BAND
THE TALK OF THE MUSIC WORLD

CARNEGIE HALL
Sunday Evening, January 16th, at 8:30

S. HUROK

presents

(by arrangement with Music Corporation of America)

BENNY GOODMAN
and his
SWING ORCHESTRA

I.

"Don't Be That Way" .... *Edgar Sampson*
"Sometimes I'm Happy" (from "Hit the Deck")..........*Irving Caesar &*
Vincent Youmans
"One O'clock Jump" ....*William (Count) Basie*

II.

TWENTY YEARS OF JAZZ
"Sensation Rag" (as played c. 1917 by the Dixieland Jazz Band)
E. B. Edwards

PROGRAM CONTINUED ON SECOND PAGE FOLLOWING

(Opposite Page) Benny Goodman's Music Hall band recorded *Take My Word, Bugle Call Rag,* and others for Columbia in 1934 before closing in mid-October. Six weeks later they were playing on NBC's new three-hour dance program (Top, M), alternating with (Top, R, M and extreme R) Kel Murray and Xavier Cugat. Singer Helen Ward (Top, L) who auditioned with Goodman for the Music Hall job, joined the sponsored program, which budgeted for special arrangements. Goodman hired Spud Murphy, Fletcher Henderson, Joe Lippman, Dean Kincaide, Benny Carter, and Edgar Sampson and switched to Victor in April 1935 to record *Blue Skies, Sometimes I'm Happy, King Porter Stomp,* and the first trio sides with Teddy Wilson and Gene Krupa (Above, Middle, L), including *After You've Gone.* The band went on tour for ten months, playing ballrooms like Elitch's Gardens in Denver (Middle, L) with (L to R) Jess Stacy, p; Dick Clark, ts; Hymie Shertzer, as; Harry Goodman, sb; Gene Krupa, dms; Joe Harris, tb-vo; Jack Lacey, tb; Helen Ward, vo; Goodman, clt; Bunny Berigan, tp; Bill DePew, as; Nate Kazebier, tp; Art Rollini, ts; Ralph Muzzillo, tp; Red Ballard, tb, and Allen Reuss, gtr. Elitch's patrons preferred sweet music, so Goodman played stock arrangements. The morale of the band was low when they began at the Palomar (Middle, R), August 21. After playing two sets to an unresponsive crowd, Goodman, realizing his bandleading career was about to end, decided to go out in style. He wrote: "I called out some of our big Fletcher Henderson arrangements for the next set, and the boys seemed to get the idea. From the moment I kicked them off, they dug in with some of the best playing I'd heard since we left New York. To our complete amazement half the crowd stopped dancing and came surging around the bandstand. That was the moment that decided things for me.... That first big roar from the crowd was one of the sweetest sounds I ever heard in my life...." Now billed as a swing band, the group had its month-long booking at Chicago's Congress Hotel (Bottom) extended to six; and a new radio sponsor, Elgin Watch Company, took them back to New York, after Teddy Wilson made his debut with the trio at a concert in April 1936. Earl Hines's arranger, Jimmy Mundy, joined, contributing *Madhouse, House Hop,* and *Swingtime in the Rockies* to the library. They returned to the Palomar in 1936, made their first movie, and added Lionel Hampton on vibes to make the Goodman Quartet's *More Than You Know* and *Lady Be Good.* Goodman's brass team became the most powerful when within four months in 1936–37 Ziggy Elman and Harry James (Bottom, L, extreme L and M) joined. Swing achieved its official sanction with the crowds dancing in the aisles at the Paramount Theatre, the twelve-inch *Sing, Sing, Sing* recording, the Hotel Pennsylvania, and the culmination, the 1938 Carnegie Hall concert (Top, R).

When Goodman switched to Columbia Records in 1939, only Lionel Hampton (Top, R) remained of his old stars. He was joined by Fletcher Henderson (whose own band had split up) and new guitarist Charlie Christian (Top, L, extreme L with Goodman and his guitarist Arnold Covarrubias) on Goodman's Sextet recordings *Rose Room* and *Stardust,* adding new dimensions to guitar sound and style that the next generation would follow. New members (Middle, R) included Johnny Guarnieri, piano (third from L); George Auld, tenor sax (fourth from L and Middle, L, with Charlie Christian); Cootie Williams, trumpet (third from R); Billy Butterfield, trumpet (second from R); and Lou McGarity, trombone (extreme R). Williams and Auld joined Goodman and Christian in the Sextet after Hampton left to start his own band in 1940, making *Airmail Special, On the Alamo,* and *Breakfast Feud;* new arranger Eddie Sauter contributed his adventurous harmonies and dynamics to *Moonlight on the Ganges, Superman,* and *Clarinet a la King.* Vocalist Peggy Lee (Bottom, L) replaced Helen Forrest in 1941 and made *Let's Do It, Why Don't You Do Right?,* and *My Old Flame.* During the war Goodman's band underwent many personnel changes. Stan Getz (Bottom, M) joined for several months, 1945–46, soloing on *Swing Angel* and *Rattle and Roll.* Wardell Gray and Billy Bauer, guitar (Bottom, R), were part of his 1948 Sextet, which did not record because of a ban that year.

Drummer Chick Webb (Top, L) struggled to overcome tuberculosis of the spine, which left him hunchbacked and eventually killed him, and the loss of his stars Johnny Hodges and Cootie Williams, who left for other bands. His band was hitting its stride, the fiercest competitor in the Savoy Ballroom with *Stompin' at the Savoy, Let's Get Together,* and others, when vocalist Ella Fitzgerald (Top, L) was added in 1935. Gradually her singing overshadowed fine instrumentals such as *Blue Lou, Liza,* and *Spinnin' the Webb,* which showcased Bobby Stark (Middle, R). Alto man and singer Louis Jordan (Middle) left to start his own band in 1938, not long after the band was in Chicago: (Bottom, L to R) Wayman Carver, ts-flute; Mario Bauza, tp; Bill Johnson, gtr; Beverly Peer, sb; Tommy Fulford, p; Taft Jordan, tp; Webb; Nat Story, tb; Jordan, as; Charlie Linton, vo; Bardu Ali, dir; Teddy McRae, ts; and Chauncey Haughton, as-clt. Buddy Rich aptly described Webb: "...a tiny man... and this big face, and big, stiff shoulders. He sat way up on a kind of throne and used twenty-eight-inch bass drums which had special pedals for his feet and he had those old gooseneck cymbal holders. Every beat was like a bell." Ella Fitzgerald's hits kept the band together after Webb died in 1939.

Jimmy Dorsey (Top, L) took over the Dorsey Brothers band, finishing the season at Glen Island Casino, and continued on Decca Records under his own name, his first important hit being *Parade of the Milk Bottle Caps*. Bing Crosby invited him and his band to join the "Kraft Music Hall" radio program in California. After the show was over he toured with (Bottom, L to R) Fud Livingston, tenor sax and arranger; Roc Hillman, guitar; George Thow, trumpet; Skeets Herfurt, tenor sax; Bobby Van Eps, piano; Jack Stacey, alto sax; Martha Tilton, vocals; Jim Taft, bass; Ray McKinley, drums; Bob Eberly, vocals; Joe Yukl, Don Mattison, and Bobby Byrne, trombones; and Toots Camarata, trumpet and arranger. Tilton joined Benny Goodman later that year, but by 1939 Helen O'Connell (Top, R) joined Bob Eberly, and their duets on *Amapola, Yours, Green Eyes*, and *Tangerine* were highly successful. Dorsey's records of *John Silver, Dusk in Upper Sandusky, Charleston Alley*, and *Deep Purple* were all well regarded, but his biggest successes came during the war when no recordings were made and his band rivaled Tommy's for musicianship. Decca recorded fewer instrumentals with Jimmy Dorsey than with any other name band, despite his many good players like Herb Ellis, Red Rodney, Jimmy Guiffre, Babe Russin, and Karl Kiffe.

Tommy Dorsey (Top, L) revamped Joe Haymes's band and by 1936 was in the Commodore Hotel with (Middle, R, L to R) Les Jenkins, Joe Bauer, Axel Stordahl, Steve Lipkins, Walt Mercurio, Max Kaminsky, (Dorsey), Dave Tough, Joe Dixon, Fred Stulce, Carmen Mastren, Bud Freeman, Edythe Wright, Gene Traxler, Clyde Rounds, Jack Leonard, and Dick Jones. Stordahl, Mastren (Top, M, with guitar), and Paul Weston wrote most of his arrangements like *At the Codfish Ball, Song of India,* and *Marie* (which came from the Sunset Royal Orchestra) with scores coming in later from Larry Clinton such as *Dipsy Doodle* and *Satan Takes a Holiday.* At the Texas Centennial, 1936: (Top, R, L to R) Kaminsky, Leonard, Stordahl, Tough (also Bottom, L), and Freeman. Later drummer Buddy Rich (Middle, L) and trumpeter Ziggy Elman drove the forties band, which featured Sy Oliver's arrangements of *Chicago, Easy Does It, Yes, Indeed, Well, Git It!, Not So Quiet, Please, Sunny Side of the Street,* and *Opus Number One.* Oliver emphasized the same kind of styling he'd done for Jimmie Lunceford in the thirties, and coupled with the popularity of Frank Sinatra, 1940–42, Dorsey's was one of the hottest bands in the business. Charlie Shavers, trumpet, and Louis Bellson, drums (Bottom, R, second from R and extreme R), were part of his postwar band.

Singer Bob Crosby became leader of Ben Pollack's old band in 1935 with Gil Rodin as director. Their first hit on Decca was *In a Little Gypsy Tea Room,* which took them to the Hotel Lexington (Middle, R) in 1936. (L to R) Nappy Lamare, gtr; Ward Silloway, tb; Mark Bennett, tb; Gil Bowers, p; Matty Matlock, clt; Bobby Haggart, sb; Bob Crosby; Yank Lawson, tp; Gil Rodin, as-dir; Eddie Bergman, vln; Ray Bauduc, dms; Eddie Miller, ts; Noni Bernardi, as; Andy Ferretti, tp. Arranging was done by Haggart and Matlock and saxist Dean Kincaide, who played in the band at times. Best of all were the Bobcats units — (Top, L, L to R) Irving Fazola, Gil Rodin, Joe Sullivan, Bobby Haggart, Nappy Lamare, Crosby, Eddie Miller, and Ray Bauduc — and their recordings of *Who's Sorry Now, March of the Bobcats, Slow Mood,* and *Five Point Blues.* Fazola (Top, R), Bauduc (Middle, L), Lamare, and Miller (Bottom, L) were all New Orleans jazzmen, and Lawson and Matlock were from Missouri and Kentucky; hence the high percentage of Dixieland tunes done by the Bobcats or just as successfully by the whole band, like *South Rampart Street Parade, Wolverine Blues, High Society,* and *Milenberg Joys.* (Bottom, R) Bassist Bob Haggart teamed up with drummer Ray Bauduc to produce the hit *Big Noise from Winnetka,* a bass drums and whistling duet. Sterling Bose, Billy Butterfield, Warren Smith, Bob Zurke, Muggsy Spanier, and Jess Stacy were featured prior to Crosby's joining the Marine Corps late in 1942. (Opposite Page) The ultra-smart *Vanity Fair* recognized jazz in a left-handed manner in 1936, when Armstrong starred at Connie's Inn on Broadway. The club and the magazine shut down for good that year.

Impossible interview

Fritz Kreisler vs.

Louis Armstrong

FRITZ: With your talent, you, the most famous trumpeter in America, should be in a symphony orchestra. LOUIS: But Ah don' wanna be in no symphony. Ah wanna swing . . . (*he plays* Nagasaki). FRITZ: O, Handel! O, Haydn! LOUIS: O, Nagi! O, Saki! FRITZ: I'm sure *they* couldn't appreciate Paganini. (*He plays the* Moonlight Sonata.) LOUIS: But, pops, yo' ain't *swingin'* it! Go to town, man! FRITZ: Profane Beethoven? Never! (*Louis begins to play the* Moonlight *with hot variations. Gradually Kreisler's playing perks up.*) FRITZ: Hmmm. Maybe there's something to this swing business, after all. How'm I doin'? LOUIS: Yo' sendin' me, man. FRITZ: Perhaps you'd teach me to sing, too. (*He essays a reproduction of Louis' throatiness.*) La da da de skeeten skatten da booten. Let's try that *Nagasaki* opus. (*They play a genuinely barrelhouse duet.*) LOUIS: Ah'll give yo' a job playin' fiddle in mah band. FRITZ: Hot ginger and dynamite! Wait until Heifetz and Zimbalist hear me now. (*Picks up his violin.*) O, Nagi! O, Saki!

Bunny Berigan laid it all on the line, playing everything to the limit, and his limit exceeded everyone else's until alcohol finished his career shortly before his death in 1942. He was in demand as a studio player (Inset, L) in the early thirties, and with Benny Goodman with his solos on *King Porter Stomp* and *Blue Skies;* with Billie Holiday on *Billie's Blues* and *Did I Remember;* and with his own 52nd Street band on *Swing Mr. Charlie* and the first version of *I Can't Get Started with You,* which he later redid with his own big band for Victor in 1937. Tommy Dorsey's *Marie* and *Song of India* would be less valuable without his solos (Inset, R), and he confidently stepped into the bandleading role with a swinging band of undisciplined young soloists including Georgie Auld, tenor sax; Joe Dixon, clarinet; Joe Bushkin, piano; and George Wettling or Dave Tough, drums. Over a three-year period his band produced some good records like *Mahogany Hall Stomp, Little Gates Special,* and *Davenport Blues.* He went back to Tommy Dorsey for a while in 1940, then tried his own band again until illness finally overcame him. He was thirty-three when he died.

Count Basie's path to stardom was a long one, despite his having one of the greatest soloists in jazz history, Lester Young (Top, L), whose incredible flowing style with its light, nearly vibratoless sound contrasted starkly with the moaning, southwestern tenor sax of Texan Herschel Evans (Top, R), a Coleman Hawkins admirer. Basie's band played mostly head arrangements with blues vocals by Jimmy Rushing (Bottom, L) and ballads by Billie Holiday (who did not record with the band) and Helen Humes (Bottom, R). Rushing's *Good Morning Blues* and *Sent for You Yesterday* had audiences in an uproar; Humes won them over with *My Wanderin' Man* or *Blame It on My Last Affair* in her four-year stay. When Eddie Durham and Jimmy Mundy began writing arrangements in 1937–38 and Basie strengthened his personnel with the addition of New Yorkers Benny Morton and Dickie Wells on trombones and Harry Edison, whose broad, powerful trumpet solos contrasted with Buck Clayton's more emotional and warmer style, he began making an impact, at the Famous Door on 52nd Street and on dozens of records like *One O'Clock Jump*, *Taxi War Dance*, *Out the Window*, *Texas Shuffle*, *Swingin' the Blues*, and *Jumpin' at the Woodside*. It helped, too, that both Young and Evans were fine clarinetists with individual styles.

The heart of Basie's band was the rhythm section—(Middle, R) Jo Jones, drums, and Walter Page (second from R), bass, with guitarist Freddie Green (Top, R), playing with Basie, who lightened his piano to mesh with them as one. They fed soloists Buck Clayton and Herschel Evans (Middle, M, R and L) or new trumpeters Joe Newman and Al Killian (Bottom, R, L and second from R), with powerful lead man Ed Lewis (second from L) and soloist Harry "Sweets" Edison (R). The Basie band at its pinnacle on Treasure Island (Top, L) for the San Francisco World's Fair in 1939: (L to R) Buddy Tate, Benny Morton, Earl Warren, Harry Edison, Dickie Wells, Jack Washington, and Dan Minor, as Lester Young (R) takes off on *Song of the Islands.* The year before, another achievement: Lionel Hampton (Bottom, L, with Lester's sax) and Lester (R) backstage at the 1938 Carnegie Hall concert. Don Byas (Middle, L) was possibly the only man capable of replacing Lester Young in 1941. He was an incredibly fluent, big-toned player whose accompaniment to Jimmy Rushing on *Harvard Blues* is superb. Other outstanding solos are on *Jump the Blues Away, Tuesday at Ten,* and some small-group titles including *Sugar Blues.* After John Hammond enlisted in the service, Basie got less attention from Columbia, and his instrumentals were fewer in number—*Avenue C, Rambo,* and *The King* are among the better ones—which caused him to move to Victor in 1947. The move didn't matter; the band business was going under. Basie broke up his band in late 1949 and used a combo for the next two years.

Artie Shaw (Top, L) started a small group with strings in 1936, which recorded *Streamline* and *Sweet Lorraine* on Brunswick. Two years later (Bottom) he switched to a standard big-band lineup with key men Cliff Leeman (third from L) on drums, trombonist George Arus (fifth from L), tenor man and singer Tony Pastor (sixth from L), and trumpeter Johnny Best (R) and recorded *Begin the Beguine, Indian Love Call,* and *Back Bay Shuffle* for Bluebird. In 1939 Georgie Auld and Buddy Rich added an extra spark on *Traffic Jam, Rosalie,* and *Lady, Be Good.* After dropping out for a time, Shaw returned in 1940 with a thirty-two-piece band with strings and recorded the hit *Frenesi.* His small combo, the Gramercy Five, used trumpet, clarinet, and harpsichord on numbers like *Special Delivery Stomp* and *Summit Ridge Drive.* His swan song before joining the navy in 1942 was adding trumpeter Hot Lips Page (Top, R, L) and drummer Dave Tough (Middle, L, third from R) for swinging numbers like *Carnival.* During his navy term in 1943 (Middle, L), Shaw's band toured the South Pacific, and a year later, mustered out, he reorganized a new Gramercy Five (Middle, R) with younger players, featuring (L to R) Dodo Marmarosa, Roy Eldridge, (Shaw), Barney Kessel, and Morris Rayman. They recorded *Grabtown Grapple* and *The Sad Sack.* Shaw, through his force of will, left as high a standard of recording as any of his competitors.

Les Brown (Top, L) played clarinet and alto sax, led the Duke University Blue Devils, and had a good dance and swing band for a decade, but is remembered as much as anything because Doris Day (Top, L) made a recording of *Sentimental Journey* with him that became a big hit. Brown was fortunate while working at the Log Cabin in Armonk, New York, to record disc jockey Alan Courtney's *Joltin' Joe DiMaggio* (Top, R) for the famed Yankee Clipper (L), who hit safely in fifty-six consecutive games in 1941. Trombonist Si Zentner (extreme R) later led his own bands. Brown worked a great deal with Bob Hope after the band era. Woody Herman's (Middle, L) start as a Ted Lewis imitator in vaudeville did nothing to hurt his playing, and when he became a leader in 1937 (Middle, M) he specialized in the blues for quite a few years. (Bottom, L to R) Hy White, Walt Yoder, Malcolm Crain, Saxie Mansfield, Clarence Willard, Frankie Carlson, Herman, Joe Bishop, Pete Johns, Tommy Linehan, Neil Reid, Ray Hopfner, Joe Estren. *Bishop's Blues, Dupree Blues,* and *Doctor Jazz* were typical of Herman's repertoire. By 1941 he had recorded *Woodchopper's Ball, Fan It,* and *Blue Flame* with (Middle, R, L to R) Saxie Mansfield, Jimmy Horvath, Sam Rubinowitch, and Herbie Haymer, and *Woodsheddin' with Woody* and *Las Chiapanecas.* During the war years arranger Dave Matthews began experimenting with Basie and Ellington styles. The first of Herman's many Herds started in 1944.

Charlie Barnet, the uninhibited son of well-to-do parents, played tenor, alto, and soprano saxes with abandon and lost most of his jobs (and bands) because he refused to play commercial music. He finally got what he wanted: a good band, a good job—at the Famous Door on 52nd Street—and a recording contract, all in 1939. At the Apollo Theatre, where Barnet was very popular as far back as 1934, in December 1939: (Top, L to R) Claude Murphy, Lyman Vunk, Billy May, Bill Robertson, Johnny Owens, Don Ruppersberg, Bobby Burnet, Bill Miller, and Barnet. This band recorded *Cherokee, The Last Jump, The Duke's Idea, Comanche War Dance,* and *Leapin' at the Lincoln,* and slightly later, after Bernie Privin replaced Burnet on trumpet, *Pompton Turnpike, Southern Fried,* and *Redskin Rhumba.* Between those instrumentals, Barnet's band got burned out of the Palomar Ballroom in Los Angeles, 1939, and he hired vocalist Mary Ann McCall, who did *Between 18th and 19th on Chestnut Street.* In 1941 Lena Horne sang *You're My Thrill* and *Haunted Town;* Horace Henderson arranged *Ponce De Leon, Charleston Alley,* and *Little Dip.* When Barnet switched to Decca in 1942, black trumpeter Peanuts Holland (Bottom, second from R) became his main soloist, joined in 1943 by (L to R) Howard McGhee, Trummy Young, and Oscar Pettiford.

Earl Hines (Top, L) was in limbo when the swing era started, after making fine records like *Cavernism, Madhouse, Darkness,* and *Swingin' Down* on Brunswick, 1933–34, and *That's a Plenty* on Decca, which dropped him early in 1935. Two years later he began recording for Vocalion, again turning out records like *Pianology, Hines Rhythm, Inspiration,* and *Solid Mama,* but began revamping his band in 1938 and signed with RCA for its Bluebird label in 1939 using the new band: (Bottom, L to R) Milton Fletcher, Walter Fuller, Ed Simms, Hurley Ramey, George Dixon, Quinn Wilson, (Hines), Alvin Burroughs, Ed Burke, Leroy Harris, John Ewing, Omer Simeon, Joe McLewis, Budd Johnson, and Bob Crowder. Many Budd Johnson arrangements poured forth: *Father Steps In, Piano Man, Grand Terrace Shuffle, XYZ,* and his first big hit, *Boogie Woogie on the St. Louis Blues.* Singer Billy Eckstine (Top, R) and alto man Scoops Carry (R) joined in 1940, and the hit *Jelly Jelly* resulted. Carry's unusual sound and phrasing influenced Charlie Parker. Eckstine's other big hit, *Stormy Monday Blues,* made in only one take, features Shorty McConnell's inspired trumpet solo. The recording ban left Hines's 1943 band with Dizzy Gillespie, Charlie Parker, and Sarah Vaughan undocumented, and only a few of his good postwar bands with Wardell Gray, Benny Green, and trumpeter Billy Douglas got recorded. ARA, a California-based company, recorded a dozen sides, but only two instrumentals, *Straight Life* and *At the El Grotto,* were released. Deeply in debt with his El Grotto club, Hines joined Louis Armstrong's All-Stars for the Nice Festival in February of 1948.

Glenn Miller's (Top, L) first two attempts at leading a band ended in dismal failure. Success came only when he hit upon a particular saxophone sound with clarinet lead that became his hallmark. His 1938 reeds were (Top, R, L to R) Stanley Aronson, Bill Stegmeyer, Wilbur Schwartz, Hal McIntyre, and Tex Beneke. One difficulty was finding the right drummer, and in Maurice "Mo" Purtill (Middle, L) he got what he wanted. Although it is credited to Miller on the Bluebird label, his first big hit, *Little Brown Jug,* was arranged by Bill Finegan, as were many other tunes until arranger Jerry Gray went over from Artie Shaw's band. Miller struck the right note, 1939–42, with the shimmering sax work on *Moonlight Serenade,* his radio theme song for Chesterfield cigarettes; swing numbers like Joe Garland's *In the Mood* featured sax chase choruses by Tex Beneke (Middle, R) and Al Klink. He had a major hit with Erskine Hawkins's *Tuxedo Junction* and with Jerry Gray's *Pennsylvania 6-5000.* His band was strengthened considerably with the addition of Ernie Caceres on sax and clarinet, and Johnny Best and Bobby Hackett on trumpet. Hackett's solo on *String of Pearls* is one of his best. Vocalist Marion Hutton (Middle R) supplied much of the personality along with Beneke. The Andrews Sisters (Bottom, L) broadcast with Miller frequently. Miller dissolved the band in late 1942 to accept a commission to head an all-star air force band.

Gene Krupa's animated, gum-chewing good looks and wild drum solos with Benny Goodman's band made him popular enough to start his own band in 1938. He staffed it mostly with little-known players, some of whom, like tenor men Sam Donahue and Charlie Ventura and trumpeters Shorty Sherock and Corky Cornelius, became stars during their tenure with him. Krupa's first hit was *Wire Brush Stomp* (Brunswick, 1938), followed by *Drummin' Man* with vocal by Irene Daye (who later married Cornelius) and *Drum Boogie*, also with Irene Daye. Right after that, vocalist Anita O'Day (Inset, R) replaced Irene Daye, and Roy Eldridge (Inset, L) joined and made *Let Me Off Uptown*. "... Anita, oh, Anita, say I feel something.... Well, blow, Roy, blow...." Some of Eldridge's best solos were recorded with Krupa's band on Okeh and Columbia, 1941–42, including *After You've Gone, Rockin' Chair, Knock Me a Kiss,* and *That Drummer's Band.* The recording ban of August 1942 kept a lot more good music off discs, and a trumped-up narcotics charge (later dropped for lack of evidence) caused Krupa's band to break up in May 1943. Six months later Krupa rejoined Benny Goodman at the Hotel New Yorker until December, then switched to Tommy Dorsey's band until July 1944. Then he began again, with a large band including strings and younger, more modern players.

JACK TEAGARDEN AND HIS BAND
APPEARING AT THE BLACKHAWK CAFE

TEAGARDEN & SIX OF

Jan Savitt (Top, L) was Leopold Stokowski's concertmaster with the Philadelphia Orchestra, musical director at KYW, and then leader of a well-disciplined shuffle rhythm band (Top, R, L to R): Freddie Ohms, Jack Hansen, Morris Rayman, Jimmy Campbell, Miff Sines, Johnny Austin, Cutty Cutshall, Russ Isaacs, (Savitt), Jack Pleis (piano), and Eddie Clausen. Their hits *Quaker City Jazz, Sugarfoot Stomp,* and *720 in the Books* on Bluebird and Decca kept them working, but Savitt died in debt on a one-nighter in 1948. Trumpeter-trombonist and arranger Larry Clinton (Middle, extreme L) wrote hits for Casa Loma and the Dorseys before forming his own band, which played Glen Island Casino in 1938 featuring Walter Smith (eighth from L), Tony Zimmers (extreme R), and vocalist Bea Wain. Clinton hits with Wain vocals were *Martha, Heart and Soul, Deep Purple,* and *My Reverie.* He became a flight instructor and pilot during the war, returned briefly to music, and then retired. Jack Teagarden started his band in 1939, played the Blackhawk Café (Bottom), and recorded *I Gotta Right to Sing the Blues, Red Wing,* and *Peg o' My Heart* for Columbia and Brunswick. Trumpeters Charlie Spivak and Lee Castle (fourth and fifth from L), Ernie Caceres (fourth from R), and guitarist Allen Reuss cost him a fortune. A year later he had to reorganize with less expensive musicians; they played their hearts out and still made a fine band, but he had little luck, wound up deeply in debt, and broke up the band in 1946. The next year he joined Louis Armstrong's All-Stars.

Best Chesterfield Wishes Corky Corcoran

Harry James's (Top, L) first band was loaded with hard-blowing southwesterners. (Bottom) At the Hotel Sherman, Chicago, October 1939: (L to R) Thurman Teague, Jack Gardner, Ralph Hawkins, Red Kent, Frank Sinatra, (James), Jack Palmer, Dalton Rizzotto, Claude Bowen, Claude Lakey, Bruce Squires, Jack Schaeffer, Truett Jones, Dave Matthews, Drew Page. *Two O'Clock Jump, Flash,* and *Cross Country Jump* are all riff-filled swingers. Frank Sinatra's *All or Nothing at All,* later released on Columbia, sold nearly a million copies when he starred with Tommy Dorsey. James made it with flashy numbers like *Ciribiribin* and later, with strings added, *You Made Me Love You.* Corky Corcoran (Top, R) became James's most featured soloist throughout the next twenty years, along with Lunceford alto star Willie Smith, who joined in 1944. Andy Gibson was responsible for many of James's driving originals in the early years; Jack Mathias, Johnny Thompson, Jimmy Mundy, and Ray Conniff wrote most of his later material. A few instrumentals like *The Clipper, Moten Swing, Cotton Tail,* and *Easy* or *Man with a Horn,* which was a Willie Smith feature, were recorded, but Columbia was less interested in swing after 1947. James kept his band working throughout the fifties.

Zoot Sims (Top, L) played with Bobby Sherwood, Sonny Dunham, and Benny Goodman, 1942–43, until he was drafted; returned to Goodman briefly in 1946; and then became part of Woody Herman's Four Brothers Band in 1947. Hal McIntyre's band played Glen Island Casino in 1942 (Top, R); his best sidemen were pianist-arranger Danny Hurd (fifth from R) and bassist Eddie Safranski. Arranger Dave Matthews's scores — *Bayou Shuffle* and *The Commando Serenade* — were released on Bluebird. High-note trumpeter Pete Candoli (Middle, L) played with Will Bradley, Tommy Dorsey, and Teddy Powell during the war years. Powell's band in 1941 (Middle, R) featured trumpeter Dickie Mains, clarinetist Irving Fazola, and pianist Tony Aless. *Steady Teddy* and *Ode to Spring* on Bluebird were arranged by Matthews and Bob Mersey. Powell had bad luck: the Famous Door closed on him in 1941, and when the Rustic Cabin burned down in New Jersey, he lost most of his library of arrangements. Pianist-arranger Claude Thornhill's band (Bottom) went for a whole ensemble sound, six clarinets in unison against his one-finger romantic piano; solos by Irving Fazola (seventh from R) and brilliant brass led by Conrad Gozzo (fifth from L); and attention to dynamics at Glen Island Casino in 1941. His Columbia records *Snowfall* (his theme), *Portrait of a Guinea Farm,* and *Sleepy Serenade* contrasted with arranger Gil Evans's *There's a Small Hotel* and *Buster's Last Stand.* Thornhill joined the navy in late 1942. His postwar band lasted from 1946 until 1948.

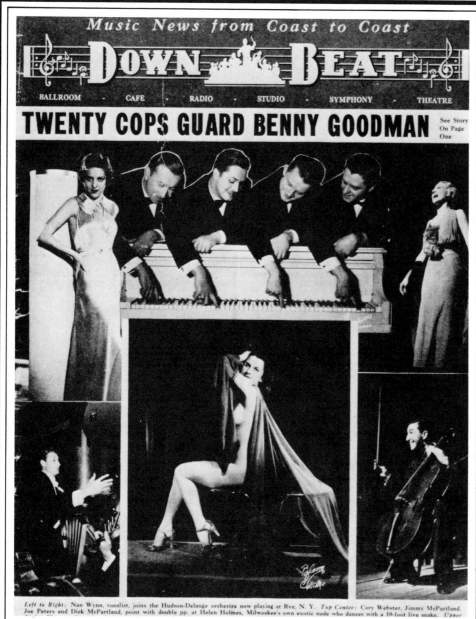

Music News from Coast to Coast

DOWN BEAT

BALLROOM · CAFE · RADIO · STUDIO · SYMPHONY · THEATRE

TWENTY COPS GUARD BENNY GOODMAN
See Story On Page One

Left to Right: Nan Wynn, vocalist, joins the Hudson-Delange orchestra now playing at Rye, N. Y. *Top Center:* Cory Webster, Jimmy McPartland, Joe Peters and Dick McPartland, point with double pp. at Helen Holmes, Milwaukee's own exotic nude who dances with a 10-foot live snake. *Upper*

Music News from Coast to Coast
DOWN BEAT
BALLROOM · CAFE · RADIO · STUDIO · SYMPHONY · THEATRE
DO BEST WHITE BANDS COPY NEGROES?
SEE STORY ON PAGE A

Music News from Coast to Coast
DOWN BEAT
BALLROOM · CAFE · RADIO · STUDIO · SYMPHONY · THEATRE
"W. C. HANDY IS A LIAR!" SAYS JELLY ROLL
See Story on Page 3

August '38   15c

DOWN BEAT

Duke, Stan, Hamp—Win Place, Show
(See Page 2)

Recording Starts Again
(See Page 3)

BG, Barnet Bands Bop
(See Page 2)

On The Cover
Patti Page

DOWN BEAT

Monte Out Of Bop City, May Sue
(See Page 1)

Herb Haymer Life Story
(See Page 3)

Artie's Answer To Critics
(See Page 1)

On The Cover
Joe Venuti
Kay Starr

DOWN BEAT
WHITEMAN CONDEMNS SWING MUSIC!
See Story On Page 2

Down Beat started as a musicians' paper in mid-1934 on newsprint (the early issues are priceless) and gradually evolved into a headline-hunting tabloid that rivaled the old *New York Daily Mirror* at its yellow journalism worst. Cheesecake covers and gag shots typified editor Carl Cons's and owner Glenn Burrs's breezy approach to music journalism in the thirties, but *Down Beat* covered the news somewhat more thoroughly and pictorially than its archrival, the much older and more staid (and better printed) *Metronome*. John Hammond, Dave Dexter, and Leonard Feather all wrote for "The Beat," as its loyal readers called it, and columnist George Hoefer's "Hot Box" supplied valuable discographical information and capsule biographies of many jazz pioneers through the years. *Down Beat* absorbed the West Coast magazine *Tempo* when it stopped publishing in 1940. The original newspaper-size format, which often caused prewar issues to fall apart, was discontinued in the fifties. It is still publishing.

Metronome

MODERN MUSIC AND ITS MAKERS

JULY 1938 25c

METRONOME CONTEST WINNERS

HAL

BENNY

TOMMY

• CONTEST SURPRISES

• ORCHESTRATION— MY OLD KENTUCKY HOME

• WEBER-PETRILLO BURY HATCHET

THE ORCHESTRA · WORLD

January, 1944

15c

Foreign Canada 22c

HARRY JAMES AND THE MUSIC MAKERS

Metro-Goldwyn-Mayer
Columbia Records
Chesterfield

FLASH

WEEKLY NEWSPICTURE MAGAZINE

10¢

DEC. 1937

Metronome

MUSIC AND ITS MAKERS

25 cents

Greetings

Bunny Berigan

THE MODERN MUSICAL NEWSMAGAZINE

TEMPO

Intimate Stories of Musicians and Entertainers

Music and Rhythm

JULY 1942 15c Canada 20c

Carol Bruce and Jimmy Lytell Like Their Swing Mellow

Metronome, the oldest music magazine (1889), held little of interest for jazz fans before George Simon joined the staff in 1935 (he became editor in 1939). This *Life*-size slick-paper magazine was conservative, dominated to an extent by instrument manufacturers and music publishers. Simon gradually shifted emphasis to strong coverage of bands and recordings (much of which he wrote himself under pseudonyms until Barry Ulanov and others were hired), and he began featuring Berigan, Goodman, Dorsey, and the others on its covers. *Orchestra World* (Top, R) started in 1925 with some good dance-band coverage and later swing. It became more or less a publicity magazine and almost anyone could get written up for the right deal. *Tempo,* oriented toward film and radio studio bands, started in Los Angeles in 1933 and never really came east. In *Music and Rhythm* Dave Dexter and John Hammond attempted to dig into the business with some hard-hitting articles, but it was too much like *Down Beat* and the other pictorials. *Flash* (Middle, R) was a black version of *Look* that occasionally ran swing band features.

Women in swing were unheralded, except for Billie Holiday (Top, L), Mildred Bailey (Top, R), and talented newcomer Maxine Sullivan (Middle, R) who became a major star after *Loch Lomond* came out in 1937. Instrumentalists, except pianists like Mary Lou Williams, Lil Armstrong, Cleo Brown, and a few others, went nearly unnoticed. The harp work of Adele Girard (Middle, L) might have remained unrecognized save for the fact she was Joe Marsala's wife and was featured in all his fine groups. Guitarist Mary Osborne (Middle, M) played somewhat like her idol Charlie Christian in the bands of Terry Shand and Joe Venuti until she joined vibist Marge Hyams and tenor soloist L'Ana Webster (Top, M), who played in an airy style somewhat like Lester Young and Ben Webster, in a group called the Hip Chicks. Trumpeter-vocalist Billie Rogers (Bottom, R) joined Woody Herman's band as a specialty act in 1941, later joined the trumpet section, and then led her own band, 1944–45, playing with a big tone in a style somewhat like Roy Eldridge's. Johnny Mandel and Harry Babasin were members of this band, which made no records. The International Sweethearts of Rhythm (Bottom, L) managed to record for Victor in 1946 and featured tenor star Vi Burnside on *Vi Vigor*. They went overseas on a USO tour later that year, but none of the fine instrumentalists ever really got credit or publicity for their work during those years.

Joe Venuti (Bottom, L) followed Benny Goodman at the Palomar, but his penchant for practical jokes often backfired, costing him thousands of dollars, and his bands largely went unrecorded. Lester Young's band (Top, R) played Kelly's Stables in March 1941 with Clyde Hart, piano; John Collins, guitar; Shad Collins, trumpet; Nick Fenton, bass; and Harold "Doc" West, drums. Except for a backup date for Una Mae Carlisle on Bluebird *(Blitzkrieg Baby),* it went unrecorded, a shameful oversight in 1941. Young, his pants pressed to razor sharpness, took his B-flat Conn tenor sax to Los Angeles, where he reorganized with his brother Lee on drums. This group was also unrecorded. Louis Prima (Middle, L, seated) enjoyed widespread popularity with his touring swing band, 1936–37, which recorded *Pennies from Heaven, Rosalie,* and *Exactly Like You* for Brunswick and featured Julian Laine (second from L), trombone; Pee Wee Russell, (fifth from R), clarinet; and Sal Franzella (second from R), alto sax. Violinist Eddie South (Middle, R) mixed sweet and swing at Ben Marden's Riviera in 1936 with (L to R) Jimmy Bertrand, drums; Zinky Cohn, piano; (South); Wright Smith, violin; Ed Burke, trombone; Harold Scott, clarinet; Everett Barksdale, guitar; and Milt Hinton, bass. The piano artistry of Fats Waller (Bottom, R, extreme L) and his sense of humor made Victor records *Us on a Bus, Baby Brown, Christopher Columbus, My Very Good Friend — the Milkman,* and others valuable; on trumpet, John Hamilton; tenor sax, Gene Sedric; guitar, John Smith; bass, Cedric Wallace; and drums, Slick Jones.

The 1942 band of Ray McKinley (Top, L) with arrangements by Brad Gowans was dispersed by the draft. His postwar band featured Nick Travis, Vern Friley, and Ray Beller and played Eddie Sauter's arrangements on *Sandstorm* and *Hangover Square* for Majestic. Pee Wee Erwin (Top, M) took over Bunny Berigan's band in 1940 and led it for two years. After seven years in studio work he came back to lead a Dixieland band in 1949. Drummer George Wettling (Top, R) worked with Artie Shaw, Red Norvo, Bunny Berigan, Muggsy Spanier, Benny Goodman, and Paul Whiteman before doing studio work. The Mills Cavalcade Orchestra (Middle, L) mixed male and female players, featured Paul Ricci (second from L), and was led for a time by trombonist George Brunis in 1935. They recorded *Rhythm Lullaby* for Columbia but spent more time rehearsing than working. Red Norvo's band (Middle, R) played Eddie Sauter's exquisite arrangements on *Smoke Dreams, Remember,* and others for Brunswick. At the Steel Pier in 1937, Lee Castle, trumpet (fifth from L); Maurice Purtill, drums (fourth from L); Hank D'Amico, clarinet (L); and tenor man Herbie Haymer, (sixth from L) were featured along with leader (M) and his wife, who were billed then as "Mr. and Mrs. Swing." The Spirits of Rhythm (Bottom, L), the first group to play 52nd Street, were successful throughout the swing era. Teddy Bunn (second from L), Wilbur and Douglas Daniels (extreme L and R), Leo Watson (third from L), and Virgil Scoggins, whisk broom, recorded *My Old Man* on Brunswick. Virtuoso trombonist, slide saxophonist, and singer Snub Mosley (Bottom, R) led his own bands, 1937–49, after working with Claude Hopkins, Louis Armstrong, and Fats Waller. This group, with drummer Tommy Benford, trumpeter Bob Carroll, and alto man Frank Cahill, played the Flame Supper Club in Duluth, Minnesota, in 1946. Earlier groups featuring Buster Smith, Willard Brown, and A. G. Godley recorded *Blues at High Noon, Snub's Blues,* and *Hey Man Hey Man (Amen)* for Decca. Mosley never got credit for the tune that became a big hit for Woody Herman. After 1950 Mosley worked with trios around New York and in the Catskills.

Slim (Gaillard) and Slam's (Stewart) *Flat Foot Floogie* was the novelty hit of 1938. Gaillard (Bottom, L, R) became a star at Billy Berg's and other clubs in Hollywood during the war. Despite having an original style and showmanship, Hot Lips Page (Middle, L) never enjoyed much success. His records varied from *Skullduggery* and *Jumpin'* with his big band on Bluebird, to the superb *Gee, Baby Ain't I Good to You* on Continental, one of the great vocal records. Pianist Harry "The Hipster" Gibson (Middle, M) subverted his musical skills for showmanship, typified by *Who Put the Benzedrine in Mrs. Murphy's Ovaltine* and *4-F Ferdinand the Frantic Freak* on Musicraft in 1944. Illinois Jacquet (Middle, R) achieved stardom with his tenor solo on *Flying Home* in Lionel Hampton's band, 1941–42. Later he joined Cab Calloway and Count Basie, who featured him on *The King* before he started his own band in 1947. His Apollo and Victor records *Bottoms Up, Merle's Mood, Robbins Nest,* and *Black Velvet* are good examples of his fluent work. Lester Young (Top, L) and Nat "King" Cole (Top, R, at piano) crossed paths after Young left Basie to start his own band. Both worked 52nd Street clubs in 1941, when Cole began recording, for Decca, *Sweet Lorraine* and *Call the Police.* Young was less fortunate. His sextet recorded only as backup for Una Mae Carlisle on Bluebird. Nor was his 1942 septet with his brother Lee on drums recorded. But a twenty-four-year-old MGM film editor named Norman Granz got Cole and Young and bassist Red Callendar together on July 15, 1942, and recorded four twelve-inch masterpieces for a new firm called Philo. They were *Indiana, Body and Soul, Tea for Two,* and *I Can't Get Started with You.*

Lionel Hampton (Bottom, seated L) was a major celebrity after four years with Benny Goodman's Quartet and big band. He organized a new band in California in November 1940 with (L to R) (Hampton), Illinois Jacquet, Jack McVea, Marshall Royal, Dexter Gordon, Sonny Craven, Ernie Royal, Joe Newman, and Karl George. Hampton had to wait until the contract he signed with Victor in 1937 expired, since they would not record his band; then he signed with Decca, recording *Flying Home* and *In the Bag*. But Decca was able to record only three sessions before the ban in August 1942. Marshall Royal organized the band and led it so that Hampton could concentrate on vibes and his flashy drum solos or join with pianist Milt Buckner (Top, R) for one-finger vibes-style piano solos. Buckner developed a locked-hands, chord-style solo style that was a big crowd pleaser. Shown at the Savoy Ballroom in 1942 (Top, L) are Marshall Royal and alto and violin soloist Ray Perry (extreme R). Later, during the war, Hampton began emphasizing heavy back-beat and hand-clapping routines that put over *Hamp's Boogie Woogie* and *Chop Chop*. Singer Dinah Washington (Top, M), a Hampton discovery who joined the band in 1943, recorded only two titles, *Evil Gal Blues* and *Blow Top Blues*, before setting out on her own in 1945. For a while Joe Williams sang in the band at the same time.

DECCA
MANUFACTURED IN U.S.A · BY DECCA RECORDS, INC.

(DLA 543)

Fox Trot
Vocal Chorus by
Louis Armstrong

SWING THAT MUSIC
(Horace Gerlach-Louis Armstrong)

LOUIS ARMSTRONG
With
Jimmy Dorsey and His Orchestra

3105 A

DECCA
MANUFACTURED IN U.S.A · BY DECCA RECORDS, INC

(62263)

Fox Trot

FOR DANCERS ONLY
(Sy Oliver)

JIMMIE LUNCEFORD
And His Orchestra

1340 B

Swing Classic

VICTOR

Not Licensed for
Radio Broadcast

25616-A

FRANKIE AND JOHNNIE—Fox Trot
Bunny Berigan and his Orchestra
Featuring H. Berigan, I. Goodman, S. Lipkins, Trumpets—
M. Samel, S. Lee, Trombones—S. Pearlmutter,
J. Dixon, G. Auld, C. Rounds, Saxophones—
T. Morgan, Guitar-A. Fishkind, String Bass-
J. Lippman, Piano-G. Wettling, Drums.

RCA Manufacturing Co., Inc.
Camden, N.J.U.S.A.

DECCA
MANUFACTURED IN U.S.A · BY DECCA RECORDS, INC

(63423)

Fox Trot

MARCH OF THE BOB CATS
(Bob Haggart)

BOB CROSBY'S BOB CATS
Bob Zurke, piano; Yank Lawson, trumpet;
Warren Smith, trombone; Eddie Miller, saxophone;
Matty Matlock, clarinet; Nappy Lamare, guitar;
Bob Haggart, bass; Ray Bauduc, drums.

1865 B

BLUEBIRD

B-7759-B

BACK BAY SHUFFLE—Fox Trot
(Macrae-Shaw)

Art Shaw and his Orchestra

RCA MANUFACTURING CO., INC., CAMDEN, N.J.U.S.A.

DECCA
MANUFACTURED IN U.S.A · BY DECCA RECORDS, INC.

(64474)

Fox Trot

JUMPIN' AT THE WOODSIDE
(Count Basie)

COUNT BASIE
And His Orchestra

2212 A

VICTOR
REG. U.S. PAT. OFF.   MARCAS REGISTRADAS

For best results use
RCA Victor Needles

26170-A

AND THE ANGELS SING—Fox Trot
(....Y Los Angeles Cantan)
(Johnny Mercer-Ziggie Elman)

Benny Goodman and his Orch.
Vocal refrain by Martha Tilton

RADIO CORPORATION OF AMERICA, CAMDEN, N.J. MADE IN U.S.A.

BLUEBIRD

B-10373-A

CHEROKEE—Fox Trot
(Ray Noble)

Charlie Barnet and his Orchestra

RADIO CORPORATION OF AMERICA, CAMDEN, N.J. MADE IN U.S.A.

BLUEBIRD

B-10286-A

LITTLE BROWN JUG—Fox Trot
(Arr. by Glenn Miller)

Glenn Miller and his Orchestra

RCA MANUFACTURING CO., INC., CAMDEN, N.J.U.S.A.

OKeh
Registered U.S. Patent Office

6046
(C 3530)

DRUM BOOGIE
Fox-Trot - Vocal Chorus by
Irene Daye and Ensemble
-Krupa-arr: Elton Hill.
GENE KRUPA and his ORCHESTRA

VICTOR

For best results use
RCA Victor Needles

27869-B

NOT SO QUIET PLEASE—Fox Trot
(Sy Oliver)

Tommy Dorsey and his Orch.

RCA MANUFACTURING CO., INC., CAMDEN, N.J.U.S.A.

Decca
MANUFACTURED BY DECCA RECORDS, INC., NEW YORK, U.S.A.

(L 4009)

Fox Trot
Vocal Chorus by
Lionel Hampton

HEY! BA-BA-RE-BOP
(Curley Hamner-Lionel Hampton)

LIONEL HAMPTON
And His Orchestra

18754 A

Now's The Time
1944-1950

Swing Low, Sweet Cadillac, coming for to carry me home/Swing Low, Sweet Cadillac, coming for to carry me home/I looked over Jordan and what did I see/A band of Fleetwoods coming for to carry me home.

—Diz 'n' Bird in Concert

"Bird, Bird—A gennulman just called in from the Bronx…The gennulman wants to know if you'd play for him A *White Christmas?*"

—"Symphony Sid" Torin, *Birdland*, Opening Night, December 15, 1949

"Negro music doesn't have to have continuous swing... a steady swing can become monotonous," Art Tatum stated in 1935. He liked to recast the harmonies of songs by using substitute chords for those most always chosen by other instrumentalists. It was all done with a dazzling technique at blinding speed which left everyone in jazz, and classical pianists like Vladimir Horowitz, gasping in admiration.

Like Tatum, and many years before him, Louis Armstrong succeeded in freeing himself from the ground beat in breaks: at different spots in *Potato Head Blues;* his way of telling a story with a beginning, middle, and end in *West End Blues;* and the way he ended phrases on the fourth beat on *I Double Dare You.*

Coleman Hawkins studied music—composition, theory, harmony, and arranging. After hearing Art Tatum play in the late 1920s, Hawkins began building his solos on the potential available in chord sequences rather than on melody. It led to his famous *Body and Soul* recording in 1939, full of passing chords and sixteenth notes.

Players dissatisfied with embellishing the melody or playing strictly on the beat could be found in abundance in Oklahoma City and Kansas City in the late 1920s and early 1930s. Guitarist Eddie Durham was fond of dissonances and advanced harmonies, which he taught to Jim Daddy Walker, and both passed them on to Charlie Christian. Lester Young had a sense of melodic form and was fond of alternate fingering on certain notes to vary the sound. Alto men Tommy Douglas and Buster Smith knew advanced harmony. Douglas was a conservatory graduate, while Smith liked to run series of sixteenth-note passages. All three were studied intently by a teenaged Charlie Parker, who worked with the latter two early in his career.

In St. Louis, a slender, shy bassist named Jimmy Blanton played hornlike solos with a fine, clean tone and impeccable time with the Jeter-Pillars band at the Club Plantation in 1938. With Duke Ellington in 1939-41 he revolutionized bass playing.

In New York, trumpeter Roy Eldridge was setting the pace after 1935 with a fast chromatic style built on what Benny Carter was doing on alto sax. His speed and range overwhelmed everyone, and he was widely copied and admired, particularly by John "Dizzy" Gillespie. Around 1939 Gillespie started using extremely fast tempos and showers of sixteenth notes (*Hot Mallets*, with Lionel Hampton) and showed a growing fondness for ending on the weak beat. In Hill's band in 1939, Gillespie found drummer Kenny Clarke keeping time on the ride cymbal and using his bass drum for accents, something Jo Jones was fond of doing, and used it to build his own style. Hill fired Clarke for "messing with the rhythm," but Roy Eldridge hired him later and encouraged his experiments.

In a turnabout, Hill, after becoming manager of Minton's Playhouse in 1940, asked Clarke to form a house band, which included pianist Thelonious Monk, already working on a style that omitted notes from the chords. Every night Gillespie came after his job with Cab Calloway, as did Charlie Christian, working with Benny Goodman, or Don Byas, with Count Basie's band, Lester Young, from Kelly's Stables, and sometimes Jimmy Blanton. Early in 1942 they were joined by Charlie Parker, whose nightly solo on *Cherokee* with Jay McShann's band was being broadcast throughout the country from the Savoy Ballroom. Clarke recalled: "Bird was playing stuff we'd never heard before. He was into figures I thought I invented for drums. He was twice as fast as Lester Young and into harmony Lester hadn't touched. Bird was running the same way we were, but he was way ahead of us."

In addition to their Minton's experiments, the new men were listening to Artie Shaw because he was felt to be more conceptually modern than Goodman; to Bobby Hackett, whose full knowledge of chords was evident on his flowing legato solo on *Embraceable You;* to Benny Carter's solos, cool, flowing, and elegant on alto sax; and to pianist Teddy Wilson's dry, unsentimental way of laying out a solo with perfect placement of notes and harmonies.

The new style coalesced on Fifty-second Street, brought about by Gillespie, Parker, bassist Oscar Pettiford, drummer Max Roach, and others in 1944-45. They shifted the rhythmic emphasis from the swing players' first and third beats, to the second and fourth (weak), and played their series of sixteenth-note solos without inflection at tempos twice as fast, using substitute chords with rapid shifts into seemingly unrelated keys. Pianists like Clyde Hart, George Wallington, and Joe Albany comped with the left hand and played single-note runs, leaving the bass to maintain the rhythm line and the drums to accent solos and ensembles while keeping tempo on the ride cymbal.

Bebop was fully formed by 1945, a revolution through evolution, which completely changed the jazz world, finished the Swing Era, and set the stage for the next development, one centered around the playing of Miles Davis, John Lewis, Gerry Mulligan, Lee Konitz, and arranger Gil Evans. The dry, undramatic style was called cool jazz, a reaction to the highly charged, emotional playing of Gillespie, Parker, Fats Navarro, and others. Gillespie and Parker kept working. But cool or hot, the liberation of the rhythmic structure was permanent. Jazz wouldn't go backward; subtlety and complexity had become second nature.

It was February 19, 1947, at the C. P. MacGregor Recording Studios on Western Avenue, south of Wilshire Boulevard in Los Angeles. Charlie Parker—the creative force of modern jazz, the equal, in some minds, of Schoenberg, Bach, and Beethoven—helped a thin, nervous, but promising baritone named Earl Coleman struggle through two ballads, absorbing two hours of precious studio time for Ross Russell's Dial label. Russell had no desire whatsoever to record ballads by anyone, let alone an unknown, but without further preparation, Parker plus pianist Erroll Garner, bassist Red Callendar, and drummer Harold "Doc" West completed seven usable takes of three new tunes—*Bird's Nest, Blow Top Blues,* and *Cool Blues*—all within thirty minutes. Seven months before, in July 1946, Parker had recorded *Lover Man* and *Bebop* for Dial, barely able to complete the date; he wound up, after being jailed for narcotics and abusive behavior, in Camarillo State Hospital, an hour and a half outside Los Angeles. When he recovered completely, Parker's ideas burst forth incessantly on his E-flat Selmer alto saxophone with number 5 Rico reed. He symbolized the vitality and brilliance of modern jazz.

© William P. Gottlieb

Minton's Playhouse (Top, R) on West 118th Street in Harlem became a focal point for after-hours sessions in which all the major developers of modern jazz—Dizzy Gillespie (Top, L) Thelonious Monk (Top, R, L), drummer Kenny Clarke, and others—were given a free hand by manager and former bandleader Teddy Hill (extreme R). There went Charlie Christian, from his job with Benny Goodman at the Meadowbrook; Roy Eldridge (second from R), from Gene Krupa's band at the Hotel Pennsylvania; Howard McGhee (second from L), from his job with Charlie Barnet at the Park Central Hotel; and Charlie Parker, from Jay McShann's band at the Savoy Ballroom. The group rehearsed and polished their ideas in rhythm, time, chord progressions, and new melodies there until Gillespie brought it downtown to 52nd Street in 1943. Just before this, in 1942–43, most of the experimenters happened to work for Earl Hines's band: (Bottom, L to R) Dizzy Gillespie, Gus Chappell, Benny Harris, Benny Green, Gail Brockman, Shadow Wilson, Shorty McConnell, Jesse Simpkins, Huey Long, (Hines), Scoops Carry, Andy Gardner, Tommy Crump, and, barely visible, Charlie Parker, who played tenor sax. Because of Mr. Pertillo's ban on recording, which began in August 1942 and lasted until November 1943, none of the early sounds of modern jazz were preserved for posterity. A year later many of these same men were with Billy Eckstine's big band.

Billy Eckstine remembered: "Bird [Top, L] used to miss as many shows as he would make, and Earl used to fine him blind. He was the only man I know who could sleep with his jaws poked out to look like he was playing, see?...it came time for his solo, so Scoops Carry nudged him, 'Hey, Bird, you're on.' And Bird ran right out to the mike in his stocking feet, just jumped up and forgot his shoes and then ran out front and started wailing. Oh, we used to have some wonderful times in those bands." Among the many other talents were vocalist Sarah Vaughan (Top, R), who also doubled on piano. She recalled, "I loved it. Oh, listen, I was going to school. I really didn't have to go to Juilliard. I was right there in it. It was just something I've never heard before, and since the first time I heard it, I haven't stopped listening to it since." Everybody wanted Freddy Webster (Top, M) as a first trumpeter because he had one of the greatest sounds of all time. He played with Hines, Millinder, Eckstine, Gillespie, Calloway, Carter, and Lunceford. He was noted for his solo on *Stardust* with Millinder and Lunceford, though his best work rarely got recorded. He did record his own tune, *Reverse the Charges,* with Sonny Boy Williams on Decca, and again with Frankie Socolow on Duke in 1945. He died, one of modern jazz's earliest casualties, in 1947. His accompaniments to Sarah Vaughan's *If You Could See Me Now* on Musicraft and to Viola Wells (Miss Rhapsody) on Savoy, *I Fell for You,* are superb. Coleman Hawkins (Bottom, L) went to all the jam sessions, listened to the new music, and hired Thelonious Monk to play piano in his band at the Downbeat in fall 1944. Little Benny Harris was on trumpet, Eddie "Bass" Robinson on bass, and Denzil Best on drums; Hawkins's alter ego, Don Byas (third from L), was there as a challenge, to keep the master on his toes. This rhythm section plus Hawkins made *Recollections, Drifting on a Reed,* and *Flying Hawk,* Monk's first records, for Joe Davis that year.

Modern jazz burst out in Billy Eckstine's band (Top), which recorded in rehearsal, April 1944, *Opus X* and *Blowing the Blues Away* for DeLuxe. At the Apollo Theatre in December 1944, key men were Tommy Potter (third from L), Leo Parker (fifth from L), Dizzy Gillespie (sixth from L), John Jackson (eighth from L), Art Blakey (sixth from R), Dexter Gordon (fifth from R), and Eckstine (fourth from R). Shown in May 1945 (Middle, R) are Art Blakey (extreme L), Tommy Potter (second from L), Budd Johnson (third from L), Fats Navarro (sixth from L), and Gene Ammons (extreme R). (Bottom, L) Eckstine doubled on valve trombone with Dexter Gordon on *Lonesome Lover Blues*. (Middle, L) Billy Eckstine (third from L) on trumpet and Gene Ammons (fifth from R), Savannah, early 1945. Miles Davis replaced Fats Navarro in 1946. Called the "Trumpet Machine" by the band, he made Eckstine hire white trumpeter Doug Mettome just to provide some competition. Agency pressure and the uneasy mix of bebop and Eckstine's obvious commercial potential caused him to give up the band in January 1947. Eckstine then began his reign with ballads and sex appeal on the MGM label.

(L and Bottom, R) Dizzy Gillespie's playing overawed all but a handful of musicians in the mid-forties. Few had his technical skill and lightning-fast execution, or his ability to hear the seemingly infinite variety of new patterns it was possible to create as he and Charlie Parker evolved a new way to play jazz. As his popularity and public presence increased, so did the number of his fans, who bought berets, music clips, double-breasted chalk-striped drape suits, and later floppy bow ties and bebop dark glasses. Cartoonist Gene "The Cat" Deitch's work (Top, R) appeared mainly in the *Record Changer,* a traditionalist magazine that gave space to Ross Russell's cogent explanations of modern rhythm and solo development and to Paul Bacon's reviews of modern music on Bluenote, Savoy, Prestige, and other labels from the late forties. Shown at the Onyx Club, 1944 (Middle, R), are (L to R) Max Roach, Budd Johnson, Oscar Pettiford, George Wallington, and Dizzy Gillespie. At Coleman Hawkins's request, Johnson took the group, minus Wallington, to Apollo in February to make *Woodyn'you, Bu-Dee-Daht,* and *Disorder at the Border,* plus three ballads. Because of the inexperience of the Apollo people and some of the younger players, it took two days to record the six sides.

In August 1945 Billy Shaw told Dizzy Gillespie to get a big band together to play concert dates. With arranger Gil Fuller's help, they rounded one up: (Top, R, L to R) Howard Anderson, (Fuller), Lloyd Buchanan, Ed DeVerteuil, Harry Proy, Kenny Dorham, Charlie Rouse, Max Roach, (Gillespie), Leo Williams, Elman Wright, John Smith, Johnny Walker, Alphonso King, Ed Lewis, Ted Kelly, and Warren Lucky. The tour started in September in Virginia, playing—dances! Dizzy and Fuller had rewritten all of Dizzy's tunes for big band, only to find angry black dancers: "Can't you nigguhs play no blues?" On the road Charlie Parker, Freddy Webster, Benny Harris, and Rudy Williams replaced some of the less experienced players, and the group quickly threw together a show, dubbed *Hepsations of 1945*, starring the Nicholas Brothers, Patterson, Jackson, and June Eckstine, so that promoters could book them into theaters. They struggled down to New Orleans and back, and Dizzy disbanded at the end of October. By the end of the year he and Charlie Parker were at Billy Berg's in Hollywood. Clark Monroe kicked off Dizzy's second big band with eight weeks at his Spotlite Club on 52nd Street in 1946. Dizzy borrowed arrangements from Billy Eckstine, wrote some with Gil Fuller, and recorded the blazing *Things to Come* for Musicraft in 1946. A year later the band, playing better, signed with Victor, played the Downbeat Club on 52nd Street, and featured (Bottom) Cecil Payne (extreme L), James Moody (fourth from L), Joe Gayles (third from R), Ray Brown (second from R), and Dizzy. This band made *Two Bass Hit* and *Stay on It* and recorded twice more in December, before the 1948 ban went into effect. They toured Europe in 1948, recorded again for Victor in 1949, then signed with Capitol, with vocalist Joe Carroll (Top, L, L), who did *Jump Di-Le-Ba, Hey Pete*, and others. New sidemen included Jimmy Heath, John Coltrane, and Paul Gonsalves. Dizzy disbanded in 1950.

Town Hall, West 43rd Street between Sixth Avenue and Broadway, May 1945. This was one of a series of modern jazz concerts produced by Monte Kay, later a well-known artists' manager in Hollywood, and then an avid jazz fan who produced sessions and concerts. This was the New Jazz Foundation; Dizzy and Bird filled the hall with a mixture of intent fans of the new music and older fans, curious but not yet decided. Harold "Doc" West was on drums, Curly Russell on bass, with Dizzy (Top). Dizzy and Charlie (Bottom, R) were then at the Three Deuces, playing (and recording for Guild) *Dizzy Atmosphere, Hot House, Shaw Nuff, Salt Peanuts,* and *All the Things You Are,* the objects of intense hatred from the jazz establishment, quoted in the press—Tommy Dorsey: "Bebop has set music back twenty years." But modern jazz had found an audience that would grow each year, an audience that came to listen, not to dance. Jazz was being regarded for the first time in its history as an art form, and by the end of the decade almost all jazz would be played in nightclubs or theaters, no longer in ballrooms and rarely in hotels.

In January 1946 at Billy Berg's, Charlie Parker and Dizzy Gillespie, along with Milt Jackson, Ray Brown, Al Haig, and drummer Stan Levey, found that their audience had dwindled to a small, intense, hard-core group of hipsters. Berg's was the city's only interracial club, a showcase for the diverse talents of Zutty Singleton, Snub Mosley, Cee Pee Johnson, and Frankie Laine. Parker's drug problems escalated until he met Emery Byrd, the infamous "Moose the Mooche" whose Central Avenue shoeshine parlor doubled as an outlet for jazz and blues records, but whose real action was pushing dope. Parker and Gillespie recorded with Slim Gaillard on Beltone *(Popity Pop)* and did two "Jazz at the Philharmonic" shows for Norman Granz. Most important for Parker, he made his first Dial date, using handpicked sidemen Miles Davis, Lucky Thompson, and Dodo Marmarosa for *Ornithology, Yardbird Suite, Night in Tunisia,* and *Moose the Mooche.* Back in New York (Top, L, cued by Pincus, 52nd Street's "official greeter"), Parker opened the Three Deuces in April 1947 with (Bottom, L to R) Tommy Potter, Miles Davis, Duke Jordan, and Max Roach, drums. For Savoy the group (with Bud Powell on piano) made *Donna Lee, Chasin' the Bird,* and later, under Miles's name (with John Lewis on piano), *Milestones* and *Little Willie Leaps.* In November Dial recorded the whole band doing *Scrapple from the Apple* and *Klactoveesedstene.* (Russell vainly sought the source of the name in obscure etymological reference works until he got it from Parker's number-one fan, Dean Benedetti: "... Why man, it's just a sound.") (Top, R) Trumpeter Kenny Dorham replaced Davis at the Royal Roost. Parker signed with Mercury; Norman Granz, in charge of jazz production, placed him in various contexts (with strings and Latin bands) but only once, on *Passport,* with his working band. (Middle, R) After Dizzy's big band broke up, he often appeared at Birdland with Parker. Granz teamed them in 1950 on *Bloomdido* and *Mohawk.*

After leading a society band for a decade, multi-reed man Boyd Raeburn changed to swing in 1943 and then to modern jazz when he played the Lincoln Hotel in New York (Top) in 1944, featuring Emmett Carls (sixth from R), Johnny Bothwell (seventh from L), drummer Don Lamond (fifth from R), and pianist-arranger George Handy, who had studied with Aaron Copland. Handy, who was heavily influenced by Duke Ellington, rarely cared to sustain a mood or tempo more than a few bars at a time; his arrangements of *Tonsillectomy, Yerxa,* and *Dalvatore Sally* for Ben Pollack's Jewel label in 1946 contrast with Eddie Finckel's *Little Boyd Blew.* Both men later left Raeburn over credits and copyright claims. Dodo Marmarosa replaced Handy in 1946. The leader described his music as "...modern classical music applied to swing. We've based it on the theory of modern music as presented by Hindemith...and we follow the lines of the great contemporary moderns, Stravinsky and Shostakovitch. Actually we are presenting new sounds in jazz by introducing extra notes in chords." The band used French and English horns and swelled to more than twenty men (fortunately financed by a wealthy friend, Stillman Pond, who also paid for Raeburn's last recordings on Atlantic in 1947) with fifty new Johnny Richards scores. They opened the Vanity Fair nightclub in January 1947 with Pete Candoli, trumpet; Buddy DeFranco, clarinet; and Hal Schaefer, piano, among the new sidemen. Raeburn declared bankruptcy later that year but returned to an old haunt, the Commodore Hotel, in 1948 with Eddie Bert, trombone; Frankie Socolow, tenor sax; and Tiny Kahn, drums. Another band in 1950 featured Fats Ford, trumpet, and Rae DeGeer, tenor sax; but Raeburn's day in the sun was past. Buddy Rich (Middle) started his band in December 1945 at the Terrace Room in Newark and signed with Mercury, which featured Eddie Finckel's arrangement of *Dateless Brown* and Billy Moore's *Desperate Desmond* with solos by Bill "Bitsy" Mullens (fifth from R), trombonist Earl Swope, and tenor man George Berg. Later, Red Rodney and Tony Scott were in the band, but Rich refused to compromise: "I liked what we had—a big brassy band with up-tempo numbers as well as ballads, played with a jazz feeling. My band was equal to my own talent. I thought why should I change my band to satisfy the no-talent ballroom operators." In 1947 Al Cohn soloed on *Tacos, Enchiladas and Beans,* his only MGM release. Later Allen Eager was featured, but he threw in the towel in 1949 and joined Les Brown for six months. Georgie Auld's band (Bottom) started in 1943, with the leader featuring himself on alto, tenor, and soprano saxes like Charlie Barnet, and recorded for Guild and Musicraft, with Dizzy Gillespie and Erroll Garner sitting in on *In the Middle* and *Co-Pilot.* Most of his arrangements were by Tadd Dameron, guitarist Turk Van Lake, and veteran Budd Johnson. On *Stompin' at the Savoy, Jump, Georgie, Jump,* and *Daily Double* (arranged by Al Cohn) he featured Al Porcino, trumpet, and Joe Albany, piano. He disbanded after playing the Tune Town Ballroom in St. Louis. In 1947 Red Rodney on trumpet, Serge Chaloff, and Tiny Kahn were in his nine-piece band, which did not record.

The N.J.F.'s Last and Maddest Session at Lincoln Square Center

MONTE KAY and SYMPHONY SID
present a

REBOP JAM SESSION

starring

CHARLEY VENTURA
Gene Krupa's Terrific Tenor Saxophonist

RED RODNEY
Krupa's Phenomenal Trumpeter

J. J. JOHNSON
Great Trombone Star

DEXTER GORDON

SONNY STITT

Exciting, Creative Tenor and Alto Men, Both Formerly with Billy Eckstine
and the Outstanding Female Vocalist of Our Time

SARAH VAUGHN
Discovered by Billy Eckstine, Now at Cafe Society Downtown

This session is dedicated to a very talented young man whose magnificent
voice and modern musical ideas have established him as the new king of
swing in 1946.

BILLY ECKSTINE
Who Will Present Six New Stars of His Sensational Band

GENE AMMONS
Tenor Sax

ART BLAKELY
Drums

FATS NAVARRO
Trumpet

LEO PARKER
Baritone Sax

RED GARLAND
Piano

BILL McMAHON
Bass

SUNDAY AFTERNOON MAY 12, at 3 P. M.

LINCOLN SQUARE CENTER, 53 WEST 66th STREET, N. Y.
(Between Central Park West and Columbus Avenue)

Young modernists were drawn to 52nd Street throughout the 1940s. Jamming at the Downbeat (Top, R, L to R) were Herbie Fields, Vic Dickenson, Jimmy Hamilton, Joe Albany, and Buster Bailey. Albany worked with everyone from Max Kaminsky to Charlie Parker and recorded *New Lester Leaps In* and *You're Driving Me Crazy* with Lester Young on Aladdin; he was rarely heard from after 1950. (Middle, R, L to R) Benny Harris, Johnny Bothwell, and Allen Eager at the Three Deuces, October 1945. Bothwell loved Johnny Hodges and starred with Boyd Raeburn, 1943–45. He began his recording career on Bob Thiele's Signature label, led his own band for a year with *I'll Remember April,* his only hit, but pretty much dropped out of sight after 1950. (Bottom, R) Slam Stewart's combo—(L to R) (Stewart), Mike Bryan, Doc West, and Erroll Garner—were at the Three Deuces in 1945 and recorded *Three Blind Micesky* on Savoy. Garner, under his own name, recorded for half a dozen other labels, blending a highly personal style from stride, a lag-along bass, and florid punctuated single notes and chords to become a major star in the fifties and sixties. (Bottom, L) Erroll Garner returned to the Three Deuces as a headliner in 1948. Some of Georgie Auld's sidemen (Middle, L) recorded under Serge Chaloff's name for Savoy, March 5, 1947—*Pumpernickel, Gabardine and Serge,* and two other titles. (L to R) George Wallington, Curly Russell, Red Rodney, Tiny Kahn, Earl Swope, Serge Chaloff. All were sought-after players.

Fats Navarro sought perfection all his life. In 1947 he told Barry Ulanov in *Metronome:* "I'd like to just play a perfect melody of my own, all the chord progressions right, the melody fresh and original—my own." To that end he practiced incessantly, and some considered him Dizzy Gillespie's equal. He replaced Gillespie in Billy Eckstine's band and was not out of work again. His full tone, effortless flow of ideas, melodic beauty, and harmonic awareness are captured on dozens of records, including *Half Step Down Please* with Coleman Hawkins on Victor, *Move* on Dial, and *Double Talk* on Bluenote, where he surpassed his mentor, Howard McGhee. He became, like too many others of his generation, a heroin addict. That addiction undoubtedly contributed to the tuberculosis that killed him at age twenty-six in July 1950.

(Bottom) At the Onyx Club, May 1944: (L to R) Freddy Webster, Sid Catlett, Scoops Carry, Trummy Young, Leonard Gaskin, Budd Johnson, Snags Allen, Dizzy Gillespie, Doc West. This was a gathering of jazz eagles under Monte Kay's auspices. Dizzy and Budd Johnson were working there, perfecting the unison lines that Dizzy and Bird would record in 1945 as *Hot House* and *Dizzy Atmosphere*. Kay was active in promoting jam sessions (Top, L) and concerts and in managing Tadd Dameron's career. (Top, R) Dial prexy Ross Russell (second from L) checks the lead sheets with new-comer baritone Earl Coleman (second from R), of the two songs *This Is Always* and *Dark Shadows*, that Charlie Parker (extreme L) asked Russell to record upon Parker's return to Dial after a six-month recovery at Camarillo State Hospital in February 1947. Drummer Doc West is behind Russell; composer Shifty Henry, at the right. Russell made more money from *This is Always* than from anything else in his catalog. Parker's solo on *Dark Shadows* was later transcribed for Woody Herman's reed section on their Columbia record *I've Got News For You*. After Coleman struggled for two hours to make satisfactory masters of the two songs, Parker, with Erroll Garner on piano, Red Callendar on bass, and West on drums, turned out *Cool Blues* and *Bird's Nest* with no prior rehearsal in just thirty minutes. A week later, with Howard McGhee, Wardell Gray, and Dodo Marmarosa, he made *Relaxin' at Camarillo, Carvin' the Bird, Cheers,* and *Stupendous.* With that he resolved, "That's all she wrote. When I lay my hair down next it's going to be in the Apple."

It was January 29, 1947. Producer Harry Lim had brought to the Keynote studios the three best white modern jazzmen, who among them had been featured in more than a dozen bands, including Sonny Dunham's, Woody Herman's, Jimmy and Tommy Dorsey's, Gene Krupa's, Les Brown's, and Tony Pastor's. Because of the shortage of players during the war, these young musicians (Chaloff being the oldest at twenty-four) had gained valuable experience crisscrossing the country in big bands. All were inspired by swing-era stars: Serge Chaloff (L), by Harry Carney and Jack Washington; Red Rodney (M), by Harry James; and Allen Eager (R), by Lester Young. Dizzy Gillespie's and Charlie Parker's playing in person and on records (Rodney joined Gene Krupa in 1945 with the express purpose of going to California with the band to hear Dizzy and Bird at Billy Berg's) turned them all around. All developed flowing, big-toned styles. Eager played on a 1946 Coleman Hawkins date, and the master gave him solo space on *Allen's Alley.* Chaloff recorded *Nocturne* with Sonny Berman on Dial. Rodney's earliest solo on record was with Jimmy Dorsey in 1944, *Oh What a Beautiful Morning* on Decca. For Harry Lim they did Al Cohn's tune and arrangement *The Goof and I* (Chaloff used it later with Woody Herman's band); and Gerry Mulligan's tunes and arrangements of *Elevation, Fine and Dandy,* and *All God's Chillun Got Rhythm,* ably supported by Al Haig, piano; Chubby Jackson, bass; and Tiny Kahn, drums. Rodney and Eager worked with Buddy Rich later that year, Rodney soloing on Rich's *Oop Bop Sh' Bam.*

Pianist Dodo Marmarosa (L) recorded *Skyliner* and *The Moose* with Charlie Barnet, *D. B. Blues* with Lester Young, with Artie Shaw on Victor and Musicraft, frequently with other groups, and on this date at Atomic in 1946 with Ray Brown, bass, and Jackie Mills, drums, which produced *How High the Moon*. Later, on Dial, he did *Bopmatism* and *Dary Departs* but disappeared after 1950. The 1946 *Esquire* award winners (R) recorded *Indiana Winter* and *Blow the Man Down* for Victor, produced by Leonard Feather with (L to R) Harry Carney, J. J. Johnson, and Coleman Hawkins. Johnson was with Count Basie's band; he would join Illinois Jacquet in 1947 and work with Coleman Hawkins at Birdland in 1950.

Pianist-arranger Sir Charles Thompson played in a spare, Basie-like solo style starting with the Lloyd Hunter and Nat Towles bands in the Midwest. Later, when he worked with Lionel Hampton, Floyd Ray, Lester Young, Roy Eldridge, and Hot Lips Page on 52nd Street, Bess Berman, owner and producer of Apollo Records, noticed him. On September 4, 1945, Thompson brought together veteran players like Sergeant Buck Clayton, then stationed at Camp Kilmer, on trumpet; Danny Barker, guitar; J. C. Heard, drums; and bassist Jimmy Butts. Both Barker and Heard were with Cab Calloway's band at the Café Zanzibar; Butts was with Noble Sissle's band at Billy Rose's Diamond Horseshoe. Thompson, then working with Charlie Parker's group at the Spotlite with Dexter Gordon on tenor, wisely chose the two new style setters. Of the four sides, *20th Century Blues* and *The Street Beat* show Parker and Gordon to best advantage. Drummer J. C. Heard accented with bombs for their benefit but played straight for Clayton, who later worked on 52nd Street with advanced pianist Kenny Kersey in his group. Thompson wrote *Robbins Nest* and other tunes popularized during his years with Illinois Jacquet's jumping band.

330

WRITTEN BY AMERICA'S No. 1 AUTHORITY ON BE-BOP

INSIDE
BE·BOP

LEONARD FEATHER

The first critic to herald the new movement in jazz. He tells the fascinating inside story of how it all began, with new exclusive stories and pictures. A thorough technical explanation of be bop with musical illustrations and one hundred biographies of your favorite modern musicians.

J. J. ROBBINS & SONS, Inc.
221 WEST 47th STREET, NEW YORK 19

Six-foot-five tenor star Dexter Gordon (R) asserted his personality with such unmistakable authority, with a huge sound and sometimes sardonic quotes, that he became the most influential figure on his horn throughout the decade. He played well in any setting, as *Ghost of a Chance* on Dial and *Dexter's Mood* on Savoy show, but he thrived in the heat of combat, as in his famous Dial duets with Wardell Gray on *The Chase* and Teddy Edwards on *The Duel,* or in driving up-tempo pieces like *Dexter's Minor Mad.* Because modern jazz bewildered many potential fans, critic, composer, and author Leonard Feather, with Barry Ulanov of *Metronome,* the first to get the new music's message, showed in his 1949 *Inside Bebop* (L) how it all came about with biographies, musical examples, and records.

Big-toned tenor man Charlie Ventura became popular in Gene Krupa's and Teddy Powell's bands, 1942–46, with *Dark Eyes* and *Body and Soul* (with Krupa's trio). He formed his own big band in 1946 and made a hit with a florid version of *How High the Moon* for National. A year later he and trombonist Bill Harris had a group that made *Stop and Go* and, with Kai Winding replacing Harris, *East of Suez.* In 1948 with Benny Green on trombone and arrangements by Jackie Cain (extreme R) and pianist Roy Kral, his Bop for the People became extremely popular with *Euphoria* and *I'm Forever Blowing Bubbles.* In 1949 he switched to Victor and a year later started another big band with Red Rodney on trumpet and Dave McKenna on piano, which played Ellington tunes and had a hit with *Ha.*

Thelonious Sphere Monk (R) could play like Art Tatum, Earl Hines, or Teddy Wilson, but he heard music differently and developed a completely original and idiosyncratic style that was blues-based but angular and spare. He worked mostly at Minton's Playhouse and spent his time composing tunes like *'Round Midnight, Well You Needn't, Ruby My Dear, Criss Cross,* and *In Walked Bud,* which he recorded for Bluenote in the late forties. He was a melodist and once stated that bebop sounded like Dixieland to him because he felt most young musicians did little more than run changes. Many people preferred Cootie Williams's band version of *'Round Midnight* to Monk's, however. (L), Williams's brilliant young pianist, Earl "Bud" Powell, later worked and recorded with Parker and Gillespie, nearly the only pianist who could play with their endless inventiveness and at their blinding speed. Powell was known as "Hammerfingers" for his clean execution at tempo; his *Indiana* and *I Got Rhythm, Bud's Bubble,* and others show the ceaseless flow of his ideas.

Howard McGhee (L, extreme L) and Oscar Pettiford were influential players throughout the forties. McGhee played like Roy Eldridge on *McGhee Special* with Andy Kirk, but changed to Dizzy Gillespie's style after his 1943 stand with Pettiford in Charlie Barnet's band. He had speed, technique, and a good sound, as *Dialated Pupils, Turnip Blood,* and *Night Mist* on Dial show, and was known for the beauty of his middle-register playing. He won the 1949 *Down Beat* poll. Pettiford was the major bassist in the wake of Jimmy Blanton's death and became well known during his stay with Duke Ellington, 1945–48. Tenor man Wardell Gray (R) played like Lester Young in Earl Hines's band and moved gradually toward Charlie Parker's harder, driving sound on *Twisted* and *Move* on Prestige.

Illinois Jacquet (L, extreme L) occupied center stage with his swinging, exhibitionistic tenor solo on *Flying Home* with Lionel Hampton's band, 1941–42. Later, with Count Basie, 1945–46, he played fluently on *The King* and *Muttonleg* and then formed his own band with Joe Newman, J. J. Johnson, and baritone saxist Leo Parker (R). They cut *Bottoms Up, Robbins Nest,* and *Merle's Mood* for Apollo, and *Black Velvet* for Victor. By 1949 he showed his capable modern work on *Riffin' at 24th Street*. James Moody (R) mixed swing and modern with his tenor sax on *Emanon* (Musicraft) and *Oopapada* (Victor). Conga drummer Chano Pozo (M) began Dizzy Gillespie's use of African and Latin rhythms in modern jazz on *Algo Bueno, Manteca,* and *Cubana Be, Cubana Bop.* Pozo was murdered in Harlem in 1948; Gillespie used his cousin Chino Pozo and others afterward.

Bassist Charlie Mingus (L) worked with Louis Armstrong, Kid Ory, Cee Pee Johnson, Mercer Ellington, and others and came to prominence with Lionel Hampton's band, which recorded his *Mingus Fingers* on Decca. He recorded as Baron Mingus on Four Star doing *Love on a Greyhound Bus* and *Bedspread,* and with a big band on Fentone for *The Story of Love.* As the new decade arrived, he came into his own with Red Norvo's trio, with guitarist Tal Farlow, on *Swedish Pastry* and *Move* for Discovery. A year later the iconoclastic bassist started his own record label, Debut. (R) Sarah Vaughan's range, harmonic awareness, and daring made her a standout among a wealth of good singers when she started in Earl Hines's band in 1943 and then moved to the completely modern Billy Eckstine band in 1944. Her first date, recorded by Leonard Feather for Continental, featured *Signing Off* and *No Smokes Blues.* Later, on Musicraft, she did the beautiful *If You Could See Me Now* with Freddy Webster's accompaniment, and on Columbia in 1950, *Nice Work If You Can Get It* with a Miles Davis accompaniment.

Clyde Hart (Top, R) was one swing star who, like Budd Johnson, adapted to modern jazz. In Oscar Pettiford's view, "Clyde was the only pianist who could play those things without any trouble. He was the first to play modern left hand." Hart died in 1945. Lucky Thompson (Top, M) was not a bopper, but he was harmonically advanced; he played with the Eckstine band in 1944 and Ike Carpenter's band at the Trianon, as well as with Boyd Raeburn and Johnny Richards. *Just One More Chance* shows his debt to Hawkins and Byas, and *Stay on It* with Count Basie, his swinging side. Aside from Monk, Tadd Dameron (Top, L) was the most prolific composer in modern jazz, an arranger who insisted on form and beauty in modern music. His career peaked at the Royal Roost and Bop City with Fats Navarro and Allen Eager in the late forties. He was Miles Davis's pianist at the Jazz Festival in Paris in 1949 and remained there until 1951. Milt Jackson (Middle, R) and Terry Gibbs (Middle, L) rose to prominence with Dizzy Gillespie in 1946 and Woody Herman in 1949. Gibbs was a hard-charging swinger; Jackson worked out a unique bell-like sound that became notable with the Modern Jazz Quartet in the fifties. Buddy DeFranco (Middle, M) played clarinet like no one else, but somehow, despite his fine work for Tommy Dorsey and Count Basie's septet in 1950–51, and his recording of *Extrovert* on Capitol, he never received the accolades his gifts so richly deserved. Clarinet was almost completely out of favor in modern jazz. (Bottom, L) Clark Terry's unique soft sound and speed stood out in Count Basie's combo in 1950–51, particularly on *Little White Lies,* and with Wardell Gray on *Move* for Prestige. Billy Taylor and Barbara Carroll (Bottom, M and R) followed Art Tatum and Bud Powell respectively, recorded prolifically, and worked steadily.

Drummer Kenny Clarke (Top, M) switched the timekeeping role from bass drum to top cymbal in Edgar Hayes's and Teddy Hill's bands, 1938–39, and later led the house rhythm section at Minton's Playhouse. His tunes *Epistrophy (Fly Right)* and *Salt Peanuts* were drum licks set to music, and he adapted his style with Red Allen and Sidney Bechet to Dizzy Gillespie and Charlie Parker with ease. Denzil Best (Bottom, R) played trumpet and piano until tuberculosis forced him to change to drums. He wrote *Bemsha Swing, Allen's Alley, Move,* and *Dee Dee's Dance,* and his superb brush work with George Shearing's Quintet made him a major name by the end of the forties. Tenor stars Paul Gonsalves (Top, L) and Eddie "Lockjaw" Davis (Middle, L) were not beboppers, although the former worked in Dizzy Gillespie's big band, 1949–50. Lockjaw Davis's extrovert tenor featured Fats Navarro on *Hollerin' and Screamin'* and *Spinal* on Savoy. Later Davis became prominent with Count Basie's revived big band in 1952–53. Charlie Kennedy (Top, R) was a fine alto man with Gene Krupa whose feature was *I Wake Up Dreaming.* Herbie Steward (Middle, R) played alto and tenor equally well and was one of the original Four Brothers in Woody Herman's 1947–48 band. Featured on *Love of My Life* and *The Hornet* with Artie Shaw, Steward stuck with dance-band work and faded out of the picture. Don Lanphere (Middle, M) was equally gifted, as his work with Fats Navarro on *Move* on Dial in 1948 proves, but he rarely received his due. Pianist Hank Jones (Bottom, M) worked with Andy Kirk, Hot Lips Page, and Howard McGhee, who featured him on *Night Music* and *Coolie Rini* on Dial; he also made *Star Eyes* with Charlie Parker. Pianist Herbie Nichols (Bottom, L) worked mostly in swing, Dixie, and jump bands, although he had a modern style. In 1952 Mary Lou Williams recorded his *Bebop Waltz.*

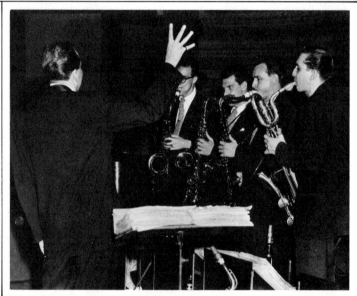

(Opposite Page) Woody Herman's First Herd, 1944–46, leaped into national celebrity and became a million-dollar grosser by parlaying a driving, shouting style built on Dizzy Gillespie and Charlie Parker trumpet and sax figures in arrangements written mainly by pianist Ralph Burns and trumpeter Neal Hefti. They gained publicity via the Old Gold radio show in 1944 and the Wildroot show in 1945. Their many Columbia Records hits, like *Caldonia, Apple Honey, Wildroot, The Good Earth,* and *Northwest Passage,* showed off Herman's superb rhythm team of Chubby Jackson, bass, and Dave Tough, drums, as well as the high-flying brass section and soloists Sonny Berman, Bill Harris, and Flip Phillips. Berman (Top, L) and Harris had special features like *Sidewalks of Cuba, Everywhere,* and *Bijou* written to display their fine original talent. The Woodchoppers small unit with the soloists plus Margie Hyams or Red Norvo, vibes, made *Pam, Steps,* and other superb records. With some changes late in 1946 the First Herd (Bottom) featured Jimmy Rowles, p (foreground L); Chuck Wayne, gtr (third from L); Red Norvo, vbs (extreme L); Flip Phillips, ts (sixth from L); Woody Herman, clt (front, M); Don Lamond, dms (seventh from L); Bill Harris, tb (fifth from R); Pete Candoli, tp (eighth from R); and Shorty Rogers (seventh from R). (Middle, L, L to R) Berman, Rogers, Lamond, Jackson. Rogers, a fine arranger, demonstrates a point, 1946. This Herd disbanded in December 1946. With many new faces Herman had his Second Herd (Top, R) at the Commodore Hotel in 1948: (L to R) Fred Otis, Mary Ann McCall, Harry Babasin, Jimmy Raney, Don Lamond, Stan Getz, Ernie Royal, Al Cohn, (Herman), Bob Swift, Zoot Sims, and Serge Chaloff. Al Cohn wrote *The Goof and I.* Burns did *Summer Sequence,* which featured Stan Getz on the fourth part, later known as *Early Autumn;* and Jimmy Guiffre wrote *Four Brothers.* (Middle, R, L to R) Herman signals the 1949 saxes: Don Lanphere, Buddy Savitt, Jimmy Guiffre, and Serge Chaloff. (Above) Tenor men Zoot Sims (Top, L) and Stan Getz (Top, R) were the best of many Lester Young followers who played in Herman's bands. A month after their November 4, 1949, Carnegie Hall concert (Bottom) with Shelly Manne, drums, and Buddy Childers (fourth from L), trumpet, they disbanded.

Stan Kenton (Top, L) featured (Top, R) Stan Getz (third from R) and Dave Matthews's (extreme L) arrangements in his Artistry in Rhythm Band in 1944. By 1946 (Middle, R) Pete Rugolo (extreme L) was the chief arranger, contributing *Unison Riff, Bongo Riff, Monotony, Prologue Suite,* and *Fugue for Rhythm Section* with Kai Winding (third from L), Buddy Childers (third from R), and Shelly Manne (extreme R). Trumpeter-arranger Ken Hanna's (second from R) *Somnambulism* and Bob Graettinger's *Thermopolae* were part of Kenton's new Progressive Jazz; they used one book for dances, another for concerts. Art Pepper (Middle, L, and Bottom, M), Conte Candoli (extreme L), and Bob Cooper (extreme R) were part of the Progressive Jazz Concert at the Hollywood Bowl that drew fifteen thousand people in June 1948. Six months later Kenton wrote, "...we're nervous, sick, unhappy, and our music is going to become all of those things too if we don't watch out." He disbanded on December 17, 1948, then launched a thirty-piece orchestra, billed as Innovations in Modern Music, for a concert tour in 1950.

Gene Krupa, impressed by Tommy Dorsey's band with strings, followed suit in 1944 and eased into the new sounds with arrangers like Eddie Finckel, who wrote *Leave Us Leap,* which featured a good young trumpet player named Don Fagerquist (Top, L). Veteran arranger Budd Johnson wrote the first bop vocal, *What's This,* for vocalists Dave Lambert and Buddy Stewart in 1945. Equally important was tenor star Charlie Ventura (Middle, R, extreme R), who put over his Hawkins-Webster style on trio numbers like *Dark Eyes* and *Body and Soul.* When Fagerquist left in 1946, Red Rodney (Middle, L) joined at the 400 Club because he knew Krupa's band was headed for the Palladium in Hollywood, where he'd have a chance to hear Dizzy Gillespie and Charlie Parker. Rodney, the best white modern trumpeter with a fat sound, soloed on *How High the Moon* and sang on *It's Just a Matter of Opinion* with Buddy Stewart and Carolyn Gray. During Rodney's stay (Bottom) he was joined by Gerry Mulligan (seventh from R), Charlie Kennedy (extreme R), and Buddy Wise (fifth from R), all of whom soloed on Mulligan's *Disc Jockey Jump* in 1947, made after Fagerquist returned. Gene's new theme, *Starburst* by Eddie Finckel, featured Al Porcino on trumpet. *I May Be Wrong (but I Think You're Wonderful)* featured Kennedy, Wise, and a new trombonist, Urbie Green. Other good sides included *Calling Dr. Gillespie* and *Up and Atom,* both by Finckel, which were recorded in late December 1947. When they resumed recording (Top, R) for Columbia in 1949 after the ban, Roy Eldridge had rejoined; he soloed on *Bop Boogie, Swiss Lullaby,* and *Watch Out (Whatcha Tryin' to Do),* the last a duet with singer Dolores Hawkins. Trombonist Frank Rosolino sang and played on *Lemon Drop.* In 1950 Krupa switched to Victor and recorded a group of Fats Waller tunes that featured tenor man Buddy Wise. A year later he cut back to eleven men.

Pianist Elliott Lawrence (Top, extreme L) studied with conductor Leon Barzin and led the staff orchestra at station WCAU in Philadelphia. Their broadcasts attracted attention, and Lawrence signed with Columbia Records. Gerry Mulligan wrote for the band *Five O'Clock Shadow* and *Elevation* and other scores, which featured sidemen like trumpeter Alec Fila (top row, third from R) and trombonist Willie Dennis. Mulligan played baritone for a while in 1949, along with alto man Phil Urso. Earl Swope was featured on trombone when they changed to Decca in 1950. Later Lawrence did television and Broadway shows. Pianist-arranger Claude Thornhill (Middle) reformed his band after his discharge from the navy in 1946, aided immeasurably by arranger Gil Evans, who rehearsed them carefully. Thornhill, on the bandstand from the piano, would play an identifying introduction, which allowed the sidemen time to get out the arrangements and the drummer to find the right tempo. Evans gradually got the band to enjoy playing his arrangements of Dizzy Gillespie's and Charlie Parker's *Anthropology, Donna Lee,* and *Yardbird Suite,* which featured soloists Lee Konitz (with glasses) and Danny Polo (seventh from R). Red Rodney and later Emil Terry were trumpet soloists. Singers Fran Warren and Gene Williams (seated) both had hits on *A Sunday Kind of Love* and *Sorta Kinda,* which helped overcome the public's increasing indifference to Thornhill's unusual instrumentation and original style on *The Troubadour* and *La Paloma.* Thornhill liked the suspended sound with melody, and harmony and rhythm moving at minimum speed. "The sound hung like a cloud," stated Gil Evans. When he felt the sound had gotten too somber, Evans left. Thornhill disbanded because of illness in June 1948. He regrouped later that year, but his key men, except for Danny Polo, tuba player Bill Barber, and drummer Billy Exiner, had gone. Jobs became scarcer, especially for a leader with the unique style and instrumentation that Claude Thornhill had pioneered with french horns and tuba. He led other bands well into the fifties, but abandoned his original style and shifted to bread-and-butter dance music. One who wrote some arrangements after Thornhill's 1948 reorganization was blind British pianist George Shearing (Bottom). Born in London in 1919, Shearing came to Leonard Feather's attention as early as 1937. He began recording for British Decca and later won the *Melody Maker* poll as best British pianist for seven years. He made his first record for Savoy, *Have You Met Miss Jones,* in 1946, then settled here at the end of 1947, working in a trio at the Three Deuces and then at the Clique in 1949. Feather organized a date for Albert Marx's Discovery label with Margie Hyams, vibes; John Levy, bass; Chuck Wayne, guitar; and Denzil Best, drums. They recorded *Bebop Fables,* then switched to MGM and hit right away with *September in the Rain, Nothing but D Best, East of the Sun,* and others to become the most popular new group in the fifties.

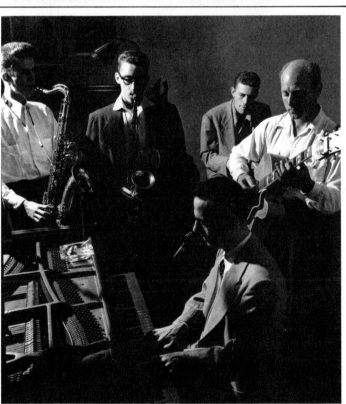

Blind pianist Lennie Tristano (Bottom, L) possessed a fantastic technique and claimed to be able to play anything of Art Tatum's—and faster. He rarely worked nightclubs, because after he evolved his ideas with (L to R) Warne Marsh, Lee Konitz, Jeff Morton, and Billy Bauer, they sometimes played in three keys at once, a frightening sound to someone expecting to make money from music. He recorded *Out on a Limb* and *Atonement* for Keynote in 1946; and three years later, after playing a short stint at the Clique, which later became Bop City (Top, L, and Middle, R), he recorded with this same group for Capitol—*Crosscurrent, Wow, Digression,* and *Intuition*—and rarely appeared in public after that. The Royal Roost (Top, R) a fried-chicked emporium at 1674 Broadway, opened in spring 1948 when 52nd Street was going rapidly downhill. Lester Young's band (Bottom, R) worked there in November: (L to R) Ted Kelly, (Young), Dennis Briscoe, Jesse Drakes, Roy Haynes. With Jerry Elliot on trombone, Lester cut *Ding Dong* and *Crazy Over Jazz* for Savoy in 1949. Both clubs lost ground when Birdland opened in mid-December 1949.

Charlie Parker's doctor advised him to slow down in 1948—advice he rarely acted upon. After the recording ban was lifted, Parker's agent, Billy Shaw, signed him with Mercury, where Norman Granz was responsible for all jazz recording. Granz ignored Parker's quintet for the most part, preferring to record him with Machito's band on *Mango Mangue* and *Okiedoke,* and later with strings, which produced the hit *Just Friends,* one of Parker's own favorites. When Shaw left the Gale firm to start Shaw Artists, he took Parker to the First International Jazz Festival in Paris. Later in 1949 he showed Parker a cellar club that was being redecorated with stripes and portraits of star musicians and told him it would be the greatest jazz club ever, capable of seating four hundred people, with no admission policy, just like the Royal Roost. Parker, eager to play there, was finally shown the name: Birdland. It was the first time a nightclub had been named for a jazzman—the only one, his admirers thought, worthy of the honor. He opened it that December. Parker recorded twenty-one sides for Mercury and Granz that year, only two, *Passport* and *Visa* (with trombonist Tommy Turk added), with his own working band.

Jamming informally behind Voice of America microphones at Birdland's opening, December 15, 1949, were (L to R) Max Kaminsky, Lester Young, Hot Lips Page, Charlie Parker, and Lennie Tristano. "...Charlie Parker liked my band better than anyone else he heard there," Kaminsky recalled. "We had nothing else in common...but we became good friends musically. He and Lester Young were the only two musicians down there who would go out of their way to speak to me. They always made a point of coming over to the table to talk about something musical." Bird cages holding tame finches hung around the club, and an even larger empty cage was ready for a myna bird. Host and greeter was Pee Wee Marquette, last seen on Broadway at the old Café Zanzibar. WJZ hired Symphony Sid Torin to broadcast live, from the "Jazz Corner of the World," from midnight to four. Red Rodney and Roy Haynes were new members of Parker's quintet, which Norman Granz did not record until the *Swedish Schnapps* date in August 1951.

Charlie Parker headlined at Birdland in 1950. After Dizzy Gillespie's big band broke up early that year, he often joined Parker there, a situation that Norman Granz decided was perfect for recording. On June 6—with Thelonious Monk, piano; Curly Russell, bass; and Buddy Rich, drums—they recorded *Bloomdido, Mohawk, An Oscar for Treadwell, Relaxin' with Lee,* and two other titles. A month later Parker did another string session, with arrangements by Joe Lippman, which included *East of the Sun* and *Laura.* John Coltrane (extreme R), a member of Gillespie's 1949–50 big band. Dizzy did only one date that year, with a sextet with Jimmy Heath and Milt Jackson for Prestige, which included *Nice Work If You Can Get It.* The tenor man was Jimmy Oliver. Coltrane doubled on alto and tenor in his 1951 sextet and recorded *Tin Tin Deo* and *Birk's Works.*

Miles Davis (Top, L) admired Gil Evans's and Gerry Mulligan's arrangements for Claude Thornhill's bands, as well as the sound of Lee Konitz's alto. He arranged a booking for this group at the Roost and the Clique in 1948–49 and a group of dates at Capitol Records. Recorded were Mulligan's *Jeru, Venus De Milo,* and *Godchild;* Evans's *Bobplicity* (Miles's tune) and *Moondreams;* Johnny Carisi's *Israel;* and John Lewis's arrangement of *Move.* The warm but cool ensemble and low-flame solos initiated a movement away from the driving, highly charged playing of Gillespie and Parker that centered around Davis and Mulligan, who became major factors in the West Coast cool school of the fifties. Charlie Parker's first date with strings (Top. R)—with Buddy Rich, drums; Ray Brown, bass; and Mitch Miller, oboe—produced *April in Paris, Summertime,* and *Just Friends.* Later Parker played Birdland with an ensemble like this and toured. Jimbo's Bop City (Bottom), an after-hours club in San Francisco, was home base for Dexter Gordon (extreme L), Sonny Criss (third from R), Roy Porter (fifth from L), and Hampton Hawes (sixth from R) off and on from 1949 to 1953. Porter had led his own 17 Beboppers in 1948–49; they recorded *Little Wig* for Savoy and featured Art Farmer, Joe Maini, and Eric Dolphy, among others. An accident on the road finished the group in 1949. Jimmy Heath (second from L), Eric Miller (fourth from L), Milt Jackson (sixth from L), Percy Heath (seventh from L), and Chuck Thompson (second from R) were regulars in sessions there. This was 1951.

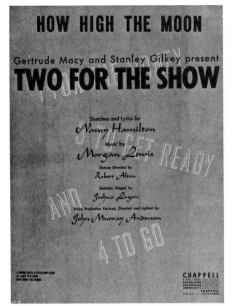

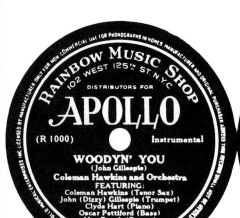

RAINBOW MUSIC SHOP
102 WEST 125TH ST. N.Y.C.
DISTRIBUTORS FOR
APOLLO
(R 1000) Instrumental
WOODYN' YOU
(John Gillespie)
Coleman Hawkins and Orchestra
FEATURING:
Coleman Hawkins (Tenor Sax)
John (Dizzy) Gillespie (Trumpet)
Clyde Hart (Piano)
Oscar Pettiford (Bass)
Max Roach (Drums)
751

COLUMBIA
36803
(CO 34289)
For perfect tone
use Columbia Needles
APPLE HONEY
Fox Trot
- Herman -
WOODY HERMAN
and his ORCHESTRA

DeLuxe
RECORDS ● LINDEN, N.J.
(121-2)
Collector's Series
OPUS X
Written and arranged by John Malachi)
BILLY ECKSTINE
and His ORCHESTRA
Featuring: Dizzy Gillespie,
Trumpet; John Jackson,
Alto Sax
3002-B

Guild
REG.
543-145   ORCHESTRA
MARCH OF THE BOYDS
[RAEBURN]
BOYD RAEBURN
AND HIS ORCHESTRA
111

Guild
REG.
565-545   ALL STAR QUINTETTE
SALT PEANUTS
(CLARKE-GILLESPIE)
DIZZY GILLESPIE
AND
CHARLIE PARKER-SYDNEY CATLETT
AL HAIG-CURLY RUSSELL
1003 A

SAVOY
BILLIES BOUNCE
(Charles Parker)
CHARLEY PARKER'S REE BOPPERS
Charles Parker, alto sax; Miles Davis,
trumpet; Curley Russell, bass; Hen
Gates, piano; Max Roach, drums
573-A
(SAV-5850)

DIAL
RECORDS
11-4-47   1021-A
Contemporary
American Music
SCRAPPLE FROM THE APPLE
CHARLIE PARKER QUINTET
CHARLIE PARKER .... Alto Sax
MILES DAVIS .... Trumpet
DUKE JORDAN .... Piano
TOMMY POTTER .... Bass
MAX ROACH .... Drums
(D-1113)

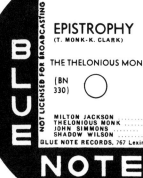

BLUE NOTE
NOT LICENSED FOR BROADCASTING
EPISTROPHY
(T. MONK-K. CLARK)
THE THELONIOUS MONK QUARTET
(BN 330)   548-B
MILTON JACKSON .... vibraphone
THELONIOUS MONK .... piano
JOHN SIMMONS .... bass
SHADOW WILSON .... drums
BLUE NOTE RECORDS, 767 Lexingt. Ave., NYC.

Capitol
REG. U.S. PAT. OFR.
(3397)   Bop
Y   Instrumental
GODCHILD
(George Wallington)
MILES DAVIS
And His Orchestra
Miles Davis, Trumpet; Kai Winding, Trombone;
Junior Collins, French Horn; Lee Konitz, Alto
Saxophone; Gerry Mulligan, Baritone
Saxophone; Bill Barber, Tuba; Al
Haig, Piano; Joe Shulman,
Bass; Max Roach, Drums.
57-60005

Capitol
REG. U.S. PAT. OFF.
Beechwood
BMI-3:02   Instrumental
3786-Y
INTUITION
(Lennie Tristano)
LENNIE TRISTANO
and His Sextette
Lennie Tristano, piano; Billy Bauer, guitar;
Arnold Fishkin, bass; Denzil Best, drums;
Warne Marsh, tenor sax; Lee
Konitz, alto sax.
7-1224

PRESTIGE
Disk Jock Record   Not For Sale
758
STRIKE UP THE BAND
(Geo. Gershwin)
**SONNY STITT and
BUD POWELL QUARTET**
Sonny Stitt — tenor
Bud Powell — piano
Curley Russell — bass
Max Roach — drums
(1004)
RELEASED BY PRESTIGE RECORD CO., 754-10TH AVENUE, NEW YORK, N.Y.

NEW JAZZ
NEW JAZZ RECORD CO., 782-8th Ave., N.Y.C. 19
FOR DISC JOCKEY USE ONLY
805   (JR C-25)
(Comp. S. Getz)
LONG ISLAND SOUND
STAN GETZ QUARTET
AL HAIG—piano
GENE RAMEY—bass
STAN LEVEY—drums
STAN GETZ—tenor

Index